In Memory
of two
Canadian Bolsheviks

Reg Bullock
(1905-1979)

and

Peter Schulz
(1940-1970)

CANADIAN
BOLSHEVIKS

THE EARLY YEARS OF THE COMMUNIST PARTY OF CANADA

By Ian Angus

VANGUARD PUBLICATIONS, MONTREAL

Canadian Cataloguing in Publication Data
Angus, Ian, 1945—
  Canadian Bolsheviks

Bibliography: p.
Includes index.
ISBN 0-88758-044-0 (bound). — ISBN 0-88758-045-9 (paper)

1. Communist Party of Canada—History. I. Title.

HX103.A53   324.271'0975   C81-090096-3

Published by Vanguard Publications
Distributed by Pathfinder Press
1317 est, rue Ste-Catherine
Montreal, Quebec H2L 2H4
U.S. Distributor: Pathfinder Press Inc.
410 West Street, New York, NY 10014

Printed and bound at
Payette & Simms Inc.
300 Ave. Arran
St-Lambert, Quebec

Dépôts légaux: 2e trimestre 1981
Bibliothèque nationale du Québec
Bibliothèque nationale du Canada

Legal deposits: 2nd trimester 1981
National Library of Quebec
National Library of Canada

Contents

Early Canadian Communist leaders. From left to right: William Moriarty, Tim Buck, Jack MacDonald, and Maurice Spector.

PREFACE

I

Canadian Bolsheviks is a study of the birth and death of a revolutionary party.

At the end of World War I many of the leaders of the left wing of the Canadian labor movement concluded that the existing organizations of the left were inadequate to the task of overthrowing capitalism and creating a new society. They established a new party—a new *kind* of party—that attempted to combine the experiences of Canadian labor with the lessons of the Russian Revolution. They called their new organization the Communist Party of Canada.

They made mistakes, but they learned from their errors. They learned quickly and well, founding a party of great promise. They united revolutionary socialists from every part of the country in a single organization with a common program and a common approach to political activity. This had never been done before in Canada. They extended their influence through consistent activity in the labor movement and through cooperation with the non-communist left. The Communist Party soon became the largest organization of the Canadian left.

A decade later, the Communist Party of Canada was in a state of collapse. Three-quarters of its membership left its ranks in one two-year period. Almost every one of the founding leaders of the party was expelled. Tim Buck rose dramatically from a secondary leadership position to undisputed control of the party apparatus. The CPC was soon to describe itself as "Tim Buck's Party."

This organizational collapse and transformation was accompanied by an equally dramatic change in the party's political direction. The CPC abandoned the program it had adopted in its early years, walked out of the unions, and isolated itself in a mindless binge of sectarian ultraleftism that deprived it of all allies and left it wide open to attack. The party turned its back on its principles.

When the crisis was over, an organization with the name "Communist Party of Canada" remained, but it was not the party that bore that name through the 1920s

The chief characteristic of the old party had been dedication to the cause of proletarian revolution. It had welcomed the leadership of the Communist International, but it had accepted orders from no one. The Russian leaders of the International were first among equals, but no more.

The chief characteristic of the new party—of "Tim Buck's Party"—was unquestioning submission to the dictates of the Kremlin. From 1930 until today the Communist Party of Canada has followed every twist and turn of Soviet foreign policy. Its program and policies are determined not by the needs of the working class in Canada and abroad, but by the narrowly perceived diplomatic concerns of the Soviet bureaucracy.

The Communist Party of Canada was transformed, at the end of its first decade, from a revolutionary party into a border guard for the Soviet Union. In *Canadian Bolsheviks* I have tried to explain how and why that change took place.

II

The major thesis of this book is that the transformation of the Canadian Communist Party paralleled, and largely resulted from, the degeneration of the Russian Revolution following Lenin's death. A detailed analysis of the triumph of the bureaucratic counterrevolution in the Soviet Union is outside the scope of this volume. However, where necessary I have traced the history of the major international events and issues that provided the backdrop to the crisis that overtook the Canadian CP in the latter half of the 1920s. The victory of Stalinism in the Soviet Union was a disaster of world historic importance. It profoundly disoriented working people around the globe who had been inspired by the promise and achievements of the world's first workers republic. It was used by the opponents of Marxism to discredit the program of revolutionary socialism associated with the ideas and method of Marxism. And by destroying the revolutionary Communist International, it gave a new lease on life to world capitalism. Humanity has paid a heavy price for this setback.

Today, when a new generation of radicalizing youth are attracted to Marxism in their search for an alternative to crisis-wracked capitalism, it is all the more necessary to probe and understand the achievements and failings of those pioneers who set out more than sixty years ago to build a mass revolutionary Marxist party in this country. We have much to learn from them.

Canadian Bolsheviks is not an impartial book. One can write impartial mathematics texts. But writers on the history of our species who claim to be impartial are only deceiving their readers, and perhaps themselves. Very often, when the topic is working-class history, the vaunted "impartiality" conceals a lack of sympathy for those who form the subject matter. As Trotsky wrote, in introducing his monumental *History of the Russian Revolution*: "The serious and critical reader will not want a treacherous impartiality, which offers him a cup of conciliation with a well-settled poison of reactionary hate at the bottom, but a scientific conscientiousness, which for its sympathies and antipathies—open and undisguised—seeks support in an honest study of the facts, a determination of their real connections, an exposure of the causal laws of their movement."

I have no sympathy for those who use the rise of Stalinism as a pretext for rejection of Marxism, who declare that the experience of the past fifty years proves our hope for a liberated humanity through socialism to be an empty dream. Quick to deny that there is any lawfulness in human history, they nevertheless see Stalinism as the inevitable product of some iron law. Whether they blame Bolshevism or revolution or human nature, those who see totalitarian dictatorship as the inevitable product of socialism betray a profound pessimism about the future of humanity.

As a Marxist, I am optimistic about our future. One of the grounds for that optimism is our ability to study the mistakes and betrayals of the past, to learn from them, and to take steps to see that they do not happen again. In this sense, *Canadian Bolsheviks* is intended not only as an attempt to recover our past, but also as a contribution to our future.

It is the responsibility of historians to state their opinions clearly, and to label them as opinions. It is also their responsibility not to allow their opinions to get in the way of an accurate reconstruction of the past. I have sought to meet those responsibilities.

III

Canadian Bolsheviks does not attempt to provide a comprehensive history of the Communist Party, even for the decade on which it focuses. It is devoted to one central topic: the making and unmaking of a revolutionary party.

As a result, many important subjects are left unexamined, and I hope that future historians will examine them in more detail. Two omissions in particular must be singled out.

Most obvious is the omission of any discussion of the CPC's activity and policy in Quebec. Since Confederation, the Quebec national question has been a central issue in Canadian politics. The growth of the Quebec working class and the resurgence of Quebec nationalism since 1960 have put Quebec at the center of the debate over the political future of this country.

In the 1920s, Quebec's importance was not so obvious to radicals in English Canada. Indeed, there was a widespread tendency to write off Quebec as a clerical, reactionary backwater. The CPC did not make that error, but neither did it sink deep roots in Quebec. It won, and then lost, a small group of Québécois radicals in the early part of the decade: from then on its strength in Quebec was limited to English-and Yiddish-speaking workers in Montreal. Rather than explore this problem superficially, I have left the subject for other writers more versed in the history and problems of the labor movement in Quebec.

Another omission is the CPC's policy toward women. The suffrage movement collapsed at the beginning of World War I, and it was not until the 1960s that the struggle for the emancipation of women equalled and surpassed the impact it had gained in the prewar years.

The Communist Party was virtually the only holdout against this reactionary trend. Its newspaper *The Worker* campaigned for women's rights, in particular for equal pay for women workers, but also for women's right to birth control and abortion. The party established Women's Labor Leagues wherever possible. Florence Custance, the only woman on the CPC's Central Committee, deserves to be remembered as a pioneer fighter for women's rights in Canada. Again, I hope that other writers will be able to do her and her cause more justice than is possible here.

IV

This is not an "official history" of any kind. Histories written to meet the needs of a party line are a Stalinist innovation the world could well do without. I take full responsibility for the political views expressed in this book, for the historical account and its interpretation, and for any errors that may appear.

Nevertheless, I owe a great debt to many people who assisted me with my research and writing.

William Rodney, author of the pioneering study of the CPC, *Soldiers of the International*, conducted an extended correspondence with me over several years, and graciously sent me copies of two documents by Maurice Spector that were unavailable from any other source.

The Royal Canadian Mounted Police, as noted in the bibliography, refused to open their files to research. This crude attempt to block historical study was partially offset by Ron Adams, a historian who was granted access to the RCMP files before the doors were locked. He made all of his notes and copies of documents available to me. While Mr. Adams will probably disagree with the political views expressed in this book, his assistance had much to do with its completion.

Theodore Draper, Norman Penner, Jaroslav Petryshyn, Jim Upton, and Dan Schwartz also gave me copies of unpublished papers and documents uncovered in their own work.

Karen Levine, then with the Multicultural History Society of Ontario, directed me to several important collections of material. Barbara West of the Library of Social History in New York guided me through the then-unsorted documents in the James P. Cannon archives, and promptly answered several letters asking for assistance.

Earle Birney granted me two lengthy interviews, from which I learned a great deal about Maurice Spector and Jack MacDonald; he also gave me permission to examine the closed section of the Birney Papers and to quote from relevant correspondence.

John Riddell, Arthur Young, Samantha Anderson, Darrel Furlotte, Norman Penner and George Breitman all read various stages of the manuscript and offered comments, suggestions and criticisms, most of which I accepted. Without the assistance of Barbara Stewart and Robert Simms, *Canadian Bolsheviks* would not have an index.

Richard Fidler's assistance as an editor and in preparing the manuscript for publication was invaluable. He went far beyond normal copy editing, making literally hundreds of suggestions for changes, most of which are incorporated in the final draft.

And this book would not have appeared at all were it not for the constant support, encouragement, and patience of Lis Angus. Her suggestions are incorporated on almost every page.

To these and many others, my sincere thanks. I hope that the final product justifies their efforts.

Ian Angus

Toronto, November 1980

List of Abbreviations

ACCL	All-Canadian Confederation of Labor
ACW	Amalgamated Clothing Workers
AFL	American Federation of Labor
ARC	Anglo-Russian Committee
BLP	British Labor Party
CBRE	Canadian Brotherhood of Railway Employees
CCF	Cooperative Commonwealth Federation
CEC	Central Executive Committee (of the Communist Party of Canada)
CI	Communist International
CIO	Congress of Industrial Organizations
CLDL	Canadian Labor Defense League
CLP	Canadian Labor Party
CPA	Communist Party of America
CPC	Communist Party of Canada
CPGB	Communist Party of Great Britain
CPSU	Communist Party of the Soviet Union
ECCI	Executive Committee of the Communist International
FOC	Finnish Organization of Canada
ILP	Independent Labor Party
IUNTW	Industrial Union of Needle Trades Workers
IWW	Industrial Workers of the World
IFTU	International Federation of Trade Unions
ILD	International Labor Defense
ILGWU	International Ladies Garment Workers Union
KMT	Kuomintang
KPD	Communist Party of Germany
LWIU	Lumber Workers Industrial Union
MWUC	Mine Workers Union of Canada
OBU	One Big Union
PB	Political Bureau (of CPC)
RILU	Red International of Labor Unions
SDP	Social Democratic Party of Canada
SPC	Socialist Party of Canada
SPD	Social Democratic Party of Germany

SPNA	Socialist Party of North America
TLC	Trades and Labor Congress (Canada)
TUC	Trades Union Congress (Britain)
TUEL	Trade Union Educational League
UCPA	United Communist Party of America
ULFTA	Ukrainian Labor-Farmer Temple Association
UMWA	United Mine Workers of America
WPC	Workers Party of Canada
WPDL	Workers Political Defense League
WUL	Workers Unity League
YCL	Young Communist League
YCI	Young Communist International

PART ONE

A NEW KIND OF PARTY

It will be a party of action, seeking contact with the workers, a party in which the theorists and doctrinaires as such will find small place, a party of the workers, and with them in their daily struggles against capitalist oppression, seeking always to build up a united front of the working class for Industrial Freedom and Emancipation from wage slavery.

—*The Workers Guard,* December 17, 1921

1. War and Revolution

Canadian Communism did not spring out of the ground suddenly at the end of World War I, and it was not smuggled into the country by Russian agents. The men and women who created the new movement were long-time socialist and labor militants, most of whom had a decade or more of experience as leaders of the working class in Canada. Two related developments shaped their decision to create a new type of party, a Communist party. One was the experience of the Canadian labor movement, its victories and defeats, during and immediately after the War. The other was the October 1917 revolution in Russia, which in this country as elsewhere gave rise to a fundamental realignment of the left.

The new party built on an already long tradition in Canada of socialist organization and activity. But it also represented a deepgoing break with two characteristics of much of the prewar left: the sectarian abstention of some currents from participation in everyday struggles of working people, and the liberal nostrums of other currents that sought only to reform capitalism, not to overthrow it.

In 1914, on the eve of the War, two organizations dominated the Canadian left: the Socialist Party of Canada (SPC) and the Social Democratic Party of Canada (SDP). Each had about 3,000 members. The Socialist Party, the older of the two, was based in Vancouver and the great majority of its members were in the four western provinces. The SDP's Dominion Executive Committee was located in Berlin, Ontario (the city's name was changed to Kitchener during the war) and most of its members were in Ontario, although it had important groups of members in Montreal, Winnipeg, and on the West Coast.

The Socialist Party of Canada prided itself on its doctrinal puri-
ty. It would have no truck or trade with reformers or reforms: it was
for revolution, and nothing less. The SPC even refused to join the
Second International, on the grounds that the British Labor Party
was a member. In the language of the time, the SPC was an "impos-
sibilist" party: the word was coined as a contrast to the "possibil-
ist" socialists who favored trying to win whatever reforms were
possible within the framework of capitalist society. In the SPC's
view, reforms were at best a waste of time, at worst a diversion from
the struggle for socialism. It should be noted, however, that the
party deviated from this policy in practice: the socialists elected to
provincial legislatures (three in British Columbia, one in Alberta)
fought for and won a number of important reforms, most notably
improved working conditions in the mines.

Until 1912 the Socialist Party had held itself aloof from the trade
union movement. Although a majority of its members were unionists, and although some union locals expressed support for the
Socialists, the party's principal spokesmen were openly critical of,
even hostile to, the organized labor movement. The party's best-
known theoretician, E.T. Kingsley, argued that the conflicts
between employers and workers were not part of the class struggle
at all—they were mere "commodity struggles," disputes over the
division of wealth in capitalist society, and hence of no interest to
socialists. The class struggle, according to Kingsley and the SPC
leadership, existed only on the political level: in practice this meant
that the class struggle was limited to election campaigns. For all its
"impossiblism," the SPC was expounding a view not far removed
from reformism.

In 1912 a new generation took over the leadership of the Socialist
Party. The process by which this change was effected has not been
recorded, but the new leaders were, in their majority, active union
men. They included Jack Kavanaugh, W.A. "Bill" Pritchard, Joe
Naylor, Ginger Goodwin, and others, all of them men with long
experience in the labor movement. Under the leadership of this
group the Socialist Party won a majority of the executive positions
in the recently-formed B.C. Federation of Labor, and won leading
positions in many major unions, most importantly District 18 of the
United Mine Workers, which organized miners in Alberta and eastern B.C. The change in the party's policy towards the labor movement was demonstrated dramatically in the summer of 1913, when
the SPC played a leading role in the defense of striking miners on
Vancouver Island, campaigning for a general strike to force the

provincial government to remove the militia from the mines. This
turn in party policy laid the basis for the SPC's winning of the
leadership of the entire western labor movement in 1919.

The Social Democratic Party was formed in 1911 by a number of
groups which had split away from the Socialist Party during the
previous four years. The common denominator in all of the splits
was opposition to the SPC's fixed policy of refusing to cooperate
with non-socialist groups in the labor movement. The SDP favored,
and actively sought, alliances with the various small "Labour Parties" which existed on a local level in many cities.* In Toronto, for
example, the SDP was instrumental in the creation of a Labour
Representation Committee which included itself, the Independent
Labour Party, and the Toronto Trades and Labour Council. It made
a strong showing in the 1912 municipal elections, and in 1913 won
the election of prominent SDPer James Simpson to the Toronto
Board of Control, with a higher vote than any other candidate.

The SDP was much more heterogeneous than the Socialist Party.
While the SDP's "Platform" was generally Marxist in form and
content, the party included a very wide range of socialist opinion,
from revolutionary to purely reformist. It included, for example,
members of the Christian Socialist Fellowship, two of whom were
SDP candidates for public office in Toronto in 1914; one of them
expressed the view that "there is no room for intelligent difference
between the working class movement and the church, and that
both should work together to secure more ideal conditions than
prevail today."[1] Such opinions would never have been allowed in
the Socialist Party. Nor would the SPC have accepted into membership the group of Social Democrats at the University of
Toronto whose statement of principles included this singularly
un-Marxist clause:

There is nothing narrow about our Socialism. Socialism is the problem of
people living together. Democracy is the problem of rule by all the people.
The Social-Democratic Party aims, not at class hatred, but at the harmony
which is the ultimate well being of all the individuals in the state.[2]

---

*Most of these parties were "labor" in name only. Some of them were
electoral machines for ambitious union leaders: the Toronto Independent
Labour Party, for example, existed only to support the annual aldermanic
campaign of a leader of the Street Railway Men's union. Others had even
less connection to organized labor: they were composed of reformers who
were vaguely sympathetic to the program of the British Labor Party.

On the other hand, the SDP included a large number of socialists whose views corresponded to those of the orthodox Marxists of European Social Democracy. In general, although there were no firm factional lines, the division between the left and the right in the SDP corresponded to ethnic distinctions. Socialist immigrants from Eastern Europe—Ukrainians, Poles, Finns, and Jews in particular—made up a clear majority of the SDP membership. These SDPers, organized in separate "language branches" or separate federations, tended to stand on the party's left. They had brought with them to Canada their experiences in the fight against Czarist or Hapsburg tyranny: they were revolutionaries, trained in a far different school from that of the university socialists. But the ethnic groups tended to stay out of the public eye. The language barrier, and the deep-seated xenophobia of Canadian society, led them to restrict their activities to their own communities and to express their views only through the ethnic socialist press. The leadership of the SDP fell by default to the Anglo-Canadian wing of the party. People such as James Simpson, who was simultaneously a member of the SDP, the Methodist Church, and the Loyal Orange Lodge, ran the party.

Like the Socialist Party, the SDP had a very strong presence in the labor movement. R. Parm Pettipiece was editor of the West Coast labor weekly *B.C. Federationist*. R.A. Rigg was secretary of the Winnipeg Trades and Labor Council. James Simpson, Fred Bancroft, and James Watters were on the executive of the Trades and Labor Congress, forerunner of today's Canadian Labor Congress. These men were on the right wing of the socialist movement but in the labor movement as a whole they were on the left: the conservative American labor leader Samuel Gompers did not conceal his opinion that Simpson was a very dangerous radical.[3]

The absence of any significant Anglo-Canadian element in the SDP left wing is explained by the presence of other political organizations which attracted English-speaking revolutionists. In the far west and in Winnipeg, the Socialist Party played this role. In Southern Ontario the revolutionary pole of attraction was the Socialist Party of North America.

The SPNA, despite its name, never had more than 100 members, organized in three or four locals in Southern Ontario. It was formed in March 1911 by Local 24 of the Socialist Party of Canada. Its members objected strenuously to the pro-reform policies of the SPC's elected representatives, and to the SPC's support for restrictions on Oriental immigration.

The SPNA was strongly influenced at its founding by the sectarian and dogmatic Socialist Party of Great Britain: former SPGB leader Moses Baritz was the prime mover in the split from the SPC. Like the British party, the Socialist Party of North America took "impossibilism" to extremes. To join, a prospective member had to pass an examination in Marxist theory. Before being allowed to speak on a public platform in the party's name, more examinations had to be taken. The party's declaration of principles bound it to "wage war against all other political parties, whether alleged labor or avowedly capitalist," and rejected any support whatsoever to reforms.

Shortly after its formation, the SPNA parted company with the Socialist Party of Great Britain on a question which was later to prove of vital importance. The SPGB limited itself to abstract propaganda: it preached the socialist gospel and waited for the working class to see the light. In 1912 the SPNA abandoned that approach, adopting a resolution that its members should join trade unions whenever possible, and should propagandize for socialism within the unions. The party took on an interventionist character: though it still refused to cooperate with other socialist groups, it did regularly fight for its views in the labor movement. The organizers of any substantial labor or socialist meeting could always expect to find members of the SPNA in attendance, pressing their view that nothing less than the socialist revolution was of real interest to the working class.

The Left and the War

War was declared on August 4, 1914. On that date, as Rosa Luxemburg later wrote, German Social-Democracy abdicated and the Second International collapsed. The German SPD's "abdication" was certainly the most dramatic, since the party was the largest and most influential in the International, but desertion under fire was common throughout the world. Every major socialist party in Western Europe abandoned the principles of socialist internationalism: men who had condemned war for decades reversed themselves and urged the workers to slaughter each other in the name of the fatherland or Empire. The war exposed the deep inner rot of the Socialist International, a rot which years of peace had hidden from view.

Minorities in every party remained true to the program of revolutionary internationalism. In Germany Karl Liebknecht spoke out in the Reichstag against the war and voted against the war budget.

Together with Rosa Luxemburg and Franz Mehring, he began assembling the nucleus of revolutionists who would eventually create the German Communist Party. Similar developments took place elsewhere. In a few countries, entire parties held to an internationalist policy. The Russian Bolshevik Party, led by Lenin, condemned the International's betrayal and issued an appeal for the creation of a new International.

The Socialist Party of Canada belonged to the antiwar minority in the world socialist movement. On August 6, only two days after the declaration of war, it issued a strong statement which was widely distributed across the country:

MANIFESTO
To the Workers of Canada

In view of the European situation, and the efforts of the capitalist press and politicians to stir up a war fever in Canada, to the end that Canadian workingmen will be induced to take up arms in defense of the interests of their masters, the Socialist Party of Canada, instead of passing futile resolutions of protest, would call your attention to the following facts:

1. Inasmuch as all modern wars have their origin in the disputes of the international capitalist class for markets in which to dispose of the stolen products of labor, or to protect themselves in the possession of the markets they already have, the motive of the anticipated struggle in Europe is of no real interest to the international working class.

2. Further, as the struggle, if materialized, will claim as its victims countless thousands of the members of our class in a quarrel that is not theirs, it behoves the workers not to be carried away by the frenzied clamorings of the interested advocates of war, the vaporings of capitalist "statesmen," or the blare of martial music. In no conceivable manner, shape or form could the interests of the workers of any of the nationalities involved be furthered or protected by their participation in the conflict.

3. Since the international working class produces all the wealth of the world, and still possesses nothing, receiving in the shape of wages but sufficient to maintain a slavish existence: and since the international capitalist class occupies the position of a social parasite, producing nothing and possessing everything, which position it is able to maintain by virtue of its control of the state—the only struggle that can be of vital interest to the working class of all nations is that which has for its object the wresting of this power from the hands of the master class, and using it to remove all forms of exploitation and servitude. To this struggle the Socialist Party of Canada calls you. The only barrier standing in our way is ignorance in the ranks of our own class.

As an International Working Class, we have but one enemy—the International Capitalist Class.

WORKERS OF THE WORLD, UNITE! YOU HAVE NOTHING TO LOSE BUT YOUR CHAINS: YOU HAVE A WORLD TO GAIN.[4]

The Social Democratic Party had more difficulty than the SPC in deciding what to say about the European war: its manifesto did not appear until the end of August. When it did appear, however, the party gave it wide distribution, arranging publication in most labor newspapers and separate distribution as a handbill. Like the Socialist Party, the SDP opposed the war in sharp terms:

MANIFESTO

SOCIAL DEMOCRATIC PARTY OF CANADA

TO THE WORKERS OF CANADA

Ever since the war terror began its march through Europe, the capitalist press of Canada, acting on behalf of the capitalist class, has done its utmost to create the war spirit and arouse a patriotic cry, calling upon the workers of Canada to go forth and shed their blood in the interests of the MASTER CLASS.

We desire to emphasize the fact that this war, as all modern wars, is being waged between international capitalists. Representing as it does a struggle to secure markets for the disposal of the stolen products of labor, it can, therefore, be of no real interest to the working class.

Since capitalism is based upon wage-labor and capital, the working class receiving in the shape of wages but sufficient to maintain a bare existence and the ever-increasing surplus product taken from labor, strengthening as it does the position of the capitalist as a social parasite, we appeal to the workers of Canada to refrain from lending any assistance in this war. Let the MASTERS fight their own battles.

We further wish to emphasize the fact that the present is an opportune time of getting a larger measure as to your true class position in society. This is being pointed out everywhere by the socialists, on the street corner, in halls and through the party press. This knowledge is of vital interest. It will unfold to you the difference between social existence and social progress.

Yours for the revolution,

H. Martin, Dominion Executive Committee
Social Democratic Party[5]

It is obvious that the author of this statement had the Socialist Party's manifesto before him as he wrote: not only ideas but entire phrases have been copied. He has watered the message down somewhat, in particular by removing the SPC's emphasis on the class struggle and the idea that the working class has only one enemy— the capitalist class. This conception—comparable to Lenin's insistence that for the workers the real enemy was at home—played an important role in Socialist Party propaganda during the war, while the SDP leadership tended towards more pacifist positions. A west coast SDP newspaper, for example, devoted a full page to an article which asserted that "The only power that is greater than both militarism and hate is the power that rules the universe—the power of love."[6] Compare that statement to a protest issued by Winnipeg SPC local number 3 when the *Winnipeg Tribune* labeled them pacifists:

Mr Editor, in conclusion allow us to again protest against the label Pacifist. We are strong upholders of war, and you can rest assured that each member of our party is forced to do his bit in the class war. A war, our success in which means to the workers abolition of exploitation and the ownership of the earth and all that therein is.[7]

On the war, as on other questions, there was division in the SDP. The party's Anglo-Canadian leadership was at best pacifist, while much of its rank and file stood for revolutionary internationalism. This was especially true of the Eastern European SDPers, who had lived under the tyranny of Britain's ally, the czar. They knew from personal experience that this was no war for democracy and civilization. Their views were expressed in an unsigned Ukrainian leaflet, distributed in Montreal:

Twenty-three millions of the most beautiful bloom of humanity are led out on to the battlefield to be slaughtered—to unavoidable death. These millions are for the second year already killing each other to amuse the crowned kingly heads, to satisfy the blood-drinking capitalists: Germans, English, Austrians, Russians, French, and other nations....

Yell, you tyrants! Yell, and you, who got drunk on the blood of the people, be happy and forge new chains! Mad ones—already the black ravens are crowing about the bodies of our brothers. There will be a time of settlement, a time of reckoning and judgement, and the Proletariat will end the war. He will use his own arms which you gave him, against his tyrants and destroyers. By one move of the working class, the thrones will fall and the crowns will be thrown from the heads, and other inhuman creatures and the ancient bloody system will disappear off the face of the earth. Over the heads of the imprisoned ones, a red flag of brotherhood and freedom will wave, and all will be happy and equal in the new powers of Socialism.
    This is the aim to which the present suffering people are striving, and which will certainly come in the semblance of a great holy war named "Social Revolution."[8]

This was a far cry from the SDP leadership's abstract criticism of war: it was even stronger than the Socialist Party's propaganda. So, too, was a Russian-language leaflet distributed in Toronto. It urged the soldiers to recognize that their enemies were not in the opposing trenches, but at home:

Comrade workingman, the private of the enemy's army, I know that you are not my adversary. Shake hands, comrade! We are both victims of slander and oppression. Our common chief enemy is behind our backs. Let us turn the barrels of our carbines against our true, our common enemies.[9]

As we will see, these opposing views on war eventually split the Social Democratic Party. At the beginning of the war, however, the differences were not clear. To any outsider, and to most participants, it seemed that the Canadian Left was united in its opposition to the War.*

Decline

The outbreak of war was accompanied by an unprecedented propaganda barrage depicting the German people as semicivilized, bloodthirsty monsters. The word "Hun" replaced "German" in the vocabulary of politicians and the daily press. Tales of terrible atrocities filled the newspapers. The German Army was reported to be murdering babies, raping nuns, and slaughtering thousands of innocent civilians in "poor helpless Belgium." The war was portrayed as a crusade for democracy and civilization against Hunnish tyranny.

If the most prominent socialists in Western Europe had fallen victim to the patriotic plague, it is scarcely surprising that some Canadian socialists did likewise, especially under the impact of the anti-German campaign. Perhaps the best known SPC member to abandon his principles was J.H. Burroughs, editor of the party's newspaper *Western Clarion*. An editorial by Burroughs in the October 24, 1914 issue declared support for the allies against "German culture," and expressed the hope that Germany would soon be crushed.

This editorial produced a storm of protest from the party ranks. The Toronto local demanded Burroughs' expulsion. The Winnipeg

---

*I have been unable to find any statements on the war by the Socialist Party of North America, but there is no reason to doubt SPNA leader Florence Custance's later statement that "the party did not fear to openly denounce the war, but the members were by no means pacifists."[10]

local warned that the editorial "gave a fake idea of the S.P. of C. position on the war." The Calgary SPC charged that the article was "opposed to the manifesto of the Socialist Party of Canada and the working class movement," and expressed the hope that "such capitalist punk will be confined to the waste paper basket in the future." The Vancouver local urged that steps be taken "that will prevent the repetition of such an obnoxious tirade in the party organ."

The Dominion Executive Committee voted 4 to 1 to condemn the editorial, and Burroughs was forced to resign.[11] From that point on the *Western Clarion* maintained a strong antiwar position.

The apostasy of much of the international left forced the SPC to re-evaluate its positions on a number of major questions, and it moved sharply to the left. Although the party had long had a formal position in opposition to reforms, its statement of principles had pledged to support legislation that would "advance the interests of the working class and aid the workers in their class struggle against capitalism." In 1915 the SPC deleted those words from the statement of principles: it now called for socialism and nothing else.[12]

In 1916 the party endorsed a call by the Socialist Party of Great Britain for the formation of a Third International.[13] And in October 1917—before the Bolshevik Revolution—it began discussing a proposal to change the party's name to "Communist Party of Canada."[14]

But firmness of revolutionary principle was no guarantee of organizational stability, especially in face of the great social pressure in favor of the war. The entire labor movement was weakened by the war in its first years: trade union membership dropped by 18 percent between January 1914 and December 1915, and the number of workers taking part in strikes was the lowest in many years.[15] The decline in working class combativity also affected the Socialist Party. There was no rank and file revolt, no split, simply a rapid erosion of membership and support. The smaller party locals disappeared, while the large ones declined in size and activity. Financial support fell off. In April 1915 the twice-monthly *Western Clarion* changed to a monthly, and the November 1915 issue failed to appear at all because the party could not pay the printer. The Socialist Party was paying the price for swimming against the stream.

One result of this decline was a strengthening of the sectarian currents which had dominated the party until 1912. Anti-union articles reappeared in the pages of the *Clarion,* and the paper increasingly limited itself to abstract expositions of Marxist theory. The division between the party's "intellectuals" and the trade union socialists deepened: the latter, who were fighting losing battles to retain their influence in the unions, seem to have pulled back from party life, increasing the isolation of the party.

The Social Democratic Party leaders were much more strongly influenced by prowar propaganda, and many of them adopted openly pro-imperialist positions. R. Parm Pettipiece used his position as editor of the *B.C. Federationist* to argue that "the only force capable of destroying the menace of German military bureaucracy is military force."[16] He gave full support to the Allied cause. James Simpson voted for a variety of prowar resolutions on the Toronto Board of Control: when the jingoism got to be too much for him, he would quietly absent himself so as not to disturb the unanimity of the proceedings. When he ran for re-election in December 1914, a *Toronto Daily Star* editorial noted that "everyone who knows Simpson knows he is loyal to the core."[17]

Even the most radical members of the SDP leadership began to buckle under the weight of anti-German propaganda. In August 1914 the party's Dominion Secretary, Hill Martin, had written: "We don't want other people's blood, and we refuse to waste our own. If the masters want blood, let them cut their own throats."[18] In the fall of 1915 he resigned from the party and volunteered for the Armed Forces. He was followed by Toronto SDP organizer Matthew Wayman: when Wayman returned from Europe he castigated his former comrades as traitors and German agents.[19] In 1918 R.A. Rigg resigned as secretary of the Winnipeg Trades and Labor Council in order to enlist: he told the press that he "had come to the conclusion that it mattered whether this war is won or lost."[20]

The renegacy of the party members who dominated the Trades and Labor Congress was particularly dramatic. In 1911 the TLC had endorsed a proposal for a general strike in the event of war breaking out, and subsequent TLC conventions adopted strong antiwar statements. But when the war came, the TLC Executive issued a statement which condemned war in general, promised to act to end the war "at any moment the working class in the other countries involved make a move to end this struggle," and endorsed Britain's campaign against "German despotism."[21] A year later the executive declared that it was "the duty of the Labor world to lend every possible assistance to the Allies of Great Britain...in a mighty endeavour to secure early and final victory for the cause of freedom and democracy."[22] The TLC Executive opposed plans for "registration" of labor until the Borden government actually introduced a registration scheme: then they supported it. They opposed conscription vigorously, even threatening a general strike to stop it, but, when conscription became law, they abandoned the fight with the excuse that "under our representative form of government, it is not deemed either right, patriotic, or in the interests of the Dominion or of the Labor classes" to resist enacted legislation.[23]

WHILE THE TLC LEADERSHIP was expressing its confidence in democracy and the British tradition of fair play, thousands of workers were discovering what these could mean in practice. Wartime legislation, passed by Order-in-Council without Parliamentary approval, provided for the internment without trial of "enemy aliens"—which meant anyone who had been born in Germany or in the lands ruled by the Austro-Hungarian Empire. In all, more than 8,000 "enemy aliens" were held in Canadian "internment camps." Those allowed out on parole were prohibited from taking any part in discussions of the war.* Police conducted regular round-ups in immigrant neighborhoods, arresting every man who could not produce a registration card: no such raids took place in Anglo-Saxon neighborhoods.

In part the government's repressive policies were aimed at immigrants in general; in part they were aimed directly at the left. Sometimes it was impossible to tell just which concern was uppermost in the authorities' minds. The May 2, 1918 *Toronto Daily Star,* for example, reported that Ottawa police had raided "a secret session of alien enemies" and interned a group of Austrians. The SDP's *Canadian Forward* revealed that the "secret session" was a May Day celebration organized by Ottawa local 56 of the SDP, and that the "Austrians" arrested were in fact seventeen socialists of Ukrainian origin. They were described as Austrians solely because their home towns were within the boundaries of the Austro-Hungarian Empire.[24]

Direct suppression of socialist views was also widespread. In 1915 Socialist Party members in Red Deer, Alberta and Saint John, New Brunswick, were jailed for sedition. Isaac Bainbridge, editor of *Canadian Forward*, was arrested repeatedly and served a number

---

*On Sunday, June 10, 1917, Toronto police raided a meeting of the Ukrainian branch of the SDP. Over 80 people were arrested on the grounds that simply attending such a meeting, called to discuss conscription, was a violation of their parole.

of short prison terms for publishing articles critical of the war. In September 1918 two radicals of Russian origin in Toronto received prison sentences of two and three years for "uttering statements detrimental to Britain and her allies."[25]

Official repression was accompanied by officially-sanctioned unofficial action. A particularly blatant case of this occurred in Toronto on June 3, 1917, when a well-organized mob of several hundred war veterans attacked an SDP anticonscription meeting in the Labor Temple, broke furniture, terrorized women and children, beat several of the organizers, then marched off in formation, unmolested by the squad of forty Toronto Police officers who watched the proceedings from beginning to end.[26]

The federal government instituted press censorship at the beginning of the war, a censorship which in practice was aimed at the left. A long list of banned periodicals was established: many of the outlawed newspapers were socialist organs from the United States. The Chief Press Censor carefully followed the socialist press and issued warnings whenever the slightest criticism of government policy appeared. The extent of the censorship may be judged from the fact that an entire issue of the University of Toronto *Varsity* was suppressed because it contained a letter mildly critical of Britain's war aims. The editor responsible for publication of that issue, 19-year-old Maurice Spector, was removed from his post.[27]

Like the Socialist Party, the SDP went into sharp decline at the beginning of the war. Early in 1915 its newspaper went bankrupt, leaving the party without any English-language press until October 1916. Party members who held municipal office were, in most cases, defeated in the December 1914 municipal elections; James Simpson, who had topped the polls in 1913, was defeated in his try for re-election to Toronto Board of Control in 1914, despite the editorial support of the *Globe,* the *Star,* and the *World.*

More serious was the rapidly growing rift between the party leadership and the immigrant socialists who formed the majority of the party's membership. The immigrant socialists bore the brunt of government repression: this intensified their disagreements with the SDP's prowar wing, and at the same time forced them more and more to limit their activities to their own communities. By late 1916, although the myth of a united party remained, there were in fact several Social Democratic Parties in Canada: a Russian SDP, a Ukrainian SDP, a Jewish SDP, and so on. When Russia's czar was overthrown in March 1917, the SDP found itself unable to organize a united celebration: on April 1 there were two meetings in

Toronto's Massey Hall in support of the Russian Revolution. In the afternoon the Ukrainian, Polish, Finnish, and Russian SDPers met, while the English and Jewish SDP met in the evening. Participants in the afternoon meeting told reporters "We won't be bossed by Jimmy Simpson," "They want to run everything," and "Simpson engineered the big meeting and we didn't want it that way." In the afternoon meeting speakers told the audience "that the Russian revolution had not gone far enough," while the evening meeting, which featured a speaker from the Liberal Party, was content to endorse the purported victory of democracy in Russia.[28]

This split deepened when the TLC leadership abandoned the extraparliamentary anticonscription fight in favor of support for anticonscription candidates in the December 1917 general election. That election was conducted under the Wartime Elections Act, which took the vote away from conscientious objectors, pacifists, and all citizens of "enemy alien" origin, if they had been naturalized later than March 31, 1902, or if they normally spoke an "enemy language."* For the Social Democrats who were not citizens, or who lost their rights by government decree, electoral activity was meaningless. What respect they retained for the party's right-wing leadership was lost forever.

Revival

The Canadian labor movement had grown rapidly in the years preceding the war: membership in trade unions rose from about 50,000 at the turn of the century to more than 175,000 in 1913. The outbreak of war brought this growth to a halt. Membership dropped to 166,000 in 1914 and to 143,000 by the end of 1915. This decline resulted in part from the enlistment of union members in the armed forces, and in part from the depression which began in 1914, producing widespread unemployment in unionized industries.†

The depression ended in 1916. Unemployment almost disappeared. Many industries experienced a severe manpower shortage. Workers pressed their advantage by taking part in militant strikes,

---

*The same act gave the vote to wives, widows, sisters, and daughters of members of the Canadian forces serving in Europe. These first women to vote in a Canadian federal election were enfranchised solely to produce an overwhelming majority for proconscription candidates.

†Union membership was concentrated in skilled trades, such as construction and printing. These trades were hurt by recession and by the diversion of capital into munitions manufacturing. The factories which converted to munitions were seldom unionized.

embittered by the glaring contrast between the employers' super-profits and the sacrifices imposed on working people by wartime conditions. In 1917 more than 50,000 workers took strike action. The number rose to 79,000 in 1918 and—as pent-up social tensions were unleashed in the wake of the war—to the phenomenal total of 148,915 strikers in 1919. The dramatic upsurge in labor militancy halted the decline in union membership and brought thousands, then hundreds of thousands of new members into the unions. By the end of 1917 there were a record 204,630 trade union members in Canada. Membership totals passed 240,000 in 1918 and reached nearly 380,000 in 1919, more than double the highest prewar total.

These figures may seem small when viewed from today's perspective: since 1966 there has never been a year in which fewer than 200,000 Canadian workers took part in strikes. But the labor upsurge of 1917-1919 must be viewed in the context of its time. Canada's population was much smaller than it is today (8,788,483 according to the 1921 census) and the majority of the population lived outside of the major cities. Farming was the most productive sector of the economy: the great production industries that were to be organized by the CIO in later decades did not yet exist. The number of workers who went on strike in 1919 was not only greater than in any previous year, it was not equalled again until 1943. In 1919 the Department of Labor began calculating the total duration of strikes as a percentage of the estimated total working time of all non-farm workers. That percentage hit 0.60 in 1919: it has never since been so high.

The rebirth of the labor movement in 1917 was paralleled by a resurgence of the left. Socialists played prominent roles in the anti-conscription movement, organizing meetings attended by thousands in cities from coast to coast. More than 1,000 people attended a Toronto SDP meeting in celebration of May Day, 1917.[29] The editor of *Canadian Forward* exuberantly reported the new mood a few weeks later:

A new spirit is abroad amongst the workers. The deadly apathy which has held them in thrall is passing away, and the long-awaited reaction against capitalist jingoism is coming swiftly. Everywhere there are evidences of a reawakened interest in Socialism and the Socialist movement. The sales of literature, especially sales of 'The Canadian Forward,' are increasing. Old comrades who became unattached and inactive are entering again into the struggle with whole-hearted energy and enthusiasm. Branches are keenly anxious to begin the open-air campaigns and new branches are being started....[30]

Events in Russia were particularly inspiring for the Canadian left. On International Women's Day, March 8, 1917, mass demonstrations developed into an uprising which overthrew the czar.* A provisional government was established, incorporating most of the non-Socialist political parties. The workers' councils (soviets) which had first appeared during Russia's 1905 revolution, were reborn.

For thousands of socialists in Canada, these events had direct personal relevance. They had fled the czar's rule, they still had relatives in Russia, they knew many of the new political leaders personally or by name. Many of them made immediate arrangements to return home to take part in the revolution.

Even socialists who had no personal ties to Russia were inspired. This was a mass popular uprising against tyranny, and as such had the full support of the entire Canadian left. The socialist press followed events in Russia as closely as it could, hindered by distance and by wartime censorship.

The first substantial analysis of events in Russia in the socialist press appeared in *Canadian Foward* on June 13, 1917. The article was written by Gregory Chicherin, a Russian Marxist then in exile in Britain. He described the class conflicts in Russia, and forecast a further deepening of the revolutionary process, including its extension to other European countries. Six months later Chicherin was a member of the Bolshevik government in Petrograd.

Inspired by the overthrow of the czar, strengthened by the revitalization of the labor movement, mobilized by the campaign against conscription, the Canadian left had begun to revive by mid-1917. But the real turning point came in November. The February Revolution in Russia was a light in the East: the October Revolution was a bolt of lightning.

Revolution in Russia

In the eight months that followed the downfall of Czar Nicholas II, government succeeded government: none was willing or able to satisfy the Russian masses' intense desire for peace, land reform, and economic justice. The first governments were restricted to the procapitalist parties; then a few moderate "socialists" were invited in. Eventually a populist, Alexander Kerensky, became prime min-

---

*In 1917 Russia was still using the Julian calendar, which was 13 days behind that used in other countries. As a result, Russia's "February Revolution" took place in March by Western reckoning, and the "October Revolution" took place on November 7.

ister, with a mixed liberal and socialist cabinet. This government too was committed to the maintenance of capitalism and to the continuation of the war. Its unpopularity grew steadily.

The Provisional Government was an arbitrarily selected group of politicians with no democratic mandate. The only democratic structures in the country were the Soviets of Workers' and Peasants' Deputies. These bodies, thrown up spontaneously in the revolutionary upsurge and constantly replenished by mandated delegates from the factories, the fields, and the front, much more accurately reflected the rapidly shifting moods of the masses. At first they were dominated by the moderate socialists, who were content to let the Provisional Government rule, but they moved rapidly to the left. The most revolutionary party in Russia, the Russian Social-Democratic Labor Party (Bolshevik)* won support in local and regional Soviets across the country. By autumn it was clear that the Bolsheviks would have a majority in the All-Russian Soviet Congress scheduled to open in Petrograd on October 25 (November 7). "All power to the Soviets!" was the Bolsheviks' principal slogan, and they meant what they said. Fearing endless wrangling with the Kerensky government, perhaps even an attempt at a military coup, the Bolshevik-led Petrograd Soviet overthrew Kerensky's government on the eve of the Congress. When the Soviet assembled, Bolshevik leaders Leon Trotsky and Vladimir Ilyich Lenin announced that power was now in the hands of the Russian workers.

Now Lenin, gripping the edge of the reading stand, letting his little winking eyes travel over the crowd as he stood there waiting, apparently oblivious to the long-rolling ovation, which lasted several minutes. When it finished, he said simply, "We shall now proceed to construct the Socialist order!"[31]

The revolution had an electrifying effect on the world socialist movement. For generations Marxists had been talking about proletarian revolution: now one was actually taking place. Marxism had been raised from theory to practice. As a founder of the U.S. Communist Party later wrote:

The whole world labor movement was overcome with depression in 1914-1917.

---

*The word "Bolshevik" means "majority." It refers to a 1903 split in the Russian Social Democratic Party. It quickly became synonymous with "Leninist" or "Communist" and is so used in this book.

But the Russian Revolution of November 7 changed all that overnight. At one blow, the revolution lifted the proletariat of Europe to its feet again. It stirred the hundreds of millions of colonial slaves who had never known political aspiration before, who had never dared to hope before. The Russian Revolution awakened them to the promise of a new life.[32]

A Winnipeg socialist expressed similar sentiments a few years after the revolution:

Those were dark days for the progressive workers, and it appeared that the work of the past was all in vain. But when the situation had assumed its blackest aspect, a bright light suddenly appeared in an unexpected quarter. The downtrodden workers of Russia, taking advantage of the situation the war had created, overthrew their age-long oppressors. This act was the greatest stimulus the workers of the world have ever received.[33]

And Canadian revolutionist Malcolm Bruce, who in 1917 was a member of the Socialist Party in Vancouver, later recalled his reaction to the revolution:

It was like a bolt out of the blue, like a blinding light when the news came over of the overthrow of the democratic government by the Bolsheviks and the establishing of the Soviet Republic. ...there was a great uplift amongst the working class. At least they saw that the working class rose in their might and took over the power of a powerful nation and they wondered if it couldn't be done here. ...Charlie Lestor, who was perhaps the greatest lecturer and propagandist they had in the Socialist Party of Canada,...said: "Malcolm, this is it! This is the beginning of the world revolution!"[34]

Enthusiasm for the Russian Revolution was universal in the Canadian left. Even James Simpson demagogically announced that he "would rather be a member of the Bolshevik government...than a member of the British House of Commons."[35] The socialists studied everything that came out of Russia. *Canadian Forward* reprinted John Reed's brilliant eyewitness reports of the Bolshevik revolution from the U.S. socialist press. These were followed by articles by immigrants from Russia, and by translations of speeches and articles by Lenin, Trotsky, and other Bolshevik leaders.*

---

*As a result, the socialists were much better educated about Russia than were those who read only the capitalist press. The *Toronto Daily Star*, for example, told its readers that "the control of Russia...is in the hands of German-paid anarchists." Between November 1917 and November 1919 the *New York Times* announced the downfall of the Bolsheviks no fewer than ninety-one times![36]

The first work by any of the Bolshevik leaders to be widely read in Canada was Leon Trotsky's *War and the International,* originally published as a pamphlet in Switzerland in 1914. A U.S. publisher rushed out a much-padded translation as a book, under the title *The Bolsheviki and World Peace.* Advertisements for the book appeared in every left-wing periodical in Canada in February 1918, accompanied by laudatory reviews. *Canadian Forward* called it "a book that should be in the library of every socialist."[37] Excerpts appeared in the pages of the Toronto *Mail and Empire.* The book was even the topic of sermons: the Reverend Dr. Horace Westwood of All-Souls Unitarian Church in Winnipeg disagreed with Trotsky's views, but paid tribute to its power and impact:

Never have I met a more consummate handling of facts, or a keener insight into the struggle of the masses. Every page is vibrant with passion, the passion of his conception of justice. Every page rings with his evident sincerity. His is no small soul. He is a great man on fire with the vision of a great cause and idea.[38]

If a religious leader reacted that way, we can imagine the response of people who considered themselves Marxists. By early in 1918, Canadian revolutionary socialists were referring to themselves as "Bolsheviki" and seeking to emulate the Russians. Four months after the Bolshevik victory, the Manitoba Social Democratic Party declared "its willingness to unite with the Socialist Party of Canada on the basis of the Bolsheviki program," sent greetings to the Soviet government, and condemned the German Social Democratic Party as "the Judas of the International working class" for not acting to block Germany's war against the Soviets.[39]

THE DEBATES AROUSED by the Russian Revolution in the Canadian labor movement pushed the Social Democratic Party further along the road to an open split. For some time the right wing of the SDP had been urging that the party dissolve itself into some broader, even more amorphous party, a Canadian version of the British Labor Party with organic links to the trade unions. James Simpson expounded this view in full-blown form in the February 24, 1918 issue of *Canadian Forward.* He recalled the steps taken by the Trades and Labor Congress leadership in 1917, when it had initiated the formation of a "Canadian Labor Party"—largely in an effort to defuse pressures for mass extraparliamentary action in the struggle against conscription. The CLP had not taken hold among the mass of workers, but Simpson held out high hopes for its prospects. He proposed that the SDP should join the CLP as a body:

> The experience of the British Labour Party proves that the intimate associa-
> tion of the Trade Unionists and Socialists in one political organization is
> mutually advantageous. Trade unionists get a clearer vision of their duty to
> those of their own class and socialists become more sympathetic with the
> psychology of the working class movement, thus compelling them to adopt
> methods of education through their propaganda that are sanely adapted to
> the real conditions that have to be faced.[40]

Simpson's proposal may have gained credibility from developments that were occurring at the same time inside the British Labor
Party, whose membership had been seized with enthusiasm by the
Bolshevik Revolution in Russia. At a conference in December 1917
the BLP adopted a manifesto with a sweeping program for "socialization of Industry." Simpson, who attended the conference,
returned to tell a Montreal audience in February 1918 that

> There are not many differences between the Bolsheviks and the British
> workers. The press has tried to belittle the Bolshevik Government, but it is
> well to recognize that the sentiment of the Russian people is at bottom that
> of the British workingmen.
> ...What the British workers want is just what the Bolsheviki have
> attained—the nationalization of all great public institutions—such as
> railways and banks.[41]

But the Canadian Labor Party, with its very tenuous, limited
roots in the unions and its lack of popular support, was not even a
pale reflection of the British Labor Party, let alone the Bolshevik
Party! In reality, Simpson, for all his praise of the Bolsheviks, was
trying to deflect popular support for the Russian revolutionists into
support for a quite different kind of political organization, a parliamentary, electoralist party. His proposal provoked a major controversy in the Social Democratic Party, and it soon became clear that
an absolute majority of the SDP membership was hostile to the idea
of joining the CLP. The Manitoba SDP, at the same convention
that offered to unite with the Socialist Party "on the basis of the
Bolsheviki program," decided that membership in the Canadian
Labor Party was incompatible with membership in the Social
Democratic Party.

The Anglo-Canadian wing of the SDP had no intention of waiting for the decision of the majority, or of respecting that majority's
wishes. When the Ontario Section of the Canadian Labor Party

was founded in March 1918, James Simpson was convention secretary, and fifty-six of the four hundred delegates present represented SDP branches. They remained in the new party even though the convention defeated every radical resolution put forward.[42]

Similarly, in Manitoba, the Anglo-Canadian wing of the party ignored the convention decision on the labor party and participated in the founding of the Dominion Labor Party in the spring of 1918.* Well-known Social Democrats Arthur Beech and Fred Tipping were on the executive of the new party. In British Columbia the SDP simply vanished: virtually of its leaders transferred their allegiance to the Federated Labor Party early in 1918: the remainder joined the Socialist Party.[43]

In effect, a cold split had taken place. In Manitoba the left wing had taken the party over and the right wing had walked out. In B.C. the party collapsed. In Ontario the party retained a semblance of unity, but the right-wing members devoted all of their political energies to the CLP, while the left moved towards Bolshevism.

Bolshevism and the SPNA

The "Bolsheviki program" offered to Canadian revolutionaries a new conception of what a socialist program should be, and a new view of the role to be played by the revolutionaries themselves. For a generation or more, in Canada and around the world, Marxism had been buried in a heap of scholarly dogmatism and bureaucratic reformism. The social revolution was relegated to the distant future: socialists were reduced either to pedantic repetitions of eternal Marxist truths, or to petty tinkering with the mechanisms of capitalist society. The Bolsheviks restored to Marxism the idea that the duty of revolutionaries is to make the revolution. They rejected fatalism: their party sought to intervene in society as an active force, to move the working class to act in its own interests, and ultimately to lead a proletarian revolution.

There was, obviously, more to Bolshevism than that. Lenin's writings on strategy and tactics display a subtlety of approach that few of his self-proclaimed followers even today appreciate, let alone emulate. But it was this commitment to revolutionary *action*, to a unity of theory and practice in which the party itself became a

---

*The Canadian Labor Party was a federation of provincial parties — it had a different name in almost every province. To add to the confusion, there were other "Labor Parties" which were not part of the CLP.

dynamic force in history, that won the allegiance of the international left.

The entire Canadian left was influenced by the Bolshevik conception of revolutionary politics, but one organization accepted it totally, and was transformed by it: the Socialist Party of North America. As a result, the SPNA played a critical role in the establishment of the Communist movement in Canada.

The actual process of transformation is virtually undocumented. Only one participant, Florence Custance, wrote about the experience. Her reminiscence, which appeared in the Canadian Communist newspaper *The Worker* in 1926, is very brief and contains few details.

According to Custance, a major debate broke out in the SPNA shortly after the Bolshevik Revolution in 1917. One group supported the Bolsheviks, while another saw the Revolution as "a wild experience of a handful of men, who had returned to Russia after living in exile." The pro-Bolshevik group won a majority.

Shortly thereafter the party launched, for the first time in its history, a newspaper, *The Marxian Socialist.* From the very first issue the paper caused disputes: it could not be limited to abstract expositions of theory, it had to take stands on current issues. A major point of contention was parliamentarism — the party had always forecast that socialism would come through elections, but that policy was now challenged. After "a heated and bitter discussion" the party adopted a policy which "was a departure from the former strictly doctrinaire attitude." Custance's summary of the new policy shows just how much of a departure was involved:

It insisted upon the necessity of work in the trade unions and that work in this connection must be considered in the light of class struggle activity and not merely a pure and simple wages question deserving only theoretical treatment.

It recognized the usefulness of the general strike in the process of revolutionary struggle. (This form of struggle had always been characterized as a syndicalist tactic.)

It insisted that parliamentarism had its limitations and that the class struggle could not be confined within the narrow scope of parliamentarism. (This conception was tantamount to heresy.)

And finally it recognized the need of armed insurrection, for the establishment of the workers power and rule. (This was the maddest of all conceptions.)[44]

From this point it was only a small step to a call for regroupment of the left, for creation of a new party uniting in a single revolutionary organization all those who agreed with this approach. The SPNA quickly took that step. Its appeal to the revolutionary left appeared as an editorial in the September 1918 *Marxian Socialist*. It deserves to be quoted at length, as the first clear Canadian appeal for a party of a new type.

The forces of Allied imperialism are battling with the forces of revolutionary Russia; intervention has become a fact. From East and West, North and South the forces of the imperialistic Bourgeoisie are invading the young proletarian republic. Their object is the destruction of the revolutionary forces and the consequent overthrow of the Soviets.

With the expropriated exploiters of Russia as their allies, the international Capitalist class is preparing to wipe out the great menace to their system. But while they are one in the desire of annihilating the revolutionary forces, they are divided as to who shall get the lion's share of the plunder; so that on the ruins of the proletarian state, there would develop a conflict for the control of the natural resources of Russia.

The proletariat of Canada must ask itself the question: What will victory of the Russian working-class mean—and what defeat?

Victory will mean the speedy establishment of Socialism not only in Russia, but throughout Europe by a series of revolutions. It will baffle the efforts of the Asiatic imperialists who attempt to erect their rule in Asia. It will weaken the power of the Capitalist class in America and Australia and so give the proletariat the opportunity of asserting itself. In fact, it will mean the end of exploitation and all wars of conquest and pave the way for the peaceful development of society on a communistic basis.

Defeat of the revolution will bring the world-war to new life, will temporarily weaken the proletariat everywhere. Victory of Imperialism will give rise to new world wars and the most abject slavery, which in turn again leads to the greatest sharpening of the class struggle and must therefore lead to new political eruptions. In the words of Lenine: "The proletariat must choose between years if not decades of wars between the great imperialist powers, or revolution."

What must be done under such circumstances? The most powerful propaganda must be started at once, to arouse the indifferent. Locally and nationally the various revolutionary groups must cooperate in a united effort for the purpose of counteracting through an extensive education the work of the forces of reaction.

The time is ripe for unity of the Revolutionaries in Canada. The need for an organization which is nation wide, not in name only, but in fact, and which will not hesitate to combat the political forces of the master class is imperative in these days of rapidly moving events.

Instead of localized spasmodic efforts, we need a country-wide effort, instead of mere philosophizing we need action. The next step in this direction is the calling of a convention for the purpose of uniting the revolutionaries in the fight against the ruling class as well as the opportunists.[45]

This is a remarkable document. In the first place, its appeal for a new organization is posed in a totally internationalist framework. The new party is seen as an element in an international proletarian army, doing its part on Canadian soil to advance the world revolution. One would search in vain for any earlier document that stated the responsibilities of Canadian socialists in such terms. Secondly, the appeal focuses on the need for coordinated country-wide *action* against the "political forces of the master class." Again, this breaks with tradition. Even the campaign against conscription in 1917 had involved a variety of local actions, rather than a common and coordinated drive against the government. The SPNA was proposing a party of a new type: a party that was internationalist in ideology and in deed; a party prepared for political combat with capitalism at home and abroad.

The appeal received a favorable response. The Socialist Party column in Winnipeg's *Western Labor News* called it a "fine editorial," and reported that the Manitoba and Alberta executives of the SPC, as well as "many locals of the SDP in this city" were in favor of a convention which would establish such an organization as the Socialist Party of North America proposed.[46]

The SPNA's appeal appeared early in September, 1918. The unity convention it proposed would no doubt have occurred by year-end: but on September 27 the government outlawed the left.

2. The First Communist Party

Early in 1918, government and police officials began to express concern about the growth of the radical left. The Royal Northwest Mounted Police reported that the Industrial Workers of the World were gaining ground, and launched an investigation.[1] The Chief Press Censor noted an increase in the volume of radical literature published, and complained that he "found it pretty difficult to know just what to do in dealing with publications printed in Ukrainian, Russian, Lithuanian, Estonian and Finnish..."[2] The Acting Chief of the Dominion Police proposed that meetings in foreign languages be banned and that radical literature be outlawed.[3]

In the summer of 1918, Prime Minister Borden appointed C.H. Cahan, a conservative lawyer from Montreal who was later to serve as a minister in the R.B. Bennett government, to investigate the situation and make recommendations "in respect to the existing regulations for safe guarding the public interests against enemy aliens."[4] The wording of Cahan's terms of reference indicates that the government had already decided how it viewed the problem. It had no difficulty in accepting Cahan's principal conclusion: "The Bolsheviki are enemy aliens."

Cahan reported that the regulations, which forced "enemy aliens" (i.e., immigrants from Germany and Austria-Hungary) to register and made them subject to internment, were effective and well-administered. There was only one problem: the law did not cover Russians, Ukrainians, and Finns, people who posed a serious danger:

The Russians, Ukrainians and Finns, who are employed in the mines, factories and other industries in Canada, are now being thoroughly saturated with the Socialistic doctrines which have been proclaimed by the Bolsheviki faction of Russia.... I have before me a mass of literature, filled with most pernicious and seditious teaching, which is even now, in large quantities, being secretly circulated in Canada.... Since the outbreak of the present war, revolutionary groups of Russians, Ukrainians and Finns have been organized throughout Canada, and are known as The Social Democratic Party of Canada, the Ukrainian Revolutionary Group, the Russian Revolutionary Group, and others.... The members of these associations of Russians, Ukrainians and Finns, who, as aliens, are carrying on a most pernicious propaganda, should be compelled to register, and thereby be made amenable to local police supervision.[5]

Cahan's report, presented to the government in mid-September, was a mixture of truth, half-truth, lies, and prejudice, buttressed by quotations from radical literature and reports from politically illiterate policemen. There was no suggestion in it that Canadians of British descent might be attracted to Bolshevik policies: Bolshevism was a foreign invention, supported only by foreigners. The report, only 17 double-spaced pages long, made no attempt to prove its case, but it did not have to. It was preaching to the converted. Less than two weeks after Cahan completed his report, the Borden government implemented measures even more severe than those recommended by Cahan.

Order-in-Council PC 2384, issued on September 27, 1918, banned thirteen organizations: the Industrial Workers of the World, the Russian Social Democratic Party, the Russian Revolutionary Group, the Russian Social Revolutionists, the Russian Workers Union, the Ukrainian Revolutionary Group, the Social Democratic Party, the Social [sic] Labor Party, the Group of Social Democrats of Bolsheviki, the Group of Social Democrats of Anarchists, the Workers International Industrial Union, the Chinese National League, and the Chinese Labor Association. One month later the Finnish Social Democratic Party and the Socialist Party of North America were added to the list.

By any standards this was a strange list. It included major organizations such as the Social Democratic Party alongside virtually non-existent ones, such as the Workers International Industrial Union, an adjunct of the tiny Socialist Labor Party. Many of the names were badly garbled. The two Chinese organizations were not even remotely Bolshevik in sympathy: they were Canadian extensions of the nationalist Kuomintang. The Socialist

Party of Canada, which was at least as large as the SDP, was not mentioned at all.

The government was not interested in precision. This was a shotgun attack on the left. Heavy fines and prison sentences were provided for anyone associated with the banned parties and groups. Even renting a room to an illegal organization could bring a $5,000 fine and five years in prison for the landlord. All meetings conducted "in the language of any country or portion of any country with which Canada is at war, or in the language or any of the languages of Russia, Ukraine or Finland," were banned—with the exception of religious services. Seditious books (the list included Plato's *Republic*!) were banned. Most socialist periodicals were outlawed. Simple possession of a banned periodical—even if it had been published before the ban—was grounds for fine and imprisonment.

These regulations, it should be noted, were in addition to existing laws which provided for the arrest, fining, and imprisonment of anyone "uttering statements detrimental to Britain and her allies." PC 2384 was one of the most determined and conscious assaults on civil rights ever seen in Canada. It made possible a coordinated, all-out drive to smash the left.

Roundups of radicals began within days of the enactment of PC 2384. The offices of most radical periodicals and organizations were raided. In Winnipeg, Michael Charitonoff, editor of *Rabochy Narod* (Working People), was charged with possession of "objectionable matter." Expecting a nominal fine, he pleaded guilty: the Magistrate imposed a $1,000 fine and sentenced him to three years in prison.[6] In Sault Ste. Marie, seven Social Democrats were charged with membership in a banned organization. They were fined a total of $16,700 and sent to prison for terms ranging from three to five years.[7] In Southern Ontario the police conducted coordinated raids the weekend of October 19-20. They arrested thirteen socialists in London, twenty-two in Stratford, twenty-three in Toronto. Forty-four members of the Chinese Nationalist Association in Toronto were arrested the same weekend.[8] A report by Dominion Police Sergeant B.H. James, dated March 24, 1919, listed twenty Ontario cities in which arrests and raids took place— Sault Ste. Marie, Subury, Copper Cliff, Timmins, South Porcupine, Toronto, Windsor, Walkerville, Ford City, Sarnia, London, Ottawa, Stratford, Brantford, Welland, St. Catharines, Galt, Kitchener, Parry Sound, and Niagara Falls.[9] In these locations and many more, the radical left learned important lessons about the fragility of Canadian democracy.

Fighting Back

These arrests had as their object the suppression of radical activity. The government hoped to root out Bolshevism—which it identified with "foreign" agitators—and to crush it. More than one government has discovered that ideas cannot be destroyed by such methods. The Canadian government was soon to learn the same lesson.

The attempt to imprison Michael Charitonoff was the first government assault to meet strong resistance. Instead of meekly accepting his punishment, Charitonoff appealed both the conviction and the sentence, and asked the Winnipeg Trades and Labor Council for help. A Defense Committee that included most of the city's union leaders was established, funds were raised for his defense, and protest rallies were arranged. After several months of stalling, the government backed off and dropped all proceedings.[10]

The case of Arthur Skidmore was even more dramatic. He was a member of the Social Democratic Party in Stratford, and a prominent member of the International Association of Machinists. After being arrested in the October 15-16 sweep, Skidmore was fined $500 and sentenced to thirty days in jail. Stratford, center of the Grand Trunk Railway, was a strong union town: the city's labor council immediately threatened a city-wide general strike if Skidmore was not released. His own union went further, threatening a country-wide strike of machinists if he were forced to serve his sentence. Skidmore was released after eleven days in jail and his fine was remitted.[11]

The campaign in support of Skidmore was part of a more general drive by the SDP against the Order-in-Council. The party brought heavy pressure to bear on the federal government through its extensive connections in the labor movement and in Ontario politics. In mid-November, over the protests of C.H. Cahan (who had just been appointed Director of Public Safety), the Social Democratic Party was removed from the list of banned organizations.[12]

But the most telling case of all occurred in Toronto. On January 1, 1919 two young workers were arrested on Queen Street. Charles Watson and Harold Cheeseman were first held on a nominal vagrancy charge but police told reporters that the charge would be changed to "disseminating Bolshevik propaganda"—the police testified at their trial that the two had been placing radical leaflets in mailboxes. The charge they actually faced was possession of illegal literature: a search of Watson's rooms had uncovered fifteen objectionable items, included a copy of Karl Marx's *Wage Labor and Capital*, Daniel DeLeon's famous pamphlet *The Preamble of the Industrial Workers of the World*, the program of the Socialist Party of North America, and an anonymous leaflet entitled "The Red Terror in Russia." Magistrate Kingsford found the last-named item to be "decidedly the most objectionable" of the lot. The magistrate was particularly upset that Cheeseman and Watson were not foreigners: "Persons of British birth or descent above all should not forget the orderly traditions of their race. It would be a disgrace if they associated themselves with the propaganda of foreign cut-throats."

On January 9 Watson was sentenced to three years in Kingston Penitentiary and fined $500. Cheeseman was bound over to January 16 when, on the grounds that he seemed "to belong more to the class of tool, which older or more cunning men use and then desert," he was given a lesser sentence: six months in jail.

The sentences provoked a storm of protest, particularly from the Carpenters Union, to which Cheeseman belonged. Since the Carpenters were the largest union in North America, and had thousands of members in Toronto, they wielded considerable influence. The union began circulating a petition for the release of Watson, Cheeseman, and all other political prisoners, and for repeal of the Order-in-Council. The petition was formally launched at a meeting on January 12 organized by the Workers Political Defense League, a group originally established to aid those arrested the previous October. Over 1,600 people turned out to hear speeches by radicals and labor leaders, including Frank Watkinson, business agent for the Carpenters, Plumbers union organizer John Bruce, and William McCutcheon, international vice-president of the Boilermakers. The meeting closed with cheers for Bolshevism, Karl Liebknecht, and Leon Trotsky.

On January 16 some twelve hundred people demonstrated in the snow in front of City Hall while Cheeseman was being sentenced. Following the trial they marched from City Hall to the Labor Temple.

On January 23 the Carpenters announced a mass public meeting to protest the Orders-in-Council and to demand the release of Watson and Cheeseman. Prestigious Massey Hall had been booked for the event and the featured speaker would be Tom Moore, president of the Trades and Labor Congress of Canada. This was no token protest: the labor movement seemed prepared for a major confrontation.

Faced with this unexpected response, the federal government capitulated. On January 24, the day the Massey Hall meeting was to take place, the Justice Department announced that Watson's fine would be remitted, and that the jail terms would be reduced to thirty days for Watson and fifteen for Cheeseman. Since Cheeseman had already spent that much time in jail, he was released immediately. Watson had a few more days to serve. The labor movement, justifiably, celebrated a victory.[13]

These were important victories which illustrated the depth of the labor radicalization that was taking place, and which exploded the myth (still promoted by some historians) that the radical left was isolated from the mainstream of Canadian labor. But important as these victories were, they won justice for only a minority of those facing persecution. Immigrant socialists in particular were very vulnerable to attack: few of them were able to win release as Charitonoff did. In Toronto, for example, while Anglo-Saxon SDPers Isaac Bainbridge, James Reid, and Thomas Shew received suspended sentences following the October raids, Russian and Ukrainian leaders arrested in the same round-up were jailed for terms ranging from three months to one year. And while the English-speaking SDP branches regained legality, the immigrant groups remained on the outlaw list and their newspapers remained illegal. The ban on meetings in Ukrainian, Russian, and Finnish meant that many socialists were excluded from all legal political activity. They had no choice but to continue it illegally.

The government could not destroy the left—but it could drive the radicals underground.

Raising the Flag

The outlawing of radical political organizations and of meetings in most foreign languages temporarily stunned the left. Before it too fell under the ban the Socialist Party of North America held public meetings in Toronto on the Russian Revolution, but it avoided any direct challenge to the law. The activities of the left were largely confined to raising funds for the defense of imprisoned comrades.

On November 5, revolution broke out in Germany. Sailors mutinied, workers took over factories, tens of thousands stormed into the streets. The monarchy was quickly overthrown, and the new government sued for peace. On November 11 an armistice was signed, bringing the war to an end.

The Toronto Trades and Labor Council immediately called a meeting for November 16, to demand the lifting of wartime restrictions on the right to strike. On November 15, however, the government lifted the restrictions so the conservative leaders of the Council saw no reason to proceed with their plans. They went to the Labor Temple solely to inform anyone who showed up that the meeting was cancelled. What happened was described in the *Toronto Daily Star*:

President Conn and other officers were on hand at the hour set for the gathering. So were the Socialists. Hundreds were present, long before eight o'clock. They filled the big hall to capacity. They climbed up and sat on the beams and supports of the roof. They filled the body of the hall and galleries and crowded on the steps of the platform. It was one of the biggest crowds that has ever packed the Labour Temple Auditorium.

After opening the meeting, President Conn attempted to avoid trouble by announcing that as the order-in-council had been cancelled, the protest meeting was unnecessary and an adjournment would therefore be in order. That started the uproar. "Traitor! Fakir!" came from all parts of the hall, while a regular howl of derision went up from the crowd. "We'll elect another chairman," called a "comrade," and an outburst of applause greeted the suggestion.

The Labor Council executive let the meeting proceed for a few minutes. A "Delegate Lewis, of the Machinists" proposed a motion condemning PC 2384, charging that the Cabinet "has illegally usurped the functions that belonged to the elected representatives of the people." According to the *Star*, the resolution would have passed easily, but Lewis drew the ire of Labor Council president Conn by the speech he made in support of it.

He demanded that all persons imprisoned for violating the order-in-council be at once liberated; that all aliens who had been interned during the war be at once given their freedom; and concluded by declaring that the war had been won by the working men of Germany, not by Great Britain and her allies.

Lewis's final reference to the November Revolution in Germany outraged Conn. To suggest that this event had been a major factor in bringing the war to a close was, the Labor Council president declared, "a gross reflection" on the British and Canadian trade unionists who had fought and died "in the interests and defense of freedom." He immediately called a halt to the proceedings, turned out the lights in the hall, and threatened to call the police. The audience poured out onto Church Street and held an outdoor meeting.

For over two hours and a half the speakers unburdened their minds on the question of governments in general and the Canadian government in particular. It was denounced as the foe to human liberty. Everyone in authority came in for a round of abuse, and the working classes were called upon to "show that they had fighting blood in their veins" by vigorously protesting autocracy in Canada.

According to another report, "the addresses were interspersed by the singing of Socialist songs and cheers for the revolutionists of Russia and Germany." The following night a group of socialists attempted to hold another outdoor meeting in the same location, but were prevented from doing so by police: two men were arrested.[14]

Events such as the takeover of the Labor Temple meeting do not occur without at least some advance organization. The large turnout—the *Toronto Daily News* estimated the crowd as "a thousand socialists, mostly foreigners"—and Lewis's readiness to take the floor with a prepared resolution and a speech, indicate that the left had organized for the meeting. On the other hand Conn's success in evacuating the hall suggests that the organization was fairly minimal.

The organization steadily improved. Prevented from organizing their own meetings, the radical left organized for other public events. In late 1918 and early 1919, anyone sponsoring a public meeting in Toronto on any topic vaguely related to political or social problems could expect a considerable turnout of radicals determined to turn the discussion period into a discussion of the lessons of the German and Russian revolutions. For the radical left, such events provided otherwise unavailable opportunities to raise the flag, to prove that repression could not kill their ideas.

The high point of this activity came on January 24, 1919, at a meeting in Massey Hall. This was the meeting, described earlier in this chapter, which the Carpenters Union called to protest the jailing of Watson and Cheeseman. The featured speaker was Tom Moore, president of the Trades and Labor Congress of Canada. To the dismay of the organizers, the meeting became as much a protest against Moore as against the government.

Moore's election to the TLC presidency in 1918 was part of a right-wing takeover of the Congress. He was a supporter of the Samuel Gompers school of business unionism, and had been among the most conservative of Canadian labor leaders during the war: he was one of the few who gave full support to conscription. He was enough of an opportunist to see that refusal to attend the January 24 meeting would undermine his position in the TLC—but by attending it he opened himself to the attacks of the radicals, who opposed everything Moore stood for.

Between two and three thousand people attended the meeting. It was clear from the beginning that the organizers were in trouble: when the chairman announced that a petition for repeal of the orders-in-council would be circulated in the hall, a member of the audience stood up and proposed that instead of petitions, a nation-wide General Strike should be called. This, reported the *Evening Telegram*, "provoked great cheers and clapping, which was the first indication to everyone that there was a noisy element in the audience."

The "noisy element" was quiet during speeches by William Varley of the Great War Veterans Association, labor lawyer Arthur Roebuck, Machinists' vice-president J.A. McLelland, and Carpenters' business agent Frank Watkinson. John Bruce, organizer of the Plumbers and Steamfitters, received loud cheers when he called for the release of the two Russians, both machinists, who had been in prison since September, and of the Social Democrats imprisoned in Sault Ste. Marie.

But when Tom Moore took the podium, pandemonium broke out. The *Evening Telegram*'s report caught the mood well. Moore began, the *Telegram* reported, by criticizing members of the audience who had booed a clergyman who attempted to speak from the floor.

"You come here in the interests of free speech," shot out President Moore when he took the platform, "and yet you will not allow an old grey-haired man to speak. I regret such an exhibition."

"Sit down!" "Say something!" "Shut up!" "What do you know?" and similar cries of resentment were shouted.

"I come from Ottawa," resumed Moore.

"Go back to Ottawa," called a voice.

"I come from Ottawa," continued the speaker, "to offer my protest at this meeting. Someone has spoken of a general strike. You don't know what that means."

All kinds of interruption broke forth again. "Hail the general strike!" and "Long live the international revolution!" were heard among the shouts.

And so it continued. At one point Moore's speech was interrupted for ten full minutes by jeering and booing from the crowd. When he finally finished, the podium was taken over by Robert Truman, a leader of Machinists Local 438. (The organizers later claimed that Truman, one of the best-known socialists in the Toronto Labor Council, was not a scheduled speaker and took the platform without their sanction.) Truman introduced himself as a revolutionary socialist, and challenged Moore's insistence on constitutional methods as the way to achieve labor's goals.

Do you think the capitalists are going to allow us to gain our ends by constitutional means? Might is right and we must use our might to get our rights, to establish a world after our ideals. We want a cooperative commonwealth. Now all we have is the oppression of the revolution, which really represents the workers of the world.

You have never had your rights. Your oppressors have allowed you a few privileges, that is all. We can give food, clothing, shelter and comfort for all on one and a half hours work a day. We must stand behind the Bolshevists who are struggling for freedom. (Prolonged Cheers)

It is the white terror, not the red, we must fear. I say our slogan must be "Down with the exploiter! Long live the social revolution!"

Truman concluded his speech by calling on the audience to stand in protest against the murder of German revolutionists Karl Liebknecht and Rosa Luxemburg, who had been beaten and shot to death by *Freikorps* officers in Berlin just nine days earlier. Nearly everyone present stood and cheered the revolution and the memory of the murdered revolutionists. The radical left in Toronto had demonstrated very clearly that it was not dead, despite the government's efforts.[15]

The Bolshevik Underground

Three months later, on April 30, 1919, residents of working class neighborhoods in Montreal and in the Southern Ontario cities of Toronto, Hamilton, Brantford, and St. Catharines found leaflets tucked into their mailboxes. The eight-by-twelve inch flyers were covered with small print. One side headed "MAY DAY!" urged Canadian workers to "resolve not to stay slaves any longer, but to struggle uneasingly [sic] against the capitalist class until you conquer power and establish the rule of the workers."

Your only hope lies in revolution—the sweeping away of this rotten system of exploitation. You must achieve a victory over the capitalist class so that you can celebrate May Day along with your fellow-workers in Russia.

Long live the revolution of the workers against the capitalists! Workers, Unite!

The other side went into more detail. It put forward a seven-point program, beginning with "the forcible seizure of the governmental power and the establishment of the dictatorship of the proletariat." It called for "The complete destruction of all capitalist political institutions," including "abolition of the standing army," "confiscation of all private property without compensation," and "handing over the land to the agricultural laborers and poor farmers." Society, the leaflet declared, "must be run in the interest of the worker alone."

That side of the leaflet was headed "Programme of the Communist Party of Canada," and both sides were signed by the "Central Executive Committee of the Communist Party of Canada."

Communism had come to Canada.[16]

THIS "COMMUNIST PARTY" WAS AN UNDERGROUND organization—so much so that historians of the Canadian left have completely ignored it. Neither the Communist Party's own historians nor the major academic studies of the party mention it at all. According to the universally accepted account, the CP of C was founded in May 1921, by the fusion of the Canadian branches of the U.S. Communist movement. And yet, as the evidence clearly shows, there was an organization styling itself the Communist Party of Canada two years earlier.

It is in the nature of underground organizations that they do not publish membership lists, or hold press conferences, or sign their members' names to leaflets, or otherwise provide the documentation which historians later use to trace the evolution of political groups. In other countries the files of police spies and provocateurs have provided much valuable information not available elsewhere: the RCMP, however, still has its files from that period under lock and key, and Canadian law provides no means of access to 60-year-old documents. As a result, any account of the origins of the first Communist Party of Canada must be to some degree speculative. What follows is only an outline, based on those official records that are available, on newspaper reports, and on other fragmentary sources. Future historians may well change this outline: at the very least they will add detail.

The first evidence that the left was doing more than organizing to heckle at public meetings came in November 1918, shortly after the

Armistice, when thousands of copies of a leaflet were inserted in mailboxes in several Southern Ontario cities. The leaflet, headed "Peace and the Workers," ridiculed the victory celebrations then taking place. It urged the workers and soldiers of Canada to unite, to win over the police, and to form Soldiers' and Workers' Councils. "...nothing short of the complete overthrow of the capitalists and their institutions can prepare the ground for the building of the Workers' Republic where the workers shall control their own destiny."[17]

The leaflet did not cause a proletarian uprising, but it did produce considerable distress in ruling class circles. The Toronto *Daily News* on December 2 devoted an editorial to a condemnation of the "dangerous pamphlet." The Reverend Newton Powell of Trinity Methodist Church made "The Threat of Revolution in Canada" the subject of his December 8 sermon: "Mr. Powell dealt with the seditious pamphlet recently circulated through the city, which aimed to incite workers to rebellion and to Bolshevik methods...." On December 17, Police Magistrate Colonel George T. Dennison fired twelve Toronto Police officers who had attempted to organize a union: he took this action, although it provoked a police strike, because he believed that unionized policemen could not be depended on. He cited as proof of his contention "an absolutely extreme Bolshevik pamphlet...circulated by the thousands in this city," which had urged revolutionary workers to win over the soldiers and police.[18]

The December 6 *Labor News,* a weekly published in Hamilton, commented wryly on the uproar:

A snake in a seraglio could scarcely cause such a shrill cacophony of fear, horror and general indignation as the appearance of alleged Bolshevism occasions to the ancient beldames of the kept press. These literary lackeys and ladies-in-waiting of the "Big interests" have discovered evidence of propaganda in certain industrial sections of Hamilton and Toronto which was promptly labelled Bolshevist, and the editorial columns of most of the dailies have been ringing with denunciation for days. In proof of the existence of such a movement a leaflet entitled "Peace and the Worker" is quoted extensively.

In their hysterical demand for instant suppression of this fragmentary essay in anti-capitalist agitation, this tract, variously characterized as "damnable, dangerous and subversive of the present (moral) order," the somewhat staccato sentences amplified and annotated and the alleged diabolic import interpreted for the unknowing, is practically quoted in its entirety when the various excerpts are placed side by side. This in the judgement of the sapient commentators is the first step towards suppression. All of which must be exceedingly gratifying to the anonymous author and his friends.

The editors of *Labor News* suggested that the fact that the identity of the author of the leaflet remained unknown to the police was proof of "the growing strength of the solidarity of the workers."

"Peace and the Workers," was unsigned. It was followed, however, by two more manifestos signed by the "Provisional Council of Workers and Soldiers Deputies of Canada," and addressed to "Comrade Soldiers and Workers." One appeared in mailboxes on New Years Day, 1919, the other early in February: both were distributed in the same group of Southern Ontario cities, including Toronto, Hamilton, Brantford, and St. Catharines.

Again these leaflets caused concern among the spokesmen of the established order. The *Toronto Daily Star* described one of them as "wholly mischievous and incendiary," while the Great War Veterans Association protested that "the Earlscourt District of Toronto has been flooded with Bolshevik literature...distributed from door to door...in the early hours of New Years Day." *The Globe* reported that Brantford was "flooded" with literature which was "redolant of Bolshevism."[20]

The clandestine leafleting continued through the early months of 1919, while the police prepared to crush the Bolshevik menace in the bud. On March 23, 1919, Toronto police raided two downtown rooming houses, arresting three people: Arthur Brown, Annie Bancourt, and Charles Charnie.

Charnie was easily the best-known of the three. He was twenty-four years old, a Russian Jew who had lived in New York but was now attending the University of Toronto. He had come into prominence very suddenly in January 1919, speaking at public meetings organized by various groups. His flamboyant style made him a popular speaker and ensured that his speeches would be quoted at length in the daily press. On January 13, for example, he had been included on the platform with other speakers at the meeting organized by the Workers Political Defense Committee to protest the conviction of Watson and Cheeseman. He finished his talk with a ringing declaration: "The war is not over. A national war is over, yes, but the great international war, the war of the classes, is not over. Long live the class war!"[21] A week later he was among the speakers at a rally organized during the Social Democratic Party's national convention. His speech included passages such as these:

The German revolution is the hope of the world. If it falls completely there will be no hope for years. If it succeeds there will be a revolution in France, Italy, the United States, Canada, and everywhere....

You won't have a revolution by shouting "Hurrah!" Bite your lips, clench your fists and be determined to answer as clearly as possible the clarion call of our brothers on the other side!

...Who tells us that we want to spill blood? For four and a half years the battle fields of Europe have been soaked with rivers of blood. They, the murderers of humanity—the capitalist classes—tell us we want bloodshed. (Loud cheers here interrupted the speaker.)

This same blood cries out to the working classes of the world and says "Revenge!" This blood is going to make an international social revolution and nothing else.[22]

The arrest of the three was scarcely noticed by the Toronto press, although the *Globe* and the *Times* did report that a large number of police had been mobilized on April 6 to prevent "socialists and radical trade unionists" from holding a meeting in Spadina Hall to protest the arrest of "three local socialists."[23] The police held the three incommunicado for more than a month. On April 28 they took the story to the press. There were headlines in every Toronto daily.

BOLSHEVIST GANG IN POLICE GRIP—*Mail and Empire*
Police Arrest Leaders of Toronto Bolsheviks—*Toronto World*
WILL DEPORT THREE ALIENS—*The Globe*
Bolshevik Propaganda in Canada Traced to Agents
   in Germany and Russia—*Toronto Times*

The police offered the press three major revelations. First, this was not a routine arrest of local radicals. Involved were not only the Toronto Police, but the Ontario Provincial Police, the Federal Immigration authorities, and the Dominion Police.* The Acting Chief Commissioner of the Dominion Police, A.J. Cawdron, was personally involved. Such an alliance of forces would scarcely have been formed unless the authorities believed that this was an arrest of considerable importance.

Second, the authorities revealed that the three radicals were living under assumed names. "Brown" was really Arthur Ewart; "Bancourt" was Lita Zaborowski; "Charnie" was Lieb Samsonovitch. Ewart and Zaborowski, who had been "living together as man and wife,"† were German immigrants who had come to Canada before

---

*The Dominion Police was a predecessor of the RCMP. It merged with the Royal North West Mounted Police in 1920.
†The press and the police appear to have thought this was as great a crime as Bolshevism.

the war; Samsonovitch was a Russian exile who had entered Canada illegally at the end of 1918 after being expelled from New York's Columbia University for subversive activities.

Third, the police charged that the three were at the center of a major Bolshevik conspiracy. They "formed the nucleus of a Communist Party." Police reported finding "three brand new Colt automatics, one small German weapon, and a plentiful supply of cartridges" in Ewart's rooms. "In addition there was a quantity of Bolshevik literature including the Communist platform, one of the articles of which is the overthrow of constituted government in Canada." From the descriptions which appeared in the press, it is clear that this "Communist platform" was the leaflet which would be distributed in Southern Ontario and Montreal on April 30.

According to police, the evidence showed that the three had established connections with radicals across the country. Ewart had letters from socialists in Winnipeg, Kitchener, Hamilton, Brantford, Detroit, and Vancouver. He was also in correspondence with "people acting for Liebknecht and Luxemburg." Ewart, the police believed, was the main instigator of the organization, and the author of the leaflets.

Inspector of Detectives Guthrie told the *Toronto Times* that the police had obtained "a list of possibly 1000 men and women, the majority of whom are of foreign birth, who were actively participating in this Bolshevist agitation. We know also their names and where they are employed. At any moment they can be picked up, and from now on they will be closely watched." The *Mail and Empire* claimed that "The compilation shows the bulk of the membership is comprised of Russians, Germans, Austrians, Jews, with a sprinkling of Canadians and Englishmen. Among the various leaders in the movement are one Irishman, a Finlander, two Dutch brothers, two Englishmen, and their wives."

Ewart was placed in an internment camp for "enemy aliens" and Samsonovitch was locked in the City Jail. Before the end of May both were deported to the United States. The police promised further arrests.*[24]

Further arrests came on Sunday, June 1. At 11:00 a.m., a squad of plainclothesmen and uniformed police, led by A.J. Cawdron of the

---

*I have been unable to learn anything about Samsonovitch's later life. Zaborowski was reported to be still in a Toronto jail late in 1919, but her subsequent movements are also unknown. Ewart lived briefly in Detroit, then returned to Germany, where he became a Central Committee member of the Communist Party.

Dominion Police, raided offices at 553 Queen Street West in downtown Toronto. This was the former headquarters of the outlawed Ukrainian Social Democratic Party: now it was rented by a group calling itself the "International Workers Association." There, and at a residence at 354 Huron Street, thirteen men were arrested and large quantities of literature (including stacks of the April 30 leaflet) were confiscated. The authorities told reporters that those arrested were friends of Charles Charnie and the "two other Bolshevik agitators"; more concretely, the police announced that the arrests had rounded up the entire Central Committee of the Communist Party of Canada.

On June 10 the men appeared in court charged with possession of objectionable literature. The trial itself was bizarre. Magistrate Kingsford, who had a well-established reputation for imposing heavy fines and prison sentences on radicals and union organizers, walked into court with his judgment already written. After hearing evidence for one day, and without the majority of the accused being allowed to state their cases, Kingsford pronounced all of them guilty and sentenced them to prison terms ranging from six months to three years. Five of them successfully fought for new trials on the grounds that they had had no trial at all, but the new trials did not change the outcome. All thirteen went to prison. As they were led out of court, one of them shouted "Hurray for the Bolsheviki!"[25]

The Origins of Canadian Communism

Who were the organizers of this first and long-forgotten attempt to create a Communist Party of Canada? The available evidence suggests that three political currents were involved.

In addition to the first three arrested—Ewart, Zaborowski, and Samsonovitch—we know from press reports the names of the thirteen "Central Committee" members arrested in June 1919. They were: Thomas J. Bell, Matthew Blochuck, John Boychuck, Chester Clarke, Benjamin Davis, John C. Ford, Herbert Hite, Antony Madwicki, Luke Maryleski, Max Rotchyld, Assey Soloski, Andrio Vallerio, and George Vaskleck. To these sixteen names we can add five others, men who were probably involved although no direct connection can be proven. They are: Charles Watson and Harold Cheeseman, arrested in the act of placing leaflets in mailboxes on New Years Day, the day that the underground organization's "Second Manifesto" was distributed in just that manner; Anton Tretak or Trejak, arrested in Brantford on New Years Day for distributing leaflets; and Agnew Swigach and Adam

Emolinsky, arrested in a Sullivan Street, Toronto, rooming house in August 1919. Like Ewart, Swigach was reported to have had connections in Detroit, which was the most important organizing center of the U.S. Communist movement in 1919. It has not been possible to trace all of these individuals, but there is enough information to provide a clear picture of the groups that came together in the Bolshevik underground in 1918-1919.

First, the party included at least a section of the Socialist Party of North America. Thomas J. Bell had represented the SPNA at the founding convention of the Ontario Section of the Canadian Labor Party in the spring of 1918.[26] According to Tim Buck, Arthur Ewart was also an SPNA member.[27] And there is circumstantial evidence that Charles Watson was involved in that organization: he had a copy of the SPNA program in his rooms at the time of his arrest; SPNA organizer Arthur Taylor appeared as a character witness on his behalf at his trial; and Independent Labor Party leader Joseph Gibbons charged that Watson had once "denounced Christianity" at an ILP meeting—public attacks on religion were a trademark of the SPNA.[28] The pattern of leaflet distribution in Southern Ontario conforms to the distribution of the SPNA's membership: particularly noteworthy is the inclusion of Brantford, a city of 30,000 people in which the Socialist Party of North America had long been the only radical organization.

The inclusion of Detroit on the list of cities which Ewart had contacts in and Swigach visited is also significant. Detroit was the center of the Michigan Socialist Party, a section of the Socialist Party of America which had long been influenced by the SPNA, the Socialist Party of Great Britain, and the Socialist Party of Canada. In 1919 the Michigan socialists were one of the driving forces behind the creation of the Communist Party of America.*

The SPNA had always been a small, tightly-knit organization which demanded a high degree of commitment and activity from its membership. That organizational heritage, combined with the political lessons it learned from the Russian Revolution, made the party a natural focus for underground revolutionary activity in the fall of 1918. We can only speculate as to whether the SPNA as a whole participated in the creation of a new party, or whether its forces divided. It is noteworthy that Arthur Taylor and Florence Custance, both of whom had been founding members of the SPNA,

---

*The Michigan socialists did not last long in the Third International. They soon split and formed the Proletarian Party, led by indefatigable propagandist John Keracher.

played central roles in the Workers Political Defense League, the organization which organized the campaign in support of Watson and Cheeseman, and which was mentioned in the press as a group raising support for Samsonovitch in May.[29] At the very least there were close ties between the WPDL and the undergound Communist Party: quite possibly the League was a "front" for Canada's first Bolsheviks.

THE SECOND CURRENT involved in the creation of the first Communist Party came from the language federations associated with the Social Democratic Party. Two of the men arrested on June 1, 1918 were prominent in the SDP: Max Rotchyld had spoken on behalf of the party at a meeting in March 1917 to mark the overthrow of the czar in Russia, and John Boychuck was a well-known leader of the Ukrainian Social Democratic Party.[29] It is also significant that the June 1 arrests took place in the former head-quarters of the Ukrainian SDP. It is probable that the "International Workers Association" was simply the Ukrainian SDP in a new guise.

If there was any semblance of truth in the police claim that 1,000 or more people were involved in the underground Bolshevik agitation in 1919, there can be no doubt that the majority of those people came from the SDP. In Eastern Canada only the SDP language groups had that kind of support spread over a considerable number of cities.

The involvement of the SPNA and SDP language federations in the creation of the underground Bolshevik organization is not surprising. As we have seen, these two currents were the first on the left to move towards Bolshevism and to propose the creation of a new revolutionary party. What may be surprising to many is the fact that the first CPC included a group of radicals whose views were closer to anarchism or anarcho-syndicalism than to Marxism.

In many countries revolutionary anarchists were attracted to Bolshevism. These radicals, whose anarchism was more a reaction to the conservatism of the Second International than a deep commitment to the ideas of Bakunin or Kropotkin, saw in the Bolshevik movement a commitment to revolutionary action like their own. Lenin noted that "very many anarchist workers are now becoming sincere supporters of Soviet power, and that being so, it proves them to be our best comrades and friends, the best of revolutionaries...."[30] One of the best-known converts from anarchism was Victor Serge, a leader of the anarchist movement in France and Spain, who became editor of the Communist International's official magazine in 1919. Prominent syndicalists, including Alfred Rosmer and Pierre Monatte of France, and "Big Bill" Haywood of the Industrial Workers of the World, also declared their support for the Third International.

Within Russia itself the Left Socialist Revolutionary Party participated in a coalition government with the Bolshevik Party from November 1917 through mid-1918, and many Left S-Rs joined Lenin's party. The Left S-Rs were the heirs of the anarchist-terrorist *Narodnaya Volya* (People's Will) organization, which had assassinated Czar Alexander in 1881, and they remained strongly influenced by anarchist conceptions. The supporters of the Left S-Rs in Russian emigré communities in North America were strong supporters of the Russian Revolution. They created an organization called the Russian Workers Union and an associated group calling itself the "Soviet of Workmen's Deputies of the United States and Canada." The Russian Workers Union was estimated in 1919 to have some 7,000 members in North America; seventeen of its locals were in Canada.[31]

C.H. Cahan's 1918 report to the Borden government had reported that the motto "Anarchy and Communism" had been adopted by many "Bolsheviki" in Canada: "it has been generally adopted as a form of greeting or salutation, until it is now used as a sort of a password." Cahan also noted that "the Bolsheviki Associations have gone so far as to form their own Soviets." It is likely that these passages refer to the Russian Workers Union.

A final link connecting the anarchist-communists of the Russian Workers Union to the 1919 Communist Party appears in the August 1919 *Marxian Socialist*, the official organ of the SPNA. That issue contains an appeal by "the local Soviet of Russian Workers and Peasants Deputies" calling on the Canadian government to recognize the Soviet government in Russia and condemning the invasion of Russia by imperialist troops. That appeal did not appear in any other English-language radical periodical: evidently there was a special relationship between this group and the SPNA. The "Provisional Council of Workers and Soldiers Deputies of Canada," which made its appearance late in 1918 and which evolved into the Communist Party of Canada, was a direct offspring of that special relationship.

Agnew Swigach, who was arrested in August 1919, was described in October 1918 as a member of the Russian Social Revolutionary Party: since he was the only member of that party arrested in

Toronto in the first wave of arrests under PC 2384, we can assume that he was a leader of the organization.[32] Less certain, but probable, is the connection of one of the most prominent of the 1919 Communists to the anarchist-communist wing of the Russian immigrant community. Lieb Samsonovitch—Charles Charnie—frequently spoke in terms which had more in common with anarchism than with Marxism. At a public meeting in January 1919, for example, he spoke of issuing "spiritual orders-in-council" against the government. He had previously been active in the left in New York City, where the Russian Workers Union had its headquarters: he may have been sent to Canada to cement the alliance the Toronto branch had established with the Marxists of the SPNA and the SDP.

The Politics of the Underground

The alliance of the SPNA, the SDP Left, and the Russian Workers Union seems to have been established in the summer of 1918. Forced underground in September, the three groups constituted themselves as a "Soviet" and began distributing propaganda just after the war ended in November. The name "Provisional Council of Workers and Soldiers Deputies of Canada" was still being used in February 1919: by March 23, when Ewart, Samsonovitch, and Zaborowski were arrested, the name had been changed to "Communist Party of Canada" and a platform adopted. Since the first reports of the formation of the Communist International did not appear in the Canadian press until March 24, and since the Platform makes no reference to the new International, adoption of the name "Communist" must have been the result of a local decision, reflecting the general revulsion against the Second, Socialist International.

The political views expressed by the 1919 Communist Party were typical of the mixture of anarchist, syndicalist, and generally "leftist" views that were common in Western Europe and North American communist circles in 1918-1921, and which Lenin was to criticize in the pamphlet *"Left-Wing" Communism: An Infantile Disorder.* The most systematic exponents of these views were Anton Pannekoek and Herman Gorter, two early proponents of a Third International, leaders of the Amsterdam-based *De Tribune* group. Their response to the degeneration of the Second International was, for the most part, to place a minus sign wherever the reformists placed a plus sign. Thus, the reformists favored electoral activity, the *Tribunists* opposed it; the reformists favored trade

union organization, the *Tribunists* opposed it. The views of
Pannekoek and Gorter were well-known in North America through
translations of their articles which appeared in the journals *International Socialist Review* and *New Review,* both influential organs
of the left wing of the Socialist Party of America. A historian of the
early years of U.S. communism has pointed out that "Pannekoek
and Gorter were familiar names to many American Socialists when
Lenin and Trotsky were virtually unknown."[33] That influence
extended into the Canadian revolutionary left as well.*

The influence of the Dutch Left can be clearly seen in the
Communist Platform published in Toronto in 1919. Much of it was
devoted to a denunciation of those socialists who sought to enter
Parliament, even those who claimed to use it for purposes of
"agitation" only. "We oppose the use of parliamentary action as a
snare and delusion," it declared unequivocally. "Instead of relying
upon capitalist institutions, our business is to urge the workers to
seize power and destroy the rule of the bourgeois." The disdainful
attitude of the Dutch Left towards trade unions is also clearly
evident:

The Communist Party does not worry about reorganizing the Trade Union
movement; we do not propose to fritter away our forces in guerrilla warfare
with the capitalist class about better conditions under capitalism. It is
inevitable that the workers, in their instinctive revolt against the
conditions imposed upon them under capitalism should seek some means of
defence against this oppression. Thus rises trades unionism and later
industrial unionism. It is our duty to point out the limitations of these
means of defence and urge them to take offensive measures against
capitalism.

The successes of the Russian Bolsheviks had depended on their
ability to implement a strategy based on what the Communist
International would later call *transitional demands*—a strategy
that linked the present struggles of the masses to the goal of
proletarian revolution. The strategy depended on a very profound
understanding of the shifting moods of the Russian workers, and
an ability to put forward slogans and demands which both met the
needs of the instant and helped to organize and educate the workers
for future battles. The 1919 Communist Party of Canada had none

---

*The influence of Pannekoek and Gorter may well account for the otherwise
inexplicable police assertion that "two Dutch brothers" played a role in the
leadership of the 1919 Communist Party of Canada.

of Lenin's subtlety: for them the struggles of today were one thing ("guerrilla warfare") and the revolution was another entirely. The organization was formed in the midst of the greatest labor upsurge Canada has ever seen. General strikes had broken out in a dozen or more cities (see next chapter). The Communists could find no better way to respond to this crisis than to urge the strikers to see the error of their ways, to tell them to abandon their strikes in favor of insurrection. A CPC leaflet distributed during the Toronto General Strike in June 1919 gave faint support to the strike ("The Communist Party of Canada is not opposed to your strike"!) but went on:

You machinists who made so many splendid machine guns, rifles and small arms for your masters to sell, why did you neglect to provide yourselves with them before you struck? If you had done that you would not be at the mercy of a gang of policemen who are hired to protect the property of your masters. You packing-house workers who slaved so nobly to provide your masters' army with food, are you willing to toil and provide for the feeding of the workers in their battle for freedom? The time is ripe for the battle for power; the workers will respond if you workers give the rallying cry; the soldiers will not shoot at their brothers, they are tired of fighting for the capitalist gang of useless wasters.[34]

This abstract "revolutionism" had very little appeal and even less influence among the workers the Communists hoped to lead to power. One of the principal themes of the history of the Canadian Bolshevik movement over the next three years would be a struggle to escape from this type of "leftism" and adopt policies which corresponded to the realities of Canadian life, while maintaining the commitment to revolution which the first Canadian Bolsheviks displayed.

The arrests of the spring and summer of 1919 disrupted the new party, driving it further underground. It seems likely that it shattered into isolated local groups carrying on little public activity and having little contact with each other. The formation of two Communist parties in the United States in September 1919 was both a source of strength and a source of division: some of the groups allied themselves with one of the U.S. parties, some with the other. As we will see in chapter 4, by the beginning of 1920 there were branches of the two U.S. parties active in major Canadian cities: these branches were, at least in part, the remnants of the first attempt to create a Communist Party of Canada.

3. Canadian Labor in Revolt

The Communist Party that was formed in 1919 drew its membership and support from circles which had long been committed to
some form of revolutionary socialism. These currents—the SPNA,
the SDP Left, the Social-Revolutionary Party—were the first to
commit themselves wholeheartedly to the cause of Bolshevism. But
although they had close ties to the labor movement, they were
really outside of the mainstream of Canadian working-class
politics. The majority of left-wing activists in the labor movement,
in the SDP and the SPC, were excited about the Russian Revolution
and admired the Bolsheviks, but they were not convinced of the
need to emulate the Russians in Canada. Bolshevism was still a
foreign force in Canadian life: it had yet to sink roots in the labor
movement, to win the allegiance of the labor militants who could
combine the political program of Bolshevism with an intimate
knowledge of the realities of Canadian working-class life. These
militants were eventually won to Communism, not through
abstract propaganda (although that played a part) but through
their practical experiences as leaders of the great labor revolt of
1919.

The West Moves Left

As noted in chapter 1, the War resulted in a decline in the labor
movement and in its left wing: membership and support for both
fell off sharply in 1914, and did not begin to recover until 1916. In
Western Canada, this meant a brief eclipse for the Socialist Party,
which lost most of its influence in the labor movement to Social
Democratic and Labor Party politicians. With the revival of the

labor movement in 1917-18, the SPC again moved into the forefront west of the Lakehead. The *Western Clarion* resumed twice-monthly publication in 1918 and weekly publication (under the name *Red Flag*) by the end of the year. In March 1918, SPCer A.S. Wells took over as editor of the influential labor weekly *B.C. Federationist*. Members of the SPC soon won election to all of the executive positions in the Vancouver Trades and Labor Council and, for the first time since 1912, won a majority of the executive of the B.C. Federation of Labor.

Socialist Party meetings grew rapidly at the end of 1918 and in early 1919. After several weeks when hundreds of workers had to be turned away from the party's regular Sunday afternoon propaganda meetings in Vancouver, the party in January 1919 decided to hold two simultaneous meetings every week, at the Columbia and Royal theaters. One month later it consolidated these into a single weekly meeting at the Empress Theater, which was larger than the other two combined—and still it attracted overflow crowds to hear Jack Kavanaugh, Bill Pritchard, Ernest Winch, and other party leaders explain the principles of Marxism. Similar meetings took place in Nanaimo, Victoria, Prince George, and other cities.

A parallel swing to the left was taking place in the labor movement in Winnipeg. For two decades *The Voice*, owned by labor reformer Arthur Puttee, had been the newspaper of the city's labor movement. In 1918, Puttee opposed a brief general strike called by civic workers, and condemned the strikers in his newspaper. The Trades and Labor Council retaliated by withdrawing support from *The Voice* and launching its own newspaper, *Western Labor News*. The new paper declared:

When a war is on it is serious beyond measure to have your own heavy artillery firing on your infantry at the moment the enemy is making his charge. Yet this is exactly what happened to us in this strike. It was a real war and while the master class was attacking us in front, we found the labor paper at our back actually attacking us to such an extent that the daily press used whole editorials from The Voice in their own press to attack us. This made it absolutely clear to the workers on strike that we must have our own paper.[1]

Puttee's newspaper folded, leaving *Western Labor News* as the most widely read labor paper on the prairies. This radical victory was followed by the removal of Labor Party supporter Fred Tipping from the presidency of the Winnipeg TLC. The leadership of

Winnipeg and Manitoba labor, by the end of 1918, was in the hands of a coalition of radicals dominated by Socialist Party members Bob Russell and Dick Johns, and a group of Christian radicals associated with the Winnipeg Labor Church. The best-known of the latter was William Ivens, editor of the *Western Labor News*.

As in Vancouver, Winnipeg's shift to the left saw a notable increase in the number and size of public meetings sponsored by the left. The most famous of the Winnipeg meetings was held on December 22, 1918, in the Walker Theater, under the auspices of the Trades and Labor Council. Thousands of workers jammed the theater to hear speakers from the Labor Party, the Socialist Party, and the Labor Church denounce the federal government's campaign against the left, call for withdrawal of Allied troops from Russian soil, and demand the release of all political prisoners in Canada. According to the report in *Western Labor News*:

Chairman [John] Queen then called for three cheers for the Russian Revolution. The meeting ended with deafening cries of "Long live the Russian Soviet Republic! Long live Karl Liebknecht! Long live the working class!" The meeting ordered that, if possible, the message of congratulations be cabled to the Bolsheviki.[2]

By the end of 1918, then, the radical left had the leadership of the largest labor organizations west of Ontario. Their position was reinforced in January 1919 when the Socialist Party made a very strong showing at the Alberta Federation of Labor convention, and later the same month when SPCer P.M. Christophers won the presidency of District 18, United Mine Workers. Now the left had to show what it could do with the power it wielded.

The Western Labor Conference

The left's strength in the West was not matched in Eastern Canada, where conservative labor leaders still held sway. Following the 1918 convention of the Trades and Labor Congress of Canada, which was wholly dominated by the conservative East, western labor leaders resolved to be prepared for the next convention. A coalition of socialist and non-socialist unionists proposed that the western unions should caucus before the 1919 TLC convention, to adopt a common strategy. That caucus became the Western Labor Conference, held in Calgary March 13-15, 1919.

The new socialist leaders of the western unions made every effort to ensure that the left would dominate the conference. Edmonton socialist Sarah Knight, who had played a major role in the 1919

Alberta Federation of Labor convention, wrote to R.B. Russell in
Winnipeg:

With a big representation at Calgary in March we ought to make things
hum. Wherever possible get reds as delegates. We will put every effort forth
in that direction ourselves and maybe we might be able to turn it into an
S.P. Convention.[3]

Russell wrote to the SPC's Dominion Secretary: "We are getting a
number of Reds elected by the locals—so let's hope we will be able to
start something."[4]

Every prominent socialist trade unionist in the West attended the
conference. From British Columbia: Jack Kavanaugh, Bill Pritchard, Victor Midgley, and Joe Naylor. From Alberta: Sarah
Knight, Joe Knight, and Carl Berg. From Manitoba: Dick Johns
and Bob Russell. These were the leaders of western labor, elected by
thousands of workers in union locals across almost half the
country. From the minute it opened, the proceedings of the
conference were entirely dominated by members of the Socialist
Party.

On the first day Jack Kavanaugh, representing the Resolutions
Committee, proposed a resolution calling for "abolition of the
present system of production for profit and substitution therefor of
production for use." After lengthy discussion the resolution
passed—"without a dissenting voice, amid prolonged cheers." If
anyone had doubted the strength of the left, those doubts were now
stilled. Other resolutions demanded withdrawal of Allied troops
from Russia, the six-hour day, and the end of capitalist propaganda
against immigrant workers. Many resolutions included a call for a
General Strike if the government failed to meet the conference's
demands by June 1. One resolution which subsequently gained
wide publicity declared "full acceptance of the principle of
'Proletariat Dictatorship' as being absolute and efficient for the
transformation of capitalistic private property to communal
wealth."

For practical purposes, however, the most important resolutions
adopted were those concerning the immediate future of Canadian
labor. The original objective of the conference—planning strategy
for the coming TLC convention—was forgotten. Instead the
delegates voted to work for *secession* from the TLC, secession
which would lead to the creation of a new organization, the One Big
Union. The Western Labor Conference did not actually found the
OBU: it elected representatives who would arrange a referendum

on the question in unions across the country. The OBU was formally established in June.

THE SENTIMENTS EXPRESSED at the Western Labor Conference, and in the One Big Union, are often termed "syndicalist." There is an element of truth in that description, but it is misleading. Syndicalism, properly speaking, is a political viewpoint that rejects electoral activity in favor of economic organization through labor unions. Characteristically, syndicalists see union activity as the main or only road to the overthrow of capitalist society. The classic North American syndicalist organization was the Industrial Workers of the World (IWW), founded in 1905.

The One Big Union did not adhere to any of the classical variants of syndicalist thought. While it placed great importance on the creation of a revolutionary union movement, it was led by men and women who were members of the Socialist Party, which was firmly committed to the goal of building a political party to capture political power. These Socialists sought to build a socialist-led economic organization *parallel to* the socialist political organization, not in place of it.

In fact, the founders of the One Big Union seem to have had only the vaguest idea of the nature of the union they proposed to build. It was to be an industrial union, encompassing all workers, but what its structure was to be, what tactics it would follow, what relationship it would have to other labor organizations—these questions were left unanswered, and subsequent experience would show that there was no agreement on what the answers might be.

The Western Labor Conference was not a serious planning session for revolutionary unionists. The Socialists won the support of western labor, and in their euphoria passed a host of resolutions which they could not implement. The delegates gave no thought whatsoever to the practical problems posed by the votes they took: for example, they made no practical preparations for the various general strikes they threatened to call. They would soon discover that good intentions and radical resolutions are not enough. When the test came, the leaders of the OBU would be found wanting.

General Strike

At the beginning of May, 1919, the metal and building trades in Winnipeg were shut down by strikes. The employers refused to bargain: in response, the Winnipeg Trades and Labor Council held a referendum on the question of calling a general strike. More than

11,000 workers voted in favor, only 500 against. On Thursday, May 15, the Winnipeg General Strike began.

More than 22,000 workers, many of them not union members, answered the call within twenty-four hours. Eventually more than 30,000 walked out, representing a clear majority of Winnipeg's working people. Even the police association voted to strike: the police remained on the job at the request of the Strike Committee. Bread and milk wagons carried placards announcing that they were operating "By Permission of the Strike Committee." The strikers were in *de facto* control of the city.

Workers across Canada were inspired to emulate their comrades in Winnipeg. General strikes of varying duration and extent took place in Calgary, Lethbridge, Edmonton, Regina, Saskatoon, Prince Albert, Brandon, Fort William, Port Arthur, Amherst, Sydney, Toronto, and Vancouver, with lesser strikes in many other centers. Many of these strikes were called in sympathy with the Winnipeg workers. Others stemmed from local conflicts: the Toronto General Strike, for example, was called to aid striking metalworkers and packinghouse workers in that city.

The Vancouver General Strike actually was longer and involved more workers than the strike in Winnipeg: estimates of the number of strikers go as high as 60,000. The demands of the Socialist leadership of the Vancouver labor movement also went beyond those of the Winnipeg strikers, who were fighting primarily for improved wages and union recognition. A manifesto issued by the Vancouver Trades and Labor Council called for:

1. The reinstatement of the postal workers who struck in Winnipeg.
2. The immediate settlement of the postal workers' grievances.
3. The right of collective bargaining through any organization that the workers deem most suited to their needs.
4. Pensions for soldiers and their dependents on the basis laid down by the soldiers' organizations.
5. The minimum recompense for service overseas by the granting of the sum of $2,000 gratuity.
6. The nationalization of all cold storage plants, abattoirs, and elevators, with a view to removing the evil hoarding of foodstuffs.
7. The enactment of legislation for the six-hour day in all industries where unemployment is prevalent.[5]

If these measures were not implemented, the manifesto warned, the workers would "continue the strike until the present government resigns and places these matters before the electorate."

But it was in Winnipeg that the labor uprising of 1919 was fought to a conclusion. There more than anywhere else the actions of the workers posed the most fundamental question of all: Who shall rule?

A general strike by its very nature is a challenge to the established order. If it is not to be a brief, symbolic act of protest, a general strike must raise, if only implicitly, the question of control of society. The bread and milk wagons carrying "By Permission of the Strike Committee" placards were symbolic of this. Whether they knew it or not, the strikers had radically undermined the ability of the ruling class to rule. The basic day-to-day decisions about the functioning of society were being made, at least in part, by the strikers and their leaders.

But the leaders of the Winnipeg strike, including the socialists, failed to see the revolutionary implications of their actions. They did their utmost to confine the strike to simple questions of trade union rights and wages. They exerted every effort to avoid conflict with the government. Again and again they exhorted the workers to "Do Nothing," to stay off the streets, to avoid parades and demonstrations. The pro-strike parades that did take place were organized not by the Strike Committee but by the veterans' organizations.

Winnipeg's capitalist class recognized the stakes in the strike much more clearly than the strike leaders did. The city's businessmen organized a "Citizen's Committee" to combat the strike. They stated their analysis of the situation in no uncertain terms:

This is not a strike at all, in the ordinary sense of the term—it is Revolution.

It is a serious attempt to overturn British institutions in this Western country and to supplant them with the Russian Bolshevik system of Soviet rule.

Winnipeg, as a plain matter of fact, is governed by the Central Strike Committee of the Trades and Labor Council.[6]

Similar statements appeared in almost every daily newspaper, and in the speeches of Liberal and Conservative politicians. The spokesmen of the ruling class deliberately overstated the amount of conscious planning involved in the supposed Bolshevik plot, but their statements show a clear understanding of the dynamics of the crisis.

The OBU as such did not lead the Winnipeg General Strike: it had not yet been formally founded. But the Winnipeg strike and the parallel actions in other cities were a critical test of the ability of the pro-OBU radicals to provide an alternative to the traditional labor leadership in Canada. They failed the test completely. The wave of general strikes exposed, as nothing else could, the Socialist Party's total lack of anything even resembling a revolutionary strategy. Historians may argue about whether a socialist revolution was possible in Canada in 1919, but there is no doubt that this was the greatest social crisis Canada has yet seen. In this situation the SPCers could only support the Christian radicals who urged the workers to remain passive. There was no serious effort to coordinate the strikes in the various cities, no effort to involve the strikers in decision making on a regular basis, no effort to extend the Strike Committee's authority. Above all, there was no preparation for the clash with the state that would inevitably come.

The ruling class was not sitting still. The Winnipeg contingent of the Royal North West Mounted Police was strengthened, as was the army. The federal Parliament, in record time (forty-five minutes for three readings in both Houses and Royal Assent!), adopted a government bill permitting the deportation without trial of naturalized citizens suspected of sedition. The entire Winnipeg police force, which had shown itself sympathetic to the strikers, was fired: the cops were replaced with thugs recruited by the Citizens Committee.

On June 16 the federal government struck, arresting the main strike leaders in the middle of the night and locking them in Stony Mountain Prison. Five days later the police "specials" and the Mounties attacked a silent parade of workers, killing one man and injuring at least thirty more. On June 26, more than forty days after it began, the Winnipeg General Strike came to an end.

The strike in Vancouver continued for several more weeks, and the wave of radical sentiment which had swept the western labor movement did not subside for many months, but the defeat of the Winnipeg General Strike was a decisive turning point. It marked the beginning of the end for the labor revolt of 1919.

The Eastern Labor Revolt

Before turning to the aftermath of the defeat in June 1919, it is important to consider developments in the labor movement in Central and Eastern Canada. The year 1919 is so often spoken of in terms of the "Western Labor Revolt" that one is left with the impression that the labor movement elsewhere was completely quiescent, or even hopelessly reactionary. This is not true. While events in Ontario, Quebec, and the Maritimes did not have the drama of the great confrontations in the West, nevertheless there were clear signs of rising militancy and radicalization among the workers east of the Lakehead.

Little has been written about the labor movement in the Maritimes in 1919, although there was a one-month general strike in Amherst, Nova Scotia, and mass rallies in support of the imprisoned Winnipeg strike leaders took place in many other areas. The years 1918 and 1919 were also marked by a series of important local victories. In 1918 labor slates won majorities on the city councils of Sydney and Glace Bay. In the same year Nova Scotia's miners voted to affiliate their provincial association to the United Mine Workers of America, creating UMW District 26, which was to be one of the most militant unions in Canada during the 1920s. In 1919 the miners won the eight-hour day.[7]

In Montreal, a series of major labor battles was fought during this period. Thirty-two hundred Montreal textile workers took part in a two-month strike in 1919; 4,000 carters struck for fifteen days; 3,000 ship-builders walked out for six weeks; 2,000 wire-cutters struck for seventeen days. The strikes varied in outcome, from partial victory to total defeat, but the number and size of the conflicts demonstrated that Montreal was not immune to the radical virus that was sweeping the West.

The most important center of radical political activity east of the Lakehead was Toronto. The strength of the labor left there was demonstrated clearly on May Day 1919, when a rally organized by socialist unionists drew an unprecedented turnout: press estimates of attendance ranged from 3,000 to 6,000, while the left claimed 8,000. All agreed that it was a particularly militant gathering, with most of the participants wearing red badges reading "Workers of the World Unite!" and all of the speakers, even the most moderate, declaring solidarity with the Bolsheviks and opposition to Allied intervention in Russia. By a standing vote, amidst great cheering, the rally endorsed a resolution threatening General Strike if the government did not immediately release all political prisoners in Canadian jails.

The speakers at the rally included James Simpson, representing the Social Democratic Party; Jack MacDonald, a patternmaker (die-maker) and vice-president of the Metal Trades Council; Max Armstrong, a machinist who supported the OBU; Herbert Lewis, also a machinist, editor of the militant *Ontario Labor News*; Harry Kirwin, Dave Morgan, and R.C. Brown of the Metal Workers, and others. These men were all immigrants from the British Isles; all were skilled workers, most of them in the metal trades; all had years of activity in the socialist and labor movements behind them. Now they were taking the leadership of Toronto labor. Though it has not been well remembered by historians, the May Day Rally in Mutual Arena in Toronto in 1919 was Central Canada's counterpart to the Winnipeg meeting in the Walker Theater.

Toronto labor was heading towards a major clash with Capital. Forty-six hundred metal trades workers went on strike May 1 to win the eight-hour day. They were joined, on May 5, by 3,100 packinghouse workers. Demonstrations were held in the city's streets almost daily, with mass rallies every weekend. Twenty-five hundred marched to the provincial Legislature in Queen's Park on May 9. Five thousand demonstrated for the eight-hour day on May 17: they were joined by a group of veterans carrying a banner reading "We Fought for Democracy, Not for Capitalists." Jack MacDonald told the rally: "We want the world for the workers, and we are going to have it."[8]

By mid-May the radicals had a majority in the Toronto Trades and Labor Council. Over the opposition of the council's conservative executive, the left forced through a call for a General Strike in support of the metal trades workers. A Central Strike Committee was established, composed of fifteen representatives of the major unions—the newspapers claimed that twelve of the fifteen were socialists and that Toronto, like Winnipeg, would soon be under control of the strikers. On May 30 the General Strike began. Twelve thousand workers answered the call.

The radicals had seriously overestimated their ability to carry a general strike against the opposition of the more conservative sections of the labor movement. In Winnipeg support for the strike had been unanimous: in Toronto important unions, notably the streetcar drivers and the civic workers, refused to come out. After only four days the General Strike was called off. The meat packers eventually won a partial victory, a wage increase but no union recognition. The Metal Trades strike lasted until July 28, ending with minor gains for the workers.

The collapse of the General Strike took some of the spirit out of the left, but they continued to organize. Toronto was the scene of several major protest rallies in support of the arrested Winnipeg strike leaders—one, addressed by Winnipeg Alderman John

Canadian Labor in Revolt   59

Queen, drew some 6,000 participants to Queen's Park. And on July 17, in a 171 to 148 vote, the radicals captured all of the executive offices in the Toronto Trades and Labor Council.[9] The left wasn't beaten yet.

Using the Ballot Box

Historian Martin Robin entitled his account of the events that followed the strike wave in 1919 "Return to Politics."[10] This is very misleading, reflecting Robin's prejudice that politics is identical to parliamentary activity. The radicals who led the labor movement, east and west, had never left politics. Unlike the early Socialist Party, and unlike today's social democrats, they did not *limit* politics to electoral activity. Though they had no overall strategy and not much of a program, they were determined to use all available means to advance the cause of socialism. Insofar as they tried to understand the relationship between different forms of political activity, they saw electoral activity as most important, with economic activity subordinated to it. It required no great shift for them to decide to participate in the municipal, provincial, and federal elections in late 1919.

Labor's chances at the ballot box were strengthened by the radicalization of two other important social groups: the returned soldiers and the farmers. These groups were affected by and contributed to the unrest of the spring and summer of 1919; during the fall they began to make common cause with labor.

The veterans, by 1919, had begun to realize that they had won nothing at all in the War. They had returned to unemployment and poverty, under a government which wanted to ignore them. In September 1919, thousands of Toronto veterans broke with the Great War Veterans Association, which they saw as a tool of the government; they formed the Returned Soldiers Gratuity League (later renamed the United Veterans League) to fight for a grant of $2,000 for each returned soldier. One rally held by the League, on September 11, drew an estimated 20,000 participants, making it the largest political demonstration ever held in Toronto.[11]

In 1918 the national farmers' organization, the Canadian Council of Agriculture, adopted a new program which demanded reduced tariffs, taxes on business profits, public ownership of utilities, and such classic populist reforms as direct legislation and the right of voters to recall elected representatives. The provincial United Farmers organizations took up this program and entered candidates in provincial elections. In 1920 the Council of

Agriculture launched the National Progressive Party to run for federal office.

The first test of the labor-farmer-soldier alliance came in October 1919, in the Ontario general election. The Independent Labor Party nominated 25 candidates, including such radicals as James Simpson and Jack MacDonald. In several ridings Soldier or Soldier-Labor candidates ran. The United Farmers of Ontario contested most of the remaining seats.

More than one historian has described the outcome of that election as a minor revolution. The Conservative government was swept out of office. Six cabinet members, including the Premier, lost their seats. Conservative representation fell from 78 seats to 25. The Liberals dropped from 30 seats to 28. The United Farmers increased their representation from 2 seats to 45, making them the largest party in the House, while the Independent Labor Party, which had never had more than one sitting member, and which held no seats at the time of dissolution, elected 11 of its candidates.

After a week of negotiating, the UFO agreed to form a government, with the support of the ILP. Walter Rollo of the Labor Party was named minister of labor in Canada's first Farmer-Labor government.

Similar electoral victories were won by Labor slates in other parts of the country. In the Winnipeg municipal elections in late autumn, a joint slate that included the Dominion Labor Party, the Socialist Party, and the Social Democratic Party won 7 of 14 seats on City Council, and almost 45 percent of the mayoralty vote. The following spring the three parties and the United Farmers of Manitoba ran strong campaigns for the provincial legislature. In Winnipeg itself the labor candidates received nearly 43 percent of the vote. Three of the four labor candidates elected in the city were still in prison for their roles in the General Strike; a fourth prisoner, R.B. Russell, was eliminated only after 37 counts in Manitoba's complex proportional representation system. In all, eleven labor and nine farm candidates were elected: they formed the official opposition to the Liberals, who had won a small plurality in the voting.

A Farmers government was elected in Alberta in July 1921, and in the same month a Farmer-Soldier-Labor slate won election as the official opposition in Nova Scotia. In December two labor candidates, J.S. Woodsworth and William Irvine, were elected to the federal House of Commons, along with 64 members of the farm-based National Progressive Party.

To many radicals, and to many supporters of the status quo, it seemed that a revolution by the ballot box was under way.

Disillusionment

The defeat of the Winnipeg General Strike had revealed the inadequacy of the Socialist Party as a revolutionary organization, and the dangers of relying on the general strike as a cure-all for labor's ills. The experience of the Farmer-Labor parliamentary groups elected in 1919-1921 had a similar impact, shattering the illusions many radicals had in the electoral, "labor party" road to socialism. The Farmer-Labor groups proved completely incapable of implementing any fundamental changes in society.

Almost from the beginning Ontario labor found itself in conflict with the Farmer-Labor government. Workers on the provincially-owned Hydro Power Canal at Chippewa went on strike to win the eight-hour day in July 1920. The Cabinet, composed largely of farmers with holdings large enough to employ hired labor, would not legislate the eight-hour day. It resorted instead to a time-honored method of killing the issue: a committee was appointed to study it.

With a few honorable exceptions, the labor members elected to provincial and federal parliaments in 1919, 1920, and 1921 proved unworthy of labor's support. The Labor caucus in Ontario was rent by petty personal jealousies and ambitions from the day it took office. It proved unable to put forward any common program, or to work together to advance labor's interests: holding office and dispensing patronage were more important than the needs of the class its members supposedly represented. Many of the Labor members elected were in fact Liberals or Conservatives who had found it convenient to run under the labor banner: they had changed their label, but not their politics. By early 1921 the Labor contingent in the Ontario legislature was quite thoroughly discredited. Similarly, in Manitoba, the labor caucus split in two shortly after the election, and neither group accomplished anything noteworthy.[12]

Revolution by the ballot box had proved a dismal failure.

THE LABOR REVOLT of 1919 raised entirely new questions for the Canadian left. The socialist movement had long restricted itself to educational activities, to "making socialists." The transition from capitalism to socialism was a matter for the far distant future. The unspoken assumption most socialists made was that their movement would grow until it encompassed a majority of the population, and then take power peacefully, through parliamentary means.

Now another possibility appeared, one which some European Marxists and a very few North Americans had been discussing for decades: the possibility of a transition to socialism that would result from a revolutionary crisis in which the working class would suddenly rebel against the established order. Such a rebellion actually occurred, in a chaotic and unconscious fashion, in 1919. A socialist victory resulting from this type of crisis would be much closer to the predictions of Marx and Engels—and to the actual experience of Russia and Germany in 1917 and 1918—than the gradual growth of socialism which most Canadian socialists had expected.

Such a crisis, whether it took the form of mass strikes, or massive shifts in voting patterns, or some combination of the two, or some other variant entirely, would pose major questions of leadership and strategy. The ruling class had demonstrated in Winnipeg that it would not be passive in face of a challenge to its power. The Canadian left had never considered such matters. Raising them meant adopting a new approach to socialist politics—and that meant building a new kind of party.

4. Regrouping the Left

Three political currents came together to create the first Communist Party of Canada in 1919: the Socialist Party of North America, a part of the left wing of the Social Democratic Party, and a group of Russian populist-anarchists. During 1919 and 1920 three more groups moved rapidly towards the Third International: the remainder of the SDP left wing, a group of radical trade unionists, and the left wing of the Socialist Party of Canada. Each group followed a different road to Bolshevism.

The Social Democratic Party

The SDP was banned under Order-in-Council PC 2384 in September 1918, but was restored to legality in November on the grounds that it favored gradual constitutional change, not revolution. The party's right wing was silent on the suppression of its Finnish, Russian, and Ukrainian affiliates, perhaps hoping that the Order-in-Council would rid the SDP of its troublesome left wing.

If that was their expectation, they were quickly disillusioned. Two months after the SDP regained legality, it held its first national convention since the outbreak of the War. As the *Toronto Star*'s report indicated, the results were by no means to the liking of the right wing.

Extremists in the Social Democratic Party won a decisive victory over the moderate faction during Saturday's and Sunday's session of the SDP convention, and a drastic policy to force action by the Government in granting the needs of the party will be the result. The extremists gained control of the convention at the opening session, and as a result all palliative measures were struck out of the platform. . . . Direct agitation for the abolition of the capitalist system was. . . seen as the only alternative, and the convention pledged itself to that end rather than to the advocating of any individual measures of reform.[1]

The *Star*'s report, which is very short on details, probably over-states the extent of the left wing victory. A brief article in *Labor News*, evidently written by an SDP member, reported that the delegates "were almost unanimous on all points of importance," and that the convention agreed to affiliate to the Labor Party. According to *Labor News*, all reforms were dropped from the SDP program "in view of the fact that the new Ontario Labor party would probably concentrate its efforts along these lines."[2]

These two rather different evaluations of the SDP convention reflect two sides of a contradictory process. The left wing clearly had a numerical majority in the SDP. Its influence is reflected in the fact that one of the featured speakers at a public rally during the convention was Charles Charnie (Lieb Samsonovitch) of the underground Bolshevik organization. We can be sure that he was not invited by the Simpson wing of the SDP!* At the same time, the left wing was quite aware of the value of the connections and influence of the right wing, and was not prepared to push matters to the point of split at the convention. The result was a number of compromises designed to keep the party together while the executive was taken over by the left.

But the centrifugal tendencies in the party were simply too strong to be resisted. Part of the left wing devoted its energies to the new Communist Party, and most of the right wing spent its time building the Labor Party. After January 1919 such men as James Simpson and Isaac Bainbridge simply stopped referring to themselves as Social Democrats. The party began to disintegrate. A proposed SDP newspaper never materialized, and the new national executive, dominated by Jewish and Anglo-Canadian radicals who were looking more and more towards Bolshevism, never really functioned. The SDP could not survive.

Maurice Spector, a member of the SDP executive elected at the January 1919 convention, explained the collapse of the SDP in an article written in 1922:

---

*Charnie's presence suggests that there was no sharp organizational distinction between the underground and the SDP Left. The underground may have remained in the SDP in order to win over more revolutionists to their cause.

The Social Democratic Party vanished from the political scene for two reasons. First, the right wing perceiving that the war had sufficiently quickened the sense of independent political action among the moderate trade union elements, threw themselves into the work of getting control of that development by the organization of an Independent Labor Party; secondly, the left wing developed by the repercussion of the Russian Revolution succeeded in putting a successful referendum on affiliation to the Communist International (1919). But this achievement was little more than a revolutionary gesture, a demonstration of ideal revolutionary solidarity, since the party was rapidly disintegrating, and was finally liquidated by its revolutionary Central Committee to prevent the treasury funds and party name being exploited by the former Social Democratic element in the I.L.P. for its own political ends.[3]

By the beginning of 1920 the Social Democratic Party had disappeared. In its place were underground groups devoted to revolutionary political goals. These groups carried on legal (i.e., public) propaganda through a variety of front groups, while discussing Bolshevism in private.

The first and best-known of the front groups was the Ontario Labor College, formed early in January 1920, with offices at 28 Wellington Street West, in downtown Toronto. The College was an adjunct of the Plebs League, formed at the same time, with the same offices, by the same people. The two organizations held weekly educational classes in Marxist theory in their offices at the Occident Hall in the Ukrainian section of Toronto, in West Toronto, and in Hamilton. The best-known leaders of the organizations were former SDP executive member Maurice Spector; former SPNA leaders Florence Custance and Tom Bell; and Max Armstrong, a popular speaker and educator who had at various times been active in the SDP, the SPNA, and the One Big Union.[4]

A parallel organization was established in Quebec. The Montreal Labor College, initiated by Social Democrats Mike Buhay, Rebecca Buhay, Annie Buller, and Bella Gauld, attracted a broader range of speakers than its Toronto counterpart—non-Marxists, including J.S. Woodsworth, participated in its program of classes and public meetings.[5]

It is unclear whether the Plebs League saw itself as a Communist organization from its foundation. William Rodney, in *Soldiers of the International*, states that the Plebs League affiliated with the United Communist Party of America (one of two Communist Parties in the U.S.) in January 1921.[6] It seems unlikely that the decision to establish a party was delayed that long. In the first place, the group included Tom Bell and Florence Custance, both of whom had been involved in the 1919 Communist Party—Bell had served a prison term for his part in it. Secondly, it included Maurice Spector, who had initiated the referendum for the Third International in the SDP. These three would have needed very little convincing to establish a Communist organization, although formal affiliation to the UCPA may have taken longer.

The division of the U.S. Communist movement into two parties was to a large degree ethnically based. The UCPA's leadership was composed largely of English-speaking radicals, while the rival Communist Party of America was led and dominated by radicals of Russian and other East European origins. This division spread into Canada. The Ukrainian and Finnish Communist groups affiliated to the CPA, giving that organization a much larger membership base than the UCPA. John Boychuck, who had gone to prison with Bell for creating a Communist Party in 1919, became a prominent member of the CPA branch in Toronto.

Both of these groups had their origins in the Social Democratic Party. The UCPA brought together Jewish and Anglo-Canadian radicals, most of them intellectuals, from the SDP and the Socialist Party of North America; the CPA was based in the leadership of the ethnic organizations which had long formed the majority of the SDP's membership. In 1921 these groups were joined by another which also came from the SDP, but by a more roundabout route.

The Labor Left

When the SDP's right wing left the party in 1919 to participate in the Labor Party movement, they were themselves a divided force. Some—James Simpson is the best example—were social democrats in the modern sense, liberal reformers with an eye on parliamentary careers. Others saw the Labor Party as a step towards the Socialist Commonwealth: they were the left wing of the right wing. This group included a large number of dedicated socialist leaders, of whom the best known was Jack MacDonald.

MacDonald was born in Scotland in 1888, and played a prominent role in socialist and labor politics in his native city, Falkirk. He was, like most of the Labor left, a highly-skilled industrial worker, what was then called a pattern-maker, what we today would call a die-maker. When he emigrated to Canada and settled in Toronto in 1912, MacDonald joined the Pattern Makers Lodge, becoming one of that union's principal spokesmen in the Toronto and District Labor Council. In 1919 he was vice-president of the Metal Trades Council, the organization which initiated the

Toronto General Strike. MacDonald does not seem to have held any
executive positions in the SDP, and he was not a regular contributor
to the socialist or labor press, but his skill as an orator made him
famous. During the great labor radicalization of 1919 there was
seldom a radical or labor meeting in Toronto that did not feature
Jack MacDonald in some prominent capacity.

On July 7, 1919, the *Toronto Times'* labor column featured a
"Chat With An Agent Of The Secret Bolshevism." Though the
"agent" was not named, anyone familiar with the Toronto labor
left could have identified MacDonald. He was Scottish, "about 30
years old," an official of a union which had just finished a
sympathetic strike, and so on. The *Times'* reporter expressed great
indignation that this man "appeared in the guise of a labor leader"
when in reality he was only "hiding under that honored name to
play upon the hopes and grievances of real workingmen and lead
them to revolt." The interview provides a valuable insight into the
thinking of men such as MacDonald in 1919. Labor, he said, was
fighting for "control of the means of production. All of them." The
best weapon at labor's disposal was the general strike—"We can't
win by the ballot. That's been proved. We always get tricked." He
endorsed the goals of the Russian Revolution:

We all have copies of the Russian soviet constitution here. We've read it and
studied it. About the methods they used I'm saying nothing, you
understand. They may be right or they may be wrong. But I will say this: the
Russian soviet constitution is the greatest thing for the workingmen that
has ever been devised.... And we'll get it right here, too.

MacDonald was typical of hundreds of labor radicals, both in his
British origins and training as a skilled worker, and in his political
outlook. He and his co-thinkers were profoundly attracted to the
Russian Revolution and to the Bolsheviks' dedication to the cause
of proletarian liberation, but they knew very little about Bolshevik
"methods." What they thought of as Bolshevik methods were the
slogans and policies of the Canadian Bolshevik underground:
slogans and policies which a man with MacDonald's experience
knew to be out of touch with reality. MacDonald defended the
underground against government persecution—he was the
featured speaker at demonstrations opposing the conviction of the
thirteen Communists in June—but he did not accept their political
ideas. He and his circle vacillated between the traditional social
democratic, electoral approach to socialism, and a semi-syndicalist
enthusiasm for the general strike, until they were convinced there

was a better way. In the end it was their own experience that convinced them.

The defeat of the general strike movement of the spring and summer of 1919 was followed by a widespread enthusiasm for labor parties and candidates. MacDonald himself ran as a candidate for the Independent Labor Party in the Ontario provincial elections, coming second in his riding with more than 7,000 votes. He was elected second vice-president of the ILP and president of the smaller, more radical Canadian Labor Party (Ontario Section). When the CLP and ILP formed a Labor Representation Committee to coordinate efforts in the 1919 Toronto municipal elections, MacDonald was chosen as chairman. From July 1919 until January 1921 he served on the executive of the Toronto Trades and Labor Council, representing the TLC on a host of committees and councils.

MacDonald's participation in labor electoral politics did not blunt or mute his radical views. In February 1920 he told a public meeting in Toronto: "I believe in the Soviet system as now practiced in Russia today. While there have been barbarities under that system we must remember that they have established this system while they have had the whole Capitalist class of the world at their throats."[7] Such remarks ensured that he was in constant conflict with the labor reformers who ran the ILP. MacDonald in turn looked with increasing disfavor on the ILP legislative caucus, as personal ambition, petty jealousy, and above all the alliance with the procapitalist United Farmers prevented the party from achieving even the most moderate of gains for the working class.

The turning point for MacDonald was the North East Toronto provincial by-election in November 1920. James Higgins, a member of the committee which organized the Toronto general strike, was nominated jointly by the ILP, the United Veterans, and the Trades and Labor Council. MacDonald and other radicals campaigned on Higgins's behalf, but the Farmer-Labor government refused to support him. (The legislators objected to the radical planks in Higgins's platform, especially his call for withdrawal of troops from Russia and his support for Irish self-determination.) The ILP right wing attributed Higgins's defeat in the by-election to the involvement and influence of socialists. The party executive, in a joint meeting with the legislative caucus, declared its opposition to the appearance of ILP spokesmen at meetings at which views were expressed which were "not in accordance with the fundamental principles of British democracy or the platform of the ILP." A second resolution expressed the opinion that socialists should not hold office in the ILP, and requested socialists to decline if nominated![8]

For the radicals, already disenchanted with the ILP, this was the last straw. They broke with not only the ILP right wing, but with such former Social Democrats as James Simpson who favored unity at all costs. In early January 1921, MacDonald's supporters in the Labor Council nominated him for president; he opposed not only the right wing candidate but also James Scott, one of Simpson's associates. Following the elections, in which he trailed badly, MacDonald announced to a crowded ILP Forum that he was leaving the party:

I have been in the Labor Party for what assistance I could render to the workers and for want of a better party. I can't possibly remain in it any longer. I believe it is the duty of class-conscious Socialists to form Left wings affiliated with the Third Internationale.

MacDonald heaped scorn on the very idea of winning socialism through parliamentary means:

Hyndman, Clynes, Thomas and others of the Second Internationale talk of Socialism, social ownership, nationalization, the capture of Parliament and other reforms. Their followers imagine that by some enactment of Parliament capitalism will slide from the backs of the workers....

Don't have any illusions! There never was a class that got off the backs of the workers unless it was thrown off. Do you think the capitalist class, which is preparing to shed blood to destroy the Soviet of Russia is going to sit around a table to hand over the means of production?...

Soft words will not get the workers over the barricades....

That meeting, on January 23, 1921, caused a sensation in the Toronto labor movement. Every newspaper reported it—several made it front page news. ("John MacDonald...threw off his camouflage last night," said the Tory *Mail and Empire*.) In an attempt to undo some of the damage caused by MacDonald's defection, and to restrain some of MacDonald's associates from following him, the ILP held another meeting two weeks later, featuring James Simpson speaking on the desirability of reform through constitutional means. Simpson, however, was hissed and booed by members of the audience. When he finished, MacDonald took the floor. "The ILP is moribund," he said. "It is dead. It does not function except through a forum.... Communists in Toronto are much stronger than the members of the ILP. The ILP is not a Socialist organization, it is a Liberal Party. Talk on Communism. Talk on something real!" That confrontation caused almost as great a stir as the first meeting did.[9]

Representatives of both underground Communist parties had been present at the January 23 meeting. Thomas Bell of the United Communist Party of America expressed doubts about MacDonald's sincerity, and argued that he could not be permitted to join the Communist movement in view of his record, but George Wiltshaw of the Communist Party of America disagreed, pointing out that the Third International had appealed to supporters of the Second International to come over to the new organization. MacDonald accepted Wiltshaw's invitation, joining the Toronto CPA branch shortly after the meeting. He brought with him a group of labor militants who were as disgusted with the ILP as he was: they included such people as Fred Peel, Robert Shoesmith, Tim Buck, Joe Knight, and Sarah Knight, all of whom were to play leading roles in the Communist Party of Canada in the 1920s. They transformed the CPA from an ingrown organization limited to the East European immigrant community into a party that attempted to win broad influence in the labor movement. Under their initiative the CPA launched a legal front, similar to the UCPA's Ontario Labor College, called the Workers Educational Association. MacDonald's adherence to the Communist movement was a major turning point in the history of Canadian Bolshevism.

Fusion

There were now two Communist parties in Toronto and in most other cities east of Winnipeg. The split had no political justification: the parties had similar programs and objectives and conducted similar activities. That the split lasted any time at all reflected not Canadian conditions but the paralyzing factionalism that had divided the Communist movement in the United States since 1919. The Comintern repeatedly urged the U.S. parties to overcome their differences and merge, but to no avail. Finally, early in 1921, the International established a Pan-American Agency with instructions to unite the two parties by June 1, 1921. If unity could not be achieved the Agency had the authority to create a new party "without regard to the existing parties," in effect reading the opponents of unity out of the International. Early in May, at a secret convention in Woodstock, New York, the two organizations united to form a single party, the Communist Party of America.[10]

The Comintern's instructions also applied, by extension, to Canada. Early in April the Pan-American Agency sent Caleb Harrison to Toronto to initiate unity talks. Harrison, who used the pseudonym "Atwood," soon had negotiations under way. The first concrete result of his efforts was the production of issue number one of *The Communist*, published to mark May Day by the "Committee of the Third International in Canada."*

The unity talks moved very quickly. As late as May Day 1921 the two parties held separate rallies in Toronto, and the unity convention actually assembled on May 23.

The delegates travelled in the greatest secrecy to a small farm on the outskirts of Guelph, Ontario, owned by UCPA member Fred Farley. Twenty-two people attended in all—fifteen from the CPA, five from the UCPA, and two from the Socialist Party of Canada. The disproportionate strength of the CPA delegation reflected the size of the large immigrant organizations in the CPA, whose delegation included Matthew Popowich and John Navisisky of the Ukrainian Labor Temple Association in Winnipeg, and John Ahlqvist and John Latva of the Canadian Finnish Organization. The CPA group also included Jack MacDonald and George Wiltshaw. The UCPA was represented by Maurice Spector, Tom Bell, Florence Custance, and two others whose names are not known. The members of the SPC did not officially represent their party, although they may have been sent by their branches: one of them was Toronto SPC secretary William Moriarty; the other may have been Fred Kaplan from Winnipeg.†

The convention, under Harrison's chairmanship, lasted only one day. In contrast to the U.S. unity convention, which almost collapsed as a result of the constituent organizations' failure to agree on major issues, the Canadian meeting was unanimous on every significant point. It adopted a constitution and a program—both of them modified versions of those adopted in the United States—

---

*The first English-language Communist periodical in Canada was *The Communist Bulletin*, published by the UCPA early in 1921.[11] Only one issue appeared. The UCPA does not seem to have published an English magazine or newspaper in Canada. Both organizations circulated the Communist newspapers published in the United States.

†No full list of the delegates exists. The list given by Tim Buck in his *Reminiscences*, pp. 97-98, is contradictory and unreliable. Despite his claims to the contrary, the evidence indicates that Buck was not present at the Guelph convention. See the Appendix to this chapter.

chose the name Communist Party of Canada, accepted the discipline of the Communist International "as binding upon all delegates present and...its entire membership, without any reservations," and chose a provisional Central Committee.[12] With that done, and after the singing of The Internationale, the delegates dispersed. The June issue of *The Communist*, edited by Maurice Spector, announced the formation of the new party:

The result of the Constituent Convention is the organization of the Canadian working class into the Communist Party of Canada, section of the Communist International, with a program of mass-action as the vital form of proletarian activity, armed insurrection, civil war as the decisive form of mass-action, for the destruction of the Capitalist State, proletarian dictatorship in the form of soviet power as the lever of the Communist reconstruction of society. And now Comrades, there is tremendous work before us. Ours is an age of revolution versus imperialism. History is with us. Socialism is no longer the possession of a cloistered sect, nor a subject of parliamentary diplomacy. It is a bitter, relentless mass-struggle against the most monstrous coalition of oppression and destruction that history has record of. Therefore all shoulders to the wheel.

Long live the Communist Party of Canada!
Long live the Communist International!

The Socialist Party of Canada

The May 1921 convention united the main body of revolutionary Marxists east of Manitoba into a single party. The only significant group of socialists remaining outside of the Communist Party was the Socialist Party of Canada. The SPC remained dominant on the left in Western Canada, as the largest or only working-class political organization in most cities. To the members of the new party the addition of all or part of the SPC membership to their ranks was a matter of primary importance.

The Socialist Party, as we have seen, had long considered itself to be on the left wing of the international socialist movement. It had refused to join the Second International because reformists were allowed in, and it had declared itself in favor of a Third International as early as 1916. Its newspaper *Western Clarion* had been the first Canadian periodical to print articles by leaders of the Bolshevik revolution ("Pacifism in the Service of Imperialism," by Leon Trotsky, appeared in the January 1918 issue) and it had given constant, if not always uncritical, support to the Soviet government. Charlie O'Brien, long the Socialist Party's representative in the Alberta legislature, had moved to the United States during the

War and had become a founding member of the Communist Party of America. Add to this the leading role SPC members played in the labor revolt of 1919, and it seemed not unreasonable to expect that the party would adhere to the Communist International and form the nucleus of a Communist Party in the West.

But the SPC was no semi-Bolshevik Party just waiting for the call. Intransigence in the name of Marxist principle may mean a genuine commitment to proletarian revolution—but it may also mean sectarian sterility. For an important part of the SPC's leadership that is just what it did mean. Their Marxism was academic and abstract, divorced from the day-to-day life of the working class they hoped to lead. Even some of those who had opposed the party's former rejection of trade unionism, who had plunged into the battle in 1919 (W.A. Pritchard is a good example), drew a dividing line between their union activity and their political activity. It was characteristic that the party, though its members had control of the One Big Union, never took a formal position *as a* party on the division in the labor movement. Indeed it refused to do so, on the grounds that "the comparative merits of various forms of industrial activity do not come within the field of S.P. of C. activity."[13] It was also characteristic that the pages of the *Western Clarion*, during the 1919 labor revolt, were devoted almost exclusively to abstract expositions of Marxist theory.

The militant unionists and the abstract theoreticians had long co-existed in the Socialist Party. Some, like Pritchard, managed to belong to both camps. In 1921 the question of affiliation to the Third International ended the co-existence, and the party blew apart.

Although the issue of affiliation to the Third International had been a subject for discussion in the party ranks from March 1919 on, the SPC did not begin a formal discussion until January 1921. In October 1920 the Winnipeg local of the party voted to ask the Dominion Executive to organize a referendum vote on affiliation. Instead, the executive opened the pages of the *Western Clarion* to a debate, with the statement that "the date of the referendum will necessarily depend upon the discussion that arises."

As it happened, the debate lasted nearly a year, occupying all the time of party members and most of the pages of the *Clarion*. The lines were clearly drawn from the beginning. Opposed to affiliation were the party's intellectuals, led by J. Harrington and W.A. Pritchard. Foremost among the pro-affiliation group was Jack Kavanaugh, former president of the B.C. Federation of Labor,

chairman of the 1919 Western Labor Conference, and probably
B.C.'s best-known socialist labor leader.

Members of the underground Communist parties also played a
role in the discussion. William Moriarty of Toronto and Fred
Kaplan of Winnipeg were two who had already joined the Third
International when they submitted their discussion articles to the
Western Clarion. That others did likewise is indicated by an
editorial in the *Clarion* that darkly referred to an unnamed
Vancouver member who had "joined the party [a few months ago]
in order to vote us into the Third."[14]

Some positions taken by the opponents of affiliation were frankly
reactionary. Harrington argued seriously and vehemently that
joining the Third International would commit the SPC to support
for colonial liberation movements, and that socialists had no
business involving themselves in such activities.

But the real issue, from the beginning to the end of the long
debate, was "What kind of party is the SPC to be?" or, to express it
in other terms, "What is the proper activity for Marxists to engage
in?"

For Harrington and his circle, the answer was simple enough: the
task of Marxists was education, the role of the party was
educational. They understood education in a very narrow sense: the
dissemination, through lectures, pamphlets and books, of Marxist
ideas. The workings of capitalist society would inevitably bring
about a socialist revolution; in the meantime socialists should
prepare by educating themselves and others, by "making
socialists." Plunging into the labor movement, combatting
reformism, fighting to win the leadership of unions—the Third
International made such activities compulsory for member
parties—such work would, in Harrington's opinion, "hamper and
in the end nullify our educational work...use up all the precious
time and energy, at present limited enough, for the work we are
engaged in."[15]

In Harrington's view, Marxism was "a method of understanding
social institutions, their development or decay," and the task of the
party was to explain that method to the working class. Here was the
crux of the debate. Jack Kavanaugh, quoting Harrington's definition of Marxism, replied:

Marxism, as I understand it, is something more than the foregoing. It is also
the application of the foregoing for the purpose of organizing the working
class for the capture of political power.[16]

The issue, as William Moriarty expressed it, was whether the SPC should devote itself to "a philosophy of action...[or] a philosophy of erudition."[17] Moriarty won no friends on the *Clarion* editorial board by stating the issue so bluntly, but reading the discussion today it is difficult to doubt the justness of his statement.

THE DEBATE DRAGGED ON for months, filling the pages of the *Clarion* with articles that added nothing to the originally stated positions. By the end of May most of the debate was superfluous in any event: the SPC was trying to decide whether to become the Canadian section of the Comintern, when such an organization already existed. For the advocates of affiliation (and especially for the CPC members who were taking part in the debate) the need to end discussion and *act* took on added urgency when the CPC Central Committee, in September, decided to launch a "legal party" to campaign for communist principles in Canada.* Even if they won the referendum, the pro-affiliation forces could foresee endless wrangles about interpretation and implementation of the decision.

In mid-December 1921 the Communist current decided to split the Socialist Party. The Provisional Organization Committee of the Workers Party of Canada (the "legal party" formed on December 11) assigned Florence Custance, Fred Peel, and William Moriarty to write an Appeal to the left wing of the SPC.[18] The Appeal was issued in mimeographed form just before Christmas, and published in both the January 6 *B.C. Federationist* and the January 7 *Workers Guard*, the newspaper of the Workers Party. "A split is now inevitable," it declared. "The educationists will reorganize and continue their philosophical readings. But you—the Left Wingers, who stand out clearly and strongly for the Third, what will you do?" The Appeal urged the left wing to break with the SPC, which it branded "an educational sect...out of touch with the masses of the workers," and to join in building "a strong party of struggle."

The response came quickly, so quickly that there is no doubt that support within the SPC had been arranged before publication of the Appeal. The Winnipeg SPC local voted 25 to 11 to sever its connections with the Dominion Executive Committee, and joined the Workers Party.[19] After the Vancouver local failed to follow suit, four supporters of the Third International—Jack Kavanaugh, A.S.

---

*That decision, which led to the launching of the Workers Party of Canada, will be discussed at more length in chapter 5.

Wells, J.G. Smith, and R.W. Hartley—issued a statement "on behalf of twenty members of the S.P. of C." announcing their intention to join the Workers Party:

> Those whom we have hitherto looked upon as revolutionary Marxists refuse to accept the task which the International Communist movement has laid before them.
>
> To them the academy is preferable to work among the masses. In the academy let them stay. That is the real position of the party—an academic institution: not a political party of the working class....
>
> To us the road is clear. We will go forward with the revolutionary workers of the Third International. The road is hard, but the goal is worth all of the hardships of the task before us. Let the slogan of the Communist Manifesto become a reality: "Workers of all countries unite, you have nothing to lose but your chains."[20]

By the end of January 1922, the Socialist Party of Canada had all but collapsed. Local after local voted to join the Workers Party. The SPC leadership claimed not to be concerned about the losses, but there is no doubt that the splits of 1921-1922 were a deathblow for its brand of Marxism. The SPC continued its program of abstract Marxist education (one month after the Vancouver split, Harrington was giving a class on "Revolution and Counter-revolution in Early Peru") and continued to publish the *Western Clarion* for several years. But its membership and readership declined precipitously. In the summer of 1925 the Socialist Party of Canada disbanded.*

The Communist Cadre

Between the end of World War I and the beginning of 1922, a complete regroupment of the Canadian left took place. In most countries during this period the left split between a social-democratic majority and a communist minority, but that was not the case here. The Communist movement took 90 percent or more of the membership of the Social Democratic Party, all or most of the Socialist Party of North America, and a major fraction of the Socialist Party of Canada, including virtually all of its active union

---

*Another party with the same name was founded on the initiative of Ernest Winch later in the decade. It became one of the founding organizations of the CCF.

members.* By the beginning of 1922 the Communist movement had gathered into its ranks a clear majority of the organized left. It had also assembled its basic leadership cadre, the team that would guide the party through the 1920s.

Jack MacDonald's background has already been discussed. His initial political training was in Scotland, but by the time the Communist Party of Canada was formed he already had nine years of Canadian political and union activity behind him. A self-educated worker and an outstanding orator, MacDonald was one of the most popular figures in the Ontario labor movement. When he decided to join the Communist movement, he brought dozens of radical trade unionists with him.

It is impossible to exaggerate the importance of MacDonald's role in the Canadian Communist movement. He was the party's first chairman. He became national secretary in 1923, holding that post until 1929. He was a delegate to the Fourth (1922) and Sixth (1928) Congresses of the Communist International. "Moscow Jack," as the papers called him, was communism personified for many Canadian workers in the 1920s.

When MacDonald was elected national secretary in 1923, his place as party chairman was taken by *Maurice Spector*, the youngest of the party's central leaders. Spector was born on March 19, 1898 in the Ukraine, but was brought to Canada as an infant. He joined the Young Socialist League (the SDP's youth wing) in 1914, and by 1916 was contributing regularly to the SDP's *Canadian Forward*. At the beginning of 1918, as acting editor of the University of Toronto *Varsity*, Spector published a letter critical of the war and the Allies' role in it: this violation of wartime censorship got him removed from the paper and nearly expelled from university. In 1919 Spector was a member of the Dominion Executive of the SDP; in 1920 he participated in the formation of the Toronto branch of the United Communist Party of America.

Spector was, beyond doubt, *the* outstanding Canadian Marxist intellectual of his generation. He edited the CPC's underground newspaper *The Communist* in 1921, and became editor of the "legal" newspaper *The Worker* in 1922. With one interruption

---

*Whether a majority of SPCers joined the Communist movement cannot be determined. The splits took place while the referendum vote was in progress: the executive admitted that a very small majority (including many of those who split) favored affiliation. There is no doubt that a majority of the active rank and file went to the Workers Party in 1922.

(caused by travel in Europe and Russia) Spector remained editor of *The Worker* until 1928. In 1927-1928 he also edited the party's magazine *Canadian Labor Monthly*. He was a delegate to the Fourth and Sixth Comintern congresses, and in 1928 became the first Canadian to be elected to the Executive Committee of the Communist International (ECCI).

The MacDonald-Spector partnership was the axis around which the leadership of the Communist Party was organized in the 1920s. MacDonald was an organizer of great ability, and a speaker who could reach and influence masses of workers. Spector also had a reputation as an orator, but his greatest contribution to the party was as a theoretician and writer.

MacDonald and Spector were the dominant leaders of the Communist movement in its early years, but they were not the only leaders. Quite the contrary. Largely through MacDonald's efforts, the CPC assembled a team of leaders who worked together with surprisingly little friction: the bitter factional strife which marred U.S. party life in the 1920s was entirely absent in Canada. It is not possible to name every party leader. The following list includes only those who played major roles in the party's national leadership.

Tom Bell, an Irish-born lithographer, was one of those who came to Communism through the Socialist Party of North America. He was arrested for his role in the 1919 Communist Party, and later participated in the Toronto UCPA local. From 1921 to 1923 he was active in the party in Toronto and Winnipeg, then moved to Cape Breton, where he edited the *Maritime Labor Herald* and played a prominent part in the most important labor battles of the decade. Like many Canadian skilled workers, Bell was forced by economic conditions to emigrate to the United States late in 1924.

Malcolm Bruce was the only member of the party's initial leadership who was born in Canada—in Prince Edward Island, in 1881. While still in his teens, he participated in the Western Federation of Miners' attempts to win union recognition in Butte, Montana. In 1910 he settled in Regina, joining the United Brotherhood of Carpenters and the Socialist Party. He was a founding member of the One Big Union, and in 1922 became one of many OBU members to join the Workers Party. During Spector's absence in 1923-24 he was editor of *The Worker*, and he was a delegate to the Fifth (1924) Congress of the International.

Tim Buck was a machinist from Britain who came to Canada in 1910. His early political career is discussed in the appendix to this chapter. Buck served through the 1920s as the CPC's trade union director, and as head of the Canadian section of the Trade Union Educational League. He was a delegate to the Fifth Congress of the Comintern in 1924 and represented the Canadian party at the Seventh Plenum of the ECCI in 1926.

Michael Buhay, born in England in 1890, became a member of the Social Democratic Party in Montreal in 1913. He was an organizer for the Cloakmakers Union during the War, and for the Amalgamated Clothing Workers Union during the 1920s. Buhay was a founding member of the CPC and one of its most prominent union activists. In 1928 he became editor of the Party's Yiddish monthly *Der Kamf*. He was a delegate to the Fourth Congress of the Red International of Labor Unions in 1928.

Florence Custance was the only woman in the party's central leadership. Born on December 31, 1881, in England, and trained as a school teacher, Custance was a founder of the Socialist Party of North America in 1911. Though direct evidence is not available, Custance was probably a member of the 1919 Communist Party. In 1920 she helped found the Toronto UCPA branch. Through the 1920s she was prominent in such groups as Canadian Friends of Soviet Russia, the Canadian Labor Defense League, and the Women's Labor League. She was secretary of the CPC's Women's Bureau and a regular contributor to *The Worker* on topics related to women's rights and the activities of women workers. In 1925 she founded and edited the magazine *Woman Worker*.

Jack Kavanaugh was born in England in 1882. He emigrated to Vancouver in 1907, and became a longshoreman. He was elected SPC party organizer in 1910, and president of the B.C. Federation of Labor in 1912. In 1919 he played a major role in the creation of the OBU. Kavanaugh was elected to the Workers Party's National Executive Committee in 1922, and appointed editor-in-chief of *The Worker*. The latter post was largely nominal, however, because immediately after his appointment he returned to the West Coast. Kavanaugh left the party late in 1922 as a result of disagreements on trade union policy, but rejoined in 1923. In 1925 he emigrated to Australia, and later became General Secretary of the Communist Party there.

William Moriarty emigrated from England in 1910. He joined the

Socialist Party during the War, serving as party secretary in both Ottawa and Toronto. One of the first SPC members to join the Communist movement, he became a member of the Central Executive Committee at the May 1921 convention, and was elected National Secretary of the Workers Party in 1922. He subsequently became business manager of *The Worker* and, in 1926, National Organizer of the party. Moriarty was a delegate to the Fifth (1925) Plenum of the ECCI.

The great majority of the members of the party were immigrants from Finland and the Ukraine. They were organized in separate "language federations," which were affiliated to the party and entitled to their own representatives on the Central Executive Committee. The leaders of these federations tended not to involve themselves in the day-to-day work of the party as such, although they were influential in setting overall policy. They formed a set of parallel Communist leaderships, formally subordinate to the party leadership but in practice all but independent of it. In the Finnish Oranization of Canada *John Ahlqvist, Tom Hill,* and *John Latva* played pre-eminent roles; in the Ukrainian Labor Temple Association *John Boychuck, Matthew Popowich,* and *John Navisisky (Navis)* were the best-known Communist leaders.

It would be possible to name dozens more who played leadership roles of various kinds in the Canadian Communist movement in the 1920s, but those named here were clearly the party's primary leadership. At considerable personal sacrifice, and with complete dedication, they worked to build a new revolutionary party in Canada.

APPENDIX
The Early Political Career
of Tim Buck

Tim Buck was the only early leader of the Canadian Communist movement to write extensively about his experiences. During the 1930s Buck became General Secretary of the party and was hailed as the *founder* of Canadian Communism; during the 1950s and 1960s he attempted also to establish himself as the *historian* of Canadian Communism. In a series of articles, pamphlets, books, and interviews, Buck gave an account of the party's early years which placed him at center stage. There were very few, if any, events in the history of the party in which Buck did not (by his own account) play a pivotal role.

Buck never wrote a full-scale autobiography, but his writings and interviews contain a wealth of autobiographical material. This material has been used extensively by historians of the Canadian left and labor movements. Even writers who know that Buck's accuracy cannot always be guaranteed have accepted many of his "eyewitness" accounts as valid.

For example, Buck's account of the underground Bolshevik movement has been accepted by such eminent historians as William Rodney and Ivan Avakumovic. Buck's version occurs in several different works, but the content is basically the same in each:

The first attempt was made in February 1919. That time the plans were betrayed and the preliminary conference was raided by the police. John Boychuck, Tom Bell, Mrs. Florence Custance, Mr. and Mrs. Everhardt and other leading members of the committee were arrested. John Boychuck and Tom Bell were sentenced and served prison terms; the Everhardts were deported to Germany, where they immediately became active in the foundation of the Communist Party of Germany; he was elected to the Central Committee. The attempt to form a Canadian party of Communists was frustrated for the time being.[21]

Another version states that the purpose of the meeting was to form an "International Workers Association."[22] Yet another refers to an attempt to establish an "International Workers Party"; according to this account, "They weren't going to call it 'communist,' they were going to try to circumvent the War Measures Act."[23] And the most fascinating addition to the story came in Buck's *Reminiscences* (interviews tape recorded by the Canadian Broadcasting Corporation in 1965 but not published until 1977)—here he claimed to have been informed in advance that the conference was to take place by a man later suspected of being a police informer, but that he (Buck) did not know the exact location or date until afterwards.[24]

It is quite clear that the event Buck is describing was the attempt to establish a Communist Party of Canada in 1919, which has been discussed in chapter 2. But it is also quite clear that Buck really knew very little about it. We can note that he gets the date wrong;

that the Germans arrested were named "Ewart," not "Everhardt";* that the people he claims were arrested together were in fact arrested several months apart; that Florence Custance was not among those arrested; and that Buck makes no mention of the best-known of the early Bolsheviks, Charles Charnie. And, most important of all, Buck explicitly denies that a "Communist Party" was formed, though the evidence proves the opposite.† If Buck were as closely involved as he suggests in his *Reminiscences*, that detail would surely not have been missed.

Buck's errors in his account of the 1919 events can best be explained as the result of an attempt to pass off second-hand information as first-hand knowledge. The events of 1919 were no doubt discussed in party circles in the 1920s, especially since three genuine participants—Custance, Bell, and Boychuck—were on the Central Committee. Buck would have heard those discussions, and he passed them on in distorted form decades later.

But if that is the case, then a question mark must be placed over Buck's entire account of his political activity between 1910 (when he arrived in Canada) and 1921. For Buck claims, in several different works, to have been a member, *a founding member*, of the Socialist Party of North America. The SPNA played a key role in the creation of the 1919 Communist Party: as a member of that party he would surely have had more direct knowledge of the events of 1919 than his writings reveal.

A close examination of Buck's accounts of his early political activity show that the question mark is justified. There is scarcely a single point on which Buck's word can be accepted.

We have only Buck's word for his involvement in the SPNA: I have been unable to find a single contemporary reference linking him to that party. And there is very strong evidence that he never was a member.

In his *Reminiscences*, Buck states that he participated in the founding of the SPNA in 1915. In *Lenin and Canada* he gives the date as 1916.[25] In fact, the SPNA was founded on March 22, 1911:

---

*William Rodney pointed out the error in names in *Soldiers of the International*. Buck made the correction, without acknowledgement to Rodney, two years later in *Lenin and Canada*.

†Buck's claim that the name "Communist" was avoided to circumvent the War Measures Act would not make sense in any case: the name "Communist' was not illegal, and the people arrested in 1919 were never charged with that non-crime.

half a decade earlier.[26] An error of four or five years in the founding
date of an organization that lasted only eight years is a major error
indeed! The significance of the error is increased by the fact that
Buck's two dates are both after the War began: surely a participant,
even if his memory was foggy, would remember whether the
founding meeting took place before or during the War. We can only
conclude that Buck was not a founder of the SPNA.

In interviews given to the CBC in 1965, Buck described the
municipal election campaign of 1912 (the vote actually took place
on New Years Day 1913) as a major turning point in his political
evolution. A Labor Representation Committee was formed to run a
labor slate for City Hall.

The idea was that Jimmy Simpson should run as a labour candidate for the
Board of Control and Carl Lindalla, the president and leader of the Finnish
Social Democratic Party, a worker and a delegate to the Trades and Labour
Council, should run for Mayor.

Buck says that Arthur Taylor convinced him to support the
campaign and that he became heavily involved, in particular
raising money to launch the *Industrial Banner*, a weekly
newspaper edited by Simpson.

It was a completely new experience for me, and on January 1st, when
Jimmy Simpson was elected but, more than that, when Lindalla got 12,000
votes, I suddenly realized: this is Marxism in action! This is the struggle for
socialism! ... Here, for the first time in my life I realized that you don't have
to get people together and get them to sign a card before they can act and
they don't all have to be members of one organization.[27]

Buck's account of his sudden insight into the value of unity in
action was reprinted almost verbatim in Oscar Ryan's hagiographic tribute *Tim Buck: A Conscience for Canada,* and the editors of
his *Reminiscences,* which are based on the CBC interviews, do not
provide any footnotes which might suggest that his account is open
to question.

Nevertheless, it is inaccurate in almost every detail.

The Labor Representation Committee was formed in the fall of
1912. It did not run a candidate for Mayor, and Simpson, its
candidate for Board of Control, was defeated. The following year
Simpson ran for Controller again and was elected, but the LRC's
candidate for Mayor, one James Birks, ran a very poor fourth, with

only 1,511 votes. Carl Lindalla ran for alderman both times and was defeated both times.

Has Buck simply confused the two campaigns? The problem with that theory is that on his own account, Buck was working in the United States during the winter of 1914-1915, when Simpson was elected: he could not possibly have any memories of that campaign. And the story of Lindalla is clearly second-hand: Lindalla created a sensation in 1907 when he ran for Mayor and received 8,277 votes, but that was long before Buck came to Canada!*

The factual inaccuracies aside, there are political problems with Buck's account. He says that Arthur Taylor convinced him to support the Labor Representation Committee. Taylor was well-known on the Canadian left: he was a founder of the Socialist Party of North America and remained in the party through 1918. The SPNA's views on the Labor Representation Committee were also well-known; following the conference that established the LRC, the secretary of the SPNA published a statement in Simpson's *Industrial Banner*:

The policy of the SPNA was one of uncompromising hostility to all other parties there, for the good reason that they are not Socialist organizations....

[Our attitude] was, and is, one of unrelenting hostility to all such 'unity' which is not based on a class-conscious rank and file.

...as the working class have not as yet attained to class-consciousness, it is up to those who are Socialists to carry to them the message of Socialism, and not capitalist reform, as appears to be the object of this new Socialist-cum-labor federation.[28]

The SPNA would expel members for less than supporting the Labor Representation Committee. It is beyond belief that one of the party's leading spokesmen would have spent time convincing a young worker to join the LRC. And it is equally beyond belief that the same young worker, having been convinced by the LRC experience of the value of unity, would have been allowed to join (much less to found) the SPNA a year later.

According to Buck's account, his next major foray into labor political action occurred in April 1918, when he participated in the

---

*It is, by the way, stretching things to call Lindalla a "worker" as Buck does. *The Globe* on December 29, 1906 described the Socialist candidate as "a man of considerable wealth... Mr. Lindalla is a tailor, ...is a large landowner, owns the factory in which he works and employs a large number of hands."

founding of the "Ontario Labour Party." Buck includes himself in a list of the leaders of the new party, states that both socialists and non-socialists were involved, but assures us that "we were united in our desire for a united labour party."[29] He goes on to describe the 1919 Ontario elections (he gives the date as February—actually it was October) in which he supported the Labour Party campaign.

Again, this activity was totally contrary to the policies of the SPNA, which announced in its Declaration of Principles its determination "to wage war against all other political parties, whether alleged labor or avowedly capitalist." The SPNA attended the founding convention of the Canadian Labor Party, Ontario Section, in 1918, put forward a resolution calling for total socialization of the economy, and withdrew when it was defeated. If Buck's activities were as he describes them, then he was not a member of the SPNA at the end of the War either.

This conclusion is strengthened by two early biographical sketches of Buck published in *The Worker* in the 1930s, when the Tim Buck personality cult was first being created, but when there were still many workers around who would contradict any obviously false account. One of these, published just after Buck went to prison in 1932, states that "while working closely with certain members of the two socialist parties which existed in Toronto after the conclusion of the war, he did not join either." According to this account, it was not until "towards the end of the war years" that "Tim discovered Marx."[30] The other report says that Buck's first political activity in Canada took place through a Toronto branch of William Z. Foster's Syndicalist League of North America, which Buck joined in 1916. The Syndicalist League was an organization of militant, but not necessarily Marxist, trade unionists.* This report does not mention any other organized political activity prior to the establishment of the Communist Party.[31] Since Buck was out of prison when the latter article appeared, he could (and certainly would) have corrected any factual errors which understated his revolutionary credentials: no such correction was made.

Both of the early biographical sketches add an interesting fact about Buck's history that has not been mentioned since. "Early in 1919," Tim Buck left Canada to find work, settling in Rocky Mount, North Carolina. He is reported to have taken part in a railway

*The similarity of the initials SPNA and SLNA may account for some of Buck's memory problems.

strike there, and to have been run out of town for favoring racial equality. Buck heard about the Winnipeg General Strike while in North Carolina, and returned to Toronto "soon after this momentous event." If this account is reliable (and there is no reason to doubt it) then Buck was in the United States throughout the period when the first Communist Party of Canada was formed and suppressed. He could not have been informed of the founding meeting: his knowledge of the events was based on second- or third-hand reports, many years after the fact.

Finally, it should be noted that Buck's claim to have participated in the founding convention of the Communist Party of Canada in May 1921 is supported by no contemporary evidence at all. Buck's name did not begin to be associated with Canadian Communism until the establishment of the Workers Party in 1921. Maurice Spector, who certainly was present in May, wrote in 1933: "The recent canonization of Buck as the founder of the Canadian Party is little short of ludicrous.... Buck was not even a delegate to the constituent convention of the Communist Party. He did not and could not take any part in the organization of the party, under the circumstances. Nor was he on the central committee."[32] Similarly, in 1936 Jack MacDonald wrote: "Buck was not even at the Convention where the Party was founded, nor was he a member of the first Executive."[33]

Buck's attempts to back-date his revolutionary credentials are characteristic of the man. He had had an honorable career as a trade union militant during and after World War I. Like many such militants, he was attracted to Marxism as a result of the Russian Revolution, and disillusioned with reformism as a result of the Farmer-Labor experience of 1920. His experiences led him to join the Communist movement. His record as a solid and reliable unionist won him the respect of other Communists, and he quickly rose out of the rank and file into the leadership. That history should have been good enough for anyone: but it wasn't adequate to the requirements of the Buck personality cult, so he made himself a revolutionary leader retroactively. His historical writings, as a result, provide useful insights into the mind of the man who eventually took over the CPC, but they are completely unreliable as history.

5. From Leftism to Leninism: The Underground

The Russian Revolution had an electrifying effect on socialists in every country. Hundreds of thousands of workers, inspired by the world's first successful proletarian revolution, resolved to emulate the Bolsheviks.

Many of them, however, saw only the seizure of power. They could not see the years of preparatory work that created the Bolshevik party and won it the support of the majority of the Russian workers. They saw Lenin's intransigent opposition to the leaders of the Second International. They did not see his years of work to defeat sectarian policies which could have isolated the party from the Russian masses. They saw the Bolshevik call for power to the Soviets of workers, soldiers, and peasants. They did not see the years in which the Bolsheviks participated in even the pseudo-parliaments permitted under Czarist rule. They saw the Bolsheviks lead an insurrection. They did not see the careful planning that went into it, the preparation that even included preventing a premature uprising only months before they took power.

The limited knowledge of many communists, combined with their desire to make revolutions as quickly as possible, led to a rapid growth of ultraleft and sectarian political views within the Third International. Many newly made communists viewed all participation in bourgeois elections as treachery, all trade unions as agencies of the capitalist class to be smashed, all maneuvers and compromises as treason to the revolutionary cause. The Program of Canada's first Communist Party, distributed on the eve of May Day 1919, provides an illustration of this trend:

The tactics of the Bolsheviki are based upon the fact that we do not need the institutions of capitalism for our emancipation....

The Communist Party of Canada builds its facts upon this basis. We oppose the use of parliamentary action as a snare and delusion.... Instead of relying upon capitalist institutions, our business is to urge the workers to seize power and destroy the rule of the bourgeois.

The Communist Party does not worry about reorganizing the Trade Union movement; we do not propose to fritter away our forces in guerrilla warfare with the capitalist class about better conditions under capitalism.[1]

For the Communist groups in Canada and the United States in 1919-1920, the only program to be advanced, the only demand to be raised, was proletarian revolution. Anything less was betrayal. During the short-lived Toronto general strike of 1919 the Communist Party thought that a leaflet calling for the abolition of capitalism—nothing less—was the most appropriate propaganda. Similarly, the Communist Party of America intervened in a Longshoremen's strike in New York with a "Proclamation" that said nothing about the causes of the strike or the workers' demands: instead it proposed "establishment of a Workers Republic of the workers, by the workers, for the workers" as the only possible solution to their problems.[2]

It might be asked what possible reason the workers could have to pay any heed to people who refused to fight for "better conditions under capitalism," but the Communist movement on this continent had no time for such considerations. The CPA believed that anyone raising such objections was an opportunist:

This cry of "contact with the masses" holds in itself the seeds of future compromise, vacillation, and betrayal....

When the Communist Party is swamped with these politically immature masses, they will clog and hamper the revolutionary effectiveness of the Communist Party, holding it back when the time for action comes....

The Communist Party, if it is to learn anything from the bitter experiences of the past, cannot afford to get "contact with the masses" at the expense of sacrificing Communist principles and tactics. Essentially the Communist Party represents ideas and not numbers. We can afford to remain small in numbers for the present, if we shape our organization to hold Communist principles and policies unsullied and free from the base ingredients of compromise and opportunism and carry on our Communist propaganda to the workers with the full implication of all that it implies.[3]

Many more examples could be cited. The policies pursued by the Communist Party of America and the United Communist Party of

America—and by their Canadian branches—fell entirely within the ultraleft camp in the Third International. If those policies were not changed, the North American Communist movement stood every chance of ending up like the Socialist Party of Canada—an irrelevant sect, preaching to the working class from far beyond the sidelines of the class struggle.

Lenin's classic pamphlet *"Left-Wing" Communism: An Infantile Disorder*, published in 1920 on the eve of the Second Congress of the Communist International, attempted to correct the errors of the ultralefts with some comradely advice. The theme of the pamphlet was the need to go where the masses are, to meet the workers on their own ground, to express revolutionary ideas in language understood by the working class, to "patiently explain" rather than to preach from on high. "For the whole task of the Communists is to be able to *convince* the backward elements, to work *among* them, and not to *fence themselves off* from them by artificial and childishly 'Left' slogans."[4]

On this basis, Lenin urged the Communist Parties to participate not only in the existing trade unions, but in "cooperative societies, insurance societies, and similar organizations." He derided the idea that Communists should boycott elections and urged full participation in them, including attempts to reach electoral agreements with non-Communist working-class parties such as the British Labor Party. The Communists, he wrote, had to learn to combine rigidity in principles with flexibility in tactics.

Lenin viewed the growth of "leftism" in the International as a product of the movement's immaturity, as less serious than reformism because it was "a very young trend... only just coming into being." Its newness meant that it would be easily corrected: "It is only for this reason that, under certain conditions, the disease can be easily cured; and we must set to work to cure it with the utmost energy."[5]

Lenin's optimism proved misplaced. Although his pamphlet helped to correct some of the most blatant stupidities of the ultraleft, the leftist current in the International and in the Russian Communist Party grew and consolidated itself. Such prominent Russian leaders as Gregory Zinoviev and Nickolai Bukharin were sympathetic to the leftists, and a major section of the German Communist movement adopted policies that were little short of *putschism*, leading to a catastrophic attempt to seize power in 1921. There was every possibility that the ultraleft would gain a majority at the Third Comintern Congress in the summer of 1921.

Lenin did not view this possibility lightly. He told the assembled delegates, "If the Congress is not going to wage a vigorous offensive against such errors, against such 'Left' idiocies, the whole movement is doomed."[6]

Trotsky later made an equally sharp evaluation of the problems the Third Congress had faced:

It is now obvious that the change achieved at that time under the leadership of Lenin, in spite of the furious resistance of a considerable part of the congress—at the start, a majority—literally saved the International from the destruction and decomposition with which it was threatened if it went the way of automatic, uncritical 'leftism.' . . . [7]

Lenin and Trotsky worked together at the congress, demonstratively proclaiming themselves the "Right Wing." They raised the slogan "To the masses!" as the watchword of the congress and the task before the Comintern, and emphasized again and again the need for the Communist parties to adopt tactics which would win them a hearing from non-communist workers. The resolutions adopted at the congress, while in some respects a compromise with the left, were on all important questions representative of the Right Wing led by Lenin and Trotsky.*

Not everyone was convinced. The German Communist movement split, losing an important section of its leadership and rank and file to the Communist Workers Party, an ultraleft, semi-syndicalist organization. Similar splits took place in other Communist parties, including one which took more than two thousand members from the ranks of the U.S. Communist Party. The ability of the Canadian Communist Party to learn the lessons of *"Left-Wing" Communism* and the Third Congress would be a key indicator of its political maturity.

---

*Some historians describe the turn "To the Masses" as a *temporary* tactical shift forced on the Comintern by the defeat of the revolution in Europe in 1918-1920. This ignores the fact that *"Left-Wing" Communism* was written before the final ebb of the revolutionary wave. The tactics defended by Lenin and Trotsky at the Third Congress were weapons which had long been part of the Bolshevik arsenal. However, the renewed *emphasis* on these tactics reflected the Bolsheviks' recognition that the defeats of 1918-1920 were in large measure the result of the immaturity of the Communist parties, their failure to apply the lessons the Bolsheviks had learned in the past. Trotsky aptly described the Third Congress as "the school of revolutionary strategy."

"Undergroundism"

Perhaps the most blatant symptom of the leftism of the early Communist movement in North America was what might be termed "undergroundism." The Communist parties in the United States had scarcely been formed when they were hit by a wave of police raids and prosecutions; communism, for all practical purposes, was declared illegal in 1919. Similarly, the first Canadian Communist groups were formed in the shadow of the Orders-in-Council that had outlawed the left and led to the imprisonment of many radicals and the deportation of even more. For many of the young revolutionists who joined the new movement, this seemed to be the natural order of things. Revolutionists should be illegal: if they were not, then they were not revolutionists. As James Cannon, one of the founders of the U.S. Communist movement, later wrote, this conception proved to be a major obstacle to the development of American communism:

As time went on and the wave of reaction receded, possibilities for legal activities opened up. But tremendous factional struggles were necessary before the party took the slightest step in the direction of legalizing itself. The absolutely incredible idea that the party can't be revolutionary unless it is illegal was actually accepted by the majority in the Communist movement in 1921 and early 1922.[8]

This policy was fully accepted by the Canadian Communist groups in 1921. Both the CPA and UCPA branches operated as conspiratorial, "underground" parties, appearing in public only through front groups, and the establishment of a single Communist Party of Canada made no difference to that policy. The party's newspaper *The Communist* was an "illegal" newspaper: it listed no editorial board and named none of its contributors. Not only did it fail to include an address to which interested workers might apply for more information, it did not even name the city in which it was published. The first issue declared that "Those who shrink from illegal work for the accomplishment of the destruction of capitalism are unfit for a revolutionary party worthy of the name."[9] The problem, however, was not people "shrinking" from illegal work when it was necessary, but the determination of the Communists to make such work compulsory regardless of the circumstances. The CPC's founding convention actually put a clause in the party constitution declaring categorically that this party was to be "an underground, illegal organization."[10]

The Orders-in-Council banning revolutionary organizations had been repealed two years earlier, and although there was continuing police harassment, there was no general witch-hunt against the communist movement in progress: indeed, the Socialist Party was debating whether to join the Communist International in the pages of its public press. The authorities did not outlaw the CPC or its publications—the Communists did that for themselves.

The Communists' "undergroundism" was more a matter of form than content, and it deceived no one. The police certainly knew who they were, and so did the rest of the left. A review of *The Communist* in James Simpson's *Industrial Banner* reported that "in the writing and phrasing of the paper one can clearly see the hand of a university graduate."[11] To those familiar with the Toronto left, which included very few people who had had the opportunity to attend university, this was as good as an open declaration that Spector was editor.

The party's romantic infatuation with illegality also laid it open to telling criticisms by its political opponents in the labor movement. The *Western Clarion* seldom missed an opportunity to make digs at "the sewer-pipe revolutionists...our friends of the rat-hole persuasion (by choice)."*[12] Even SPCers who favored affiliation to the Third International made such criticisms, referring with scorn to "the Toronto secret outfit."[14]

These, however, were minor problems. Much more serious was the fact that being "underground" deprived the party of the possibility of winning broad influence in the labor movement—or even within that section of the left which had not yet adopted Bolshevism. As Spector later noted, it left the party in danger of being "wholly left behind in the organization of the left elements of the Canadian Labor movement which were beginning to stir."

The left wing of the S.P.C., growing tired of the interminable discussion on affiliation to the Third International...were leaving the S.P. of C. Various organizations, such as the Finnish Socialist Federation, were unattached but yet ripe for affiliation to an open Communist organization. The retro-gression of the O.B.U. in the West was leaving great numbers of workers aside of any political or economic organization.... And finally the labor

---

*Long after these phrases appeared, and while the CPC was in the process of abandoning the underground, Jack MacDonald insisted before a Van-couver meeting that "If a man is not prepared to become a sewer-pipe communist he is no communist at all."[13] Obviously the *Clarion*'s jibe had struck home.

bureaucracy were laying plans to canalize the mass movement...by the organization of a 'safe and sane' Labor Party.[15]

An anonymous party member expressed the same view very concisely: "The workers who are not yet Communists but are opposed to capitalism...are in danger of being swept into Laborism or scientific Socialism of the Western school."[16]

This issue of the "legal party" was present in the Communist Party of Canada from its foundation, if only because the question was being debated in the U.S. party. By mid-1921 there were three distinct factions in the American Communist movement; the majority of the Central Committee favored the creation of a legal, above-ground Communist Party parallel to the underground party, while a minority on the CC opposed any moves towards legal activity. The minority probably had the support of a majority of the rank and file. The third faction, which favored abolition of the illegal party and the creation of a single, legal Communist party, was not formally a part of the CPA; it was organized in the "Workers' Council," a group which split from the Socialist Party of America in April, 1921.[17]

The two factions in the CPA took their dispute to the Third Congress of the Comintern in June-July, 1921. The "Theses on Tactics" drafted by Karl Radek and submitted to the congress over the signatures of Radek, Lenin, Trotsky, Bukharin, Kamenev, and Zinoviev, left no doubt about where the Russian Bolsheviks stood on the issue. "In the United States," the theses insisted, "the communists are still only on the threshold of the first stage of forming a Communist nucleus and establishing contact with the working masses." While it had been possible to remain illegal during the period when the party was first assembling its forces, now it was the Party's "duty to attempt by all possible means to escape from illegal organizational forms and to reach the broad working masses."[18] Meeting privately with the U.S. delegation, Lenin was even more decisive:

Holding up an American edition of Bukharin's pamphlet *The Communist Program*, he asked whether it had been printed illegally. Told that it was put out by a regular printer and sold publicly, he exclaimed that there was no need for an illegal party if such a pamphlet could be printed and sold legally.[19]

Despite this strong statement, and despite the congress's Theses on Tactics, two thousand members of the CPA split rather than participate in a legal party. Those remaining could only agree on a compromise—the formation of a legal party under the strict control of the underground organization. The legal party would have a semi-communist program, while the underground party would campaign for the full program of Communism through an illegal newspaper. The Workers Party of America, as the legal party was named, was formed December 23-26, 1921, in New York City. Not until 1923 was the absurdity of two parallel parties eliminated, with the "merger" of the two into the Workers (Communist) Party of America, and not until 1925 did the legal party formally proclaim itself a section of the Communist International. Undergroundism died hard.

The Legal Party in Canada

The Canadian experience was very similar in form, but quite different in content.

The most obvious difference between Canada and the United States was the absence of factionalism in the "legal party" discussion in Canada. There were some doubts expressed, primarily by Ukrainian and Finnish communists who feared the possibility of deportation if they came out openly as Communists, but those doubts were soon stilled.* There was no split over the issue.

The first step was the launching of a public newspaper, the *Workers World*, in August 1921. The first (and only) issue of that newspaper to appear was almost totally given over to reports on the congresses of the Comintern and of the Red International of Labor Unions; the emphasis on legal, mass activity came through loud and clear. Lenin was quoted as saying "Whoever . . . fails to understand that we must conquer the majority of the working class is lost to the Communist movement. He will never learn anything." Radek, author of the "Theses on Tactics," was also quoted: "It is only in contact with the masses—in trade unions, for example— that we can win over that part of the proletariat which will accompany us in our advance. . . . We must win over the proletariat and to do that we must be in the front ranks of the fighters."

Workers World was published before the Canadians had heard a full account of the congress and of the U.S. discussion of the "legal party" in the United States. That, and the fact that most of the

---

*According to Rodney, Tim Buck was among those "who were loath to give up secrecy of underground activity. . . ."[20]

copies of the first issues were confiscated by the police, caused the party to hesitate after taking this first initiative. By the end of September, however, the party leadership had heard full reports on the congress from Joe Knight, who had been in Moscow representing the OBU at the RILU congress, and from American CP leader Max Bedacht. Bedacht, with James Cannon and Jay Lovestone, was one of the principal advocates in the United States of legal activity. He explained to a crowded Toronto membership meeting the plans of the Communist Party of America to launch a legal party while maintaining the underground apparatus intact and in control. The Canadian Communists decided to follow suit.

The Canadians moved much more quickly than the Americans. Early in October the first issue of a new, twice-monthly newspaper appeared. The *Workers Guard*, edited by Fred Peel,* marked a major advance over previous Communist publications in Canada. Its layout was lively and its contents vastly more popularly written than those of any of its predecessors. Gone was the numbing anonymity of the "underground" newspapers, including *Workers World*. The *Workers Guard* made a deliberate attempt to give the communist movement a human face. This report, from the first issue, is typical:

> An audience of unemployed gathered at Queens Park, Toronto, Saturday afternoon, and listened attentively with occasional moments of applause to the addresses of W. Moriarty, F. Cassidy, A. Preston, Max Armstrong, John MacDonald, James Simpson and Mrs. Knight. A number of secret service men were present, but they created no disturbance and conducted themselves in an orderly manner. Will it last?...
>
> Max Armstrong was in his usual form, imperturbable and convincing....
>
> John MacDonald poured a broadside into the vitals of the dear, pious *Globe*, from which she will never recover. John has a way all his own.

The article quoted from each speaker, and concluded with the text of a resolution passed by the meeting. This was not great prose, but it was a great advance over *The Communist*. Discussing the same topic, the underground press would have published a solemn proclamation in lengthy columns of solid print, signed by the

---

*Peel, like MacDonald, was a pattern maker and had played a prominent role in the 1919 strike. He had been active in the Socialist Party of Canada virtually since its foundation, and was one of the most widely-respected socialist trade unionists in Toronto.

Central Committee and calling for the proletarian revolution as the only solution to unemployment.

The third issue of the newspaper issued a call for the creation of a new party, "a party of the workers, born of themselves, a party and a platform not foisted upon them by side-stepping labor politicians." The new party would not "worship the ballot," but would "be of the working class rank and file, for the working class, with it in its daily struggle."[21]

Across the country the underground CPC units moved to set up preparatory organizations for the new party. In Montreal on November 5 a meeting of seventy or eighty people established the Workers League, "a real working class party which stands on the tenets of the 3rd International," and nominated Michael Buhay as its candidate in the federal elections in Cartier riding.[22] In Winnipeg, a "Workers Alliance" claiming two thousand members was formed: the Socialist Party's *Western Clarion* derided it as "an organization made up of various groups of social democrats, young labor leaguers, Jewish Nationalists, Communists, and others."[23] The Workers Alliance displayed no love for the SPC either: it ran Jacob Penner as a candidate in Winnipeg North, winning just enough votes to deprive SPC candidate and One Big Union leader Bob Russell of victory over the Liberal candidate.[24]

On December 11 delegates from Winnipeg, Toronto, Montreal, and several cities in Southern and Eastern Ontario met in the Toronto Labor Temple to launch the new party. They constituted themselves as a provisional conference, adopted a manifesto addressed to "Fellow Workers, to Members of the Socialist Party of Canada, to Members of Labour Parties, and to Trade Unionists," elected a Provisional Organization Committee, proclaimed the formation of the Workers Party of Canada, and called for a national convention in February. Thus, despite their later start, the Canadian Communists actually launched their "legal party" two weeks before their American counterparts.

Jack MacDonald, Acting Chairman of the new party, immediately undertook a cross-country tour to win support. He spent most of his time in the West, and most of his efforts on winning over members of the SPC: by the time he finished his tour, at a meeting attended by two thousand people in Vancouver, there was scarcely an SPC branch left intact in the country. He also concluded arrangements for the new party to take over the *B.C. Federationist,* the most widely-read labor paper in the West. This coup won the Workers Party a major propaganda voice it could never have otherwise established in the West. (It also created some problems that will be discussed in the next chapter.)*

The Workers Party of Canada was formally founded in Toronto, February 17-20, 1922, at a convention attended by 63 delegates—43 from Ontario, 16 from the West, 5 from Quebec—and by fraternal delegates from a variety of organizations ranging from the Guelph Labor Council to the Rocky Mountain Labor Party to the One Big Union. The obvious geographical imbalance was redressed by granting extra votes to the western representatives.

Numerically, the greatest gain made by the formation of the Workers Party was the adherence of the Finnish Socialist Federation with some 2,200 members—almost half of the 4,800 members claimed by the WPC. Politically, the greatest gain was the recruitment of the major figures in the SPC Left Wing. In addition to Jack Kavanaugh, J.G. Smith, and A.S. Wells of Vancouver, the convention recorded the adherence of Malcolm Bruce in Regina, Henry Bartholomew in Winnipeg, and many more. Maurice Spector summed up the achievement in his closing address to the convention: "For the first time in the Canadian labor movement, the class-conscious, militant workers of both East and West have resolved to build a united party for political action on a national scale."[26]

There remained the problem of the illegal party.

Burying the Underground

Like the U.S. Communists, the CPC had created a "legal party." Like them, they had kept the "illegal party" intact. There, however, the similarity stopped.

The Workers Party of America, as we have noted, was formed on a semi-communist basis, leaving the full program of Communism to the underground party. The Workers Party of Canada, by contrast, made "the overthrow of capitalism and capitalist dictatorship by the conquest of political power, the establishment of working class dictatorship and of the workers republic," one of the four principal points in its Platform.† Further, the WPC declared firmly that

---

*The January 21, 1922 minutes of the Provisional Organization Committee of the WPC record an "initial payment" of $500 "to the trustees of the *B.C. Federationist.*"[25] A.S. Wells, editor of the paper, had left the SPC with Jack Kavanaugh.

†There was no mention of the dictatorship of the proletariat in the WPA program.[27]

"recognizing that the Communist International is the only real centre of world revolutionary activities, the Workers Party will strive to rally the workers under the banner of the Third International."[28] There could be no doubt about the Communist nature of the WPC's program: in fact it might well be said that this was the first genuine Communist program adopted by a Canadian organization. Previous programs and platforms had been abstract declarations of principle, more or less influenced by leftist and sectarian conceptions. The WPC program was the first to translate Communist principles into language Canadian workers could understand, and to direct itself towards mass activity rather than minority discussion.

The Communist character of the WPC's program was one immediate difference between the Canadian and American situations. Another, just as important, was that *the underground party ceased all public activity in the fall of 1921.* In the United States the underground party continued to publish its newspaper *The Communist* through 1922, as the voice of the "real" Communist movement. In Canada there was no such parallel publication: any and all Communist educational material was published in the pages of the WPC's newspaper *The Worker* and all public Communist activity was conducted through the Workers Party. This meant that the Workers Party functioned, from the beginning, as a Communist Party.

Then what was the underground?

When Tim Buck was tried for sedition in 1931, there were sensational headlines about the underground party that "controlled" the WPC. In particular, much was made of the code used in underground correspondence—a quite elementary code in which the WPC was referred to as "A" while the underground party was "Z." The prosecution portrayed "Z" as the manipulative power behind everything, "A" as a mere puppet. Later historians have accepted this view:

Until 1924 [writes Ivan Avakumovic] the Communists carried out the bulk of their public activities through the WPC, which operated side by side with a shadowy body known to initiates as the "Z" party. This underground organization consisted of a small number of trusted Communists. They met in caucus before the WPC conventions to decide on the policies to be followed by the WPC and on the leaders that the delegates were to elect.[29]

Tim Buck, on the other hand, scarcely mentions the underground party in his books. In his testimony at the 1931 trial, he described it as nothing more than an informal caucus of the older members of the Workers Party.

The underground party was more than an informal caucus—but it was much less than the manipulative "real party" of anti-Communist legend. Unlike the U.S. party leadership, which was still unsure about legalization, and which had to contend with a large number of communists, both in and out of the party, who opposed legal activity altogether, the Canadian Communists from the very beginning saw the existence of two parallel parties as a temporary, transitional measure. At a convention of the underground CPC, held on the eve of the founding convention of the Workers Party, they resolved "to transform 'A' as rapidly as possible into an open 'Z' party and to transform 'Z' into an emergency apparatus of the open 'Z'."[30] This policy seemed to them to be in line with the Comintern's insistence that communists "are obliged everywhere to create a parallel illegal organization which at the decisive moment will help the party to do its duty to the revolution."[31] That is, the "emergency apparatus" would function as a *subordinate body* to be used in times of repression or insurrection. There was, as Spector and MacDonald reported to the Comintern early in 1923, no significant objection to this policy in the party:

Over this there has been no factional dispute, nor has there been any question of "mechanical control" such as agitated the American movement. In accordance with our policy we ceased publication of the underground organ [*The Communist*], and we published all documents of the Comintern in the organ of the "A" Party [*The Worker*].[32]

The East European socialists who joined the Workers Party had no difficulty in understanding and accepting the need for a parallel, illegal apparatus—it was completely in line with their experiences in their homelands, where democratic rights were virtually unknown. The SPC militants, however, were less understanding, as Spector reported (evidently to the Comintern) in 1922:

...the Western, former S.P. of C., elements, came with an original program calling for an open Communist Party with frank acceptance of the twenty-one points [the Conditions for Admission to the Comintern]. They suspected that the Eastern delegates were working for a moderate, milk-and-watery program, and since these S.P. of C. Left-wingers had split from their party on just this very issue of the twenty-one points, they felt that they would be

placed in an impossible position if they went back West with any program
short of their original conception.

This might have blown the whole WPC apart at the beginning, had
not the leaders of the underground party been prepared to be very
open with their new comrades:

A frank explanation, however, that a Canadian Section of the Comintern
already existed and that an open Communist Party would not at the present
moment be opportune, along with the explanation of the Communist
delegates that an open Communist Party was their objective also, after the
experience, activity and mass contact of the Workers' Party for a year or so,
enabled both sides to reach an accord. It was agreed, however, that the time
was ripe for the Workers' Party to recognize more or less openly the spiritual
leadership of the Communist International and the principle of proletarian
dictatorship.[33]

   As this quotation illustrates, the "underground" was not
particularly secretive, at least within the Workers Party. In fact, the
existence of the "Z" party seems to have been something of an open
secret in the Canadian Left. The *Western Clarion*, for example,
charged that the Workers Party was "a 'popular' party to attract the
masses, with a few bosses as a secret governing council to direct its
policy."[34] Bob Russell of the One Big Union stated that the question
of affiliation to the Third International (as opposed to support) was
not discussed at the WPC convention "because it was discussed in
caucus privately and decided that it was too dangerous."[35] The
justness of these comments aside, it is clear that the "underground"
wasn't much of a success as a secret organization.
   Meanwhile, relations between the legal and illegal organizations
were the subject of bitter debate in the U.S. party. A section of the
party leadership had come to the conclusion that the underground
party should be abolished altogether; they were stigmatized as
"liquidators" by their opponents. At the Fourth Congress of the
Communist International, James Cannon, who was chairman of
the Workers Party of America and a prominent "liquidator," met to
discuss the question with Trotsky.

Trotsky asked only a few questions about the actual political situation in
the country, with respect to the laws, etc. He expressed astonishment, and
even some amusement, over the theory that underground organization is a
question of principle....
   At the end of the discussion...Trotsky stated unambiguously that he

would support us, and that he was sure Lenin and the other Russian leaders would do the same....

That interview with Trotsky was the great turning point in the long struggle for the legalization of the American communist movement, which should never have accepted an illegal status in the first place.[36]

The "American Commission" of the congress met shortly after that discussion. The Russian party was represented by Zinoviev, Radek, and Bukharin. They had obviously discussed the question ahead of time, and were fully prepared.

They all spoke emphatically and unconditionally in support of the position of the liquidators.

...They especially demonstrated that the central thesis of the underground leftists, namely, that the party had to maintain its underground organization as a matter of principle, was false. It was, they explained, purely a practical question of facts and possibilites in a given political atmosphere.[37]

Three Canadians sat in the galleries during the American Commission discussions: Maurice Spector, Jack MacDonald, and Florence Custance. (MacDonald and Spector were delegates to the congress; Custance had come to Russia earlier that fall as a representative of Canadian Friends of Soviet Russia.) They listened with mounting excitement. What the Russians were saying confirmed the decisions they had already made. Spector, with obvious satisfaction, reported back to Canada that the commission's decisions vindicated the policies they had been pursuing, that the instructions of the Comintern to the American party for liquidation of the underground were "in accord with the unanimous policy of our party.... Our position received full endorsation in Moscow."[38]

Spector was overstating the unanimity of the Canadian movement: there was still opposition to elimination of the underground party, primarily in the leadership of the Finnish and Ukrainian organizations. The Comintern's decisive position overcame those objections, however, and the underground party concluded, in February 1923, that "the year's experience has proved, without possibility of contradiction, that open 'Z' activity is the only practicable method of carrying our message to the masses with any measure of success."[39] The underground was to be liquidated within six months: in practice it does not seemed to have functioned in any more than a purely formal sense from February on. It was formally dissolved in April 1924; a few days later the Workers Party changed its name to Communist Party of Canada. The last vestiges of "undergroundism" had been eliminated.

6. From Leftism to Leninism: To the Masses!

"Revolution," wrote Lenin in 1920, "is impossible without a change in the views of the majority of the working class, and this change is brought about by the political experience of the masses, and never by propaganda alone."[1]

Here was the fundamental difference between the Communist Party of Canada and all of its predecessors. All Marxists agreed that revolution would require majority support, but for the earlier Canadian Marxist organizations, only propaganda and patience were necessary to win that majority. The Communists sought to be a "party of a new type." As the *Workers Guard* expressed it, they sought to create

a party of action, seeking contact with the workers, a party in which the theorists and doctrinaires as such will find small place, a party of the workers, and with them in their daily struggles against capitalist oppression, seeking always to build up a united front of the working class for Industrial Freedom and Emancipation from wage slavery.[2]

For Leninists, it is necessary to plunge into the daily life of the working class, to participate in its struggles and attempt to give them direction, to hasten and direct the process whereby the working people, *through their own experiences*, come to the conclusion that the capitalist system must be abolished and that revolution is the only road forward. In Maurice Spector's words,

Revolutionary political activity to us means disciplined work in the labor unions, agitation in election campaigns, agitation from the floor of

Parliament, mass demonstrations, organization of the unemployed, and participation in the everyday struggles of the working class. For we realize that only through their mass experiences with the Capitalist dictatorship in the everyday struggle will the working class be rallied to its vanguard, to the struggle for the proletarian dictatorship. The struggle for power will inevitably grow out of the struggle for bread.[3]

But the Communists had a considerable heritage of sectarianism to overcome. By the beginning of 1922 they had all but destroyed the underground fetish. Could they extend that success to other fields, translating into Canadian terms the Comintern's injunction, "To the Masses!"?

Indeed, the move away from political sectarianism was already well under way when the Workers Party of Canada was formed. The political correction can be illustrated by an examination of party policy towards two important institutions of Canadian working-class life: the labor parties and the trade unions.

The Canadian Labor Party

The Canadian Labor Party (CLP) was truly a unique organization: it seems to have had no parallel elsewhere in the world. It was formed in 1917 on the initiative of the Trades and Labor Congress in an attempt to divert anti-conscription sentiment into electoral activity. After launching it the TLC leaders stood aside, maintaining the impartiality in political questions that typified the approach to labor leadership taken by their counterparts in the American Federation of Labor. Some labor leaders and Social Democrats (James Simpson was the most prominent) hoped to see the CLP develop into a mass union-based political party on the model of the British Labor Party, but they were disappointed. Instead, the CLP was a loose federation of provincial parties, and the provincial organizations themselves were loose federations of heterogeneous political forces. Local labor parties, local unions, cooperatives, socialist societies, occasionally a city Labor Council—these were the basis of the Canadian Labor Party. It was less a labor party in the modern sense than "a sort of political clearing house for labor," as one contemporary observer described it.[4]

Nevertheless, by 1922 there were sections of the CLP in every province except Prince Edward Island, and the party had established a solid record of running independent labor candidates in federal, provincial, and municipal elections. The CLP and the

Workers Party were the only working-class political organizations which were organized on a Canada-wide basis.*

From 1917 on, the CLP was a subject for sharp dispute in the Canadian left. The reformists supported it; the revolutionists opposed it; it was as simple as that. The Social Democratic Party split on the question, as did the Socialist Party in Vancouver. For an important section of the WPC's leadership, disillusionment with labor party politics was a decisive factor in their evolution towards Bolshevism. Several months after Jack MacDonald broke with the Independent Labor Party in 1921, he attended a convention of the Ontario Section of the Canadian Labor Party in his capacity as outgoing president. He introduced just one resolution: that the party should dissolve itself.[5]

The attitude of the first Communist groups towards labor parties was unremittingly hostile. The United Communist Party of America, for example, declared that it would "maintain the uncompromising class struggle under all circumstances and refuse to co-operate with groups or parties not committed to the revolutionary class struggle, such as the Labor Party...."[6] If Communists wanted to win a hearing from the thousands of workers who voted for labor parties, and if they wanted to promote united actions with those workers, this policy was suicidal.

As late as December 1921, in the manifesto of the Provisional Conference of the Workers Party, this attitude of sectarian hostility to the labor parties was evident:

Labour parties have become mere tails of the capitalist parties, and, as such, have no reason for existence.

Workers of labour parties! leave those leaders who are eagerly trying to squeeze into capitalist politics and come over to the W.P. of C., which is determined to stand up and fight the battle of the workers, shunning the efforts of other parties to patronize us by adopting a few of our leaders.[7]

There was, however, some rethinking of this policy taking place in the Communist Party. An attempt was being made to apply to the Labor Party the policy of critical support which Lenin had urged the Communist Party of Great Britain to adopt towards the

---

*The CLP did not include the most successful labor politicians. The Ontario Independent Labor Party, which formed a coalition with the United Farmers, remained outside its ranks, as did J.S. Woodsworth's ILP in Manitoba.

British Labor Party. During the discussion of the creation of the
Workers Party, one branch of the underground Communist Party
urged sensitivity towards the workers who planned to vote Labor. It
listed as one "condition for the successful formation of a new party"

the avoidance of any opening being given to the Trade Union bureaucracy
organized in Labor parties to accuse the new organization of splitting the
forces of labor during the present election period. (While we may recognize
that there is no clear issue between Capital and Labor in this election
nevertheless there appears to be such an issue to many of the workers who
see increasing misery under Capitalism and vainly hope to combat it by this
method.)[8]

The founding convention of the WPC in February 1922, unlike
the provisional conference three months earlier, did not issue any
denunciations of the labor parties, and a changed attitude was
evident almost immediately. One week after the convention, Jack
MacDonald attended the convention of the Ontario Section of the
Canadian Labor Party, explained the aims and program of the new
party to the assembled delegates, and announced that the Workers
Party would discuss affiliation to the CLP.*[9] In July, MacDonald
addressed the convention of the Independent Labor Party of Nova
Scotia, a CLP affiliate, along similar lines. He was very well
received: the convention advised its branches to reform themselves
as WPC branches![10]

While MacDonald was in Nova Scotia, the Central Executive
Council of the WPC was holding a plenary meeting in Winnipeg.
The liveliest debate there concerned the party's policy towards the
CLP. The plenum, over the objections of two delegates who argued
that the decision "would be interpreted as opportunism and might
lead to reformism," decided that the Workers Party "would permit
its districts to affiliate [to the CLP] provided they maintained
independence of organization and freedom of criticism."[11]

Events moved more quickly than the plenum decision
anticipated. In August Maurice Spector and Tim Buck attended a
national convention of the CLP in Winnipeg, and raised the

---

*Since MacDonald was a former president of the CLP in Ontario, and had
attended the previous convention only to urge dissolution of the party, there
was more than a hint of irony in the *Industrial Banner's* report that
"Brother MacDonald... said he was present to learn all he could from the
convention with a view to advising the Workers Party when the question of
affiliation was considered."

question of Workers Party affiliation. The convention made no objection, but pointed out that affiliation would have to take place through the provincial sections.

On September 25, over the signature of executive secretary William Moriarty, the CEC issued a circular letter explaining to the party membership its decision to move ahead quickly on the question of affiliation.

The outstanding fact which must be considered is that by securing affiliation we should become a definite part of the organized labor movement....

It might be objected that we should [not] help to build up an organization which can definitely be stated to be as yet reactionary in its actions and outlook, but this will not free us from the responsibilities of our Party principles. Our principles declare that our reason for existence is to reach as wide a circle as possible in order to imbue them with the ideology of Communism rather than that of Capitalism and Reformism.

It was true, the statement said, that the trade unions were the "only real expression of organization" of the workers, but work in the unions alone was not sufficient.

Here we have a political movement shaping itself, and we are out to consolidate the organizations of the workers. We cannot remain outside as an independent body while the C.L.P. is shaping itself. We cannot formulate its policies from the outside. We must get inside if we are to carry weight....

The application of our party for affiliation to the C.L.P. is a concrete step in the building up of a United Front of Labor in Canada.

The statement was particularly emphatic in insisting that the WPC was seeking to affiliate to the CLP in order to participate in "the shaping of its policies so that they will be in line with the needs of the working class," not for the purely sectarian purpose of "attacking...the reactionary leaders," or for the opportunist goal of "securing...the offices of the C.L.P."[12]

While the party was developing its approach to the CLP, it was also exploring other means of "building up of a United Front of Labor in Canada." In May 1922 the Winnipeg branch initiated an attempt to establish a common working-class front in the Manitoba elections. Noting that "there are ten seats to be contested and, at the present time, there are thirteen workers' candidates," the Workers Party wrote to the Dominion Labor Party, the Independent Labor Party, and the Socialist Party, to propose "a minimum basis for a united front of labor in the coming election."

With the object of ensuring "a straight class fight—working class against capitalist class," they proposed that the parties meet to agree on a common minimum program and on a division of constituencies.

It must be understood that the above proposal does not mean that the respective parties will not possess the right to fly their own party colors and to criticize the other organizations. But it does mean that competition on the part of the workers will be done away with.[13]

While the Winnipeg initiative did not succeed in establishing a united-front electoral agreement in Manitoba, it was clearly an effective approach to the problem posed by the existence of a multitude of labor political organizations during election campaigns. On September 25, the same day that the statement on the CLP was issued, the Central Executive of the WPC issued "General Instructions" for the implementation of "the tactic of the United Front" in municipal elections. It proposed that "other working class organizations" be approached by the WPC districts "with a view to securing common action of the working class elements against the representatives of capital." The circular outlined a proposed program for such common action—concentrating primarily on the demands for better conditions for the unemployed, since relief, in those pre-unemployment-insurance days, was a major municipal concern—but emphasized that "local conditions will undoubtedly determine much of the general platform." It urged the need for "care and diplomacy" in negotiating a united front, warning against presenting ultimatums to potential participants. The object would be to secure a mutually agreeable division of seats or constituencies; the only inviolable conditions would be that only working class organizations participate, and that "the identity of parties concerned will not be sunk, but must be preserved at all costs."[14]

The new policy produced results surprisingly quickly. In December 1922 the Vancouver WPC was able to draw together a Labor Representation Committee, including most of the labor and radical political groups in the city, to contest the municipal elections: one of the committee's candidates topped the poll for city alderman.[15] In May 1923 the Toronto WPC participated in the creation of a Labour Representation Political Association that included the ILP, the Toronto TLC, the Women's Labor League, and others. Workers Party CEC members Jack MacDonald and

Malcolm Bruce were endorsed by the association as candidates in the June 1923 provincial elections.[16] By early 1923 the Quebec, Ontario, and Alberta sections of the Canadian Labor Party had accepted the Workers Party as an affiliate. The united front was moving forward.

Communists and the One Big Union

The Workers Party's success in establishing forms of united front activity for election campaigns reflected, in part, the skill of the party leadership in exercizing "care and diplomacy" in working with other groups. It also reflected the party's growing influence in the labor movement as a whole. That influence, in turn, reflected the ability of Canadian Communists to break with the sectarian policy towards the trade union movement which had characterized most of the Canadian left in 1919-1920.

Probably no one document was as influential in shaping the trade union policy of the Canadian Communist movement as Lenin's pamphlet *"Left-Wing" Communism: An Infantile Disorder*. English translations first reached Canada in smuggled newspapers from Britain and the United States. In February 1921 the *B.C. Federationist* began serializing it: the paper subsequently issued it as a pamphlet, an action that resulted in the arrest of *Federationist* editor A.S. Wells for sedition. (The charges were eventually dropped.) Not since Trotsky's *The Bolsheviki and World Peace* had a Russian work been read so widely and so avidly by Canadian Marxists.

The pamplet's general strictures against ultraleftism were read and to a greater or lesser degree heeded, but its greatest impact was in the area of trade union policy—especially with respect to the attitude of the revolutionary left towards the One Big Union. The OBU, it will be recalled, had been founded following the secession in 1919 of the western labor movement from the Trades and Labor Congress of Canada and from the international unions. Fed up with the conservatism of the eastern labor leaders, the westerners, under the leadership of members of the Socialist Party, set out to create a union free of bureaucracy, committed to the class struggle.

Lenin's pamphlet displayed no sympathy for such tactics. He described the attempt of some German Communists to set up "a brand-new, immaculate little 'Workers' Union,' which is guiltless of bourgeois-democratic prejudices and innocent of craft or narrow craft-union sins," as "ridiculous and childish nonsense"—"Greater foolishness and greater damage to the revolution than that caused by the 'Left' revolutionaries cannot be imagined!'"[17]

The labor bureaucracy of course opposed the creation of "dual unions" because it created competition for them, reduced dues payments, and so on. Lenin opposed the creation of special revolutionary unions on entirely different grounds: in his view such tactics inevitably isolated the Communists from the mass of the working class. To decide that "*because* of the reactionary and counter-revolutionary character of the trade union *top leadership*...we must leave the trade unions" would be, in Lenin's view, "the greatest service the Communists could render the bourgeoisie."

If you want to help the "masses" and to win the sympathy and support of the "masses," you must not fear difficulties, you must not fear the pinpricks, chicanery, insults and persecution on the part of the "leaders" (who, being opportunists and social chauvinists, are in most cases directly or indirectly connected with the bourgeoisie and the police) but absolutely must *work wherever the masses are to be found.*[18]

The OBU experience confirmed the truth of Lenin's statement that the "ideal unions" the ultralefts proposed to establish would inevitably encompass only a minority of the working class. Although it initially received the referendum votes of a clear majority of the organized workers west of Ontario, the One Big Union never succeeded in organizing more than a minority of them. The enthusiasm of 1919 did not survive the defeats of that year, or the depression which began in 1920. Internal squabbling lost the OBU its largest single affiliate, the Lumberworkers, and a united front of mine-owners, the government, and the United Mine Workers destroyed its base among the miners of Alberta and British Columbia. By 1921 the OBU's only stronghold was Winnipeg—and that was dwindling. The Socialist leaders of the OBU were left holding an empty shell.

That the OBU was a dead end is easy to see today. It was not so easy to see in 1921. The OBU still claimed tens of thousands of members, and it still had a continent-wide reputation as a model revolutionary union. Such future Communist leaders as Jack Kavanaugh, Max Armstrong, Joseph Knight, Sarah Knight, and Beckie Buhay had invested a great deal of time and energy in the organization; others, including Jack MacDonald, had been sympathetic to the cause, although they felt it was premature in Eastern Canada. To break with the OBU required an emotional break with one of the high points of the labor rebellion of 1919.

Some Marxists proved incapable of making the break. The most prominent, and the most tragic, was R.B. Russell. Despite his years of experience in the labor movement and in the Socialist Party, Russell refused to see that the OBU was doomed. Convinced that it was the ideal form of working class organization, Russell stayed on as leader of the One Big Union not just through the 1920s, but until 1956, when its few remaining members finally joined the Canadian Labor Congress.

Russell and the other socialists who stayed with the OBU did so fully conscious of the implications of their actions. They read *"Left-Wing" Communism* carefully, digested its arguments, and decided that they did not agree. They decided, according to an editorial in the *OBU Bulletin*, that there was "too much proneness on the part of the active workers in this country to take the happenings in Russia and the statements of Lenin in regard to tactics as an unquestionable line of action."[19] The Communists who urged a return to the TLC were described, "with all due respect to Lenin," as suffering from "a serious overdose of 'Left Wing Communism'."[20] The OBU's campaign against Lenin's views included serializing, in the pages of the *OBU Bulletin*, "An Open Letter to Comrade Lenin" by Herman Gorter, a leader of the Communist Workers Party of Germany and one of the principal theoreticians of the ultraleft in the Comintern. Gorter's long letter—it ran for four months in the OBU's weekly in 1921—was devoted to a defense of two propositions:

Since the trade unions are inadequate weapons they must be replaced or transformed into factory organizations associated on a federal basis....

Since the proletariat must make the revolution here [i.e. outside of Russia] alone and without help, it must attain a high level of intellectual and moral development. It is therefore better not to use parliamentary methods in the revolution.

The OBU rejected in theory and practice both of these propositions: its willingness to publicize Gorter's views showed that Lenin's pamphlet was making an impact on OBU supporters.

One of the first Canadian Marxists to make a public criticism of the OBU's approach to the problems of labor was William Moriarty, who was also one of the first SPC members to join the Communist movement. In the April 1, 1921 issue of the *Western Clarion*, in an article supporting the Third International, Moriarty wrote:

Lenin's remarks concerning participation in reactionary Trade Unions should be an eye-opener to the comrades in the Party who helped to invent and form the pure, class organizations which are to put the workers on their feet. The desertion of the A.F. of L. [American Federation of Labor] by many of the oldest and ablest members of the Party, at a time when their work in the A.F. of L. was most needed, was a mistake in tactics which the movement cannot afford to repeat.

Moriarty had undoubtedly discussed this article with his comrades in the underground Communist groups. When the groups unified in May 1921, they adopted a statement which took basically the same stand. While agreeing that "the sabotage by the A.F. of L. bureaucracy" was the main cause of the split in Canadian labor,

all were agreed that unfortunately the net result of this separation of a body of advanced workers from the main body had been to leave the greater part of the organized working masses more nakedly at the mercy of the A.F. of L. officialdom than ever.[21]

The Communists, then, were agreed on the need to work inside the existing unions. It remained to fight the issue out with the supporters of the One Big Union.

The major confrontation took place at the founding convention of the Workers Party, in February 1922. Among the delegates to that convention were two representatives of the OBU, including Bob Russell.

On the second day of the convention a Trade Union resolution was introduced declaring that "the policy pursued by some groups in the past of seeking to revolutionize the labor movement by splitting away to form new ideal unions [must] be completely abandoned," and calling for consolidation of the labor movement on the basis of one union for one industry. Though the OBU was not mentioned, it was clear what was meant.

Russell immediately objected. He demanded that the convention choose between the OBU form of organization and the AFL, and warned that refusal to endorse the OBU would mean inevitable failure for the Workers Party.

After an extended debate in which various ex-OBU supporters, including Kavanaugh, the Knights, and Mike Buhay, explained why it was necessary for the Left to return to the mainstream of Canadian labor, the Trade Union resolution was adopted with only two opposing votes.[22]

The sequel was a discussion in the OBU in Winnipeg. In three long membership meetings in April and May, OBU supporters debated the Workers Party before finally declaring that the Communist policy would "force the workers who have built up a modern and efficient machine to protect and advance their class interests back into the obsolete craft organizations."

"Such action," the OBU declared, "would be retrogressive and decidedly against the best interests of the working class."[23]

For several months the Workers Party continued its efforts to convince the OBU leaders that they were isolating themselves and weakening the labor movement. The final major Communist statement on the subject appeared in the August 1, 1922 *Worker*, over Jack MacDonald's signature. After reviewing the major issues in the debate, MacDonald concluded:

The formation of the O.B.U. has not tended to strengthen the ranks of labor in Canada. Nothing is to be gained by wishing that events had happened differently. A revolutionary wave swept the whole world in 1919. If in their enthusiasm the western section underestimated the task that confronts the militants in the American Labor Movement, let us hope that that fervor for working class emancipation that is expressed so tersely in the resolutions of the Calgary convention, shall make them capable of admitting their errors, and again getting their shoulders to the wheel so that with renewed vigor the militants of the working class movement shall work for the consolidation, not of any pet organization, but of the working class as a whole.

Such arguments were to no avail. Just as the SPC leadership preferred the academy to the class struggle, the OBU leadership preferred the perfection of their "pet organization" to the real labor movement. The world moved on without them.

Trade Union Policy

The founding convention of the Workers Party pledged to foster "all tendencies to consolidate the trade union movement by amalgamating the various crafts on the basis of one union for each industry," to "oppose all dual unions or secessionist efforts," and to "work in co-operation with all militant elements in the unions for the formation and development of a left wing." The Trade Union Resolution concluded:

...the membership of the Workers' Party will assist in the consolidation of the labour unions on militant lines by permeating these organizations with a revolutionary spirit, exposing the reactionary and treacherous policies of the labour unions' bureaucracy, stimulating the sense of aggressive rank and file control, and resisting to the utmost the expulsion of militants and the splitting up of the unions in general.[24]

Most of the Workers Party's trade union work was conducted through the Trade Union Educational League. The TUEL had been founded in 1920 in the United States by William Z. Foster, who for many years had been a radical labor activist, and who was one of the central leaders of the strike which tied up the U.S. steel industry for three and a half months in 1919. When the Red International of Labor Unions (RILU) was founded in Moscow in July 1921, Foster was present: the TUEL became the American section of the RILU. Shortly afterwards Foster joined the U.S. Communist Party. Early in 1922 the Trade Union Educational League launched a newspaper *Labor Herald* and in August of that year it held its first full-scale convention. According to the Constitution adopted there, the purpose of the TUEL was:

to carry on an intensified campaign of educational work within the trade unions to the end that the natural development of these bodies to ever more clear-sighted, cohesive, militant and powerful organizations may be facilitated, and thus the labor movement hastened on to the accomplishment of its great task of working class emancipation.[25]

The Canadian Communists chose Tim Buck, who had been associated with Foster's Syndicalist League during the War, to head the Canadian Section of the Trade Union Educational League. Participation in a single North American organization was a reflection of the party's general view that in the trade unions "The fate of the Canadian left wing is entirely bound up with that of the United States."[26] Every major union in Canada (with the exception of some railway unions) was an extension of a U.S.-based union.

The North America-wide organization of the TUEL continued a tradition which extended back through the IWW and Bill Haywood's Western Federation of Miners, to the Knights of Labor in the 1880s. As a B.C. miner told a Royal Commission in 1901: "There is no 49th parallel of latitude in Unionism. The Canadian and American workingmen have joined hands across the Boundary line for a common cause against a common enemy."[27]

The TUEL coordinated the party's effort to get as much of its membership into the trade unions as possible. The object was not to place individuals wherever openings occurred, but rather to concentrate on creating groups of Communists in the most important unions, particularly in heavy industry. One year after its formation, the Workers Party claimed to have established "organized groups of party members in sixteen central labour councils, over sixty local railroad bodies, throughout both districts of the coal miners, in two big metal mining camps, and a great many of the largest lumbering centres." A party resolution described these groups as "a continuous thread of militant activity stretching from coast to coast."[28]

The first year of experience in conducting Communist agitation in the trade union movement taught the party important lessons. At its February 1923 convention the Workers Party identified two recurrent problems in its work: one was "The tendency to drop into the old position of negative opposition to officialdom and everybody else who is not a revolutionist or a good left-winger"; the other, opposite, error, was "lining up with centrists, twisters, fakirs and all who pay lip service to revolutionary ideals and progressive trade unionism." For both problems the solution was the same: developing a principled program as a basis for militant action in the union.

It is essential that we...take the initiative on a positive programme of concrete demands, fight for something the rank and file want, such as amalgamation (in the case of miners, loggers, etc., international affiliation). These to-day are real needs and slogans expressing the desires of the rank and file. Organize a group around these slogans and far from dogmatically opposing officialdom, officialdom will quickly declare itself and give you a clear-cut issue.[29]

That approach—developing a program corresponding to the needs of the ranks of the unions as a basis of unity in struggle—was at the center of Communist trade union policy in the first years of the party's existence.

Theory and Practice

Thus far we have been discussing what the Communists *said* they wanted to do in the unions. It is not the purpose of this book to present a full history (or even an outline history) of Communist work in the trade unions in the 1920s, but it is important to see how the party transformed its resolutions into practical activity. Two examples, one from the West Coast and one from the East, must suffice.

The first example, from British Columbia, would have little significance if it were not for the fact that it provoked the Workers Party's first split. Defense of labor unity cost the party a major propaganda voice in the West, and led to the resignation of prominent members of its Central Executive Committee.

As noted earlier, the party late in 1921 gained control of the *B.C. Federationist,* one of the most widely read labor newspapers in Canada. The *Federationist* was founded in 1912 as the joint organ of the B.C. Federation of Labor and the Vancouver Trades and Labor Council: each body owned slightly fewer than 50 percent of the shares, while five trustees owned one share each. During 1919 and 1920 the ownership picture became very confused: the B.C. Federation of Labor dissolved itself, urging its membership to join the One Big Union, and the Vancouver TLC split into pro- and anti-OBU groups, each claiming the name Trades and Labor Council. The Trades and Labor Council (OBU) managed to maintain control of the paper, primarily because the editor was Socialist A.S. Wells, but their claim to ownership was shaky—especially since the OBU was a spent force in B.C. by 1921.

The circumstances under which the Workers Party took over the *Federationist* are far from clear, since the change in ownership was not made public: indeed the paper continued to declare itself the "Organ of the Vancouver Trades and Labor Council—OBU" after the WPC was in full control. But however it happened, it was a great assist in the party's work in B.C. to have a weekly newspaper with a wide reputation publicizing all party activities and publishing all party statements. It is also noteworthy that under WPC control the *Federationist* reversed its usual policy of publicizing all left-wing functions: despite the Socialist Party's protests, its propaganda meetings no longer rated space in the labor weekly.

Control of the *Federationist* may have produced short term gains for the party, but the political implications, in the long run, were horrendous. The WPC had declared its opposition to the One Big Union—but it was publishing a newpaper bearing the OBU label. The WPC had declared its loyalty to the labor movement—but by a more or less shady maneuver it had captured a newspaper which belonged to all of B.C. labor, not just one party. The WPC was proclaiming its desire to unite all left-wing and militant elements in the unions—but it was using the *B.C. Federationist* to squeeze out those with whom it disagreed.

The Workers Party leadership quickly recognized that the maneuver that had won them control of the *Federationist* would do neither the party nor the B.C. labor movement any good in the long run. By May of 1922, just five months after they obtained control, they had begun negotiations to return the paper to its rightful owners. The June 2, 1922 issue announced that the *Federationist* and the *B.C. Labor News* were amalgamating, using the name of the former; the July 14 issue announced that the Vancouver Trades and Labor Council (International—i.e., not OBU) had purchased control and would henceforth publish it as their official organ. Wells resigned as editor, and was replaced by a board composed of executive members of the VTLC. Part of the agreement seems to have been that the paper would continue to publicize Workers Party activities, and the WPC did have a high profile in the *Federationist* for some time, but the main point was that B.C. labor's newspaper was back in the hands of the B.C. unions. The Workers Party had maintained its principles and established its credibility with the labor movement on the West Coast.

Two leaders of the party didn't see it that way. Jack Kavanaugh and J.G. Smith, both ex-SPCers who had been elected to the party CEC in February, protested vigorously against the decision to sell the *Federationist* to the Vancouver Trades and Labor Council. Both had a long history of battles against the men who now led the VTLC; both had fought for the OBU against those men. Unity of the labor movement was one thing: selling out to the VTLC was another.

The bitterness of the dispute may be gauged from Kavanaugh's charge that the decision which "gave the control of the Federationist into the hands of the reactionaries under the guise of tactics," was proof of the "morass of opportunism into which they [the WPC leaders] have sunk with the cloak of an United Front."[30] When the party proceeded with its decision to sell the *Federationist*, Smith and Kavanaugh and a small group of their supporters left the party.* This was a major loss for the new party. Not only were Kavanaugh and Smith among the best known of the SPCers won to Communism, they also had important connections in the labor

---

*The Workers Party was completely silent about these resignations—they only became public when the *Western Clarion* announced them, many months later. Kavanaugh rejoined the Communist Party in 1923: he later moved to Australia, and became General Secretary of the Communist Party there. He was expelled from the CPA in the 1930s, but remained a left-wing labor militant until his death in 1964. During the 1940s he was a member of the Australian Trotskyist movement.

movement. Kavanaugh was the chief spokesman of the Longshoremen in B.C., Smith of the Vancouver Carpenters. Nevertheless, faced
with a choice between keeping Smith and Kavanaugh and
maintaining principle, the party chose principle. It was a good
beginning.

Class War in Cape Breton

The change in ownership of the *Federationist* is important as an
illustration of the Workers Party's commitment to labor unity, but it
was at most a minor incident in the history of the Canadian
working class. The same cannot be said of the party's involvement
in the struggles of the miners of Cape Breton, Nova Scotia. The coal
miners of Cape Breton in the 1920s were in the vanguard of labor's
fight against the employers—and the Communists were in the
vanguard of the miners.[31]

Cape Breton's miners had a long history of militant struggle
against the coal companies, going back to the formation of the
Provincial Miners' Association in 1879. By 1921, after years of
efforts by the coal bosses to destroy every vestige of unionism, the
miners were solidly organized as District 26 of the United Mine
Workers of America.

When Jack MacDonald travelled to Nova Scotia in the spring of
1922 to address a convention of the Independent Labor Party, he
found the mining districts in turmoil. The British Empire Steel
Corporation (Besco), which controlled not only the iron and steel
smelted in Nova Scotia but the mines that dug the coal used in the
smelters, had reduced wages in all collieries by one third on
January 1, virtually wiping out the gains the miners had made
during the War. The mayor of New Waterford charged that the
wage rates would "condemn thousands of men, women, and
children to live in a state of semi-starvation."

The international head office of the United Mine Workers
announced that it did not have the financial resources to support an
all-out strike in Nova Scotia, so District 26 began a slow-down.
James B. McLachlan, a leader of the union, declared that "War is
on, class war," and urged every miner to "carry that war into the
'country' of the enemy." In the first three months of 1922 coal
output was one fifth less than it had been in 1921: in some collieries
the drop was as much as two thirds. The Liberal government in
Ottawa promised, reluctantly, to appoint a conciliation board.

This was the situation when MacDonald arrived. The slowdown
was continuing, and the miners were seething. The members of the

ILP, many of them miners, listened eagerly to the Workers Party's delegate. Since the WPC constitution did not allow affiliation of parties such as the ILP, the convention voted to recommend that its branches reconstitute themselves as branches of the Workers Party, while maintaining their association with the Labor Party.

Among those who joined the Workers Party were "Red Dan" Livingstone, International board member for District 26, and James B. McLachlan, the District's secretary-treasurer. McLachlan, who had been a leader of the Cape Breton miners for nearly two decades, wrote a report on the "on the job" strike for the May 1, 1922 *Worker.* His article concluded:

The complete solidarity of the miners in Nova Scotia in carrying on their striking on the job policy is the most wonderful and hopeful thing that has ever taken place in the industrial history of this province, *and when the final conflict comes for the final uprooting of the cursed system that is starving out people in a land of plenty, the Mine Workers of Nova Scotia shall take an effective hand in that conflict.* [emphasis in original]

McLachlan and Livingstone had long been advocates of a more militant policy for the miners, but had found themselves consistently outvoted by the conservative majority on the District executive. Now, with the arrival of the Workers Party, they gained a strategy for the organization of the left wing, a strategy which combined well with the traditional rebelliousness of the Cape Breton miners.

Their success exceeded all expectations. The discontent of the miners with a leadership that would not fight the wage cuts effectively, combined with a left wing organizing campaign, secured a clear majority of left wing delegates for the District convention in June. The convention voted to affiliate District 26 to the Red International of Labor Unions, called on the Canadian government to extend $15,000,000 in long-term credits to the Soviet Union for famine relief, voted to refuse any Besco offer which did not restore the 1921 wage rates, and declared its overall political sympathies in no uncertain terms:

We proclaim openly to all the world that we are out for a complete overthrow of the capitalist system and capitalist state, peaceably if we may, forcibly if we must, and we call on all workers, soldiers, and minor law officers in Canada to join us in liberating labour.[32]

The convention was so critical of the right-wing majority in the

District Executive that the officers handed in their resignations. McLachlan and Livingstone agreed to resign too, to allow the miners a clear choice for the executive in a special general election. Two slates were nominated. The right wing, pleading the state of the economy, called for acceptance of Besco's wage cuts. The left wing slate, which was headed by Livingstone for president and included McLachlan for secretary-treasurer, campaigned for an all-out strike. When the ballots were counted on August 15, the left had swept every post, by a six-to-one margin.

Even before it was elected the left wing had called the miners out on strike. Now the walk-out became universal. Twelve thousand miners left the job.

This was a "100 percent" strike, a tactic the UMW right wing had not been willing to try. In most mine strikes, the maintenance workers continued to work, with the union's agreement, keeping the mines pumped out and dry so that work could resume when the strike ended. This time the miners refused to take any responsibility for the bosses' property: Besco had certainly shown no respect for the miners' lives.

Besco responded by having a County Court judge issue the necessary papers to have the armed forces called in. Arrangements had doubtless been made with the federal authorities ahead of time, because by evening on the first day of the strike troops were on their way from Halifax and Quebec City. Some 1,200 fully battle-equipped soldiers—more than one quarter of Canada's standing army—occupied the collieries to protect Besco's property against an attack that never came.

From time to time groups and individuals appear in the left defending the idea that pitched battles with police or soldiers are the epitome of revolutionary tactics. Such a conception found no favor with the miners of Cape Breton. They met the troops not with violence—in a physical confrontation the miners would certainly have been massacred—but with iron discipline. Picket squads were elected, with regular shifts for all strikers. Elected picket captains maintained near military discipline. In the town of New Waterford, the union sounded a bugle every morning to wake the picketers. The union enforced strict prohibition to prevent any drunkenness; even troop trains were searched to keep out booze.

On August 18 a mass march of strikers passed through the streets of Glace Bay in a silent protest against the presence of troops. Four to five thousand men marched in a parade described by the *Halifax Herald* as displaying "no chanting, no disorder, no impressive features apart from the impressiveness of a vast body of men moving methodically and purposefully through the streets of a town."

Elsewhere the Workers Party organized solidarity actions. *The Worker* was the only labor newspaper to give full coverage to the strike and the demands of the miners, and the WPC held support meetings in many cities. When the Nova Scotia government announced plans to raise a 1,000-man police force to break the strike, the Workers Party in Halifax organized regular pickets and leaflet distributions at the recruiting center, urging the unemployed not to join the scab force: recruiting went very slowly.[33]

Meanwhile, Besco's mines were filling up with water—it has often been noted that you can't dig coal with bayonets. After less than a week the corporation, which had arrogantly refused negotiations thus far, agreed to negotiate if the maintenance workers were returned to work. The miners agreed. On August 25 the corporation made an offer. While 18 percent less than the 1921 rate, it was a substantial improvement over Besco's previous offers. It also included a sixteen-month contract, which was a long period for miners in the 1920s.

In view of Besco's known intention of reducing wages further, and the decline of miners' wages across the continent, the miners saw the long contract as protection for their standard of living. The District Executive recommended acceptance, and the miners voted 7,768 to 2,920 to ratify the contract. On September 5 the strike ended. It was a partial victory, but a victory nonetheless, and the miners celebrated it.

The Workers Party had established itself firmly in the coalfields. It had won to its ranks the most capable left-wing trade unionists in Nova Scotia—some of the best on the continent. Those unionists had shown that they knew how to lead a union and a strike, and how to battle the largest corporation in the Maritimes to a standstill.

But the strike was barely over when they faced what proved to be a far more difficult battle: against the leadership of their own union.

IN THE 1930s AND '40s, when he played an important role in building the CIO, John L. Lewis earned a reputation as a militant union leader who was always ready to defy the bosses and the government in order to build the United Mine Workers. Whatever the justice of that later reputation—and it had a basis in reality—it certainly did not apply to the Lewis of the 1920s. The president of the United Mine Workers was a firm defender of capitalism, a rabid anti-Communist, a despot who allowed no dissent in "his" union.

In 1919, when the miners of District 18 (Alberta and B.C.) voted to join the OBU, Lewis lifted their charter, suspended their leaders, and cooperated with the mine-owners in restoring "order"—that is, UMW dominance—in the coalfields. In 1921, when District 14 (Kansas), under the leadership of one of Lewis's critics, called a strike in violation of a contract, Lewis, a strong believer in the sanctity of contracts, revoked the District's charter and waged a war against the rebels which destroyed most of the locals in the District. Lewis was not above destroying the union to save the bureaucracy.[34]

District 26 had trouble with Lewis during the August 1922 strike. While the miners were face-to-face with the army, Lewis publicly condemned the "100 percent" aspect of the strike.

The 1922 strike was over before that conflict could escalate, but there was another in the wings. District 26's decision to affiliate to the Red International of Labor Unions amounted to waving a (literally) red flag in front of the UMW president. The union's International Executive condemned the RILU as an organization established to destroy the trade union movement, and ordered District 26 to withdraw their application to affiliate—and backed the order up with a threat to revoke the District's charter.

The decision of the District to affiliate to the RILU had been widely hailed by the Workers Party as proof of the growing militancy of the Canadian left: in fact Tim Buck had personally urged the convention to adopt the affiliation resolution.* A party less committed to a Leninist approach to the trade unions would have been strongly tempted to take an unyielding stand towards Lewis. Undoubtedly the rank and file in District 26 would have supported their executive in such a confrontation.

The Workers Party, however, saw no point in going to the wall over this question. The big issue was winning the UMW to a class struggle program, not formal ties with the RILU. On February 1, 1923, the District 26 executive voted to withdraw its application for affiliation.

This was no passive capitulation to Lewis. In the name of the

---

*In his *Reminiscences,* Buck claims to have been surprised by the resolution on the RILU, and to have opposed it as an ultra-left action. In 1922, however, *The Worker* reported that Buck "conveyed greetings and emphasized the urgency of international affiliation," and was greeted with cheers.[35]

District executive, J.B. McLachlan published an open letter to Lewis, announcing the withdrawal of the affiliation request and stating very clearly that only the threat of losing their charter made them back down.

> We are prepared to retreat from almost any position, rather than give anybody the opportunity to smash our solidarity. The onus for splitting this District shall never rest on this Executive Board.

Having charged Lewis with an attempt to split the union, the open letter went on to defend the RILU against his accusations, and announced the District's intention to appeal Lewis's ruling to the next UMW convention.[36]

The open letter was widely circulated in the Canadian labor movement, and in the UMW it was a part of the left wing's campaign against Lewis. It was followed, in mid-April, by publication of a letter from the RILU refuting in more detail Lewis's charge that the International was out to smash the "bona-fide trade union movement," and endorsing the decision of District 26 not to affiliate for the time being.

> We do not counsel District 26 to unite formally, as a trade union, with the R.I.L.U. if such action would mean their expulsion from the U.M.W. of A.... The task of District 26 is to remain steadfastly loyal to the principles of the R.I.L.U., and also to the organization of the U.M.W. of A., while carrying on an educational campaign among their fellow members of the U.M.W. of A. in other districts in favor of the R.I.L.U.[37]

Lewis had prevented affiliation—but in every other way this first round was a victory for District 26 and the Workers Party. Anticipating an intensified conflict, the party moved Central Committee members Malcolm Bruce and Tom Bell to Cape Breton. Bell took over as editor of the *Maritime Labour Herald,* a weekly founded by McLachlan in 1921. Jack MacDonald travelled regularly to the East Coast to ensure that the full resources of the party leadership were available on a day-to-day basis to meet the challenge of leading the miners.

Several skirmishes between Lewis and the District 26 executive took place in the spring of 1923, but the executive was able to defuse them. For example, when Lewis demanded new elections for the District 26 executive, a District convention amended the District constitution to move the regular election date up from December to August, thus eliminating the need for a special poll.

The crisis came in June, when members of the Amalgamated Association of Iron, Steel and Tin Workers struck against Besco's steel plants in Sydney. Once again the armed forces were sent into Cape Breton, this time allied with a newly-recruited "provincial police" force from Halifax. A series of pitched battles between police and strikers ensued, leading to one of the most vicious police attacks on workers ever recorded in Canadian history.

On Sunday, July 1, as the people of Whitney Pier were returning from church, a mounted squad of police charged down the main street, armed with clubs. There was no demonstration or picket line in progress, only men, women and children on a Sunday walk. J.B. McLachlan described the scene:

On Sunday night last the provincial police, in the most brutal manner, rode down the people of Whitney Pier who were on the street, most of whom were coming from church. Neither age, sex, nor physical disability were proof against these brutes. One old woman over 70 years of age was beaten into insensibility and may die. A boy nine years old was trampled under the horses' hooves and had his breast bone crushed in. A woman, being beaten with a police club, gave premature birth to a child. The child is dead and the woman's life is despaired of. Men and women were beaten up inside their own homes.[38]

On Monday and Tuesday night the coal miners of Cape Breton held mass meetings in the ice rink in Glace Bay. The Tuesday meeting resolved to strike and stay out until the troops were withdrawn from Cape Breton. McLachlan cabled every local in the province:

The government of Nova Scotia is the guilty and responsible party for this crime. No miner or mineworker can remain at work while this government turns Sydney into a jungle. To do so is to sink your manhood and allow [Provincial Premier] Armstrong and his miserable bunch of grafting politicians to trample your last shred of freedom in the sand. Call a meeting of your local at once and decide to spread the fight against Armstrong to every mine in Nova Scotia. Act at once—tomorrow may be too late.[39]

Within a week every mine in Nova Scotia was closed down. This again was a 100 percent strike. Every worker was pulled out and Besco was left to maintain its mines itself.

The government responded by arresting McLachlan and Livingstone on a charge of "circulating false information"—the "false information" being McLachlan's description of the brutal police attack on the people of Whitney Pier. Since everyone except the police agreed that McLachlan's description had been correct, the charges were later changed to "seditious libel." McLachlan was convicted; after a series of appeals, he served three months in prison early in 1924.

In the meantime, however, Besco had found a new ally: John L. Lewis. On July 6 Lewis cabled District 26, charging that the strike, in violation of a contract, was "a violation of the principles and policies" of the UMW, and that withdrawal of maintenance employees "is most indefensible and constitutes a wanton destruction of property." He ordered the miners to return to work "so as to permit of full protection of property interests affected and an early resumption of mining operations."[40]

Affiliation to the RILU was one thing: this was another. District 26 was on strike to drive the troops out of Cape Breton. Continued military intervention in labor disputes threatened the very life of the labor movement in Canada. The District executive decided that a matter of principle was at stake. They refused to give way, informing the UMW president that he had no right to order them back to work: "Our international union must understand that its jurisdiction does not give it authority to prohibit workers in Canada waging a political struggle against use of armed forces which are being used to smash our labor movement."[41]

Lewis replied with a vicious tirade against Livingstone and "your evil genius McLachlan and your revolutionary masters in Moscow." The UMW, he wrote, would not be used by political fanatics seeking "to strike down the established institutions of...government," nor to "sustain officers of perverted business morals or individuals suffering from mental aberration such as yourself and the aggregation of papier-maché revolutionists who are associated with you." Lewis suspended District 26's charter, deposed all the elected officers, and replaced them with the very men who had been defeated in a six to one vote the previous August.[42]

Lewis's public attack on the District executive came at a time when the union was on strike and its officers were facing prosecution for supporting another union. Besco could not have asked for a better gift. The newly-appointed executive pledged to return the men to the mines. Silby Barrett, the appointed president, warned that anyone remaining on strike would be expelled from the UMW. By the end of July the miners, having resisted the bosses, the government, and their own union leadership for more than two weeks, returned to work. Several days later the steel strike collapsed: the steel union was smashed and a company union was imposed by Besco. John L. Lewis had shown very clearly which side he was on.

Sentiment in District 26 was now running very strong against Lewis and his hand picked executive. Several locals initiated moves to withdraw from the international union, and the One Big Union, roused from sleep by the possibility of successful raids, established locals in several towns. If the Workers Party had chosen to lead a secessionist movement, it could have taken a majority of the membership out of the UMW into an independent Nova Scotia-based organization committed to the principles of class-struggle unionism.

The Workers Party resisted the temptation. Strong as the left was in the Nova Scotia UMW, it was a minority force in the Canadian labor movement and in the UMW as a whole. Withdrawing from the international would have isolated the militants from other Canadian unions and from other miners, and it would have invited repetition of the campaign that destroyed the OBU in Western Canada. This conflict could not be treated as one involving anyone's honor: the task for the left, as Lenin had written, was to bear the "pinpricks, chicanery, insults and persecution on the part of the 'leaders,'" in order to "work wherever the masses are to be found."[43]

The Worker and *Maritime Labor Herald* campaigned against every tendency to give up the struggle against Lewis through secession. "A Split in District 26 Would Play Into the Hands of Miners' Enemies—The Corporation and Czar Lewis," a banner headline in the October 10, 1923 *Worker* proclaimed. Editorials and lead articles pointed out that simply maintaining the existing locals was an important victory—in Kansas even those had been destroyed by Lewis. Tom Bell wrote:

So far as the Cape Breton miners are concerned there will be no dual union formed. Today is the period of retreat but on the morrow it will be demonstrated that the miners who can retreat in good order can also advance once favorable ground is found for a battle for the possession of their union. It is only fools who attempt to fight their enemies on ground chosen by the enemy.[44]

It took a year, but the Workers Party's policy of waiting Lewis out paid off. The locals were kept intact, and the left did not give way to demoralization. In August 1924 Lewis returned the District's charter, with the proviso that none of the deposed officers (meaning McLachlan, Livingstone, and their comrades) could stand for election to the new District executive. Again the WPC decided that building the union was more important than any question of personal honor or pride: the Trade Union Educational League in Nova Scotia drew up a slate of candidates which did not include any of the former officers. McLachlan and Livingstone campaigned in support of the TUEL slate. Every single member of the left-wing slate was elected: the new president, John. W. McLeod, won by a majority of 4,000 votes.[45]

The class war in Cape Breton was not over yet, by any means. The next year would see one of the longest strikes in the history of coal mining in Canada, and a continued drive by Besco to destroy the United Mine Workers. But that story will have to be told elsewhere. For present purposes, the battles in Cape Breton in 1922 and 1923 demonstrate the capacity of the Canadian Communists to provide the working class movement not just militant leadership but *intelligent* militant leadership. They knew how to fight—and when not to fight. They knew when to take the offensive and when to retreat. And they were able to keep the leadership of the great majority of the coal miners through all of the maneuvers necessary to fight Besco, the government, and Lewis.

It is very unlikely that any union in Canada, before or since, ever had as fine a leadership as that provided by the Workers Party in Cape Breton in the early twenties.

PART TWO

COUNTERREVOLUTION

Whoever understands history even slightly knows that every
revolution has provoked a subsequent counter-revolution....
And the first victim of the reactionary wave as a general rule is
that layer of revolutionaries which stood at the head of the
masses in the first period of the revolution.

—Leon Trotsky, 1935

7. Canadian Labor in Decline

The Workers Party of Canada took the injunction "To the Masses!" very seriously. It directed its members into the labor movement and the labor parties to fight for a class-struggle program and to win the support and confidence of the working class. Its efforts in Nova Scotia produced the most dramatic results, but by 1923 the party had also sunk roots in District 18 (Alberta and B.C.) of the United Mine Workers, in the Longshoremen's Union in B.C., and in the garment workers' unions in Winnipeg, Toronto, and Montreal. The largely Finnish Lumber Workers Industrial Union, formerly a part of the OBU, was under Communist leadership and was the only Canadian union affiliated to the Red International of Labor Unions.

The Workers Party missed no opportunity to demonstrate its roots in the unions. The 1923 WPC convention, for example, demonstratively elected a Presidium comprised entirely of men who were both party leaders and active members of major industrial unions.* This action was given front-page coverage in *The Worker*. The Communist newspaper also reported regularly on major labor conflicts in Canada and elsewhere, and gave considerable space to articles by Comintern and RILU leaders on trade union tactics and problems. And the party demonstrated in

---

*The Presidium members were: Jan Lakeman, Brotherhood of Railway Carmen, Edmonton; J.B. McLachlan, UMW District 26, Glace Bay; Alex Gauld, International Association of Plumbers and Steamfitters, Montreal; Tim Buck, International Association of Machinists, Toronto; and Malcolm Bruce, United Brotherhood of Carpenters and Joiners, Regina.

practice its ability to lead strikes and other labor conflicts to successful conclusions.

No strike in which the party was involved was ever treated as a purely local phenomenon. At the very least the party and the TUEL would coordinate resolutions of protest and solidarity, and arrange to have petitions and telegrams sent from meetings and union locals across the country. For example, when troops were sent into Cape Breton in 1923 and McLachlan and Livingstone were arrested, the Vancouver Workers Party branch was in the process of organizing a public meeting for James Cannon, chairman of the Workers Party of America, who was on a speaking tour reporting on his recent trip to Russia. The meeting proceeded as planned, but the discussion period was transformed into a protest rally. Money was collected to aid the srikers, and a telegram was sent to Ottawa demanding withdrawal of the troops from Nova Scotia and release of the arrested leaders. Three weeks later the WPC in Vancouver held another protest meeting, this one called specifically to support the Nova Scotia strike. The workers who crowded into the Columbia Theater were addressed by eleven speakers, representing every major union and working class political current in the city. The meeting unanimously approved a resolution demanding withdrawal of the toops and proposed the establishment of a "Steel Workers' and Miners' Defense Committee" to publicize the situation in Nova Scotia and raise funds for legal aid.[1] Similar activities took place in every city in which the party had influence in the labor movement. In some parts of Alberta and British Columbia, miners staged sympathy strikes in support of District 26.

The Workers Party's campaign in support of the Nova Scotia miners illustrates well the party's general approach to labor's war with Capital. The Communists' aim was to win the battle (or, as in the 1922 miners' strike, to minimize losses) in such a way as to defend and strengthen the entire labor movement. They sought to strengthen and put into practice the conviction that "an injury to one is an injury to all." They attempted to build up the broadest possible alliance of forces in support of the workers who were on the front line: the Vancouver meeting described above, for example, was addressed by representatives of the IWW, the Federated Labor Party, the Workers Party, and the Vancouver Trades and Labor Council, as well as leaders of major unions. They did this without giving an inch to the conservative prejudices of many of their allies

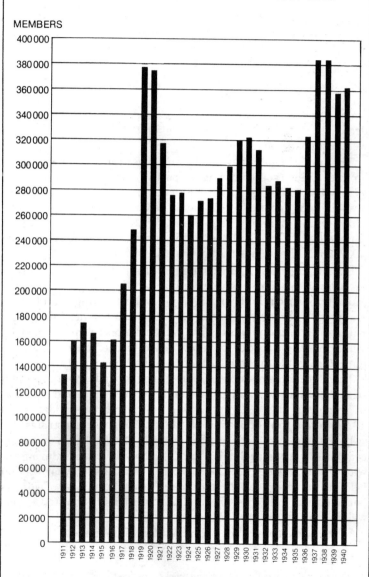

TRADE UNION MEMBERSHIP IN CANADA 1911-1940

Source: *Labor Organization in Canada, 1940*

and without muting their criticisms of labor's official leadership. Their object at all times, as the constitution of the Trade Union Educational League stated, was to help to make the unions into "ever more clear-sighted, cohesive, militant and powerful organizations."

THE COMMUNISTS PLAYED a remarkable leadership role in the labor movement in the early 1920s. There were no major labor conflicts in the decade in which they did not play some part — usually the leading part. But as the decade progressed, the number of conflicts decreased steadily. For Canadian labor, the 1920s and early 1930s were a time of decline and decay.

The statistics of union membership show the decline. Enrolment in trade unions soared during the postwar labor rebellion, reaching nearly 380,000 in 1919, more than double the prewar high. There was a slight decline in 1920, and then a precipitous drop. As the chart on the preceding page shows, by 1924 membership in trade unions had fallen by almost a third from the 1919 peak. Not until 1937 would the unions recoup the losses of the 1920s.

If anything, these figures understate the decline. Dues payments are a poor measure of the effectiveness of a union: a far better indicator, especially during a period when the wages and living standards of organized workers are stagnating or declining, is the willingness of the unions to fight in their members' interests. Strike statistics—the apostles of labor peace to the contrary—are an important guide to the health of the labor movement.

There are three possible measures of strike activity—the number of strikes in a given period, the number of strikers, and the number of workdays "lost" during strikes.* By all three standards, the 1920s were a time of decline, as the table opposite illustrates.

This table takes the prewar years 1901-1913 as a basis for comparison, thus excluding the extremely low years during the war. Beginning in 1922 the number of strikes each year was far below the prewar average, and from 1926 on the number of workers participating in each strike, and the duration of each strike, were well below the 1901-1913 average.

As the table shows, the overall statistics understate the actual

---

*A fourth widely-used measure, the workdays "lost" as a percentage of all workdays, is very valuable, but reliable statistics were not collected early enough to allow historical comparisons.

STRIKE ACTIVITY INDEX, 1914-1935
1901-1913 = 100

Year	Total All Industries			All Industries Except Coal Mining			Coal Mining Only		
	No. of Strikes	No. of Strikers	No. of Work-days	No. of Strikes	No. of Strikers	No. of Work-days	No. of Strikes	No. of Strikers	No. of Work-days
1914	50	38	68	50	34	50	45	60	93
1915	50	44	13	45	41	20	134	65	4
1916	95	102	33	94	72	39	119	266	24
1917	127	195	155	117	155	127	313	410	193
1918	183	309	117	154	267	122	183	540	43
1919	267	577	468	265	652	713	299	223	126
1920	256	234	110	241	227	165	522	267	33
1921	134	109	144	133	126	240	149	32	10
1922	83	170	210	67	81	172	313	583	263
1923	68	133	92	53	63	88	343	458	99
1924	56	133	178	46	61	49	224	467	359
1925	69	112	164	59	48	36	253	411	343
1926	60	92	37	51	72	55	239	186	12
1927	57	86	21	45	27	23	299	367	18
1928	76	68	31	70	59	32	208	111	29
1929	70	50	21	69	47	83	119	67	2
1930	53	53	13	44	35	16	224	137	8
1931	68	42	28	66	40	46	134	47	4
1932	88	91	35	70	70	29	493	70	44
1933	97	103	40	87	110	67	313	67	11
1934	150	177	79	138	161	114	388	252	30
1935	95	129	40	76	128	53	253	135	22

Compiled from *Labor Gazette*, 1935

decline. Throughout the 1920s one industry—coal mining—experienced more strikes than any other. Indeed, more than half of the strikes that took place in the decade were miners' strikes. The exceptional militancy of the coal miners distorts the figures, making it appear that the labor movement as a whole was more combative than it actually was.

It is clear that from 1923 through 1932 Canadian labor, with the notable exception of the coal miners, virtually abandoned the fight against Capital. The number of strikes and strikers, and the number of workdays lost in strikes were each year well below the prewar average. The average number of strikes per year was just one half of the 1901-1913 average. By every measure 1930 was the low point in the century for labor militancy: strike activity in that year was even lower than in 1915, when patriotism and enlistment in the armed forces had almost destroyed the labor movement. An American labor historian has written that in the United States in the 1920s, "the strike as an instrument of collective bargaining, to say nothing of social protest, had fallen into almost total disuse."[2] The same was true in Canada.

In fact, workers who did strike stood a very good chance of being totally defeated. The Department of Labor published annual statistics showing the results of each year's strikes. Between 1920 and 1932 there were only two years in which strikers won more strikes than they lost. Over the entire thirteen-year span, the Department described 352 strikes as being settled "in favor of the workers," while 549 were resolved "in favor of employers." Another 346 were said to have ended in compromise.[3] Even if the "compromise" outcomes are regarded as partial victories, *44 percent of all strikes ended in defeat for the strikers.* In reality the figure was higher than that, since "compromise" usually meant little more than saving the union from total destruction. The bosses routinely set crushing the union as a primary objective: anything less than that was "compromise." And it is important to note that one of the most common causes of strike action was an attempt to prevent a wage decrease—so victory often meant not a gain for the workers but avoidance of a loss, while compromise meant partial loss.

THE CAUSES OF THE DECLINE of the labor movement—a better term might be collapse—were many and complex. They can, however, be summarized under two headings: the changing nature of the economy, and the paralysis of the labor leadership.

The war and its aftermath, the political setback to labor following the collapse of the 1919 strikes, gave a tremendous impetus to capital investment and expansion throughout North America. Mechanized mass production, pioneered in the automobile industry, was introduced in almost every industry during the 1920s. In the United States between 1919 and 1929, according to one study, horsepower per wage-earner in manufacturing increased by 50 percent, in mining by 60 percent, and on the railroads by 74 percent. Output per man-hour rose during the same period by 72 percent in manufacturing, by 41 percent in mining, and by 33 percent on the railroads.[4] The effects of this revolution in productivity were felt in Canada as well, where the capitalist boom in the 1920s was unmistakable. It was accompanied by a wave of concentration and centralization of capital: between 1924 and 1930 there were 315 corporate mergers of various types in Canada, involving firms with assets of nearly one billion dollars. By contrast, in the following fifteen years there were only 232 mergers, involving only $399 million in corporate assets.[5]

As production expanded, the pattern of capital investment shifted. Resource industries continued to play an extremely important role in the Canadian economy, but new industries such as automobiles and electrical, rubber, and chemical products rose to challenge their dominance. The spread of assembly-line production undermined the traditional craft-based unions.

For some workers and for the growing middle class, this technological revolution meant higher wages and an improved standard of living. But for the hundreds of thousands whose livelihood depended on declining industries such as coal mining or crafts that were becoming obsolete, the boom meant falling wages and unemployment. It is a sign of the collapse of major sectors of Canadian industrial employment that a twenty-year trend in population movement between the United States and Canada was suddenly reversed in the 1920s. Between 1900 and 1920 about 1,200,000 emigrants from the U.S. entered Canada, while about 900,000 moved south. During the 1920s 900,000 more workers moved to the U.S., but only 200,000 came to Canada. Many of those who emigrated were skilled workers, unable to practise their trades in Canada. The Communist Party lost many members to this process: from its Central Executive alone it lost Malcolm Bruce to the United States for several years and Tom Bell permanently.

Canadian capitalism was bursting out of the nineteenth century, with new techniques, new products, new forms of organization.

After recovering from the profound scare it received in 1919, the capitalist class was profoundly confident of its ability to rule. The capitalists' ideological hegemony seemed to be absolute, and the prostration of the labor movement seemed complete.

Organized labor's response to the capitalist challenge has been described by historian Irving Abella:

Even though these new industries could not be accommodated within their existing craft structures, both the TLC and the AFL were unwilling to adopt different structures. They were select organizations, whose membership made up the elite of the labour movement; they wanted nothing else but to maintain their status and to be left alone.... Hidebound, TLC affiliates clung to their craft mentality. They launched no organizing campaigns, hired few organizers, and spent little money. In a period of rapid economic expansion the TLC consciously chose retrenchment and consolidation. It succeeded in neither.[6]

This, however, is description, not explanation. The conservatism of North America's labor leadership was not a new phenomenon, nor was it limited to the 1920s. The same leadership, with the same reactionary outlook, remained in office in the 1930s, when a mass uprising of American workers began in the mass-production industries. That uprising bypassed the traditional unions and leaders, creating a new organization, the Congress of Industrial Organization (CIO). Why did that upsurge not take place in the 1920s, when the objective conditions for it were fully ripe?

Part of the explanation is to be found in the normal conservatism of human social consciousness. Consciousness is a product of being—our outlook on life is shaped by the circumstances in which we live. But there is not a one-to-one correspondence between economic changes and human awareness of those changes and their implications. Quite the contrary. Consciousness is usually conservative: it lags far behind reality, refusing even to acknowledge that it is out of date, much less to comprehend the requirements of the new situation. Periodically great forward leaps occur, in which the understanding of great masses of people, like a ball at the end of a tightly-stretched rubber band, suddenly bounds into a new position. In extreme cases, such sudden leaps produce social revolutions. Such an advance was sorely needed in the North American working class in the 1920s—but it did not come until the 1930s.

Why did it take so long? In fact Canadian workers realized during World War I that major changes were needed. The general strike—a weapon far more suited to industrial rather than craft organization—became a popular form of labor action even before the war ended. There were brief general strikes in Vancouver and Winnipeg in the summer of 1918, presaging the battles that would come the following spring. The One Big Union was not just the scheme of a handful of radicals: it won the enthusiastic support of the immense majority of organized workers in Western Canada. Though the leaders of the OBU were confused about their objectives and uncertain about their methods, their union was very definitely a precursor of the industrial unions which arose in the 1930s and 1940s. Even in areas where the OBU was weak, the industrial form of organization gained ground in 1918-1919: the most important example was the rise of "Metal Trades Councils," bodies uniting all of the metal workers' craft unions into a single bargaining unit. It was the Metal Trades Councils' activities which touched off the Winnipeg and Toronto general strikes of 1919.

Had it continued, the labor revolt would, at the very least, have changed the face of Canadian labor, creating the forms of organization needed to respond to the changes in the capitalist economy.

The labor revolt did not simply end: it was defeated. Through a combination of the government's determination to prevent any substantial labor gains and the ineptness of its own leadership, Canadian labor was thrown back beyond its starting point. There was almost universal demoralization among the rank and file— and it was the rank and file who bore the brunt of the defeat. History books tell of the labor leaders who served prison terms for their part in 1919: much less is said about the Winnipeg railway workers who lost all of their seniority rights as a result of the strike, or about the workers who were blacklisted and could never again find work in their own trades, or about the untold numbers of immigrant workers who were deported without trial. Across Western Canada miners were forced to submit to inquisitions, forced to repudiate their beliefs and their organizations in order to keep their jobs. The fact that the main organizations of the labor movement endorsed and participated in the crushing of the labor revolt added to the demoralization: the working class lost faith in its organizations, and it lost faith in itself.

Defeats such as that experienced by Canadian workers in 1919-1920 are not easily overcome. The depression which set in just as the revolt was crushed intensified the despair the workers felt: they had tried to fight Capital, the outcome was misery. A generation of labor militants was lost. It was not until the late 1930s, after a series of new victories won by a new generation of workers had shown the way, that the working class began to move again.

A Major Exception: The Miners

The coal miners were a special case. From the beginning of the century the miners had been the most militant section of the North American labor movement. They fought for their rights again and again—and even when they were defeated they rose to fight again. Coal miners, E.P. Thompson writes, have always had difficulty in "comprehending the simplest of propositions as to the market regulation of wages, and they have always clung tenaciously to unscientific notions such as 'justice' and 'fair play.'"[7] Added to the miners' traditional militancy was the fact that mining towns were small, one-industry towns: when the miners went on strike the entire community was on strike. Everyone in town knew what the issues were, and above all who the enemy was. The class struggle was naked and undisguised, and solidarity was a way of life. As the table on page 135 shows, the miners' militancy survived long after the rest of the labor movement had collapsed.

The coal miners were fighting a battle of desperation: they were fighting for survival. Oil and electricity were replacing coal in the new industries: the price of coal dropped by nearly 50 percent between 1920 and 1929. Marginal mines that had been opened to meet wartime demand were being closed. These facts, and the coming of mechanization, created unemployment and falling wages, as the mine-owners sought to pass the burden of declining prices and rising capital costs on to their employees: profits, after all, are not to be touched. The mine strikes of the 1920s were almost invariably called to resist wage cuts: restoration of the 1921 wage-scale was the never-ending and never-successful battle cry of the Nova Scotia miners.

Industry-wide organization, bringing the unemployed into the union and supporting workers in allied industries such as steel, could have made victories possible for the miners. Such an approach at that time was beyond the comprehension of John L. Lewis. He tried to win by providing the mine-owners with a stable work force that wouldn't break contracts, while the owners were regularly violating contracts to bring down the wage-bill. Lewis's stubborn insistence on the sanctity of contracts enabled the mine-owners to take on the UMW one district at a time: they never had to face a continent-wide coal strike. In Canada this led to the destruction of District 18 in 1924. The UMW simply collapsed, shattering into dozens of little "home unions" across Alberta and B.C., making the best settlements they could manage. In 1925 an alliance of Communist and Social Democratic miners was able to pull together a majority of the home unions into a single Mine Workers Union of Canada, but the MWUC never included more than a fraction of the number of miners the UMW had once organized. District 26 in Nova Scotia, led by Communists who resisted Lewis's suicidal policies, remained intact, but unemployment and emigration caused its membership to drop rapidly.

The miners could not continue indefinitely as the only combative union in a quiescent labor movement. Although strikes remained a constant feature of coal mining right through the decade, as time went on the strikes became shorter and involved fewer workers than ever before: in the mines as elsewhere, the labor leadership was destroying the labor movement.

FOR THE COMMUNISTS, the decline of the labor movement was profoundly demoralizing. They had a program geared to the working class; they had a strategy and tactics which had proven their worth in practice. But as the decade progressed, their slogans received smaller and smaller responses. Their newspapers went unread by the people they were meant to reach. The party had been founded in the conviction that a mass revolutionary party could be built quickly, that proletarian revolution was on the order of the day. Now that conviction began to fade.

James P. Cannon, chairman of the Workers Party of America through the 1920s, has summarized the impact on U.S. Communists of the growth of conservatism in that period:

It was difficult to be a working revolutionist in America in those days, to sustain the agitation that brought no response, to repeat the slogans which found no echo. The party leaders were not crudely corrupted by personal benefits of the general prosperity; but they were affected indirectly by the sea of indifference around them.

. . . in revolting against their social environment and striving to change it, revolutionists nevertheless still remain a part of the environment and subject to its influences and pressures. It has happened more than once in history that unfavorable turns of the conjuncture and postponement of the expected revolution, combined with tiredness and loss of vision in the dull routine of living from day to day, have tended to make conservative even the cadres of the revolutionary party and prepare their degeneration. . . .

The prosperity, which appeared to push revolutionary perspectives far into the future, dealt heavier blows to the party than the earlier persecution. The persecution had cut down its numerical strength, but its cadres remained intact and self-confident. The prosperity sapped the confidence of the cadres in the revolutionary future. Persecution inflicted wounds on the body of the party, but the drawn-out prosperity of the Twenties killed its soul.[8]

Canadian workers did not experience as much prosperity as American workers did, but the overall impact of the decade was the same: the numbing conservatism of society as a whole, and of the working class in particular, sapped the Communists' will to fight.

For the ethnic organizations this meant turning inwards, keeping free from contamination by conservative Anglo-Saxon workers. Since Finns and Ukrainians made up some 90 percent of the Canadian Communist Party's membership, their retreat from involvement in the party's day-to-day life greatly reinforced the demoralization of the organization's small English-speaking cadre. Inevitably this demoralization tended to affect the party's program. 1924 and 1925 saw the beginning of a move away from the principles on which the party had been founded, a search for get-rich-quick formulas which would succeed where Leninism seemed to be failing. This process was all the more destructive for being unconscious: the party did not believe it was abandoning its principles, merely seeking new applications of them.

In 1920-1922 the Communist Party of Canada (like the CPs in every country) was saved from disastrous errors by the educational intervention of the leadership of the Communist International. Lenin's *"Left-Wing" Communism*, the resolutions of the Comintern congresses, the constant flow of articles and advice from the Bolshevik cadre—these works re-educated tens of thousands of revolutionary militants in dozens of countries, directing them away from ultraleftism, towards patient work among the working people. The gains that the Canadian CP made in the early 1920s were due almost entirely to the political reorientation Lenin and his comrades initiated.

But in 1923 illness removed Lenin from political life. Changes were taking place in Russia: the Bolsheviks themselves were not immune to the demoralization produced by extended isolation in a conservative and hostile world. The Communist International itself was moving onto a new course, one that none of its founders expected. In order to understand what happened to the Communist Party of Canada in the mid- and late-1920s, it is necessary to leave Canada, to consider the events which brought about a transformation of the entire world Communist movement.

8. Socialism in One Country

In August 1917 the Russian Bolshevik Party elected a Central Committee with twenty-one members. That committee led the party through its severest challenge, the October Revolution.

Seven of those twenty-one Bolshevik leaders died natural deaths. Two were killed during the 1918-1921 Civil War. Eleven of them—Zinoviev, Kamenev, Rykov, Bukharin, Miliutin, Krestinsky, Sokolnikov, Bubnov, Smilga, Berzin, and Muranov—died in Stalin's prisons during the 1930s. One, Trotsky, was assassinated in Mexico in 1940 by an agent of Stalin's secret police.

An absolute majority of the Central Committee that led the Bolshevik revolution was liquidated on Stalin's orders.

In October 1917 the Bolshevik Party elected a seven-member Political Bureau. Five of those seven Bolsheviks died in the Stalinist terror.

Between 1918 and 1921, thirty-one men and women served on the Bolshevik party's Central Committee at various times. Eighteen of them were murdered by Stalin.

Between 1917 and 1923, ten men held seats on the Bolshevik Political Bureau at various times. Eight of them were victims of the terror initiated by Stalin.

It is widely believed by Stalinists and anticommunists alike that the Stalinist regime and its associated terrors were the inevitable product of Bolshevism. In truth, as any review of the facts demonstrates, Stalin's victory in the USSR was accomplished by the physical destruction of the Bolshevik party and a complete rupture with its program and organizational principles. Not only the leaders of Lenin's party but almost the entire membership perished in the great terror of the 1930s—not only Stalin's opponents but even those who failed to support him with sufficient enthusiasm. Those killed number in the hundreds of thousands, possibly millions.

This was not just a "violation of socialist legality," as contemporary Kremlin apologists would have us believe. It was neither an accident nor the result of a personality quirk. It was a calculated counterrevolution.

As Trotsky wrote, a river of blood divides Stalinism from Bolshevism.

The Bureaucracy

The objective source of the Stalinist counterrevolution was the isolation of the Russian Revolution within the borders of a single backward country. The Bolsheviks never expected this: they saw their revolution as the first of a series of revolutions that would lead, at the very least, to the establishment of several workers states in Europe. This process was not merely desirable, it was essential, in Lenin's view:

The complete victory of the socialist revolution in one country alone is inconceivable and demands the most active cooperation of at least several advanced countries, *which do not include Russia.* Hence one of the main problems of the revolution is the extent to which we succeed in broadening the revolution in other countries too. . . .[1] [Emphasis added]

Lenin returned to this theme again and again, usually emphasizing the need for a revolution in Europe's most industrialized country: "It is the absolute truth that without a German revolution we are doomed. . .if the German revolution does not come we are doomed."[2]

The view that the efforts of several countries at least are needed to construct socialism had been expressed by Karl Marx and Frederick Engels as early as 1847,* and it remained a fundamental part of the program of every Marxist party until after Lenin's death. The insistence of the Bolsheviks on this point was not, moreover, an abstract speculation on the importance of internationalism: this was a question of life and death. The Bolsheviks were quite convinced that without successful

---

*"The communist revolution will therefore be no merely national one: it will be a revolution taking place simultaneously in all civilized countries, that is, at least in England, America, France and Germany."—Engels[3]

revolutions in advanced capitalist countries their government would fall prey to capitalist economic pressure or to capitalist armies, or both.

Russia was the most backward country in Europe before World War I. After four years of war, and three more years of civil war and imperialist invasion, the country was prostrate. The national income was less than one third of the prewar figure; industrial production was less than one fifth of the 1913 level. Coal production was one tenth its normal level, iron production one fortieth. The railways were destroyed. At the end of the civil war, the daily ration for workers in the major cities of Moscow and Petrograd was two ounces of bread and a few frozen potatoes.

And as the civil war came to an end, with the Red Army triumphant, Russia's chief agricultural areas were hit simultaneously by drought, sand storms, and locusts. Famine, one of the worst in modern history, affected 36 million peasants. Cannibalism appeared in some parts of Russia.

Not only was the infant workers republic in a state of economic collapse unparalleled in this century in any major country, but it did not have the resources to pull itself back into shape without great dislocation. The peasant economy was strong—left alone, as the experience of the soon-adopted New Economic Policy was to show, the Russian peasants could rebuild. But the cities and the industries could not be re-established as easily as family farms. Russia's working class, a small percentage of the country's total population in 1917, had been shattered by 1921. Many had died in the fighting; many more had fled to the countryside in search of food. The population of Moscow had fallen by one half, that of Petrograd by one third. Russia's highly organized and politically conscious working class simply did not exist any more.

Only 30 percent of Russia's population was literate; far fewer had the knowledge and skills needed to rebuild an industrial economy. A revolution in Germany, or France, or even Italy would have placed at the Russians' disposal the great accumulated knowledge and resources of the Western European working class. In the absence of such a revolution, the Bolsheviks had to seek the aid of experts who had little sympathy for the aims of the revolution, experts who in most cases had sided with the czarist armies during the Civil War.

The first large-scale use of nonrevolutionary experts had been in the Red Army. In 1921 the army that won the Civil War included over thirty thousand former czarist officers serving as advisors.

They had not, in most cases, been won to the program of proletarian revolution. Some were opportunists who picked the Bolsheviks as the winning side; some were nationalists who hated foreign invaders more than they hated Bolsheviks; some had spent the Civil War looking for opportunities to desert. In exchange for their desperately needed services, they had demanded and received special privileges—high salaries, unrationed food, cars, and so on.

It did not take long for such arrangements to spread to industry and government. When even literacy was rare, statisticians, engineers, administrators, and the like could claim privileges. To stay alive, the Bolsheviks had to agree.

What began as a temporary expedient congealed into a system. The small layer of highly paid experts evolved into a substantial body of people who had privileges and wielded influence solely as a result of the offices they filled. What developed was a *bureaucracy.*

In this case, bureaucracy refers not only to the existence of red tape, inefficiency, and the like. Nor does it simply result from personal attitudes. It is a social and political phenomenon. It refers to people who have power and privilege as a consequence of holding administrative office.

The young Karl Marx, in an article written before he had fully developed the ideas we know today as "Marxism," described the nature of bureacracy as he saw it in Prussia:

The general spirit of bureaucracy is secret, mystery, safeguarded inside itself by hierarchy and outside by its nature as a closed corporation. Thus public political spirit and also political mentality appear to bureaucracy as a betrayal... As far as the individual bureaucrat is concerned, the aim of the state becomes his private aim, in the form of a race for higher posts, of careerism.[4]

These were some of the chief characteristics of the bureaucracy that developed in the Soviet Union. But in the young workers state, where the capitalist class had been politically overthrown and its economic base expropriated, the rising bureaucracy took on the added features of a caste, a non-hereditary aristocracy whose heavy hand bore down on all aspects of political, social, and cultural life. The Soviet bureaucracy grew not only in the government and in industry, but in the Communist Party itself. Two parallel processes took place: careerists, eager to advance themselves, joined the party as a means to private gain; party members, exhausted by long years of struggle, succumbed to the temptation of quiet lives in secure jobs. As the bureaucracy grew, so did the party, and the percentage of dedicated and selfless revolutionists in the party declined. The Bolshevik party had 23,600 members in February 1917, 585,000 in January 1921, more than one million by 1926. *By 1927 an absolute majority of the members of the Russian Communist Party were government officials.*[5]

This bureaucracy was conservative, narrow-minded, and authoritarian. Its primary interest was the preservation of its own privileges, and the limitation of those privileges to the narrowest possible circle. Mighty and small bureaucrats, office holders in the Kremlin and managers in small factories—all were united in a single hierarchy of command and obedience.

This caste proceeded to remake the party and the government in its own image: rigid, hierarchical, secretive, and tyrannical. It had no theory, no vision: what passed for Marxist theory under Stalin's rule would have been ignored by Marx, Engels, and Lenin as beneath consideration. Its method was based on the crudest empiricism: there was no planning, no foresight. Under Stalin's leadership, the Soviet bureaucracy led the country (and the Communist International) through a series of panic-stricken turns, each one brought on by a catastrophe resulting from the previous turn. Thus the policy of major concessions to the peasantry ("Enrich yourselves!" was the slogan of the hour) suddenly gave way to forced collectivization when the peasants used their new wealth to resist Soviet rule. These zig-zags had their complement in foreign policy, as we shall see.

This was not the counterrevolution Lenin had feared, but it was a counterrevolution nonetheless. Although the state remained based on noncapitalist property relations, and such fundamental gains as nationalized property, centralized planning, and the state monopoly of foreign trade remained intact, the bureaucracy effectively disenfranchised the working class and usurped control of the state apparatus. Analyzing the class nature of the Soviet workers state during the late 1930s, Trotsky used an analogy with a trade union: "In the last analysis a workers' state is a trade union which has conquered power."[6] Under the bureaucracy's rule, he pointed out, the Soviet workers state could be likened to a trade union in which corrupt gangsters have seized the leadership; while still a trade union, its policies serve the interests of the bosses, not the workers. In doing so, they undermine the union and, carried far enough, threaten to destroy it.

At the top of the bureaucratic pyramid stood the gangster Stalin, supreme representative of the bureaucratic caste. He rose to that position only after a lengthy process in which he and his faction successively isolated and defeated their revolutionary critics within the Soviet party. That struggle, although largely waged in secret, dominated the politics of the Comintern for more than half a decade, and did not end until the late 1930s in the purges and prison camps. During the mid-1920s, the struggle took shape around key political issues of the day: the thwarted revolution in Germany, the British General Strike, and the defeat of the Second Chinese Revolution of 1925-27.

1923: Turning Point for the Comintern

The leadership of the Soviet Communist Party was the *de facto* leadership of the Communist International. This followed naturally from their prestige as the founders of the world's first workers state. In the Comintern's early years, they exercized their influence with great restraint, working out their differences with other Communists through discussion and education. Within the framework of acceptance of the Comintern's basic policies and willingness to operate under a common discipline in action, a wide variety of revolutionary views could and did coexist within the International.

As the bureaucratic degeneration of the Russian party set in, the Comintern was inevitably affected. The bureaucrats who took over the Russian party also took over the Comintern, and began to use it for their own purposes. In place of discussion and education the International was now led by command. Dissent was stamped out: the International was transformed from an association of revolutionists into an instrument of the foreign policy of the Soviet bureaucracy. The International's primary reason for being— extension of the proletarian revolution—was demoted on the list of priorities. Eventually it no longer appeared on the list at all.

The turning point for the International came in Germany, in 1923.

It would be difficult to overstate the importance of Germany to the Bolshevik leaders. Lenin went so far as to predict the defeat of the Russian revolution if revolution did not come in Germany. The German Communist Party, the largest in the world outside of Russia, had mass support among the German workers, support which grew steadily after 1920 when the largest general strike in world history blocked an attempted military coup, the Kapp putsch. The other major working-class party, the Social Democrats (SPD), were a declining force in the early twenties. To the Bolsheviks, it was clear that a German revolution was not only necessary, it was also possible.

Events moved towards a climax in 1923, as the country entered a period of unprecedented social crisis.[7]

World War I had ended in a defeat for German imperialism. Germany's imperialist rivals, determined to press their advantage, declared Germany guilty of causing the war, and demanded reparations. By early 1923 these forced payments had all but bankrupted the German economy, and the government defaulted on its "debts." France responded by sending its army into the highly industrialized Ruhr Valley, seizing industry and mines.

The German ruling class was incapable of defending the country's sovereignty: it announced a program of passive resistance, which collapsed after a few months. Meanwhile the already shaky German economy was shattered by the invasion. The greatest inflation of modern times impoverished the working class and small farmers and shopkeepers. The Mark, which under normal conditions exchanged at a rate of 20 to 40 for a British Pound, became worthless: in January 1923, at the time of the invasion of the Ruhr, the exchange rate hit 33,500 to 1; by June it was 344,500 to 1; by July 30, 5,000,000 to 1; and on August 31, 47,000,000 to 1.

The German workers responded heroically. In the Ruhr district there were mass strikes against the occupation. In some towns armed workers' militias were established, and workers' committees fought the inflation by fixing prices in the markets.

It was a classic revolutionary situation. The ruling class could not rule; the masses were totally disillusioned with the existing system. This was the best opportunity since 1918 for extending the revolution beyond Russia's borders.

The Comintern leadership, however, virtually ignored the German crisis until mid-summer. The Third Plenum of the Executive Committee of the Comintern (ECCI), held under Zinoviev's chairmanship (it was the first ever held in which Lenin did not play an active role), was silent on the German situation. The German Communist Party (KPD), under the leadership of Heinrich Brandler, floundered aimlessly without a serious policy. Its activity remained routine, as though nothing noteworthy was happening.

In the summer the situation became so severe that no one could ignore it. Brandler was summoned to Moscow and ordered to prepare for an insurrection. But instead of political direction, the

Zinoviev leadership provided only technical recipes: obtain weapons, organize a workers' militia, resist the army. Zinoviev, who in 1917 had denounced the October revolution as premature, was now trying to force an insurrection without any political preparation.

This purely technical approach to insurrection reached its nadir in Saxony, where Brandler joined the left Social-Democratic government, *solely in order to obtain access to arms.* That participating in a Social Democratic government might actually weaken the KPD's position does not seem to have occurred to Brandler or to the Comintern officials who approved the "maneuver." One week after Brandler joined the government, the central government sent 60,000 troops into Saxony to overthrow the Social Democratic-Communist coalition. The Social Democrats refused to organize any resistance, and Brandler followed suit: he called off an insurrection scheduled for the first week in October. The coalition in Saxony collapsed without firing a shot.

There are no permanently revolutionary crises. The opportunities for revolution are fleeting—they must be seized at the flood. Once past, the ruling class can re-establish its authority. A defeat in battle can provide the basis for rebuilding the revolutionary movement; a defeat without battle leads only to demoralization and decay.

Such was the case in Germany. The bourgeoisie re-established itself after October 1923, and the KPD went into decline. The SPD, whose influence had been on the wane, regained its former strength.

A correct policy in the face of defeat might at least have enabled the Communists to minimize their losses. But the Comintern leadership refused even to admit that a defeat had taken place! After taxing Brandler with full responsibility for the ECCI's own errors, and imposing a new leadership from the KPD's ultraleft Fischer-Maslow faction, Zinoviev declared that the October defeat had been only an episode.

In practically the whole of Europe the situation is such that we need expect no period now, no matter how brief, of even an external pacifism, or any kind of lull.... Europe is entering into the stage of decisive events.... Germany is apparently heading towards a violent civil war....[8]

Trotsky, who urged the ECCI to adopt a realistic evaluation of the defeat, was branded a rightist, a defeatist, a pessimist.

The Fifth Congress of the Comintern, in June and July 1924, intensified the error. At the very time when the European political situation was stabilizing, when capitalism had entered a period of growth and relative prosperity, the International proclaimed the imminence of the revolution. Throughout 1924 and early 1925 the Comintern engaged in ultraleft posturing and irresponsible adventures, all with the same objective of making the revolution by bureaucratic-technical means alone, regardless of the attitude of the masses. In Estonia, for example, 227 armed Communists attempted to carry out an insurrection on December 1, 1924. Government buildings were attacked at 5:15 a.m. By 9:00 a.m. this attempted putsch was totally crushed.

At the same time, under the banner of "Bolshevization," the Russian party leadership began the purges of the International which were to characterize the next decade. Every party was required to declare its opposition to "Trotskyism"—those who hesitated were lost.

Socialism in One Country

The defeat of the German workers in 1923 was profoundly demoralizing to the most politically-aware layers of the Soviet working class. The effect was somewhat delayed by the fraudulent optimism of the majority of the CI leadership in 1924, but as the weeks turned into months, it became clear to more and more people that capitalism had won itself another breathing space. Tired and disappointed, the Russian workers turned away from politics.

At the same time, the German defeat strengthened conservative and nationalist attitudes in the bureaucracy. The characteristic bureaucratic desire for peace and quiet expressed itself in a growing opposition to the international activities of the Comintern: the bureaucracy wanted to be left alone by the rest of the world, and to get on with things in Russia.

The ultraleft policies of 1924 can be seen as an attempt to carry out the traditional internationalist policy of Bolshevism by bureaucratic and administrative means. The International was attempting to extend the revolution by administrative *diktat*. Extending the revolution had since 1917 been the main consideration in Bolshevik policy. In his usual pedestrian style, Stalin expressed the theoretical basis for this policy in April 1924:

The overthrow of the power of the bourgeoisie and the establishment of the power of the proletariat in one country alone does not, per se, mean the complete victory of socialism. The chief task, the organization of socialist production, still lies ahead. Can this task be performed, can the final victory of socialism be gained, in one country alone, and without the joint efforts of the proletarians in several of the most advanced countries? No, this is out of the question. The history of the Russian revolution shows that the proletarian strength of one country alone can overthrow the bourgeoisie of that country. But for the final victory of socialism, for the organization of socialist production, the strength of one country (especially a peasant country, such as Russia) does not suffice. For this, the united strength of the proletarians in several of the most advanced countries is needed.[9]

Stalin was reciting by rote here: he had never been a Marxist theoretician of any ability, nor was he familiar with the international workers' movement. His instinctive reactions were nationalist, not internationalist. His policies as Commissar of Nationalities had been marked by gross insensitivity to the smaller national groups within the Soviet Union: although Stalin himself was a Georgian originally, his Russianizing policies prompted Lenin to describe him as "a real and true 'nationalist-socialist', and even a vulgar Great Russian bully."[10]

It is not surprising, then, that Stalin jettisoned the excess baggage of Bolshevik internationalism and emerged as the principal "theoretician" of the bureaucracy's parochial nationalism. A few months after the statement quoted above was published, Stalin made a typically Stalinist "self-criticism" of it:

...two different questions are here confounded in one. First of all there is the question: Can socialism *possibly* be established in one country alone by that country's unaided strength? This question must be answered in the affirmative. Then there is the question: Can a country where the dictatorship of the proletariat has been established, regard itself as *fully safeguarded* against foreign intervention, and the consequent restoration of the old regime, unless the revolution has been victorious in a number of other countries? This question must be answered in the negative.[11]

The traditional Marxist view that socialism by its very nature must be an international system was now reduced to a problem of diplomacy. If the capitalist nations could be prevented from intervening then socialism could be built, even in a poverty-stricken peasant country such as Russia.

"Socialism in One Country" became the official *ideology* of the bureaucracy. It was not, strictly speaking, a theory or even a hypothesis: it was the world-view of the Russian-nationalist officials who wanted an end to international adventures.

"Socialism in One Country" provided a rationale for bureaucratic policy, couched in pseudo-Marxist terms. It also provided a club to use against the party members who remained loyal to the Bolshevik program of world revolution.* They could be accused of lack of faith in the Russian masses.

The adoption of "Socialism in One Country" as the official line of the Soviet party had immediate and profound implications for the International.

1. It implied a major revision in the very concept on which the International was founded, the need for international class struggle as the only path to proletarian emancipation. As Trotsky wrote,

> Marxism has always taught the workers that even their struggle for higher wages and shorter hours cannot be successful unless waged as an international struggle. And now it suddenly appears that the ideal of the socialist society may be achieved with the national forces alone. This is a mortal blow to the International.
>
> The invincible conviction that the fundamental class aim, even more so than the partial objectives, cannot be realized by national means or within national boundaries, constitutes the very heart of revolutionary internationalism.[12]

2. It changed the basic relationship between the USSR and the international working class. For the Bolsheviks the Soviet Union had been a *base* for world revolution, a first conquest to be extended. It was a base they were even prepared to abandon temporarily, if such an action would have brought greater victories elsewhere. For the bureaucracy the USSR was not a base but a *bastion*, a fortress to be defended at all costs. Defense of the USSR was proclaimed as the most important task of the Communist movement. Trotsky said:

> The new doctrine proclaims that socialism can be built on the basis of a national state *if only there is no intervention.* From this there can and must follow...a collaborationist policy towards the foreign bourgeoisie with the object of averting intervention, as this will guarantee the construction of socialism.... The task of the parties in the Comintern assumes, therefore,

---

*After a diligent search, Stalinist "scholars" were able to locate two passages in Lenin's works which, by ignoring the context and twisting the meaning, could be taken as proof that Lenin believed that socialism could be built in one country. Hundreds of passages clearly proclaiming the opposite were ignored.

an auxiliary character; their mission is to protect the U.S.S.R. from intervention and not to fight for the conquest of power.[13]

3. Changing the Communist parties from revolutionary parties into organizations for the support of the short-term needs of Kremlin diplomacy could not be done easily. These parties were led by revolutionists whose record of activity in the class struggle went back to the beginning of the century in many cases. Whatever their weaknesses, they were not about to submit humbly to the bureaucracy's orders, particularly when those orders meant abandoning their revolutionary ideals. The turn to "Socialism in One Country" thus ushered in a wave of intense faction fights in the International, leading to the expulsion of a large percentage of the Comintern's original cadre between 1924 and 1931. The International's membership (not counting the Soviet party) fell from 779,102 in 1922, the last year in which Lenin played any role in the Comintern, to 328,716 in 1931, by which time Stalin's conquest of power was complete.

First Fruits: Britain and China

The implications of "Socialism in One Country" were soon felt in Comintern policy. Early in 1925 Zinoviev's ultraleft policies were jettisoned (Zinoviev soon met the same fate) and a new course, directed at winning alliances with "progressives" in the capitalist states, was begun.

In Britain, which was generally seen as the primary military threat to the USSR, the bureaucracy believed it could see a potential ally in the leadership of the Trades Union Congress (TUC). The TUG leadership, although bitterly hostile to the Communist Party in Britain, had maintained a friendly attitude towards the USSR. The British labor leaders argued that trade with the Soviet Union was a means of improving the economic situation in Britain. (No doubt they also hoped that Moscow's blessings would bolster their standing on the left wing in the British unions.) In 1924 Mikhail Tomsky, president of the Soviet trade union federation, attended the convention of the TUC as a special guest; this was followed by a visit to Russia by a delegation of British union leaders. These visits and consultations led, in the fall of 1925, to the creation of the Anglo-Russian Committee (ARC), composed of representatives of the leaderships of the British and Soviet trade unions.

The aims of the ARC were never very clear to anyone, including its members. The leaders of the General Council of the TUC supported it primarily as a lever to get the Soviet Union into the International Federation of Trade Unions, and thus to destroy the Red International of Labor Unions, which had formed under Moscow's aegis in opposition to the IFTU. In addition, the British leaders saw the ARC as a sop to the increasing militancy of the British union rank and file. The Russians, on the other hand, saw it primarily as a bulwark against war. Stalin held that it should

organise a broad movement of the working class against new imperialist wars in general, and against intervention in our country by (especially) the most powerful of the European powers, by Britain in particular.[14]

No Marxist, certainly not one who accepted Lenin's tactical conceptions, could object to an alliance with the British labor leaders for specific common objectives which advanced the interests of the working class. But the ARC was not that; it was a permanent alliance, maintained by adapting the politics of the International to the ideas of the "lefts" in the TUC leadership. As the historian of the ARC points out, the formation of the ARC produced immediate changes in Communist policy in Britain.

General Council leftists might be chided occasionally, scolded. They might be urged to do much more than they already were. But it was all done with un-Bolshevik gentility and delicacy. Leftists published their views in the Communist press. Leftists and Communists sponsored meetings jointly and appeared on platforms together. So long as that sort of thing continued, the ideological lines between Communism and leftism were bound to become blurred and poorly defined.[15]

The General Council leftists were soon put to the test. British miners were faced with wage cuts, and the TUC was committed to call a general strike if the cuts took place. The TUC leaders did not want to challenge the government. They didn't want a revolution: they didn't even want to upset the status quo. Under their radical rhetoric there was no more than bureaucratic conservatism. While the Tory government was marshalling its forces, the TUC General Council did nothing to prepare for the general strike. Forced by mass sentiment to call the strike (union members voted 3,653,529 to 49,911 in favor) the TUC leadership did everything possible to undermine it, then called it off after only nine days, leaving the miners to face the government alone. The General Strike, the greatest working class mobilization in British history, ended in betrayal and defeat.

The leaders of the betrayal of the 1926 General Strike were the same "lefts" who comprised the Anglo-Russian Committee. A decisive break with them in the wake of the general strike could have substantially aided the left wing in the British labor movement, by making it clear that the TUC's policies were alien to everything Bolshevism stood for.

But the Comintern leadership placed a very low priority on the revolutionary education of the British workers. At the top of their list was "defense of the USSR," understood in strictly bureaucratic and nationalist terms. When Trotsky called for a demonstrative break with the ARC, Stalin replied:

> ...if the reactionary trade unions of Britain are prepared to join with the revolutionary trade unions in our country in a bloc against the counter-revolutionary imperialists of their country, why should we not welcome such a bloc? I stress this aspect of the matter in order that our opposition may at last understand that in trying to torpedo the Anglo-Russian Committee it is playing into the hands of the interventionists.*[16]

The TUC leadership had been unable to stop wage reductions in the face of a determined Tory government. How it would ever find the courage to stop a Tory war was not explained. In fact, when the British government moved towards a strongly anti-Soviet policy in 1927, breaking off diplomatic relations with Moscow in May, the TUC made only a few mild protests. In September the TUC followed the Tory lead, and withdrew from the Anglo-Russian Committee.

Whether or not there were revolutionary possibilities in Britain in 1926 may be debated—but there can be no debate about the non-revolutionary nature of Stalin's policies. The ruling faction had clearly demonstrated its willingness to subordinate the development of the Comintern to the diplomatic needs of the USSR, as perceived by the Kremlin bureaucracy.

IN CHINA SIMILAR POLICIES PRODUCED a truly catastrophic result. In the face of a massive revolutionary uprising, involving millions upon millions of peasants and workers, Comintern policy was

---

*Trotsky replied: "If the 'reactionary trade unions' were capable of conducting a struggle against their own imperialists they would not be reactionary. Stalin is incapable of distinguishing any longer between the conceptions *reactionary* and *revolutionary*."[17]

directed not towards building the revolutionary left but towards supporting the "progressive national bourgeoisie." That elusive class was declared to be synonymous with the country's principal capitalist party, the Kuomintang (KMT) led by Chiang Kai-shek.[18] Comintern "theory" decreed that the coming Chinese revolution was not to be proletarian in character, like Russia's, but "national democratic." The KMT, with Communist support, was to overthrow imperialist domination of China and establish a national capitalist regime that would, it was hoped, maintain friendly relations with the Soviet republic to the north. The entire program and strategy of the Communists in China were to be subordinated to the program and strategy of the KMT.

The Communist Party was ordered to join the KMT, to accept its discipline, to refrain from any criticism of its leadership or policies. Throughout the revolutionary storms of 1925-27 the Chinese Communists had no independent identity: they operated as a wing of the bourgeois nationalist movement. The KMT, in the meantime, was accorded the fullest revolutionary credentials. It was even declared to be a sympathizing party of the International, and its representatives were greeted with high honors at ECCI meetings. The KMT's anti-working class policies were never mentioned, even when it gunned down strikers and land-hungry peasants. The Communists in China were instructed to restrain the workers and peasants, in order to maintain the alliance with the KMT.

In March 1927, Chiang's armies scored their greatest victory by capturing Shanghai—a victory made possible by a city-wide general strike led by Communists. The Shanghai Communists welcomed Chiang to the city with banners hailing the KMT and Chiang himself as saviors.

Having established *de facto* control of the country, Chiang, who since early 1926 had been an "honorary member" of the Presidium of the Comintern's Executive Committee, turned on his loyal Communist supporters. On April 12 his troops began arresting Communist leaders, murdering many of them in the streets. According to the most conservative estimates, about 100,000 people were killed in the following months. Chinese Communism was all but annihilated: party membership was down to 4,000 by the end of 1927 from 60,000 early the same year.

The Communists and their supporters were completely unprepared for this onslaught. They had been taught that Chiang and the KMT were the natural leaders of the Chinese revolution; they had been ordered to submit to the KMT's political and military discipline.* In many areas they put up heroic resistance, but they went down to defeat.

As Isaac Deutscher has written, the "hidden implications" of socialism in one country "were brought out and written in blood on the pavements of Shanghai."[19]

"Socialism in One Country" meant in practice no socialism in any other countries: defense of the USSR was the central task, no matter what the cost. In the end this policy was self-defeating. It weakened British labor, it all but destroyed Chinese Communism, and it severely undermined defense of the USSR. By the end of 1927 the Soviet republic was more isolated than at any time since the end of the Civil War.

Left Turn

Stalin's preferred method for preventing war was diplomacy supplemented by alliances with "progressives" wherever they might be found. But if the "progressives" persisted in their blindness, he had another arrow for his bow.

There can scarcely be any doubt that war against the Soviet Union will mean for imperialism that it will have to wage war against its own workers and colonies. Needless to say, if our country is attacked we shall not sit with folded arms; we shall take all measures to unleash the revolutionary lion in all countries of the world. The leaders of the capitalist countries cannot but know that we have some experience in this matter.[20]

This was both a promise and a threat. Those capitalist governments that agreed not to attack the USSR, that signed treaties with Stalin or allied themselves with him against others, were implicitly promised that they would not face the "revolutionary lion." This in fact was Soviet policy during World War II, when the Kremlin and its subordinate parties did their utmost to prevent any social unrest in the countries allied with the USSR against Germany. The threat—of revolutionary uprisings in countries

---

*The leadership of the Chinese party were strongly opposed to the CI's policies, and submitted only under the threat of disciplinary measures. After the catastrophe, these same leaders were then blamed for the defeat, and expelled. The party's founder and chairman, Ch'en Tu-hsiu, and its principal theoretician, Peng Shu-tse, were among those expelled: they subsequently became Trotskyists. Ch'en died in 1942; Peng, in exile from his homeland, remains a prominent figure in the Trotskyist Fourth International to this day.

which did not fall in with the Kremlin's diplomatic goals—was held in abeyance from 1925 until the middle of 1927. Then, with typical bureaucratic arrogance, the Comintern ordered the Communists of Britain and China to reverse field. This order was given without the slightest regard for the needs of the revolutionary movement in those countries.

Since 1921 the Communist Party of Great Britain (CPGB) had given critical support to the British Labour Party as a means of winning a hearing from the party's rank and file. In 1925-1927 this policy became uncritical adaptation to the policies of the Labour "left." Now, after the defeat of the strike, with the labor movement in decline, a sensitive approach to the mass party of British labor was needed more than ever. Instead, on October 1, 1927, the CI sent a telegram to the CPGB, ordering it to

struggle against the bourgeois leadership of the Labour Party, to strengthen and prepare itself against parliamentary cretinism in all forms, to go into the forthcoming elections as an independent party with its own platform and its own candidates, even in those cases when so-called official candidates of the Labour Party will be put up against the candidates of the Communist Party.[21]

This was to lead rapidly to all-out opposition to the Labour Party (and Social Democracy everywhere) as "social-fascist."

A similar reversal took place in China, again with more catastrophic results for Chinese communism. After the Shanghai massacre, the Communists briefly entered into an alliance with a dissident Kuomintang group in the city of Hankow.* The Executive Committee of the Comintern declared:

The Hankow government, being the government of the Left Kuomintang, is not yet the dictatorship of the proletariat and the peasantry, but is on the road to it and will inevitably, in the course of the victorious class struggle of the proletariat and in discarding its radical bourgeois camp followers, develop in the direction of such dictatorship.[22]

On July 15 this organization, which was "inevitably" becoming a dictatorship of the workers and peasants, expelled the Communist Party and rejoined Chiang Kai-shek.

Until this point the Comintern had resisted any move towards

---

*Hankow was part of a three-city aggregation called "Wuhan." The dissident group was thus sometimes referred to as the Wuhan Kuomintang.

independent action by the Chinese workers and peasants against capitalism. Now, without any political or military preparation, the Chinese Communists were ordered to carry out insurrections. The Communist Party, already battered by Chiang's coup, was beaten to the ground. The climax of this insane adventure came in Canton: on December 11, 1927, a date chosen to coincide with a meeting of the Soviet CP in Moscow, the Communists seized power and formed a "soviet government," in which the masses of Canton workers played little or no part. The Canton Commune lasted three days: when the Kuomintong's avenging executioners were finished, 5,700 people were dead.

OVER THE NEXT TWO YEARS, the sudden left turn that had been carried out in China and Britain was extended to every part of the world. Comintern theoreticians announced that a "Third Period" in postwar capitalist development had begun. The "first period" was the world-wide revolutionary upsurge of 1918-1923. The "second period" was one of capitalist stabilization, between 1924 and 1927—the ultraleft adventures of 1924 were conveniently ignored in this schema. The Third Period was declared to be one of capitalist crisis and revolutionary uprisings. One of Stalin's henchmen, Molotov, declared that there would be no fourth period, because capitalism would be destroyed during the third.

Most historians explain the Third Period simply as an international extension of Stalin's domestic policy, since it occurred at the same time as the forced collectivization of agriculture, the "liquidation of the kulaks" and the drive to create an industrialized economy at an impossibly rapid pace. However, the international left turn began in 1927, while the domestic turn began in 1928. In fact both sets of policies stemmed from a single source: the bureaucracy's commitment to national autarky under the label "socialism in one country," and its need to use the Comintern as an agency of that policy. Since Stalin's non-Communist allies had failed him, he was now "unleashing the revolutionary lion" to block imperialist intervention. This bureaucratic approach to the workers' movement, which views it as something to be "unleashed" on demand, is characteristic of Stalinism. So too is the view that the primary function of the "revolutionary lion," and the only reason for unleashing it, is defense of the USSR.

To those familiar with the "peaceful coexistence" line of the Communist parties of today, the policies of the Third Period may seem completely alien. The crudest sectarianism became the order of the day. All the strategic and tactical lessons of Lenin's time were abandoned. No alliances with other working class organizations were permitted. "Social democracy is the main channel of imperialist pacifism," Stalin wrote. Therefore the most important task of the Communist parties was "to wage an unceasing struggle against Social-Democratism in all spheres. . . . [23]

Communist parties attacked and broke up Social Democratic meetings, and denounced the entire non-Stalinist left as the main enemy. "Red Unions" were created as rivals to the existing labor organizations. Everyone who disagreed was labelled a fascist.

. . . in the nightmarish hysteria that characterized the Comintern in this period, every strike became a revolt, every demonstration a near-insurrection. The presidential vote for [Democratic candidate] Mr. Alfred E. Smith became a sign of the "mass radicalization" of the American workers, the Hoover regime was already Fascist, so was the Brüning government in Germany, so was every other government. . . . There were no more social democrats, but only "social-Fascists." Anarchists became "anarcho-Fascists" (to say nothing of the more treacherous variety of "Left syndical-Fascists who use radical phrases to hide their Right deeds"). Even ordinary "counter-revolutionary Trotskyists" became "Trotskyo-Fascists" or, as the German Stalinist, Heckert, called them, "social-Hitlerites." [24]

If such policies were not abandoned, catastrophe was inevitable— and the inevitable happened, in Germany, in 1933.

As Hitler's real fascists gathered strength, the German Communist Party (KPD) directed all of its hostility at the "social-fascists," the Social-Democratic Party (SPD). Together the KPD and the SPD had the support of over 40 percent of the German electorate: together they could have stopped Hitler. But they refused to cooperate: the reformist timidity of the SPD and the ultraleft sectarianism of the KPD left the German workers disunited and powerless. The Communist Party went so far in its hostility to the Social Democrats as to support a Nazi-sponsored referendum for the removal of the Social-Democratic government in Prussia in 1931.

Leon Trotsky, in exile in Turkey, campaigned tirelessly against this insanity, for a united front of the KPD and the SPD to stop the Nazis. Ernst Thaelmann, leader of the German Communists and a member of the Executive Committee of the Communist International, replied:

In his pamphlet on how National Socialism [Nazism] is to be defeated,

Trotsky gives one answer only, and it is this: the German Communist Party must join hands with the Social Democratic Party.... This, according to Trotsky, is the only way in which the German working class can save itself from fascism. Either, says he, the Communist Party makes common cause with the Social Democrats, or the German working class is lost for ten or twenty years. This is the theory of an utter bankrupt Fascist and counter-revolutionary. This is indeed the worst, the most dangerous, the most criminal theory that Trotsky has constructed.[25]

The Communists did refuse to make common cause with the SPD, and the German working class was indeed "lost for ten or twenty years." The world is still paying for the defeat of March 1933, when Hitler triumphed over the best organized working-class movement in the world without firing a shot, without even a scuffle in the street.

It has long been fashionable to contrast Stalin's "realism" to Trotsky's "revolutionary romanticism." As so often in politics, fashion ignores facts: Stalin's "realism" invariably produced catastrophes. His policies did not even produce the peace and quiet the bureaucracy sought. The alliance with Chiang Kai-shek produced an anti-Communist regime to the east. The Third Period produced an anti-Communist regime to the west. Each of the policies Stalin initiated to prevent intervention made intervention more likely. And after each defeat there was no analysis, no balance sheet, no rethinking. Each defeat was followed by a wild swing to the opposite political pole. The ultraleftism of 1924 gave way to the opportunism of 1925-27. The right-wing policies of that period gave way to an ultraleft binge which made 1924 pale in comparison. Still later the defeats of the Third Period would lead to a right turn far beyond anything considered in 1925.

9. The Communist Party in Transition, 1923-1929

Because Jack MacDonald and Maurice Spector later became Trotskyists, writers sympathetic to Trotsky's views have sometimes viewed the CPC as untainted by Stalinism until the expulsion of Spector in 1928. Maurice Spector in particular has been presented as an independent thinker who resisted the Stalinist onslaught and reached conclusions similar to Trotsky's by his own efforts.* This opinion finds its parallel in the writings of Trotsky's foremost Canadian opponent, Tim Buck, who claimed that Spector was a Trotskyist from the earliest days of the CPC and had joined the international Trotskyist movement in 1923.

Tempting as such a view of Spector and the Canadian party may be, to supporters and opponents of Trotsky alike, it has no foundation in fact. Under the leadership of Spector and MacDonald, the Communist Party of Canada accepted and endorsed almost every important shift in Comintern policy in the years following Lenin's final stroke. (The one major exception to this will be discussed in detail in the next chapter.)

China and Britain

The CPC's faithful adherence to the Comintern line can be seen quite clearly in the *Worker*'s coverage of events in China in 1925-27. Not only did the party fully endorse the International's support of the Kuomintang, it attempted to establish similar ties with the

---

*See, for example, Gary O'Brien's M.A. thesis, "Maurice Spector and the Origin of Canadian Trotskyism," and his article, "Maurice Spector, pioneer Canadian socialist, on the national question," *Forward*, November 1974.

KMT in the Chinese community in Canada. Joint meetings with the KMT were held across Canada: the February 26, 1927 *Worker*, for example, reported with considerable satisfaction that CP leader Beckie Buhay had been guest of honor at a Kuomintang banquet in Toronto.

In the pages of the *Worker* one can follow the entire debacle of Comintern policy in China, through Stalin-tinted lenses. On March 19, 1927 a headline read "Kuomintang Armies Approach Final Victory." An April 2 article reported "The Capture of Shanghai," with a box headed "Internal Strife in Kuomintang is Denied." On April 16 the paper again hailed the KMT's capture of Shanghai: while Canadian workers were reading that report, Chiang was slaughtering the Communists who had welcomed him into Shanghai with banners reading "Hail the National Revolutionary Army! Welcome to Chiang Kai-shek!" The May 14 *Worker* denounced Chiang as a traitor.

Following the Shanghai massacre, the Chinese Communists, on Comintern instructions, attempted to salvage their political line by forming an alliance with the Wuhan KMT. The alliance was shattered within two months, when the Wuhan KMT denounced communism and rejoined Chiang. The Canadian CP dutifully followed these zigzags. Its convention in June endorsed the Wuhan Kuomintang "as the only truly National government carrying out the testament of Dr. Sun Yat Sen."[1]

One week after this resolution was printed the *Worker* revealed that the alliance with the Wuhan KMT had been broken.

The Canadian party also fully endorsed the International's British policy—the formation of the Anglo-Russian Committee and the associated campaign for "international trade union unity" as a means of preventing war. A.A. Purcell, the most prominent of the "lefts" in the ARC, received front page headlines in the *Worker* when he spoke at the American Federation of Labor convention in November 1924. When Purcell spoke in Toronto after the AFL convention, the *Worker* published a totally uncritical, exceptionally laudatory article about him, signed "S"—probably Spector.

The *Worker* followed the general Comintern policy of reporting the British general strike of 1926 as though a revolution was imminent—"Class War in Great Britain," read one headline— while remaining silent about the treacherous policies of the British members of the Anglo-Russian Committee. When the strike was defeated, the rightwing of the British Trades Union Congress was condemned, but not "lefts" such as Purcell.

The Canadian Communist Party's acceptance of Comintern policy did not stop with support of the CI line on international issues. The party also conscientiously applied that line to Canadian conditions: every shift in CI policy had its Canadian expression.

In 1923, when Soviet internal policy was increasingly conciliatory to the peasantry, the Comintern leadership suddenly became enamored with a wide variety of peasant movements. Although in many cases the programs of these organizations and the ideology of their leaders remained mired in petty-bourgeois and national-democratic illusions, and many were openly hostile to the proletarian movements in their own countries, they were portrayed as valuable international allies for the Soviet government. The Comintern assembled a mixed bag of delegates and created a Peasants International (Krestintern) which did not last long past its founding congress. Communist parties around the world were instructed to form alliances with peasant organizations: in the United States this led to the creation of a "Farmer-Labor Party," which collapsed a few months after its formation. In Canada, Maurice Spector proposed that the Communists should implement this policy by converting the Canadian Labor Party into a Farmer-Labor Party. This remained a staple of CPC policy through 1924, until the International reversed itself and the Canadians followed suit.*

Canadian Independence

During the ultraleft turn of 1924 the *Worker* was suddenly filled with flamboyant "anti-imperialism" with almost no real political

---

*Trotsky opposed the call for Farmer-Labor parties as an abandonment of the principle of independent working-class political action, an attempt to merge two classes with divergent interests. The plan in general he called a "reactionary idea" and the attempt to form such a party in the United States a "senseless and infamous adventure." The problem with the Comintern's schemas, he argued, was not the concept of an alliance of the workers with the working farmers—that had always been a central axis of the Bolshevik program and the Comintern's policy—but the illusory view that such an alliance would be formed on the basis of an independent farmers' or peasants' program. "The *task* of a long and stubborn struggle of the proletarian vanguard against the bourgeoisie and pseudo-peasant demagoguery for influence over the most disinherited strata of the peasant poor was being more and more displaced by the *hope* that the peasantry would play a direct and an independent revolutionary role on a national as well as on an international scale."[2]

content. The *Worker* proclaimed the Communists' intention to combat "a triple master class" composed of "home grown exploiters...British imperialism...and Wall Street imperialism."[3] These articles, assembled for "Anti-Imperialist-War Week" had a great many such phrases in them, but when the phrases are cleared away, there is no strategy, no concrete proposal or plan of action—nothing but phrases.

These, however, were minor shifts in policy compared to the swing to the right that took place in 1925. Parallel to the International's adoption of alliances with the "progressive national bourgeoisie" in the colonies (especially China), the Canadian party made the somewhat belated and improbable discovery that Canada was still a colony of Great Britain, that a fight for Canadian self-determination was in order, and that the progressive national bourgeoisie was represented by... the Liberal Party led by Mackenzie King! In 1924 the CP had denounced the efforts of these "home grown exploiters" to negotiate a new relationship with Britain as attempts to gain a share in the exploitation of Britain's Asian and African colonies. The first trial balloon for a new policy was released by Tim Buck in the March 21, 1925 *Worker*:

Politically...Canada is still a colony, still a part of the Empire upon which the sun never sets....

...the winning of complete independence from British political control means a great deal to the revolutionary movement of Canada and to the labor movement as a whole. In substance, it means the repeal of the British North America Act. It will strip the capitalist government of their everlasting excuse of powerlessness, and bring the workers of the country face to face with realities.

Buck admitted that "so far as the average worker is concerned, this struggle for political control has little more than a sentimental appeal," but insisted that Communists could not take such a view. The capitalists headed by Mackenzie King were conducting a fight for self-determination, and "In their fight for complete independence from Downing Street, the Communists of Canada will help them with all their might." He expected that a parting of the ways would occur after the achievement of independence. For the capitalists independence would only be a step towards incorporation into the U.S. empire, while "To us the Communists, it is a step towards a Workers' and Farmers' Republic."

Norman Penner has commented that this article was "written outside the usual Communist frame of reference."[4] If anything, that understates the case. Not only did it contain nothing even resembling a Marxist analysis of Canada's supposed colonial status (it borrowed all of its arguments from the Liberal theorist J.S. Ewart), but the conclusions it reached broke sharply with Leninism. One of the most important additions to Marxist theory made by Lenin was the theory of Imperialism: the analysis of capitalism in the era of monopoly capital. Fundamental to this analysis is a sharp distinction between the colonial and semi-colonial countries on one hand, and the imperialist countries on the other. The former have still to achieve many of the gains won by the latter in the great bourgeois-democratic revolutions of the seventeenth, eighteenth, and nineteenth centuries: in the colonies and semicolonies, nationalist movements, even under capitalist leadership, can and do play progressive roles. In the imperialist countries, by contrast, nationalist movements of the dominant nations and nationalities are reactionary, diverting the attention of the working class from its enemies at home to some imaginary foreign foe.

The Comintern had explicitly characterized Canada as an imperialist power in several major resolutions and statements, and Communist Party policy in Canada had been consistent with this: it had never, prior to 1925, suggested that the Canadian capitalist class could play a progressive social role. In 1922 the party had placed the choice between "Capitalist State and Workers Republic" at the center of its program. By this it meant that the struggle for state independence had long ago been won in Canada. Notwithstanding a few remaining vestiges of colonial rule—legal and constitutional appeals to the Judicial Committee of the Privy Council in Britain were not abolished until 1949, for example—the Canadian capitalist class held all the effective reins of power in its own hands. Where Ottawa's policies coincided with those of Westminister, as they often did, it was not because of the latter's compulsion but because Canada's rulers were so inclined, through a host of common and interlocking business, financial—class—interests.

Buck's article, in stating the contrary, marked a major turn in party policy. It added an intermediate stage involving the winning of independence under capitalist rule as a necessary step toward socialism.

The party's handling of the new line showed recognition that it involved a major shift. Buck's article was published in March 1925. The *Worker* then fell totally silent on the question until July. In the meantime, William Moriarty travelled to Moscow as a delegate to the Fifth Plenum of the Executive Committee of the Communist International. He returned with the ECCI's full approval for the turn: "the CPC should understand that the question of Canadian independence is the central question of the entire political strategy of our Party," the ECCI wrote.[5]

With the ECCI's approval, "Canadian independence" became the focus of all of the party's propaganda.* An editorial in the *Worker* expressed the issue as the CP then saw it:

The growth of the movement for Canadian independence implies a demand for the abolition of the British North America Act and the subsequent calling of a Constituent Assembly to form a new Canadian constitution.

The Communist Party, while taking an active part in the move for Canadian independence, has no illusions. An exclusive class of Canadian capitalists will exploit the workers just as much as the British and American, but the disintegration of the British Empire will be hastened, and another step towards a Workers and Farmers Republic in Canada ascended.[6]

Canadian independence under capitalist rule was thus to be an intermediate step between Canada's existing colonial status and the socialist revolution. This was to be the "central question of the entire strategy" of the Canadian Communists for the rest of the decade. During the constitutional crisis of 1926, for example, when Governor-General Byng refused to call a general election on the demand of Prime Minister King, the *Worker* said that this proved that Canada was a colony ("a second Egypt") under Byng's dictatorship. When an election was called, Tim Buck wrote:

The issue that should overshadow all others in the forthcoming election, is the one created by Byng: is Canada to slip back to the position of Egypt, or are we to throw the British North America Act overboard? Is Canada to become really self-governing, or is it to remain the stamping ground of jobless underlings of British aristocracy?[7]

---

*It is noteworthy that for all of its new-found concern with national independence, the CPC did not pay any attention to the problem of national oppression in Quebec, which did clearly correspond to Lenin's definition of an oppressed nation.

After the election the *Worker* concluded that the victory of Mackenzie King and the Liberals constituted "a stunning blow to the interests of British imperialism."[8]

It is impossible to read Spector's articles on this subject and believe that when he wrote them he was a supporter of Trotsky in the Russian party disputes. Trotsky had opposed subordination to the national bourgeoisie in China, a country which was clearly an oppressed, semicolonial power. He would scarcely have endorsed it in an imperialist country, even a lesser imperialist country such as Canada. It is also worth noting that the Trotskyist organization Spector formed in 1929 did not include "Canadian independence" in its program, and that when Jack MacDonald joined Spector in 1932, he listed "the fight against the British monarchy, demand for constituent assembly . . . national independence, etc etc" as examples of slogans imposed on the CPC by Trotsky's opponents.[9]

The idea that Mackenzie King and the Liberal Party represented the progressive national bourgeoisie fighting for independence suffered a death blow in 1927, when King followed Britain's lead and broke off diplomatic relations with the USSR. A special statement by the CPC leadership expressed "the deepest disappointment" with King's action, and concluded that "this country is still at the mercy of whatever the British Foreign Office decides." The same article warned that the break increased "the danger of another world war."[10]

The "war danger" was now raised in every issue of the Communist paper, as in similar publications around the world. During September of that year, Stalin, reacting to the setbacks his policies had experienced in Britain and China, announced that "the idea of the threat of war, the idea of the need to combat the war danger . . . is now the main question of the day all over Europe."[11]

And not only in Europe. Moscow was quick to instruct the Canadian party to adapt the Canadian independence line to the new situation. The party had sent Young Communist League secretary Stewart Smith to the badly misnamed "Lenin School" which the Comintern had established in Moscow. The school became the conduit through which the latest changes in line were transmitted from the Kremlin to Toronto. Articles and documents by Lenin School students were recognized as having a special status, reflecting the policies of the International leadership.

The first such article from Smith appeared in the September 17, 1927 *Worker*. It was entitled "The Danger of War and the Struggle for Real Canadian Independence." The alliance with the progressive national bourgeoisie was dropped for Canada, as it had been for China. Now the independence struggle would serve a new end: "The struggle against war is synonymous with the struggle for Canadian independence."

It was left for the Canadians to flesh out the new line. The January and February 1928 issues of the party's new *Canadian Labor Monthly* featured a long article by Spector on "Canada, the Empire and the War Danger." According to his analysis, the rulers of Canada had "gone as far in their demands for 'national status' as they desired and dared." The Imperial Conference of 1926 had produced a new relationship in which the Canadian capitalists were "partners" to the British. "They will take all the share they can get in the exploitation of the colored colonies, but they will continue to protect their industries against both Great Britain and the United States." Canda's rulers had given their full support to "the main lines of British foreign and military policy."

Since Britain was the main power threatening aggressive action against the USSR, "the fight of the workers and farmers of Canada against the imperialist war danger must therefore be aimed against the Canadian bourgeoisie as joint partner of British imperialism." It was important, however, to "oppose American imperialism no less than the British."

We must link up the struggle against the war danger with the struggle against the capitalist government of this country and fight to obtain the real independence of Canada in a Workers and Farmers Republic allied with the workers of the United States and Great Britain.

Spector's article totally abandoned the argument, made in 1925, that the Canadian capitalist class had some objective interest in struggling for state independence from Britain. It returned, for all practical purposes, to the "triple master class" conception of 1924. Now the main obstacle to Canada's independence was the "home-grown exploiters," who were collaborating cheek by jowl with the imperialists of London and Wall Street. However, if Canada's ruling class was now sufficiently independent to be viewed as a "joint partner" with British imperialism, then why should the Canadian Communists be demanding state independence?

The contradiction was not only Spector's, but the Comintern's.

The Canadian party, like the International, was straddling two periods in the evolution of Stalinism. The defeats in Britain and China destroyed the premises for the right-wing policies then in effect, but the all-out turn to Third Period ultraleftism did not take place until the spring of 1929. The Canadian Communists had to live in that limbo for almost two years.

National Unions

A parallel change took place in the Communist Party's trade union policy, beginning in 1925. From the founding of the Workers Party in 1922, the CPC had followed an orthodox Leninist policy towards the unions, working to build a left wing on a class struggle program, in the form of the Trade Union Educational League (TUEL), an organization that united militant unionists in Canada and the United States. In the Workers Party's opinion, "the fate of the Canadian left wing is entirely bound up with that of the United States. National autonomy is an illusion; international unity the need." The TUEL fought for amalgamation of the craft unions into industrial unions, for union support to the Labor Party, and for support to the Red International of Labor Unions. Its purpose was to unite rank and file unionists "fighting for militant leadership, as against the passive and reformist bureaucracy."[12]

In 1924 the CPC changed its stand on Canadian autonomy on the purely practical grounds that autonomy in its internal affairs would enable the Trades and Labor Congress to provide more effective leadership:

Power to initiate action and to extend and lead the class struggle within the confines of Canada, as well as to levy assessments for the assistance of affiliated organizations on strike, would make the Trades Congress a real centre for Canadian unionism and by rallying our small locals for united struggles, would completely change the face of the Canadian trade union movement.

To this end, we must fight for autonomy. Through a systematic campaign among the rank and file we must strive to bring about the organization of all Canadian locals of each international into Canadian departments, each of which must have full freedom of action on both economic and political issues.[13]

This was not a nationalist position. The resolution insisted that "autonomy does not mean a cleavage between the movement of Canada and that of the United States." Autonomy was proposed as a means of maintaining a single North American union movement, while recognizing that the class struggle moved at a different pace in each country. An editorial in the May 17, 1924 *Worker* was very explicit on this point:

> The Canadian "ends" of the Internationals must be given complete economic and political autonomy in Canadian affairs. We have our "own" injunctions, laws, thugs and troops to cope with.... The movement for Canadian autonomy is a movement within the International unions. It starts out from the premise that national secession is bad. But the A.F. of L. must recognize that Canada is no mere state of the American Union whose workers form a State Federation.... The trade unions in this country recognize the importance of international affiliation. But they can no longer be held in tutelage.

This position was radically changed when "Canadian independence" was adopted as the central question of Communist strategy. In 1926, at a plenum of the Comintern's Executive Committee, Tim Buck and Matthew Popowich described the American Federation of Labor as a tool of U.S. imperialism and insisted that "the autonomy movement was visualized as the transitional organizational steps to complete independence." They reported to the party's convention in June 1927 that "our policy regarding Canadian independence and a Canadian independent trade union movement was finally agreed upon and approved unanimously."[14]

This shift from "autonomy" to "independence" was part of a larger turn in the party's trade union work, reflecting the International's turn towards alliances with "progressives" in the labor bureaucracy—the policy of the Anglo-Russian Committee. The steady decline of the Canadian labor movement in the 1920s predisposed the Canadian Communists to accept this policy, which promised results without the often thankless task of rank and file organizing. Under the label "international trade union unity" (which meant unity with the Soviet trade unions) the International was abandoning its traditional trade union policies, and the Canadian party was faithfully following suit.

Late in 1925, Spector reported to the *Worker*'s readers that the recent convention of the Canadian Brotherhood of Railroad Employees "went on record for international trade union unity along the lines proposed by the British and Russian trade union movements." The convention of the CBRE, Spector concluded, "was one of the most encouraging in its history."[15]

The CBRE, led by A.R. Mosher, was an independent Canadian

union excluded from the Trades and Labor Congress because of jurisdictional disputes. Mosher himself was a Canadian nationalist and a social democrat, whose views were certainly to the left of those of the majority of Canadian labor leaders. He later became a founder of the CCF.

In 1925 Mosher apparently decided to extend his influence beyond the CBRE by uniting all non-TLC unions into a rival federation. His willingness to include all non-TLC groups, including unions led by the Communists, made his project attractive to the CPC at the time of the "international unity" drive; his Canadian nationalism corresponded to the party's recent programmatic shift.

The full story of the negotiations in 1926 between the Communist Party and Mosher remains to be told: what is known is that in November 1926 a meeting in Toronto issued a call for a convention to unite all the independent unions. Participating in the meeting were Mosher's CBRE, the Mine Workers and Lumber Workers unions in which the CP had considerable influence, and a number of small organizations such as the Canadian Federation of Labor, which was a remnant of the once-powerful Knights of Labor. In March 1927 the same groups and several others (including what was left of the One Big Union) met in Montreal to form the All-Canadian Confederation of Labor (ACCL).

The nature of the ACCL is perhaps best illustrated by the preamble to its constitution, which announced that the new organization was convinced that

(a) the Canadian labor movement must be freed from the reactionary influence of United States-controlled unions;

(b) Canadian workers require a new organization through which they may collectively promote their general welfare and raise their economic and social standard;

(c) while the workers, under the present system cannot obtain the full value of their labour, it is nevertheless necessary to strive at all times to procure higher real wages and better conditions of labour;

(d) it is necessary to promote among the workers a thorough understanding of working-class economics;

Therefore, be it resolved that a central body composed of the national and independent unions of Canada be here established to give collective expression to these aims and objects.[16]

The Communist Party's support for this mildly radical and thoroughly nationalist organization involved a considerable degree of self-deception. The party's official policy was that the ACCL should work for unity with the TLC, and organize industrial unions. After the founding convention, Tim Buck had to report that neither policy was accepted:

It is regrettable that the Montreal convention failed to make a gesture of unity in the direction of the Congress, or to make the unity of the whole movement through amalgamation of the two centres part of their objective. It was in such questions of principle as this and the question of industrial unionism, that the weakest side of the convention was shown.[17]

Nevertheless, in Buck's estimation the founding of the ACCL "was objectively a step toward National [trade union] unity."

In fact it was nothing of the kind. The *Worker* that summer and fall carried a series of articles and letters by Tim Buck, Jack MacDonald, and A.R. Mosher which exposed the ACCL's real character for anyone who wanted to see. The Communist spokesmen tried gently to persuade Mosher that unity of all the unions would be a positive step. Mosher was having none of it. His attitude towards the TLC was purely nationalist and secessionist: he wanted to destroy it. Why should anyone bother with the old unions when better were available, Mosher asked.

Reactionary elements not only oppose cooperative action with non-A.F. of L. unions, but have left-wingers thrown out whenever possible. I believe that the latter should wake up to the fact that they are bucking a stone wall, immovable and unprogressive, and should give themselves wholeheartedly to the building up of national unions and federations.[18]

As for Buck's call for amalgamation of all unions in a single trade union federation, Mosher ridiculed the idea:

Brother Buck...wishes to amalgamate all unions, irrespective of any vitally distinctive difference which there may be in their principles or policy.... [The ACCL Executive] cannot so blithely propose the amalgamation of the All-Canadian Congress with the Trades and Labour Congress of Canada any more than they would hope to break a natural law by an effort to make a permanent mixture of oil and water.[19]

Trade union unity, in Mosher's view, could only come about through the destruction of the TLC:

Reactionary craft union leaders will disappear like snow before a midsummer sun, when contributions in fees and dues cease flowing in their direction For the workers to continue to pay into organizations which are not only useless, but harmful, is like feeding fuel to the flame we wish to extinguish.[20]

In 1923, summing up its first year of experience in the trade union movement and identifying problems in that work, the Workers Party had identified one trend as "the greatest danger of all." That was "lining up with centrists, twisters, fakirs and all who pay lip service to revolutionary ideals and progressive trade unionism." To guard against such dangers, the party urged its trade union militants to make it "impossible for any man to align himself with you without declaring himself definitely for a programme at least as advanced as that of the T.U.E.L."[21] If ever a unionist fitted the description given in the 1923 resolution it was A.R. Mosher. For all his protestations of progressive intent, his actions and words revealed him as just another self-interested bureaucrat. The program of the TUEL would have required him to stand for trade union unity, the most important "question of principle" cited by Buck. But Mosher did no such thing.

Still the CP did not break its declared alliance with Mosher and the rest of the ACCL leadership—it did not even make more than token criticisms of his policies. The ACCL met the same criteria as the Anglo-Russian Committee: it allowed Communists to work in a single organization with social-democratic union leaders, for unspecified goals. To achieve such an arrangement the Comintern was quite ready to abandon the principles it had once defended.

For the Comintern in 1925-1927, the "unity" achieved between Soviet and British union leaders in the Anglo-Russian Committee was a substitute for building a mass international left wing in the labor movement. The Red International of Labor Unions was put on ice: during the lifetime of the ARC it neither met nor issued any significant policy statements. The Communist Party of Canada followed the same policy towards the ACCL. The Trade Union Educational League all but vanished when the ACCL was formed: its magazine *Left Wing* ceased publication in 1927. In October 1928 Tim Buck, the purported leader of the TUEL, admitted that the "TUEL is virtually non-existent as a leading and an organizing centre."[22]

Ironically, the CPC's success in the All-Canadian Confederation of Labor coincided with the beginning of a turn away from the unity line by the International. The left social democrats who were idolized from 1925 until the fall of 1927 became the main enemy. In place of "unity" the International was soon to urge the creation of Communist-led "Red Unions."

The Labor Party

Finally, the 1925 right turn had a notable impact on the Canadian CP's policy towards the Canadian Labor Party.

The CLP, as we saw in chapter 6, was a product of the postwar labor upsurge. It united a wide variety of working class organizations, including, after 1922, the Communists. The CPC saw it as "the instrument for establishing a common front on all the vital issues of the labor movement."[23]

Until about 1924, this was indeed a correct description of the CLP. In it all the currents in the labor left met to work out a common approach toward political problems. It ensured that working-class candidates did not oppose one another for office and supported a commonly accepted minimum program.

The sharp decline that hit the labor movement in the 1920s inevitably affected the CLP. The Trades and Labor Congress pulled back from the mildly radical positions it had adopted, and returned to its traditional policy of depending on Liberals and Conservatives for legislative support. In 1926 Trades and Labor Congress president Tom Moore told a meeting of the Empire Club in Toronto that "the Labor Political Party is in no way representative of organized labor in Canada."[24] Many unions dropped their affiliation: by 1926 the organizations affiliated to the CLP had a combined membership of only 9,000 workers. As one historian has noted, "there was little doubt that by 1927 the organized labor movement had washed its hands of the party."*[25]

By 1926 the Communists were an absolute majority of the active membership of the CLP. At the convention of the Ontario section of the CLP that year, seven of the ten executive members elected were Communists. The only serious allies the CPC had in the party were the group of social democrats around James Simpson. To maintain its alliance with Simpson the Communists refrained from any but the mildest criticism of him, in spite of the fact that his

---

*The party also collapsed electorally. In the 1923 Ontario elections there were twenty-one Labor candidates, of whom four were elected. In 1926 there were only three candidates, and none was elected.

strong pro-British views directly contradicted the "Independence" policy of the CP.

It was Simpson who finally made the break in October 1927, by introducing an amendment to the constitution of the Toronto Trades and Labor Council to bar all ACCL supporters from membership. Adoption of the amendment resulted in the removal of Jack MacDonald and Tim Buck from the council. The Communists retaliated by using their majority in the CLP to remove Simpson's name from the slate of CLP nominees in the Toronto municipal elections. Simpson responded by resigning from the CLP, taking with him a majority of the non-Communists. The Trades and Labor Council subsequently withdrew its affiliation from the CLP and endorsed the new "Independent Labor Party" established by Simpson. The Communist Party was left holding the Canadian Labor Party as an empty shell.

From a Communist point of view, the CLP had no reason to exist except as a means of promoting united action between different currents in the labor movement. Since it had ceased to be that, it should logically have been abandoned in the fall of 1927. Instead the Communist Party maintained the fiction that the CLP was still a real force, and operated it as a front, pure and simple. In both 1927 and 1928 the CLP fielded slates of candidates in Toronto municipal elections—slates composed entirely of CP members.

This took to the point of absurdity the policy of unity at any price the party had been following since 1925. The CLP fiasco was the exact equivalent of the ACCL—but in the CLP there was nothing to ally with!

On the principal issues of international and domestic policy, then, the Communist Party of Canada accepted and implemented the Comintern's policies completely. It is therefore surprising to discover that there was one major exception to this general policy of acquiescence in the Stalinization of the International. On one issue the party stubbornly refused to carry out the Comintern's instructions for three full years.

That issue was the campaign against Trotsky.

10. Canadian Communists and the Left Opposition

Immense social processes such as the rise of the Soviet bureaucracy shape the lives of millions of people who neither control nor understand what is happening. But social processes do not take place in the abstract: they occur through the actions of individuals. Many historians, unable or unwilling to penetrate appearances, see only the individuals and reduce history to a series of personal conflicts.

Such has been the treatment by most historians of the conflicts that racked the USSR from 1923 to 1929. Western historians have viewed them as a simple power struggle in which Joseph Stalin, the cleverest politician, outmaneuvered his rivals. Soviet writers have from time to time changed the labels they apply to the participants in the battle, but in general they have viewed the conflict as a personal fight between the all-wise General Secretary (or Central Committee) and the petty-bourgeois adventurer (or German agent, or British spy) Leon Trotsky. Both interpretations ignore the social roots of the conflict.

Indeed, if it was only a personal fight between Trotsky and Stalin, its outcome is inexplicable. Leon Trotsky was one of the finest political leaders of this century. In the history of the 1917 Russian revolution his name is inextricably linked with Lenin's: there were parts of Russia in which the peasants believed that "Lenin-Trotsky" was one man. It was Trotsky who planned the day-to-day maneuvers that brought the Bolsheviks to power in 1917. After the revolution it was Trotsky who built the Red Army into a powerful force that saved the workers state. Lenin, no mean judge of character, described Trotsky as "perhaps the most capable man" in the Central Committee.

Stalin, by contrast, was a grey figure who played at most a secondary role in the party leadership before the 1920s.* His only notable contribution in 1917 was to give editorial support, in the Bolshevik newspaper *Pravda*, to the capitalist Provisional Government: when Lenin returned to Russia this position was reversed.

The idea that Stalin was a "better politician" than Trotsky is absurd. But Stalin's particular talents—for administrative manipulation and back-room dealing—were in tune with the needs of the new rising bureaucracy. The struggle of Trotsky and the Left Opposition against Stalin was not a battle of personalities: it was the last stand of the cadre of the revolutionary party against the bureaucracy. Trotsky's defeat was the defeat of the party, and the victory of the bureaucratic caste.

The fight against Stalin and the bureaucracy was begun by Lenin in 1922, as his final letters and articles attest. Lenin's last political act, in letters written March 5 and 6, 1923, was to break off all relations with Stalin and to form an alliance with Trotsky against Stalin. Only a stroke which removed him forever from political activity on March 6 (he died ten months later) prevented Lenin from carrying this fight through.[1]

The history of the CPSU from 1923 to 1929 is the history of the Stalin faction's drive, as the representatives of the developing bureaucratic caste, for totalitarian control of the Soviet Union. Stalin carried out this fight in alliance with various groups in the party and state apparatus, using each and then casting it aside. By 1930 Stalin and his associates were in unchallenged control of the country.

Throughout this period Trotsky was the one central leader who consistently opposed the bureaucracy, consistently pressed for a return to a Bolshevik policy. On both national and international issues he and thousands of other Bolsheviks, organized in the Left Opposition, campaigned against the party's abandonment of its program and principles.

As a result, Trotsky was singled out for the bureaucracy's most

---

*"I will probably not sin against the truth when I say that 99 per cent of the persons present here heard and knew very little about Stalin before the year 1924," said Nikita Khrushchev at the Twentieth Congress of the Soviet Communist Party in 1956.

venomous attacks. Beginning in December 1923, an all-out campaign to discredit Trotsky in Russia and the International was waged with unprecedented ferocity. Every disagreement Trotsky had ever had with Lenin was dragged out to prove that Trotsky was an inveterate opponent of Leninism. Books were rewritten to delete Trotsky's name. New histories of the Revolution were produced to play down Trotsky's role and build up Stalin's.*

The International was brought into the act: all of the parties were called upon to condemn "Trotskyism," a term invented by Zinoviev in 1923. They were to condemn Trotsky and his ideas unheard: many communists were later to regret their willingness to accede to Moscow's demands on this issue.

In many countries individual Communists resisted the campaign against Trotsky and found themselves expelled from the International. Some parties (notably in Poland) resisted for a time, but gave way after threatened or actual purges of their leaders. One party refused to go along, and held out against Comintern policy for three years. In this the Communist Party of Canada stood alone.

The chief architect of the Canadian CP's policy towards the anti-Trotsky campaign was Maurice Spector. His heretical views had their origin in the defeated German revolution of 1923.

The entire International expected great events in Germany in the fall of 1923. The Canadian party thought the situation important enough that it raised the money to send Maurice Spector to Germany, to report firsthand. What Spector saw was the debacle described in chapter 8. The German experience left many observers doubting the wisdom of the German party leadership, and Spector was no exception. In an unpublished letter to the Central Executive Committee of the Workers Party he was sharply critical of the Brandler leadership.

The prospects for victory were great. But the party should have taken up the

---

*Trotsky's actual role in the Russian Revolution may be seen in this passage from *Pravda*, November 6, 1918, on the revolution's first anniversary: "All the work of practical organization of the October insurrection was conducted under the immediate leadership of the Chairman of the Petrograd Soviet, Trotsky. It is possible to declare with certainty that the swift passing of the garrison to the side of the Soviet and the bold execution of the work of the Military Revolutionary Committee, the party owes principally and above all to comrade Trotsky." The author of these lines was Joseph Stalin.

struggle in October even in the prospect of a possible defeat. After the expectations the party had aroused in the masses by its proclaimed will to power and preparedness to assume the initiative against a counter-revolutionary stroke, a possible defeat would not have had so catastrophic an aftermath as this retreat without a struggle.[2]

The leaders of the KPD, Spector remarked sarcastically, were "no Lenin and Trotsky in energy, intelligence and forcefulness." Nevertheless, "the rank and file are lions."

So far, Spector's analysis corresponded with that of Zinoviev and of the KPD left wing, led by Ruth Fischer and Arkadi Maslow. The Comintern leadership was busy shifting the blame for the defeat onto Brandler, who was bureaucratically deposed from the KPD leadership and replaced with the Fischer-Maslow group. The Comintern described the defeats as temporary setbacks, and predicted new revolutionary advances for the immediate future.

Spector, however, held that the defeat had been "catastrophic."

The Party is outlawed, its property confiscated, its press silenced. The prisons are so overcrowded that concentration camps have been opened to hold the overflow of communists. Criticism of the police or of the financial measures of the dictatorship is met with instant suppression. . . . The unions are pale shadows of their former selves. The paying membership of the Berlin Metal Workers Union has sunk from 180,000 to 38,000. . . .

The Communist Party is itself living through a deep crisis, that for the time being cripples its effectiveness. . . . The feeling inside the communist rank and file is that of extreme depression, as also inside the proletariat as a whole.[3]

With this analysis Spector and the majority of the Comintern leadership parted company. Zinoviev, who bore a great deal of responsibility for the German defeat, attempted to deny that any defeat had taken place. He saved face by ordering a revolutionary offensive by the KPD. In *Pravda* on February 2, 1924, he wrote that "Germany is apparently heading towards a violent civil war." The ECCI wrote to the German party: "The mistake in the evaluation of the tempo of events made in October 1923 caused the party great difficulties. Nevertheless it is *only an episode*. The fundamental estimate remains the same as before."[4]

What Spector had described was not "only an episode." It was a defeat that would take years to overcome. For a Marxist (although Spector was not explicit on this point) such a defeat meant a major tactical re-orientation: the "fundamental estimate" had changed radically.

Although Spector could not have known it at the time, his evaluation of the German situation was shared, at least in its major conclusions, by one member of the Executive Committee of the International. Behind the scenes Leon Trotsky was fighting for a realistic appraisal of the German events, and against Zinoviev's ultraleft turn. When Trotsky's *Lessons of October* appeared late in 1924 (and in an English translation early in 1925) Spector would see that Trotsky's view of the 1923 German revolution was essentially the same as his own.

It is going too far to say, as William Rodney does, that by his description of the German events, "unknowingly, Spector had become one of the Western hemisphere's first Trotskyites."[5] Nevertheless, it was in the last months of 1923 that Spector's first doubts about the course of the Comintern were formed.

His doubts took a much more definite shape after he left Germany to attend the Thirteenth Conference of the Communist Party of the Soviet Union.

Spector arrived in Moscow for a three-month stay in January 1924. This was a critical time in the history of the inner-party fight in the CPSU. On October 15, 1923 a group of Trotsky's associates published the "Platform of the Forty-Six," a document inspired by Trotsky, if not actually written by him. In it, forty-six prominent party leaders called for restoration of democratic discussion within the party, and condemned the increasing alienation of the party leadership from the rank and file.

...the party is to a considerable extent ceasing to be that living independent collectivity which sensitively seizes living reality because it is bound to this reality with a thousand threads. Instead of this we observe the ever increasing, and now scarcely concealed, division of the party between a secretarial hierarchy and "quiet folk," between professional party officials recruited from above and the general mass of the party which does not participate in the common life....

The regime established within the party is completely intolerable; it destroys the independence of the party, replacing the party by a recruited bureaucratic apparatus which acts without objection in normal times, but which inevitably fails in moments of crisis, and which threatens to become completely ineffective in the face of the serious events now impending....

The factional regime must be abolished, and this must be done in the first instance by those who have created it; it must be replaced by a regime of comradely unity and internal party democracy.[6]

The Platform touched off a major debate in the CPSU. Rank and file support for it was so great that the apparatus was forced to make concessions to the demand for democratic discussion: for months the pages of *Pravda* were filled with discussion articles on the problems of bureaucracy. At the same time the Stalin-Zinoviev-Kamenev group in the party leadership began to use administrative measures to consolidate their position. The entire leadership of the Young Communist League, which had supported the Opposition, was removed from office and replaced by a pro-Stalin group. Oppositionists were transferred to isolated posts by decision of Stalin's secretariat. And the unprecedented personal campaign against Trotsky was launched.

In their Platform, the Opposition had charged the party hierarchy with manipulating the elections of delegates to party conventions to maintain their own control. This was fully borne out in early 1924. The Opposition's strong rank and file support was steadily eroded at each level of delegate selection for the 1924 party conference. In Moscow province, for example, 36 percent of the delegates to the district conventions supported the Opposition. This was reduced to 18 percent at the provincial convention which elected delegates to the All-Union conference. In many cases provincial conventions refused any representation at all to the Opposition, even though it was a substantial minority. As a result, only three of the delegates to the 1924 Conference were Oppositionists. Not surprisingly, there was little or no political debate at the conference, only a steady stream of invective directed at Trotsky.[7]

If Spector wrote an evaluation of the debate in Moscow in 1924, it has not survived. From his subsequent political actions, however, we can infer that he was appalled by the bureaucracy's drive against the man whose name, with Lenin's, had long been synonymous with the Russian Revolution. Spector did not know about Trotsky's views on international issues, and he may not have been able to follow all of the subtleties of the debate in Russian, but he knew injustice when he saw it. He probably met and discussed with members of the Opposition. He attended the party conference. He concluded that something was wrong in the workers state, and resolved to prevent the Canadian CP from joining in the anti-Trotsky chorus.

Ironically, it was only a few months after Spector's return to Canada that two other Canadian party leaders decided to support Stalin against Trotsky. Tim Buck and Malcolm Bruce were the CPC's delegates to the Fifth Congress of the Comintern, which opened in Moscow on June 17, 1924. This was the congress that extended the anti-Trotsky campaign to the International. Its watchword was "Bolshevization," a process that historian Daniel Calhoun has described concisely:

In the first place Bolshevization would involve quick and explicit condemnation of Trotsky's supporters in all Communist Parties where they still held influential positions. After that, it meant taking no decisive step without the explicit agreement of the International.[8]

None of Buck's many accounts of the period discuss the Fifth Congress, but Malcolm Bruce recorded his memories of it early in the 1960s.

There was a public meeting of party members at the Great Bolshoi theatre and sitting there in the gallery with Tim I noticed delegates from countries all over the world.... I was sitting in the gallery there before the meeting had started; from a stage door in the ground floor in walked a man with a white uniform, blouse and so on. Of course, I knew instantly it was Trotsky.... There was a tremendous ovation. I don't know that I've ever heard anything like it.... Tim leaned to me and said: "That dirty——!" (It was a very filthy word.)

I was pretty green, I couldn't understand this remark because the struggle against Trotsky had been confined almost exclusively to the Russian party and the National Executive.[9]

Bruce does not say so, but his "green-ness" quickly wore off at the Fifth Congress. When he returned to Canada, he was, with Buck, virtually the only supporter Stalin had in the Canadian Party leadership.

Why did the CPC's chairman support the Opposition while its trade union director supported Stalin? Accident probably played a role. Spector's first contact with the campaign against "Trotskyism" occurred during the dispute within the Soviet party, when little effort was made to line up foreign observers in support of Stalin, so he could draw his conclusions more or less objectively. Buck, on the other hand, experienced the same campaign at a Comintern congress, when every resource of the bureaucracy was brought to bear to convince the foreigners of the evils of Trotskyism. More fundamental in Spector's orientation, as noted earlier, was the critical frame of mind induced in him by his first-hand observation of the German debacle of 1923. As for Buck, he and the other CP leaders who eventually enlisted in the anti-

Trotsky campaign were simply swimming with the tide of Comintern opinion after 1924. Certainly Buck did not set out to become a Stalinist, and Spector did not plan to be expelled from the party he had helped to found. Nevertheless, the experiences of 1924 put each one on a path that would determine their respective political futures.

From early in 1924 the newspapers of the world's Communist parties carried a steady stream of articles denouncing Trotsky and Trotskyism as opponents of Leninism. The *Worker,* however, maintained a studied silence. There was no mention in its pages of the political disputes in the Soviet Union, or of the Comintern's support for Trotsky's opponents in the dispute. Trotsky's name continued to be reported in favorable contexts, just as it had been since 1921. In February the *Worker* published his farewell tribute to Lenin on its front page. In November it illustrated an article on the anniversary of the Russian Revolution with a picture of Lenin and Trotsky. In January 1925 the Canadian Communist paper published Trotsky's critique of Gorky's views on Lenin. There can be no doubt that Spector, who was both editor of the *Worker* and chairman of the party, had consciously decided to keep the anti-Trotsky campaign out of the Canadian party.

That is not to say that the CPC or Spector endorsed the Opposition. Spector had, as he later wrote, "reservations about the line of the Communist International"—but reservations are not a political program. He held back from expressing them, hoping "that the 'pressure of events,' the logic of history...would straighten out the official line of the Comintern."[10]

He did not fight for the Opposition program—but he did prevent the Canadian party from taking part in the campaign against Trotsky. Jack MacDonald, who had not followed the debates in the Soviet Union, and who wanted no part of the vicious factionalism that was part of it, accepted Spector's policy. The *Worker,* as a result, was steadfastly neutral.*

The Canadian party's neutrality remained unobtrusive and quite unofficial until the spring of 1925, when it was forced to take a stand. The occasion was the Fifth Plenum of the Executive Committee of the Communist International. William Moriarty attended as a delegate from Canada. On his arrival in Moscow in

---

*The publication of Trotsky's articles was not a sign that the *Worker* was supporting Trotsky. The paper was simply continuing its longstanding policy of publishing material by the Soviet leaders.

March, he discovered that the plenum was to hear a long report condemning Trotsky, and that he would be required to vote on the issue. He immediately cabled Toronto, asking the party's position. With MacDonald's agreement, Spector drafted a reply:

The Executive Committee is not convinced on the basis of evidence obtained, that the Comintern is actually menaced and confronted with a system constituting Trotskyism. Notwithstanding Trotsky's mistakes prior to 1917 and during the course of the revolution, we are unconvinced that the implications of the "permanent revolution" theory attributed to him are actually entertained by Trotsky and that he contemplates revision of Leninism. We are of the opinion that the prestige of the Comintern has not been enhanced here by the bitterness of the anti-Trotsky attack. No request from leading elements or party membership for discussion in the Party press.[11]

The minutes of the CPC's 1925 convention state that this cable was unanimously endorsed by the Central Executive Committee.[12] In 1970 Tim Buck, who had never before mentioned this incident, described it in *Lenin and Canada* and insisted that he had opposed Trotsky in a telegram he sent to the CEC from Edmonton.* Buck's claim is confirmed by a later reference made by Jack MacDonald to "one C.E.C. member, who, being unable to be present wired the C.E.C. to record his vote against Trotsky, but protested lack of information."[13] In any event, Spector's cable was sent to Moscow on April 8, and Moriarty voted accordingly. He was the only delegate to the 1925 plenum who refused to condemn Trotsky.

The Canadian cable did not endorse Trotsky; it even expressed doubts about the existence of Trotskyism. It simply refused to condemn the Russian leader on the basis of the evidence available, and registered an objection to the tone of the Comintern's polemics. It was a declaration of neutrality.

In Stalin's Comintern there were no neutrals. The Comintern let the CPC know this in no uncertain terms, in its letter to the party's 1925 convention:

We are compelled to say that considerable ideological confusion is noticeable in our Canadian brother party. The central committee of the party expressed itself in favour of Trotskyism. It did not understand the international importance of the Trotsky discussion in the Russian

---

*Buck mentioned the question only because William Rodney had reported the CEC cable in *Soldiers of the International,* published in 1968.

Communist Party and in the entire international; it even prevented the
publication of discussion articles in the Canadian Party Press.

The Executive of the Communist International places on record that by
this attitude towards Trotskyism the Central Committee of our Canadian
brother party has completely isolated itself in the Communist
International.... we urge the Central Committee of the CP of C to publish in
the Party Press the decisions of the Communist International and also
explanatory articles on the question of Trotskyism-Leninism, and to
explain to all party members the Comintern attitude to this question by
organizing discussions on it in the party organizations.[14]

The reference to complete isolation clearly threatened excommuni-
cation. Refusing to condemn Trotsky was the same as being "in
favour of Trotskyism" as far as the CI leadership was concerned.

The leaders of the Canadian party held firm. The Comintern's
letter was distributed to the party membership and reported to the
convention—but the cable to Moriarty was published in the *Worker*
as part of the CEC's official convention report to the membership,
and put up for adoption. After a thorough discussion ("Trotskyism"
was a separate item on the agenda) the convention overwhelmingly
endorsed the CEC's position. According to Tim Buck's later
account:

Not one speaker defended Trotskyism as such. Most speakers took their cue
from MacDonald and argued that the most important thing was to make it
clear that our party was independent and was not going to be drawn into
'struggles for power' in other parties or in the Comintern.*[15]

Buck viewed this as dishonest, but it was in fact the real position of
the majority of the members and leaders of the party. They didn't
understand the issues in the attack on Trotsky, and they were
appalled by the level to which it had descended. They wanted
nothing to do with it. MacDonald in particular simply wanted to
build the party in Canada, with as little interference as possible
from the International. He could see no relevance in this dispute for
Canadian Communists. Spector understood the issues better than
anyone. However, he was not yet a supporter of Trotsky in the
Russian and Comintern debates—indeed, he was largely
uninformed of the content of those debates—and he was not
prepared to take up the cudgels on Trotsky's behalf. The party was
neutral, and said so.

---

*Buck says that only seven delegates opposed the CEC position.

It may be asked why the Canadian CP was allowed to remain neutral. In Europe full-scale purges were carried out for crimes far less severe than the CPC's. Four factors seem to have been involved.

First, the lack of hardened factions in the Canadian party meant that there was no one with a motive to use "Trotskyism" as a club against the MacDonald-Spector leadership. Shortly after the convention Malcolm Bruce moved to the United States in search of work, and Tim Buck showed no inclination to carry the debate after the convention.

Secondly, the CPC was a small party in an unimportant country. Deviations which had to be stamped out quickly in Germany or France could be tolerated temporarily in Canada.

Thirdly, the intraparty struggle in the USSR entered a period of lull in 1925. The vote condemning Trotsky at the ECCI plenum was the last shot fired in the debate begun in 1923. Trotsky had been forced out of his positions as commissar of war and president of the Military Revolutionary Committee, and the "1923 Opposition" was disbanded. Not until the summer of 1926 was the battle joined again.

Fourthly, refusal to condemn Trotsky did not mean rejection of Stalin's other policies. The 1925 convention endorsed the Comintern's call for "Canadian Independence" and accepted its instruction that the "Farmer-Labor Party" slogan be dropped. The "Bolshevization" campaign was endorsed, with the implicit exception of the anti-Trotsky drive. And shortly after the convention Spector explicitly endorsed the bureaucratic and arbitrary removal of the Fischer-Maslow group from the leadership of the Communist Party of Germany: this was a major step towards the Stalinization of the International. To complete the picture, a *Worker* editorial on January 30, 1926, defended "socialism in one country."

On all the major political questions, with the sole exception of "Trotskyism," the CPC had proven its reliability: bringing the party firmly into line could wait.

The *Worker* did not simply remain silent about Trotsky. Throughout 1925 and early 1926 it continued its longstanding policy of promoting the writings of the Soviet leaders, including Trotsky. The February 20, 1926 *Worker*, for example, offered Trotsky's *Literature and Revolution* as a prize for the best article by a "worker-correspondent." An editorial in the May 15 issue declared that the British General Strike was "bearing out in life the analysis Trotsky made" in his book *Where Is Britain Going?* An advertisement in the June 12, 1926 issue decribed his *Whither Russia?* as displaying Trotsky's "accustomed vigor and brilliancy."*

There was nothing surprising in this. It had yet to be established that communists who disagreed with Stalin were subject to total censorship. Even the American CP, which had willingly condemned Trotsky unheard in 1925, continued to publish favorable reviews of Trotsky's books until mid-1926.

But the June 12, 1926 advertisement for *Whither Russia* was the last such ad to appear in the *Worker*: thereafter favorable mention of Trotsky virtually disappeared from the Canadian Communist press.

The June cut-off on Trotsky coincides with a visit to Toronto by C.E. Ruthenberg, secretary of the U.S. Communist Party. The Canadians had not been able to send a delegate to the Sixth ECCI Plenum in February and March: Ruthenberg came to report on it.[16] It is difficult not to conclude that Ruthenberg, officially or unofficially, warned the CPC to cease and desist. This is also suggested by the fact that at the same time the American CP abruptly and with no explanation halted serialization of Zinoviev's *History of the Russian Communist Party* in their magazine, *Workers' Monthly*.[17] Zinoviev was now allied with Trotsky against Stalin, and the drive to bring everyone into line was on.

Still the *Worker* maintained its silence. On August 21 it reported Zinoviev's expulsion from the CPSU Central Committee but gave no details. It was not until November 6, 1926, almost three years after the opening of the campaign against Trotsky, that the *Worker* published an article on the dispute in the CPSU. The article greatly oversimplified the conflict, ignoring many questions and distorting others: it focused almost exclusively on Zinoviev, leaving Trotsky's role aside. Nevertheless, it was the first public statement by a Canadian Communist supporting Stalin and Bukharin. Its

Whither Russia? is better known under the title *Toward Capitalism or Socialism?* (available in *Challenge of the Left Opposition*, Pathfinder Press, 1975). To readers familiar with the Russian inner-party debate, it was clearly written as a defense of Trotsky's views and as an implicit attack on "socialism in one country." It is unlikely that many persons in the Canadian CP recognized the implications of this praise.

author was Tim Buck.* He had used his appointment as acting editor while Spector was in the Maritimes to get the Stalin line into the *Worker*. Shortly thereafter he was to use another appointment to overthrow the party's policy completely.

In the fall of 1926 the Joint Opposition—an alliance of the Left Opposition led by Trotsky and forces led by Zinoviev and Kamenev—met with a major defeat in the Communist Party of the Soviet Union. Trotsky, Zinoviev, and Kamenev were not re-elected to the Politbureau, on which they had served since 1917. Zinoviev, the chairman of the Communist International since its foundation, was "withdrawn" from the Comintern by the Russian party. The Executive Committee of the Communist International was then called into session to endorse the purge. It was a matter of considerable importance for Canadian Communism that the principal Canadian spokesman at the ECCI Plenum was Tim Buck.

Many years later Buck suggested that positive reader response to his *Worker* article on the Opposition may have been a factor in the decision to make him a delegate to the ECCI Plenum.[18] This is improbable: the article appeared early in November, and the plenum opened on November 22. Since the trip to Russia took several weeks, there would scarcely have been time to weigh reader response. It is more likely that MacDonald, who was not particularly interested in the debate in the USSR, treated the choice of Buck as a routine question, and the rest of the CEC followed suit. Spector, who might have opposed the decision, was still on a speaking tour in the East. In any event, the choice was made, and the party had to live with the consequences.

Buck arrived in Moscow with a strong bias in favor of the Stalinist line. Any doubts he might have had were resolved shortly after his arrival. Buck's account is distorted by Stalinist lenses, but it has the ring of truth:

One of the first to contact the Canadian delegation after our arrival was . . . Comrade Carl Jansen† . . . [who] was perturbed by the silence of *The*

---

*It is an instructive commentary on the nature of the faction fight in the International, and on Buck's approach to it, that after defending Stalin and attacking Trotsky for two years Buck still didn't know what the major issues were.

†Jansen, using the pseudonym Scott, was a Comintern representative in North America in 1921-1923.

Worker on the crucial issues being debated in the International. We described the situation and asked for his help....

Comrade Jansen and I spent the first two days after my arrival in the library at the Comintern building. From Lenin's works, copies of *Pravda* and *Izvestia*, and mimeographed materials, "Charlie" gave me running translations of Lenin's writings on questions that I asked. I scribbled a stenographer's notebook full. Among them were the writings which cleared up, completely, my confusion about the political relationship between Lenin and Trotsky, particularly through the years before the Great October Revolution. They showed clearly that Trotsky's current opposition to the path which clearly followed the main line of Lenin's precepts was not accidental, but was consistent with the entire record of Trotsky's deviations.

It is difficult now to recapture the elation, the sense of discovery, that was inspired by learning that Lenin had written so definitely about the essentials of the problems that were then the subjects of intense debate.[19]

Buck provides a page and a half of examples of the type of material Jansen gave to him. They are the usual brief passages, torn from their historical and literary context, which have been used to "prove" that Lenin believed in the possibility of establishing a socialist society in a single country. Jansen was evidently assigned to ensure that the Canadian delegation was lined up before the plenum opened, and he came equipped with all of the anti-Trotsky material which had been produced since 1923. He fed this predigested mass to Buck, who swallowed it totally.

Until then Buck had been supporting the Stalin faction on faith alone. It is no wonder that he felt "elation" and a "sense of discovery" when he was handed the arguments he needed to fight back against the Canadian party majority. His determination to oppose Trotsky robbed him of any capacity for critical analysis he might have possessed: he wanted to be convinced, and he was.

On December 7 Stalin made a three-hour speech to the plenum. It was entirely devoted to a denunciation of the Opposition. Zinoviev was given two hours to reply, Trotsky one hour. These speeches were followed by six days of debate in which fifty delegates spoke. Only two supported the Opposition. The rest had been lined up in advance as Buck had been: the debate was monotonous and repetitive. Each delegate restated the standard accusations against the Opposition; each tried to outdo the others in vehemence.

Buck did not follow Moriarty's example. He knew what answer he would get if he asked Toronto for advice on how to vote. On December 11 he took the floor and spoke to the Plenum.

In the name of the Canadian Party, the Canadian delegation unreservedly endorses the decisions of the XV Conference of the Communist Party of the Soviet Union and expresses solidarity with it in the task of constructing Socialism in the First Workers and Peasants Republic.

...the outstanding feature of the Opposition bloc, which forced the discussion, is its absolute lack of principle....

The Opposition showed an astounding lack of contact with reality in its proposal that the Russian Unions should withdraw from the Anglo-Russian Committee....

The proposal to withdraw from the Kuomintang, which today leads the teeming millions of China in their struggle against capitalist imperialism, was similarly a proposal of either madmen or flippant adventurers....

The CP of Canada unequivocally repudiates the proposal of the Opposition bloc and stands in complete unity with the CPSU in their great historical task.[20]

Thus, writes William Rodney, "singlehandedly, Buck brought the Canadian party into line with the rest of the Comintern...."[21]

Back in Toronto, however, Spector was still trying to maintain the party's neutrality. The decisions of the Fifteenth Conference and the Seventh Plenum could not simply be ignored, but they could be played down. The December 18 and 25 issues of the *Worker* carried speeches by Stalin and Rykov denouncing the Opposition. The articles were not featured, and the *Worker* made no editorial comment on them. No news articles on the subject appeared. Having made the record as quietly as possible, the *Worker* resumed its silence, saying nothing more about the ECCI Plenum until Buck returned to Canada in March.

The April 2, 1927 *Worker* announced a public meeting featuring "Tim Buck, just returned from Russia." He was to speak on "Where is Russia Going?—'Opposition' versus 'Majority' on the Question of Russia's Development."

This meeting was the first chance Canadian Communists had had to hear the full Stalinist version of the dispute in the CPSU. But the *Worker*'s report on the meeting did not even mention the Opposition. The April 16 article simply noted that "The majority of the Soviet Communist Party were convinced that Russia could build up socialism even if the revolution abroad were delayed for a long time." One would have to be very familiar with the "Socialism in One Country" debate to realize that this sentence meant that Trotsky's views had been rejected by the Russian party.

The *Worker*'s silence now was a cover for a major dispute in the Central Executive Committee. Buck reported to the CEC on

Sunday, April 3. He sought, in effect, to win retroactive approval for his speech at the plenum. He proposed a resolution condemning the Opposition and endorsing the theory of Socialism in One Country. According to his own account, he said to the CEC: "Comrades, as the elected leaders of the Communist Party of Canada, we have to decide whether we are on Lenin's side in this struggle, or if we are against him!"[22]

The resolution produced a crisis. By early 1927 Spector had far more information about the Opposition program than before. Trotsky's *Lessons of October* had been published in English. Max Eastman's *Since Lenin Died* provided an account of the Soviet faction fight written by a man known to be close to Trotsky. At the very least Spector was opposed to the organizational measures Stalin was taking against the Opposition.

The outcome of the discussion depended on MacDonald. Until this point he had accepted Spector's policy of silence and official neutrality. His influence in the party was such as to guarantee a majority for any policy he favored. Now neutrality was out of the question. To resist the Comintern would produce a major battle, and disrupt the Canadian party. To MacDonald the debates in Russia were a diversion from the task at hand, which was to build a Communist Party in Canada. He chose the line of least resistance, and supported Buck's resolution. The condemnation of Trotsky carried, with only Spector casting a negative vote.

Spector immediately resigned as chairman of the party and editor of the *Worker*, but withdrew his resignations at MacDonald's urging. MacDonald also persuaded the CEC to reject Buck's motion that Spector be required to change his vote.*[23]

The CEC agreed to present its decision as unanimous, thus protecting Spector from the Comintern's wrath. Spector in turn agreed not to press the matter further. Tim Buck was assigned to report on the International at the coming CPC convention, Spector on the situation in Canada.

MacDonald's role in this dispute was quite out of keeping with Comintern practice. He seems to have had no fixed views of his own on the debate in the Soviet Union. (He opposed Spector's resignations on the grounds that "the line would change again.")[24] MacDonald's policy from 1924 on was consistent: he wanted to keep

---

*The idea that a Communist holding dissident views should "self-criticize" and reverse his vote was a Stalinist innovation, quite alien to Comintern practice in Lenin's time.

the Canadian party free of faction fights, by whatever means were necessary. Neither he nor Spector foresaw that their failure to take a firm stand in 1925 or 1927 would force them to fight from a much weaker position in the near future. Spector hoped that the Comintern would straighten itself out; MacDonald hoped that the entire issue would just go away.

The April 3, 1927 CEC meeting destroyed the Communist Party's neutrality. The April 23 *Worker* published Buck's resolution, and the Fifth Convention of the party, held in June, "unanimously and unreservedly" supported the CPSU majority, and condemned the Opposition.

The 5th Convention of the C.P. of C. rejects the claim of the opposition within the C.P.S.U. that the building of socialism is impossible in the U.S.S.R. and expresses complete solidarity with C.P. of the Soviet Union in its declaration that given a sufficiently long period of peace, the development of industry and agriculture into one harmonious balanced economy, completely excluding private capital, is possible.[25]

The errant party had been brought into line.

PART THREE

THE DESTRUCTION OF A PARTY

...the less the policy of the Kremlin preserved of its former internationalism, the more firmly the ruling clique clutched in its hands the rudder of the Communist International. Under the old name it was now to serve new ends. For the new ends, however, new people were needed. Beginning with the autumn of 1923, the history of the Communist International is a history of the complete renovation of its Moscow staff, and the staffs of all the national sections, by way of a series of palace revolutions, purgations from above, expulsions, etc. At the present time, the Communist International is a completely submissive apparatus in the service of Soviet foreign policy, ready at any time for any zigzag whatever.

—Leon Trotsky, *The Revolution Betrayed*, 1937

Prologue

Early in 1929 the dues-paying membership of the Communist Party of Canada was 2,876. By the beginning of 1931 it was down to 1,386, a decline of more than 50 percent.[1]

Those figures alone indicate a crisis of major proportions, but they understate its extent. There were, according to various published reports, some 700 new members recruited in 1929 and 800 in 1930. Even allowing for a very high turnover rate among the new recruits, it is clear that *at least 75 percent of the Communist Party's membership was expelled or dropped out in a two-year period.*

The extent of the decline was widely recognized within the party. Early in 1931 a Winnipeg party leader reported that in Manitoba "three-quarters of our members are new comrades who joined in the last year." An internal organization letter said that membership in Toronto, which had been as high as 500 in the past, was down to "less than 200" by February 1931.[2]

The Young Communist League experienced a similar drastic decline in membership. It had 1,200 members in 1928, and 900 in 1929. In 1930 it was claiming 800 members, but CPC organizational secretary Sam Carr admitted to Moscow that the actual dues-paying membership was only 300.[3] In some districts (B.C. for example) the YCL went completely out of existence.[4]

Both the Communist Party and the Young Communist League grew substantially during the 1930s, reaching and then surpassing the largest membership figures attained in the 1920s. But the new members were trained in a new school, in effect in a new party. Between the Communist Party of the thirties and the party that bore the same name in the twenties lay a vast gulf, marked by the crisis of 1928-1931. During those years the party lost a majority of its membership, expelled most of the men who had led the party in its first decade, and radically changed its program.

The groundwork for the crisis had been laid between 1924 and 1928, when the party gradually abandoned its political principles in response to the shifting requirements of Soviet foreign policy. The crisis was prepared by the cynicism that allowed the party leaders to vote to condemn Trotsky even though they did not know his views, and which allowed Spector to conceal his doubts with a falsely recorded "unanimous" vote.

The crisis broke into the open in November 1928, with the expulsion of Maurice Spector. It did not subside until such pioneer Communist leaders as Jack MacDonald, William Moriarty, and Michael Buhay had been driven from the party, their places taken by Tim Buck and a new generation of Moscow-trained leaders headed by Stewart Smith.

The crisis began with the birth of the Canadian Trotskyist movement. It ended with the triumph of Stalinism in the Canadian Communist Party.

11. The Expulsion of Maurice Spector

The Fifth Convention did much more than simply adopt "a resolution condemning the opposition in Russia and endorsing the decisions of the [Seventh ECCI] Plenum."[1] It confirmed that the party's most important political task was to "rally all elements willing to stand for independence" of Canada from the British Empire. It endorsed Buck's unlikely claim that "the establishment of the All-Canadian Congress of Labor marks a step forward in the struggle for an all inclusive National Trade Union Center." It discussed the progress of "Bolshevization"—and concluded that the progress so far had been very limited.[2]

And it elected a new Central Executive Committee.

Seven members were elected at large to the CEC, the Ukrainian, Finnish, Jewish, and Women's "Agit-Prop Committees" having the right to appoint their own representatives. Eight people were nominated for the seven at-large positions: Maurice Spector, Michael Buhay, William Moriarty, Tim Buck, Jack MacDonald, H. Roberts, L. Menzies, and A.E. Smith. There were 59 ballots cast, and each delegate could vote for up to seven candidates. (In fact the count shows that most voted for a full slate of seven.) The outcome of the election demonstrates how well established the central leadership of the party was:

Maurice Spector	59	Jack MacDonald	55
Michael Buhay	57	H. Roberts	52
William Moriarty	57	L. Menzies	51
Tim Buck	55	A.E. Smith	19

The votes received by the top five candidates were so close together as to make them virtually the unanimous choices of the convention. Spector's name appeared on every ballot. Roberts and Menzies, who were not as well-known as the other five, trailed them, but not significantly. A.E. Smith, a recent recruit who was not viewed as part of the central team, was far behind.[3]

Within four years of this election, four of the top five candidates would be expelled from the party. Roberts and Menzies would vanish into obscurity.* By 1931 only Tim Buck and A.E. Smith remained.

This destruction of the Communist Party's founding cadre began in 1928 with the expulsion of Maurice Spector.

Under Spector's editorship, the *Worker* in 1927 faithfully defended Comintern policy on all questions, including the dispute in the Russian party. An editorial in August called for the Opposition's expulsion from the CPSU Central Committee; subsequent articles endorsed the organizational measures taken against the Opposition, including their expulsion from the CPSU in December.

In the United States, the change from the opportunist policies of 1925-27 to the ultraleft policies of the Third Period superimposed itself on the pre-existing factions in the American Communist Party. The party majority, led by Jay Lovestone, was strongly identified with the right-wing policies of the recent past. Opposed to the Lovestone faction were groups led by William Z. Foster and James P. Cannon. Already critical of the party's conservative course, they seized upon the International's leftward course as vindiction of their criticisms.

The Canadian party had never experienced the factional warfare which characterized U.S. CP life in the 1920s. No U.S. party leader could have expressed Spector's reservations about the anti-Trotsky campaign: his factional opponents would have driven him out of the party. The Canadian leadership had long acted as a team, putting aside disagreements for the sake of building the party.

But carrying a line he strongly disagreed with began to tell on Spector by the end of 1927. His growing concern over Trotsky's fate, coupled with the tensions resulting from the party's shifting policies toward Canadian independence and toward the trade unions, tended to break down the leadership's normally cordial relationships. Late in 1927 or early in 1928, Spector came to the conclusion that the CPC's political difficulties were MacDonald's

---

*Neither was even nominated for the CEC at the next convention, 1929.

fault. An article he wrote at the beginning of 1929, after his expulsion from the party, strongly reflected the personal hostility he developed toward the party's secretary. MacDonald was "a barnacle on the ship in every situation the party could have utilized to its advantage by bold initiative." He displayed "organization conservatism and inertia," and was "the limited type of trade union-I.L.P.er with the most meagre equipment of Marxism imaginable in a party leader."[4]

Spector found an audience among the party's younger leaders, notably Annie Buller, Beckie Buhay, and Sam Carr, They formed a small personal clique around Spector, united only by hostility to MacDonald. Buhay was reported to have told party members in Windsor that "MacDonald represented the passive element and Spector the active element" in the leadership.[5] This personal infighting alienated MacDonald from Spector: by the summer of 1928 they were scarcely on speaking terms,[6] which meant that Spector had no leading member of the CPC to discuss his dissident views with, and that MacDonald was only too willing to believe the worst of Spector when political issues took the place of personal ones.

Tim Buck stood aside from the growing conflict between Spector and MacDonald. He had problems of his own. As party representative on the Young Communist League's executive, Buck became embroiled in a bitter conflict between the YCL and the party's Ukrainian wing. The Ukrainians had organized a separate Youth Section of the Ukrainian Labor-Farmer Temple Association (ULFTA), and saw no reason to allow the YCL to organize young Ukrainians; the YCL, in turn, saw the youth as its exclusive preserve and demanded control over the ULFTA youth. This debate, which reflected the general desire of the Ukrainian Communists to remain free of direct party control, led to the drafting of a resolution to the Comintern by the Ukrainians. Among other things, the document demanded immediate withdrawal of Tim Buck from the party leadership. The Anglo-American Commission smoothed the crisis over during the International's Sixth Congress, but great bitterness remained. It would become a major factor in the factional battles that racked the party in 1929 and 1930.

Spector and Cannon

In the United States, independently of Spector, James Cannon too was uneasy about the developments in the Comintern. As he later wrote:

I was never enthusiastic about the fight in the Russian party. I could not understand it. As the fight grew more intense, and the persecutions increased against the Russian Left Opposition, led by such great leaders as Trotsky, Zinoviev, Radek, and Rakovsky—doubt and dissatisfaction accumulated in my mind....[7]

Cannon, like Spector, was one of the founders of the North American Communist movement. He was elected to the Central Committee of the United Communist Party in 1920, and was named editor of *The Toiler* (predecessor to the U.S. *Worker*) in the same year. He was the first chairman of the Workers' Party of America, the American CP's legal face, formed in 1921. From 1925 through 1928 he was national secretary of International Labor Defense (ILD), the organization created by the U.S. Communist Party to aid working-class political prisoners. Through the ILD Cannon played an important role in the campaign to save anarchists Sacco and Vanzetti from the electric chair.

As one of the foremost representatives of U.S. communism, Cannon had a great deal of influence in the party: he was the leader of one of the three principal factions that dominated the U.S. party's internal life through its first decade. Nevertheless, Cannon did not use his influence to disseminate his doubts and dissatisfaction with the course the Comintern was taking. "You cannot," he later said, "make a program out of doubts."

Of course, if one had no responsibility to the party, if he were a mere commentator or observer, he could merely speak his doubts and have it over with. You can't do that in a serious political party. If you don't know what to say, you don't have to say anything. The best thing is to remain silent.[8]

This was the course Cannon followed throughout the debates in the Soviet Communist Party and the International until 1928.

I voted for stereotyped resolutions, I regret to say, but I never made a single speech or wrote a single article against Trotskyism. That was not because I was a Trotskyist.... I refused to take part in the campaigns only because I didn't understand the issues.[9]

Cannon had not followed the Soviet debate closely. He had read one Opposition resolution on the Anglo-Russian Committee and was sympathetic to its arguments ("At any rate, I was convinced that they were not the counter-revolutionists they were pictured to be"[10]) but he was far from being an Oppositionist.

In February 1928, Spector was sent as a fraternal delegate to the plenum of the Central Committee of the U.S. Communist Party. Greatly concerned by the news that Trotsky had been exiled to the remote Asian village of Alma Ata, he hoped to learn if any of the U.S. party leaders shared his concerns.

The plenum featured an extended discussion of "Trotskyism," beginning with a full-scale attack on the Opposition by Bertram D. Wolfe, and followed by a discussion period in which the various factions vied with one another to express the greatest possible hostility to Trotskyism, despite their general ignorance of the subject. Cannon, alone of the major party leaders, refused to participate, despite the urgings of his co-factionalists.

Everyone, including Spector, noticed his silence. Spector also learned from Martin Abern and Max Shachtman, Cannon's closest associates in the party and in the International Labor Defense, that Cannon was "depressed and disturbed," that he "showed a tendency to withdraw from the factional struggle in the party to the 'mass activity' of the I.L.D., as if he felt himself to be at a dead end in the party."[11] It seemed at least possible that Cannon, too, was upset about the drive against the Russian Opposition.

Spector and Cannon had met before, but they did not know each other well: certainly they had never discussed their concerns about the International. At the February 1928 plenum in New York, however, Spector sought Cannon out. Cannon later described the meeting:

We spent an entire evening together, frankly discussing our doubts and dissatisfaction with the way things were going in Russia. But neither of us knew what to do about it and made no plan or decision to do anything at that time. I think it can be safely said, however, that the thoughts we confided to each other at this meeting in February 1928 prepared the way for our getting together in Moscow at the Sixth World Congress.[12]

In this mood of "doubts and dissatisfaction," Cannon and Spector went to the Sixth Congress of the Comintern in the summer of 1928, as delegates of their respective parties. The Canadian delegation also included Jack MacDonald, John Navis, and A.G. Neal.

THE SIXTH CONGRESS HAS FREQUENTLY been viewed as the launching point for the "Third Period" ultraleftism which was so disastrous for the world Communist movement in the 1930s. In fact, the congress straddled two periods: it marked a transition from joint leadership by the Stalin and Bukharin factions to absolute control by the Stalin faction.

"On the surface," writes Bukharin's biographer, the Sixth Congress "was the high point of his career in the international movement." Bukharin chaired all the major sessions. "He opened and closed its proceedings, delivered the three main reports, and received its accolades and enthusiastic ovations."[13] But that was all on the surface. Having defeated the Left Opposition, Stalin was now ready to destroy the Right. He chose the Sixth Congress to launch his campaign against Bukharin. A whispering campaign—later known as the "corridor congress"—made clear to everyone the determination of Stalin to win total control. One of Bukharin's supporters later described the atmosphere:

The Congress was a comedy worthy of the pen of Gogol. Bukharin acted as president and made the big programmatic speech.... But in the halls and corridors a flood of dirty rumours against Bukharin was spreading, such as I have never experienced in the Comintern. It was really in the halls and corridors that a change of regime was manoeuvred while Bukharin himself was proclaiming the principles of Communism at the meetings.[14]

Even those who stood aside from the factionalism were shaken by the experience. Jack MacDonald's memories are indicative:

I recall the session of the Standing Committee where the Political Bureau of the C.P.S.U. made its declaration, drawn from it, in its own words because the delegations were "speculating" on the rumored differences within the Bureau. No such principal differences existed, ran the declaration signed by all members of the bureau and implemented by remarks from Stalin and Bukharin. Hardly had the delegations reach home before news broke out that not only were there principal differences, but that actual factions existed. And this after the lie had been given to delegates who had probed beneath the surface....[15]

Those who made the mistake of supporting Bukharin found themselves, with their leader, driven out of the Comintern. The classic case was that of U.S. Communist Party national secretary Jay Lovestone. The Sixth Congress explicitly denied charges by his factional opponents that he represented a right-wing group in the U.S. party. At a convention held in March 1929, Lovestone and his supporters received the votes of 90 per cent of the members of the party. Three months later he was labelled a representative of the Right Danger and expelled from the party and the International.[16]

While the majority of the 515 delegates were trying to choose between Stalin and Bukharin, Cannon and Spector were engaged in a "corridor congress" of their own. Both were members of the Program Commission, a congress subcommittee charged with reviewing proposals for amendments to the Draft Program which Bukharin had submitted.

To their surprise, one of the discussion documents they received was a book-length manuscript by the exiled Trotsky, entitled *The Draft Program of the Communist International: A Criticism of Fundamentals.*

Trotsky had written the long essay in Alma Ata. While it took the form of a criticism of Bukharin's program, it was in fact a full-scale review of the evolution of the Comintern since 1923. It remains today one of the most important and fundamental of Trotsky's works.

At the Comintern's Fifth Congress in 1924, Trotsky had been elected to the Executive Committee. He had, therefore, full rights at this congress, including the right to speak on his own behalf. But that was a formal right: in practice his expulsion from the CPSU and his exile made participation impossible. The Opposition was not represented at all at the Congress. Trotsky wrote his *Criticism* primarily for discussion within Opposition circles: he submitted it to the congress as a purely formal gesture, not expecting it to be circulated.

The Russian leaders decided to go through the formalities of submitting Trotsky's document for discussion, without actually allowing most of the delegates to see it. They made a rough and frequently inaccurate translation of two of its three sections, and distributed it to the sixty members of the Program Commission only. All copies were numbered to ensure their return at the end of the congress. The commission itself never discussed it.

Cannon and Spector, however, read it avidly. They had been concerned about the plight of the Opposition: this document rose above organizational disputes, outlining the political and social basis of the conflict in the Russian party, and showed how the crisis of the International arose from them. It was most crushing in its indictment of the theory of "socialism in one country" and in its extended discussion of the catastrophe in China. Despite the poor translation and the major omissions, Trotsky's *Criticism* convinced Spector and Cannon. Cannon later wrote:

We let the caucus meetings and the Congress go to the devil while we read and studied this document. Then I knew what I had to do, and so did he. Our doubts had been resolved. It was as clear as daylight that Marxist truth was on the side of Trotsky. We made a compact there and then—Spector and I— that we would come back home and begin a struggle under the banner of Trotskyism.[17]

They decided not to raise a fight for the Left Opposition at the congress itself: such a move would have cut them off prematurely from potential supporters in North America. When the issue was voted on at the congress, they absented themselves. Even this brought them under suspicion. The GPU (secret police) interrogated Spector and investigated Cannon. Stalinist Heinz Neumann made a special point of speaking to Spector, warning him that "there are rumors that you are meeting with the wrong people." Neumann offered to arrange a meeting with Stalin, an honor Spector turned down.[18]

The newly-committed Trotskyists managed to allay the GPU's suspicions. Spector's prestige in the Canadian party so outweighed the suspicion that he harbored Trotskyist sympathies that he was elected to the Comintern's Executive Committee. He was the first Canadian ever to hold that office.

This decision to support the Opposition was not one to be made lightly. It meant—and Spector and Cannon knew this—certain expulsion from the parties they had helped to found and lead. It meant cutting themselves off from their careers as party leaders and functionaries. Had Cannon not made his decision at the Sixth Congress, there is every possibility that he, not Earl Browder, would have succeeded Lovestone as national secretary of the U.S. party. Spector too had long been a party functionary.

However, if they were to adhere to the goals they had adopted upon joining the movement years earlier, the choice was clear, no matter what the likely results. In Cannon's words:

I never deceived myself for a moment about the most probable consequences of my decision to support Trotsky in the summer of 1928. I knew it was going to cost me my head and also my swivel chair, but I thought: What the hell—better men than I have risked their heads and their swivel chairs for truth and justice. Trotsky and his associates were doing it at that very moment in the exile camps and prisons of the Soviet Union. It was no more than right that one man, no matter how limited his qualifications, should remember what he had started out in his youth to fight for, and speak out for their cause and try to make the world hear, or at least to let the exiled and imprisoned Russian Oppositionists know that they had found a new friend and supporter.[19]

Spector arrived in Toronto on October 9, 1928, after spending two weeks in Western Europe establishing contacts with opposition groups in France and Germany. On the day of his arrival he learned that Cannon had already won over his principal co-workers in International Labor Defense—Max Shachtman, Martin Abern, and Rose Karsner. These three were to remain Trotskyist stalwarts for many years: Abern and Shachtman until 1940, Karsner until her death in 1968.

Spector was less successful in winning support. He resumed contact with the leftist "ginger group" he had been connected with earlier, but, in Spector's words, they "lacked the courage in the test to face the fact that the MacDonalds, the Peppers, the Lovestones, Thaelmanns and Fosters are all either part and parcel or aspirants of the Stalinist regime."[20] They did not report Spector's views to the Political Bureau, but neither would they support him.*

Cannon wrote that his group had "secured the means of reaching the party whether we get official permission or not." They had obtained copies of mailing lists containing 10,000 names and urged Spector to do the same. "Once you get cut off from the official channels, you will fully appreciate what a list of addresses means." Once again Spector was not so fortunate:

I am afraid you will be disappointed to learn that I have only been able to get the mailing list of the secretaries of the labor defense so far (most of whom are leading local functionaries). As if they had a premonition of what was coming, the mailing list of the *Monthly* and *Worker* have been kept under lock and key all the time I have been in the city. I may be able to do something with the *Kamf* list, and I have not given up hope that we may be able to "suborn" somebody in the office. This is unfortunate, but you comrades were in a different position as far as the I.L.D. was concerned.†

More seriously, Spector was immediately confronted with the problem of discussions of the Sixth Congress. He had been elected

---

*Beckie Buhay's participation in a meeting at which "Spector made it clear that he was prepared to lead an opposition movement," and submitted "definite plans...for a fight aginst the Comintern" was described in the *Worker*, April 13, 1929, by veteran party member Robert Shoesmith. Buhay did not deny the charge.

†Excerpts from the Cannon-Spector correspondence of October-November 1928 were published in the *Worker*, January 19, 1929. The letters were stolen from Cannon's apartment in a break-in in December 1928. All quotations from the correspondence in this chapter come from this source.

to the ECCI in Moscow, and was expected to play a leading role in presenting the decisions of the congress to the Canadian party membership.

An Enlarged Executive meeting, including the CEC, all available members of the Central Committee, and the Political Committee of the Young Communist League, was held October 20-22 to hear reports of the CPC's delegates. Spector wrote to Cannon on October 16:

Like yourself, I would have preferred more time to maneuver in.... The endorsation of the decisions of the Sixth Congress is certain to be on the agenda. The logical step for me would be to register my criticism of the Congress and my solidarity with the platform of the Opposition.

He decided instead to avoid a confrontation. At the Enlarged Executive meeting MacDonald delivered a five-hour report, including and endorsing all of the congress's decisions. Spector followed MacDonald with extensive remarks, but carefully avoided saying anything that would stamp him as an Oppositionist. (He had followed the same course in his speeches at the congress itself.) There was no direct vote on Trotskyism at the meeting, so he was able to win some time.

Scarcely had he surmounted that obstacle than he was assigned to speak on "The Soviet Union and the War Danger" at a public meeting on October 25. This meeting, held in Alhambra Hall, has gone down in Canadian Communist Party mythology as the great turning point, the occasion on which Spector finally revealed his counter-revolutionary colors. The various subsequent accounts of the meeting, written by Buck and others, are unreliable and mutually contradictory (see Appendix to this chapter). Nevertheless, Spector's own report to Cannon indicates that he did not carry the official line:

I not only spoke of the successes of the U.S.S.R. but gave a sober economic analysis of what led up to the grain crisis, stressing the role of class differentiation in the village and the menace of the kulak. Many who came chiefly to cheer went away to think.

The Alhambra Hall meeting created, as MacDonald later described it, "a mild sensation."[21] The Toronto City Committee demanded that Spector speak at another meeting, this time on lines to be dictated by the committee.[22] He was "called before the Secretariat and the Executive to explain the pessimistic and

Trotskyist character" of his speech.[23] The *Worker* carried no report of the meeting, a clear sign that his speech had caused dissension in the Central Executive.

Again Spector was able to avoid committing himself one way or another: but his success in avoiding the charge of Trotskyism lasted only a few days.

On October 27, after an eleven-day "trial," James Cannon, Max Shachtman, and Martin Abern were expelled from the Workers (Communist) Party of America for supporting Trotsky's views. There immediately followed a cross-country witch-hunt. All party members were required to state their views on Cannon and Trotskyism: those who asked for more information, or who suggested that they should be allowed to hear the views of the expelled, or who refused to state an opinion, were themselves expelled. About a hundred party members found themselves branded as Trotskyists in this way: most of those joined Cannon, Shachtman and Abern in establishing an American section of the International Left Opposition.

Cannon and Spector had expected to be expelled, and had laid plans in Moscow for the creation of a North American Trotskyist newspaper. Now Cannon wrote Spector proposing that immediate steps be taken towards this objective:

We thought in view of your position on the ECCI your most effective entry into the situation would be in the form of a letter to the ECCI against our expulsion which we would publish and which would be the signal for your openly joining us in the publication of a paper.

Events moved too quickly for this course to be followed. Even before Cannon's letter, U.S. party secretary Jay Lovestone had cabled Jack MacDonald, asking for Canadian endorsement of the expulsions. Such a motion was made at the regular Monday meeting of the CPC Political Bureau on November 5.

Spector refused to support the resolution and was immediately suspended, and ordered to explain his views on Trotskyism to a special meeting of the Central Executive Committee the following Sunday, November 11. Spector's reply to the order came in a statement dated November 6:

In reply to the question whether I am prepared "to wage an aggressive campaign against 'Trotskyism,'" I can assure the Polcom that I am prepared to wage an aggressive campaign for Leninism....

Trotsky today stands foursquare for the maintenance of the principles of Leninism, uncontaminated by the opportunist deviations that have been smuggled into [the] Comintern by the present Rykov-Stalin-Bucharin regime, and to which the lessons of the Chinese revolution, the economic situation in the USSR, the situation in the CPSU, and the experiences of the Anglo-Russian Committee bear eloquent witness.

He outlined his longstanding doubts about the course of the Comintern, and his equally longstanding hopes that the International would eventually right its own course.

It is now clear to me that it is insufficient for a revolutionist to "wait and see." His active ideological intervention is necessary if a correct line, failing which all discipline is hollow, is to be arrived at.... I fortunately came into possession of the suppressed documents of the Opposition, which I have carefully studied since and which have resolved all my doubts and brought me to my present unequivocal position.

Spector's nine-page typewritten statement recounted the course of the dispute in the CPSU and the International and presented Trotsky's positions on the principal questions, emphasizing the Chinese revolution. He called on the CPC to initiate a full discussion of the issues, beginning with publication of the documents of the Opposition. He concluded:

I have been a foundation member of the Communist Party of Canada since its organization, in which I took a joint part. I have also been a member of the CEC practically all the time since. Regardless of the immediate organizational consequences, I find myself compelled to make the above statement and to further register the fact that nothing on earth can separate me from the Revolutionary Communist movement. Everything that I have stated flows from my conviction that the deviations from Leninism in the CI can and must be corrected by a struggle within the International and its sections.
   Long Live the Communist International!
   Long Live the Proletarian Revolution!

At the November 11 CEC meeting the case for the prosecution was presented not by MacDonald, who might have attempted another compromise, but by Stewart Smith, the twenty-year-old former YCL leader who had just returned from two years at the "Lenin School" in Moscow. Like most other Lenin School students, Smith had joined the Communist movement after Lenin's death: for him acceptance of Stalinist ideas and methods required no break with the past. From 1926 until 1937 the Lenin School turned out a steady stream of fully indoctrinated Stalinists, international representatives of the Stalin faction: they played a central role in the conversion of the International into an agency of Stalin's foreign policy. Smith was no exception.*

Smith's attack on Spector was conducted with all the vitriol that he had acquired in Moscow. This relative neophyte accused the man who had chaired his party for years of "petty-bourgeois pessimism," of supporting "objectively counter-revolutionary" ideas. Spector was accused of personal responsibility for every problem the CPC had had for years. Most of the charges made against Spector were vague generalizations: some were patently false, such as the accusation that he had supported the Brandler wing of the Communist Party of Germany against the left wing.†

But the justness of the accusations was not at issue. Spector had committed the greatest crime possible in Stalin's Comintern: he had declared his support for Trotsky. This and this alone condemned him. By the end of the meeting he had been expelled from the party.

News of the expulsion spread rapidly through the Toronto labor movement. By Tuesday morning the *Globe* was reporting the story on the front page of its second section: "A sensation was created in Labor circles last night when it became known that Maurice Spector, spokesman for communism in Canada, had been expelled from the ranks of the party." [24]

The next day the same paper reported that Spector had made a public statement on his expulsion:

"I protested in a long statement that the fight against Leon Trotsky's exile which has been proceeding within Communist parties throughout the world for a year was not the real issue, but was being used to keep facts about the situation in Russia away from the rank and file," said Maurice Spector, former Chairman of the Communist Party in Canada, yesterday. "After James P. Cannon and two other outstanding leaders in the United

---

*It is no coincidence that the expulsion of Cannon in the United States and the subsequent anti-Trotsky campaign were engineered by Smith's Lenin School classmate Clarence Hathaway.

†No minutes of the November 11 meeting have survived, but the accusations against Spector were repeated in detail, in Smith's unmistakable prose style, in CEC statements in the *Worker*, November 24 and December 1.

States had been expelled, I was asked to support the action of the United States party. I refused, and was asked for my views. I stated them."

Spector was expelled from the party after serving it for eight years. He is a member of the Communist International, and, according to those in authority, is leading a minority which has for its purpose the return of Trotsky from exile and his restoration with full rights in the Communist International. Although opposed to the policies of the Government of the Soviet Union, he said he would appeal to the highest tribunal in the Communist movement against the action of the executive in Canada.

"Trotsky is not revising Leninism," declared Spector. "He has been slandered and denounced by those in power because he fought against a policy which strengthened the Nep man, and allowed private capital within the country to grow at the expense of the Socialist element. It is a significant fact that Lenin before his death offered Trotsky a bloc in the party to oppose Stalin. We want an internal democracy within the party."[25]

The labor press also reported Spector's expulsion widely. The *One Big Union Bulletin* in Winnipeg echoed the *Globe*'s view that the expulsion had created a sensation in the labor movement, and suggested that there was widespread dissatisfaction in the CP. The conservative *Labour Leader* made the expulsion front page news, as did *Canadian Labour World* and *The Labour News*. The *Trades and Labour Congress Journal* made a point of informing its readers of the expulsion. In most cases the labor papers expressed the view that this was just what could be expected among Communists, and that Spector deserved no sympathy.[26]

On November 17, the Saturday following the expulsion, the *Worker* appeared with a front page statement signed by the Central Executive Committee. Headed "The Communist Party of Canada Maintains Ideological Clarity," the statement contained very few facts and a great deal of invective. Trotskyism, it said, was "social democracy disguised with revolutionary phrases...objectively counter-revolutionary."

In succumbing to petty bourgeois pessimism, Maurice Spector has allied himself with the renegade Max Eastman, and finds himself without a single ally among the class conscious workers of Canada, or in the ranks of the Communist Party.[27]

Spector was virtually without allies—the CEC statement was correct on that point. Of course the CEC did not mention that Spector had been expelled before he could present his case to the membership, or that the Russian leadership had suppressed the documents of the Opposition and prevented its members from appealing to the International.

Since Spector had been denied access to the normal channels of internal party discussion, it took considerable gall for the CEC to condemn him for making a statement to "the reactionary Toronto Globe." Even the *OBU Bulletin* saw through that accusation:

> This expulsion was made as quickly as possible, so as to prevent Spector from stating his case in that paper which he was editing, and above all things, to stop him from revealing the documentary material that was in his possession which the party knew he could use to his advantage. Therefore the conflict is now almost totally one-sided, with the Communists fearing that Spector will use the only source left to him—the capitalist press.[28]

The expulsion and subsequent publicity did enable Spector to break out of his isolation to a degree. Now he could approach potential supporters openly—and now party members who had secretly nourished doubts about the International or sympathies for the Opposition knew who to talk to. Within two weeks Spector had gathered around him a group of about ten party members who were sympathetic to his cause. Spector's copy of Trotsky's *Criticism of the Draft Program* was passed from hand to hand (like Cannon, Spector had smuggled his copy out of Russia after the congress), but there was only one copy to read, and the issues were complex. Most of those who supported Spector in the first few weeks opposed the expulsion not because they agreed with his views, but because it was handled undemocratically: Spector wrote to Cannon that the majority of the group planned to abstain when asked to endorse the expulsion.

The Political Committee was not allowing such agnosticism. A full-scale Stalin-style campaign was under way against Spector and Trotsky, orchestrated by Stewart Smith. The membership was presented with a barrage of anti-Trotsky, anti-Spector propaganda. Membership meetings were held in every city and members were required to vote on a resolution condemning "Trotskyism and the Right Danger." Anyone who did not support the CEC was expelled. There was a parallel campaign in the Young Communist League.

Spector's earlier failure to insist on a full discussion of the anti-Trotsky campaign now hurt his cause. The CEC accused him of dishonesty for his failure to register his criticisms: since the party membership was unaware that Spector had defended his views in the Political Committee, such charges had an effect. More importantly, the party membership knew nothing about Trotskyism except what they read in the party press. Even members with doubts about the justice of Spector's expulsion would hesitate to face expulsion for the right to express those doubts. This was especially true of the members of the language federations: for them expulsion meant not only political isolation, but cultural and personal isolation as well.

Unlike James Cannon in the United States, Spector did not have a group of factional allies to approach for support, people who would give his ideas a hearing, no matter how heretical they might seem. The Canadian CP had no history of factionalism. That situation enabled the party to develop in a very healthy way during the early 1920s. But it also meant that Spector (and later MacDonald) lacked experience that would have aided them when they came up against Stalin's international faction.

Furthermore Spector, unlike Cannon—and unlike MacDonald— was not a working class leader with close ties to the rank and file. In a party whose membership was overwhelmingly proletarian, Spector was an intellectual. True, he had given himself wholly to the party, cutting himself off from a respectable career, but his role in the party had been as a writer and theoretician, not as a practical worker and organizer. This lent some credence to Smith's charge that he was "an 'intellectual revolutionary,' out of contact with the daily party problems and out of contact with the masses of the workers."29

By early in 1929, about thirty party and YCL members, almost all of them from Toronto, had been expelled for Trotskyism. Most found the isolation impossible to take and recanted, returning to the party within a few months. A dozen held their ground, and with Spector became the founders of the Canadian Trotskyist movement.

THE COMMUNIST PARTY OF CANADA HAD HELD ITS GROUND against the bureaucratization of the Comintern for a long time, longer than most national sections. It had accepted the political line of the International at every turn, but it had rejected the idea that a faction in the USSR could dictate who its leaders might be. Even when it capitulated on the question of Trotskyism, in 1927, it kept as its chairman a man known to be sympathetic to Trotsky. Spector was not only kept on as chairman of the party and editor of the *Worker*, he was made editor of the magazine *Canadian Labor Monthly*, launched in 1928. The party leadership, and MacDonald in particular, clearly believed that Spector's views were compatible with membership in the party, and saw no reason why secondary disagreements on strategy and tactics should deprive the party of Spector's services.

The expulsion of Spector in 1928 marked a decisive turn in party policy. The specific charges against Spector made by Smith were absurd, and the party leadership knew it. Spector was expelled for his political views alone. This set a dangerous precedent. By allowing factional considerations to decide who might be in the party, the leadership was preparing the way for a general purge of everyone who would not dance to Stalin's tune.*

APPENDIX
Spector's Expulsion:
The Tim Buck Version

Until the 1960s, Tim Buck had an absolute monopoly on the writing of Canadian Communist Party history. Each time he wrote about the party's early years, however, he was faced by a difficult problem: How to explain the fact that "Tim Buck's Party" had been founded and led by people who were expelled before the party was ten years old? How could the Communist Party have been led by counterrevolutionaries?

Until 1968 Buck was able to resolve this difficulty by skimming quickly over the early years of the party, mentioning names as little as possible, describing major events as briefly and as inaccurately as possible.

In 1968 William Rodney published a scholarly and carefully

---

*MacDonald may have been aware of the danger of the step he was taking. It is noteworthy that he did not write anything attacking Spector until early 1929, when he received proof that Spector had been collaborating with Cannon before the expulsion. Then he wrote an article for the *Worker* (January 19, 1929) in which he charged that Spector was guilty of building a secret faction: the ideological crimes of Trotskyism were scarcely mentioned. He may have been attempting to provide a retroactive "legal" justification for the clearly "illegal" expulsion. He may also have been attempting to head off an attack on himself from a real secret faction that was now developing in the party: the Buck-Smith grouping (described in the next chapter).

researched history of the CPC's early years, *Soldiers of the International*. It presented a very different picture of the CPC in the 1920s from the one Buck had been painting. It showed a party led, not by Tim Buck alone, but by a *team* of capable revolutionary leaders. It showed a party that was shattered by a major crisis at the end of the 1920s. And it showed a party which—horror of horrors!—had refused to condemn Trotsky when asked to do so by Moscow.

Characteristically, Buck did not reply directly to Rodney's book. Instead, in 1970 he published a new account of the CPC's first decade, *Lenin and Canada*. In content, though not in form, the book was a polemic against Rodney, an attempt to reestablish the Tim Buck version of history. Factually the book added a few footnotes to Buck's biography, but not many. It repeated many of the errors and outright falsifications that Rodney had pointed out: it even added some new ones. Almost all of the new material concerned the pernicious influence of Maurice Spector on the CPC, and the battle Tim Buck had waged against the "poisonous seeds of Trotskyism."

In the interests of providing a straightforward narrative, I have not dealt at any length in chapters 10 and 11 with Buck's version of the origins of Canadian Trotskyism. Indeed, correcting all of his misstatements would double the length of this book, and would add nothing to the reader's understanding of the events. However, in the interests of keeping the historical record straight, it seems to me valuable to deal briefly with three aspects of Buck's account: Spector's trip to Germany, the Alhambra Hall meeting, and the events leading to Spector's expulsion.

Spector in Germany

It was during his stay in Germany and Russia in 1923-1924 that Maurice Spector first began to question the wisdom of some of the policies of the Comintern leadership. Tim Buck, who is unwilling to admit that there might have been some legitimacy to Spector's doubts and questions, attempts to make this into a conspiracy.

According to Buck's 1970 version, Spector by the beginning of 1923 was beginning to tire of the hard work of building a party. He had joined the party when the labor movement was on the upswing, but now that things were difficult, "he withdrew from full-time party work in the spring of 1923 and returned to the university with the avowed intention of 'going into law.'" Such was all that could be expected of Spector, who, Buck points out, was "the son of a small shopkeeper"—i.e., a petty-bourgeois.

Shortly after returning to school, however, Spector became excited about the prospects of revolution in Germany. "He abandoned his studies again...when an ardent admirer of Lenin and supporter of the Canadian party offered to pay his expenses for an extended visit to Germany...." Although he was supposed to be studying the work of the German party, Spector "spent his time with the Trotskyites, staying in the home of one of the most committed of them." Then, "he proceeded to Moscow where, secretly, he completed his integration with the Trotskyites."

When Spector returned to Canada he resumed his position as a full-time party worker and became editor of the *Worker* again. His policies in that position were part of a deliberate Trotskyite plan to subvert the Canadian party.[30]

This is the type of story that is virtually impossible to disprove. There is no evidence offered, there are no concrete facts provided; just a string of charges. But the fact remains that Buck's account contains scarcely one word of truth.

It is interesting to note that this was not the first time that Buck told this story about Spector. An earlier version appeared in a speech Buck gave in 1937, when the Kremlin's campaign against "counter-revolutionary Trotskyism" was in full swing:

In 1923...Spector resigned as editor of *The Worker* and returned to his law studies, seeing no financial future for himself as a labor journalist. At this time he interested a wealthy sympathiser in purchasing a certain concession available in the U.S.S.R. during the difficult period of the New Economic Policy. The sympathiser was to supply $300,000 and Spector himself was to be one of the much despised Nepmen* by promoting the deal, demonstrating early his "Bolshevik steadfastness" and his faith in the toiling masses of the USSR. The deal fell through and he returned to his old position on *The Worker*.[31]

This account, though it could be used in the 1930s, was too obviously slanderous to be repeated in 1970—so Buck laundered it, eliminating the NEP, the $300,000, and much more. But the existence of the earlier version discredits the later one—especially since Spector acted as a party representative in Germany and Russia, reporting regularly to the Canadian Political Committee on his activities. All that is left is a wealthy party sympathiser (a Hamilton lawyer, J.L. Counsell) who financed the trip—this was a

---

*The "Nepmen" were capitalist entrepeneurs permitted to operate in the USSR, under license, in the years 1921-1927.

normal practice, since the party budget did not provide for major expenses of this type.

As for Spector's resignation to become a lawyer, a simple reading of the pages of the *Worker* explodes that charge. Spector ceased to function as editor of the *Worker* in December 1922, not "the spring of 1923," and not in order to return to law school but because the party was sending him to Moscow to attend the Fourth Congress of the Communist International. He was in Russia for two months. On his return he reported to the 1923 convention of the Canadian party on the congress, and wrote a long series of articles for the *Worker* on the implications of the congress's decisions for Canada. At the beginning of April he undertook a cross-country speaking tour on the Fourth Congress, starting in Sudbury and travelling to Vancouver—the tour lasted into June.[32] By that time the revolutionary events in Germany were being reported everywhere, so when Counsell offered to finance a Canadian Communist's trip there, Spector, the only party leader who spoke fluent German, was a logical choice. He was in Germany by early in September.

It is impossible, of course, to prove that Spector never expressed a desire to complete his degree—but he certainly didn't have time to do anything about it in 1923!

In Germany, Spector stayed not with a committed Trotskyist but with Hertha Sturm, the most active member of the Comintern's International Women's Secretariat.[33] And as for "completing his integration" with the Trotskyites in Moscow, there was no Trotskyist organization beyond the CPSU opposition in 1924: the first non-Russian groups sympathetic to the Left Opposition were created in Western Europe in 1925 and 1926, and these had no contact with the Russians before 1927. There was nothing for Spector to "complete his integration" with. In fact, as has been argued in chapter 10, Spector's actions in the years 1924 through 1927 can only be explained by accepting his own statement that he had doubts—but no program.

The Alhambra Hall Meeting

The October 25, 1928 Alhambra Hall meeting (page 210) has passed into Canadian CP mythology as the occasion when the Trotskyite devil finally showed his horns. A review of the various accounts that have been provided about this event provides an interesting picture of the reliability of CP historiography.

Given his prejudices, A.E. Smith's 1949 account seems to fit the known facts, except for the name of the hall:

I remember a mass meeting of party members which was held in the Spadina Hall, subsequent to the return of our delegates from an important congress of the Communist International in Moscow. M. Spector was the speaker of the evening. The address occupied well over an hour. It consisted of a calculated array of slanders against the Soviet Union and its leaders. The speech left everybody cold with astonishment. At its conclusion, the meeting seemed to disperse automatically. Members stood around in groups discussing the situation created by the speech in an animated fashion. I remember Bob Shoesmith approaching me and asking "What do you think of that, A.E.?"

I replied: "I cannot agree with his attitude. He should certainly be asked for a full explanation."

That was on a Sunday evening. Before the close of the next day, the same speaker had agreed to make a second address to the party in order to "explain" his first. But in the meantime his organized connections with the Trotskyists were exposed.[34]

Tim Buck, in 1952, wrote only that:

The content of his report was such that, following the meeting, a number of party members headed by Beckie Buhay demanded of the chairman that the matter be dealt with by the Political Committee of the party.[35]

Rebecca Buhay is certainly miscast here: as we have seen, in October 1928 she was secretly discussing Trotskyism with Spector. In the April 13, 1929 *Worker* Robert Shoesmith charged that after Spector's speech Buhay "pooh-poohed the suggestion of myself and others on the City Committee who...concluded that Spector had arrived at a Trotskyist position." Buhay did not deny the charge.

In 1965, in the interviews later published as his *Reminiscences*, Buck moved himself to center-stage. Now he claimed that he himself had been chairman of the Alhambra Hall meeting. Normally a member of the Toronto executive would have performed that task, but Buck was chosen "to lend a certain amount of weight" to the occasion. Why inclusion of the trade union director would "lend weight" to a meeting addressed by a man who was chairman of the party and editor of the *Worker* Buck does not explain—nor does he offer an explanation for the fact that the advertisements announcing the meeting do not mention his name.

Buck says that Spector's speech was very carefully prepared, and he presented his Trotskyist opinions in a guarded way. Nevertheless, Buck realized what was going on.

After Maurice had finished his speech, I got up and pointed out that as chairman I shared responsibility for what was said, as well as for keeping order, and I must disassociate myself from many of the things that Maurice had said. I didn't want to get into an argument with him at this moment, but I wanted it to be on record that the chairman did not agree and would insist upon having a more thorough discussion. As a result, the meeting broke up with a certain amount of confusion.

A group of members, including Becky Buhay, the sister of Mike, stopped me as I was going out and said, "Look Tim, you didn't say enough, you should have denounced him."[36]

Five years later, Beckie Buhay disappeared entirely from Buck's account, as did her criticism of his mildness. So too, it seems, did much of Spector's speech, which A.E. Smith had described as occupying "well over an hour."

His address was short but he succeeded in conveying such a negative impression that I, as chairman of the meeting, representing the City Committee, found it necessary to explain to the audience that I disassociated myself from it, considered parts of it to be thinly-veiled slanders of the Soviet Union, and that I intended to bring the matter before the party Secretariat. Following the meeting a group of comrades thanked me and volunteered to be on hand to support my demand for action.[37]

Oscar Ryan's hagiographic tribute to Buck, published in 1975, added the hitherto unknown detail that Buck "arranged for a special meeting of the party's Political Committee for the next day."[38]

The principal value of these accounts is that they show the impact of Stalinism on the writing of the history of the Canadian CP. Not only truth but even internal consistency is abandoned in the interests of portraying a political opponent as negatively as possible and glorifying the party leader.

It is scarcely necessary or useful to point out all the inaccuracies and inconsistencies in these reports: the reader can surely see them. The most important is the sudden addition of Buck as chairman in the 1965 and 1970 versions. If Buck had indeed publicly dissociated himself from a speech by Spector (who was chairman of the party and editor of both of its periodicals) there would have been a major sensation. It would have been reported, at least in the labor press if not in the daily press. Certainly A.E. Smith would not have failed to mention it—he goes out of his way to praise Buck on other occasions. But none of these things happened. Buck's account is entirely fictitious.

The Expulsion

In contrast to the Alhambra Hall story, Tim Buck's accounts of Spector's suspension and expulsion from the CPC were remarkably consistent (although there are minor discrepancies) through several tellings. According to the Buck version, the Political Bureau (PB) met shortly after the Alhambra Hall meeting to discuss Spector's heresies. At the PB meeting MacDonald proposed to refer the incident to the full Central Committee. In one account, an "emergency meeting" of the Central Committee was "convened immediately to investigate the 'political position of Comrade Spector.'"[39] In another, the PB meeting "adjourned with a vaguely worded motion by Jack MacDonald that it should lay on the table until the next meeting of the full Central Committee."[40] In a third, MacDonald "insisted that the PB call the full Central Committee into session (a remarkable step for MacDonald). . . ."[41]

When the Central Committee meeting opened, MacDonald surprised everyone "by producing copies of correspondence between Spector and the leaders of the Trotskyite organization in the United States, elaborating plans to split the Communist Party and establish a Trotskyite organization in Canada."[42]

Confronted with such evidence, Spector had to confess, and he was immediately expelled.

Where did the evidence come from? In the 1952 version, Buck said that it came from the secretary of the U.S. Communist Party, Jay Lovestone, who "had only recently come into possession of the evidence by a peculiar accident and had supplied it to MacDonald because of their close personal cooperation."[43] He was more explicit about the nature of this "peculiar accident" when he was interviewed in 1965: now he reported that, on MacDonald's request, "Lovestone arranged to have Jim Cannon's personal correspondence rifled and secured one or two letters and telegrams from Spector."[44] In 1970, however, he referred only to "materials that had been found in Cannon's files" and to "the seizure of Cannon's files." He is quite insistent that this "seizure" took place "before October 27th."[45]

This story had some obvious political advantages for Buck. It shows Spector being expelled for an actual antiparty conspiracy, rather than simply for endorsing Trotsky's ideas. Secondly, it ties MacDonald to Lovestone, who was shortly thereafter expelled from the U.S. party. In his *Reminiscences*, Buck adds an additional dig at MacDonald, charging that at the time of Spector's expulsion

MacDonald was secretly plotting with Lovestone to split the Canadian party. Any story that simultaneously damned both of Buck's major opponents was worth keeping alive.

But Buck's account is a tissue of lies, from beginning to end.

Spector was suspended on November 5, 1928, well after the "mild sensation" created by his October 25 Alhambra Hall speech had died down. He was expelled on November 11. Accounts of his expulsion appeared in the *Worker*, dated November 24 and December 1, with follow-up reports in subsequent issues. *Not one of those reports mentions the "evidence" MacDonald supposedly produced.* Not until the January 19, 1929 issue did the *Worker* print any evidence linking Spector and Cannon, but by that time the connection was public knowledge. The evidence consisted of letters and telegrams: the earliest was dated October 9; the latest, by internal evidence, must have been written in early December, because it refers to a Toronto party meeting held to endorse the expulsion of Spector.

This material was not published earlier because the CP did not have it earlier. It was all obtained in a burglary of James P. Cannon's apartment in New York City on December 23, 1928. The burglary was carried out by members of the U.S. Communist Party's national staff. Copies of some of the items stolen appeared in the U.S. *Daily Worker* simultaneously with the publication of excerpts in Canada.[46]

It is understandable that Buck did not want this story known. He insisted on the October 27 date because that was the date of Cannon's expulsion: any action taken before that date could be placed under the heading of "party discipline," if the definition were stretched a bit. A robbery after that was pure gangsterism, by any definition.

Readers of this book will realize by now that Tim Buck's "historical" works are at best unreliable, at worst deliberately false. This generalization applies with full force to his account of the origins of Canadian Trotskyism.

12. The Sixth Convention

Immediately after Spector's expulsion, Jack MacDonald went on a national tour to report on the Sixth Congress of the Comintern and to explain the expulsion of Spector. According to Buck (and other Communist Party historians), MacDonald's tour was cut short in Winnipeg when the local Communists, headed by Tom McEwen, accused him of "advocating...not the line of the world Communist movement but Lovestone's line of 'American exceptionalism.'"[1]* Thwarted in his attempt to smuggle this revisionist policy into Canada, MacDonald returned to Toronto and

tried to win support for the theory that Canadian economy, by virtue of its close ties with United States economy, was immune to the danger of capitalist crisis and, therefore, it was wrong to base the line of the party upon the prospect of economic crisis and the increasing radicalization of the masses.[2]

Elsewhere Buck wrote: "MacDonald declared flatly that United States monopoly capital had become so strong that it could control the economy and, therefore, there would not be an economic crisis in the U.S. or Canada."[3]

As with virtually everything else in the official version of the events of 1928-1931, these accounts are quite false. For example, Lovestone himself was not charged with "American exceptionalism" until May 1929, so Tom McEwen could not have accused

---

*"American exceptionalism" was the view that North America was immune to the general laws of capitalist development.

MacDonald of holding to "Lovestone's theory" in December of 1928.[4] The political debates of 1929 were published, at great length, in the pages of the *Worker,* and the party's internal documents for the period are available to historians in the Public Archives of Ontario: in all of this mass of documentary material there is not one scrap of evidence that MacDonald ever held or defended the opinions Buck ascribes to him. MacDonald was not even accused of holding such views until long after the party's 1929 convention.

What really happened in the battle for control of the CPC was far more complex, and far more damaging to the reputation of Buck and his faction, than any official party history will ever admit.

The "Right Danger"

Stewart Smith returned from Moscow's "Lenin School" in October 1928, just in time for the expulsion of Maurice Spector. As a recent graduate, with all the latest techniques at his fingertips, he was placed in charge of the witch-hunt. He was chief prosecutor in the Central Executive Committee; he was the author of the CEC's major resolution on Trotskyism; he spoke for the party leadership at the critical membership meeting in Toronto that endorsed Spector's expulsion.

But for those who could see the signs, it was clear that Smith was after other game as well. The major statement he wrote regarding the expulsion declared:

The main danger in the Communist International and the Canadian party at the present time is the danger from the right. While not for a moment weakening the struggle against Trotskyism, the Canadian party must set itself the task of combating the right dangers....[5]

The resolution that Smith wrote for adoption at all party meetings was not just against Trotskyism, but "Against Trotskyism and the Right Danger."

The "Right Danger" had become a catchphrase in the Comintern during 1928. At the Sixth Congress Bukharin argued that "the right deviation now represents the central danger"—early in 1929 he found that he was being identified as the principal representative of that deviation. But before direct attacks on Bukharin began, the Stalin faction moved against Bukharin's allies and potential allies in other parties. Smith's attack on the Right Danger in Canada was a part of this softening-up process.

One party leader who realized that Smith was up to something was Florence Custance. On November 27 she wrote to the Political Committee, rejecting the claim, made in Smith's resolution, that "bourgeois ideology" in the party was a major problem. She wrote another letter on the subject a few days later. When Toronto Group V of the Communist Party met, Custance, a member of the group, proposed an alternative resolution to the one the Central Executive Committee submitted:

That this group unreservedly support the action of the C.E.C. in expelling Maurice Spector from the party, owing to his unreserved stand with the Trotskyist Opposition as we consider Trotskyism is the greatest danger to the Communist Parties of the world and the Communist International.[6]

No one could fault this statement so far as its anti-Trotsky sentiments were concerned, but the Right Danger was missing entirely, and Trotskyism, contrary to the line of the CEC, was declared the "greatest danger."

Seeing his chance to concretize his charge that there existed a Right Danger in the CPC, Stewart Smith proposed in the Political Committee "that comrade Custance be censured, first of all for disobeying the instructions of the Polcom regarding the resolution, and secondly for influencing the group to vote against the Party resolution."[7] It was this motion, not a confrontation with Tom McEwen, that brought MacDonald back from his national speaking tour.*

On December 18 the Political Committee discussed Smith's motion. It was supported only by Smith and Oscar Ryan, the YCL representative on the Polcom. (Buck, who probably would have supported it, was out of the country.) A resolution proposed by MacDonald was adopted, asking Custance to "repudiate her actions and its implications" and referring her resolution back to Group V for another vote.

Custance responded with a statement to the Polcom in which she

---

*What happened when MacDonald visited Winnipeg remains obscure. He later said: "I went to Winnipeg at the time and found there two camps. I went into both camps; the opposition camp wanted to decide whether the CEC representative should be allowed in."[8] The conflict was undoubtedly related to the long-standing split in the Winnipeg CP between the Ukrainians and the "Anglo-Saxons." Shortly before he went to Winnipeg, MacDonald, in a CEC meeting, supported the Ukrainians in a debate over who should be the party's candidate in the Winnipeg municipal elections. The "Anglo-Saxon" members' choice had been Tom McEwen.[9]

apparently agreed that, as a CEC member, she ought not to have introduced an opposing resolution in her Group. As to its content, however, she was unrepentant:

In conclusion, I wish to state that the reservations I have placed before the Polcom, I still stand by. And in this connection may I make it quite clear that I do not underestimate Right Wing dangers and that these in a revolutionary movement are the greatest dangers. Since I entered the revolutionary movement some seventeen years ago, I have consistently fought reformism, class collaboration, the policies of compromise, and any action which tended to weaken the militant struggle of the workers. However, my experience in the movement has forced upon me the necessity of keeping a well-balanced viewpoint towards objective conditions, consequently I have not allowed myself to wander into the realms of impossibility and heroics, and to make the mistake that the workers can be won for the revolution simply by uttering revolutionary phrases.[10]

Smith, Buck, and Ryan did their utmost to have Custance censured for this statement as well, but were blocked by the majority. This was the first skirmish in what was to become a major war.

While Smith was launching his attack on Custance, Buck was establishing international connections. He went to New York to attend a plenum of the Central Committee of the U.S. party, December 15-19. That plenum was marked by a controversy between the majority, led by Jay Lovestone, and a minority represented by William Z. Foster, Alexander Bittelman, and Earl Browder. The latter group was hopelessly outnumbered on the Central Committee, where it was defeated 28 votes to 7, and in the U.S. party ranks, where Lovestone's resolutions consistently received 70 to 75 percent of the vote. Six months later Lovestone would be expelled from the Communist International and Browder would take his place, with Foster as his chief lieutenant.

Buck had apparently been briefed by Smith before he went to New York. In any event, he had long been closely associated with Foster in the Trade Union Educational League. At the plenum Buck gave fraternal greetings from Canada and, over the protests of Lovestone's supporters, used the occasion to declare his support for the Foster-Bittelman-Browder faction.[11] His report back to the Canadian leadership argued that the Foster group "takes as its point of departure the characterization of the present (third) period of capitalist reconstruction, given in the thesis of the Sixth World Congress of the Comintern." The unspoken implication was that Lovestone's line was not based on Comintern policy. When Buck added that he was quoting the minority's criticisms of Lovestone "because many of them apply to our work here," everyone knew what was meant.¹²

BY THE END OF DECEMBER 1928, then, Tim Buck and Stewart Smith had declared themselves to be the defenders of the Comintern line against the Right Danger, and had tacitly announced their intention to oust the old guard from office, beginning with the weakest links. The main support for Buck and Smith came from the leadership of the Young Communist League. Buck had been party representative on the YCL executive since the 1927 convention, and had inherited the leadership of the anti-MacDonald clique that Spector had been involved with. This group, including Beckie Buhay, Charles Marriott, Oscar Ryan, Sam Carr, and others, was joined by two prominent party leaders from the West. Tom McEwen, from Winnipeg, had for some time been engaged in factional battles with the Ukrainian leaders who had long been associated with MacDonald: he was a natural ally for Buck. Malcolm Bruce, now in Vancouver, had attended the 1924 Comintern congress with Buck, had opposed Spector's "Trotskyism" in 1925, and had a reputation for being hostile towards the Toronto leadership: he too was a natural ally. This group was to form the core of the leadership of the Communist Party for many years to come.

Opposing Buck and Smith stood a coalition of forces, organized around the party's old guard—MacDonald, Custance, Mike Buhay, and William Moriarty being the most prominent. This group included almost all of the party's trade unionists—such men as Fred Peel, Bob Shoesmith, and J.B. Salsberg, all well-known Communists, all recognized as leaders in the labor movement. And, most important of all, it included the leaders of the Jewish, Ukrainian and Finnish organizations, which included over 90 percent of the party membership. Their long-standing association with MacDonald and their more recent but very bitter hostility to Buck made their position a foregone conclusion.

(In 1965 Buck claimed that "those who expressed their agreement with me were very largely the old-timers.... [MacDonald] felt that he had all the new people, the younger people."¹³ In fact the line-up was just the reverse.)

Never before had there been such a split in the ranks of the Communist Party of Canada. The debate was guaranteed, in advance, to be much sharper than anything the Canadian Communists had ever seen.

The Preconvention Discussion

But whatever anyone expected beforehand, no one was prepared for the violence of the discussion itself. The Canadian party had always conducted its discussions in the most comradely way. The back-biting, scandal-mongering, mindlessly vicious faction fights that the U.S. party experienced were unknown, and the Canadians had always congratulated themselves on their ability to solve problems without resorting to that sort of thing. After 1929 they had nothing to congratulate themselves about.

The preconvention debate opened with the publication in the February 23 *Worker* of draft political theses for the party. The document, which occupied almost two full pages of the newspaper, quoted extensively from the resolutions of the Sixth Congress—by any reasonable standard, it was an orthodox resolution, following the official line. Only in the last paragraph did its author, MacDonald, suggest that he saw dangers in the new line:

The reverse side of this right danger—the greatest danger—is the "left" danger, a certain underestimation of the difficulties, a losing of contact with the masses, a rejection of the United Front policy, and failure to fight the trade union bureaucracy and its expulsion policy on grounds that the work is hopeless and fruitless, the danger of degeneration into a propaganda sect substituting revolutionary phrases for everyday work among the workers.

Stewart Smith was having none of this. In the March 9 *Worker* he published a long diatribe against MacDonald entitled "Clarity in the Struggle Against Trotskyism and the Right Danger." He accused MacDonald of deliberately using misquotation and selective quotation in order to distort the line of the Comintern. The party was making serious political errors, right-wing errors. Florence Custance and William Moriarty were cited in particular for "concrete manifestations of the right danger." Like most of Smith's contributions to this debate, this article was long on accusations and very short on facts.

In the same issue Smith and Buck jointly published a draft resolution urging the CPC to break with the Canadian Labor Party, and Buck-Smith supporters Annie Buller, Beckie Buhay, Fred Rose, and Jack Clarke accused the party leadership of everything from underestimating the war danger to failure to develop an agrarian program.

The debate went downhill from there. MacDonald replied that his theses were only a draft, that the Political Committee, with Smith present, had decided to rush them into print despite their obvious shortcomings, in order to get the preconvention discussion under way. Smith, he said, was guilty of "dishonest political intrigue."

When a comrade agrees without hesitation to amend certain sections of a thesis, as I did (and not even from suggestions from Comrade Smith) and agreed to include in the thesis not only the basis for the growth of right errors, but their manifestations, and then a comrade of the Polcom writes in a lead article in a reference to the thesis that "he has carefully left out mention of the concrete manifestations of the 'right' danger" this is dishonesty that must be condemned and is a manifestation of unprincipled factional activity. This is not the only statement which twists facts or states half-truths in Comrade Smith's article.... [14]

In the same issue of the *Worker*, Florence Custance expanded on the charge of dishonesty, and suggested what Smith's motive was:

Comrade Smith has an axe to grind, and he adopts as his policy to serve this purpose—any means to an end. Consequently, the kind of self-criticism he introduces into his contribution to the Party Discussion is based upon falsification of facts and distortion of statements. So when he makes Self-Criticism the keynote of his article and builds up his case on the basis of misrepresentation, his statement cannot be treated as a honest statement, and himself to be taken as an honest comrade. Why should he single out three comrades for special mention and criticism is well known to us. It has been whispered too often—a change in party leadership must be made—not to understand the motive for Comrade Smith's action. [15]

And so the debate went on. Its political content was almost nonexistent: there were no evident disagreements between the two sides on program or policy. Both sides claimed to be supporting the decisions of the Sixth Congress, both sides condemned Trotskyism *and* the Right Danger. One exasperated party member suggested that the Comintern be asked to "decide if there are real differences as to correct line.... This factional fighting will leave our party in a similar position to the Kilkenny cats who fought until there was nothing left." [16]

MacDonald's contributions to the debate in particular were marked by a sense of bewilderment. He was doing his utmost to interpret the Comintern line for Canada, but he could do nothing that would stop the vicious factionalism of Smith and Buck. MacDonald didn't seem to realize that he was dealing not with a rational political debate on issues related to the party's concrete experiences in Canada, but with an international faction fight whose outcome had already been decided in the Kremlin's inner circles. In December the German Communist Party leadership was purged. Bukharin's supporters on the Comintern's Executive Committee were being removed one by one. Lovestone was due to get the axe in May, just after Bukharin himself was removed from all positions of authority. Smith and Buck were determined to be on the winning side.

As well, the conflict reflected the ambiguous nature of the decisions of the Sixth Comintern Congress, which balanced between the Stalin and Bukharin factions in the Soviet party. Bukharin himself had written most of the congress's resolutions, and Stalin had voted for them: many lines could be read into them. The Buck-Smith and MacDonald wings each found what suited them in the resolutions, each emphasized different aspects—but even the differences of emphasis were slight. Until Moscow acted, no decision between the factions was possible.

The Comintern Intervenes

The Canadian convention had originally been scheduled to begin on March 29. In February, however, the Comintern's Political Secretariat cabled the CPC: "POLSEC UNANIMOUSLY REQUEST POSTPONE PARTY CONGRESS TILL THIRD WEEK IN MAY. REQUEST YOU SEND ANY CONFERENCE MATERIALS PREPARED."[17] After raising some minor objections, the Canadian party leadership agreed: the convention did not in fact convene until May 31.

Nothing like this had ever happened to the Canadian Communist Party. Maurice Spector commented wryly:

The Canadian Party whose portion in the Comintern hitherto has been the fate of "those wretched souls" Dante sings about, "who lived without praise or blame"—has achieved the dignity of those other elect whose conventions are mysteriously postponed in deference to cablegrams from "Moscow."[18]

It *was* mysterious—but it did not remain so for long. The delay allowed the Comintern to intervene, to ensure that a "correct" line was adopted. It is at least possible that Smith asked his co-factionalists for the delay—and for the intervention. Certainly when the Comintern's opinions arrived, in the form of a letter from the Political Secretariat, dated April 8, 1929, they were cause for celebration in the Buck-Smith camp.

From a close study of our Canadian brother party [the letter read], we see numerous manifestations of Right tendencies, persistence of Social Democratic forms of organization (federalism and independent language groups), underestimation of radicalization of the masses, insufficient attention to trade union work and activity among the unorganized, subordination of Party to Labor Party, no agrarian program, underestimation of war danger.[19]

MacDonald's resolution "Situation and Tasks of the Party" came in for sharp criticism. It contained "needless repetition of the resolutions of the VI Congress" and was "overloaded with statistics to the exclusion of an adequate treatment of the actual problems facing the Communist Party of Canada." Even more seriously, it failed to "examine thoroughly the productive relations within the country and the prospect of crises," and "over-stressed the 'prosperity' of Canada."

The letter attacked "the maintenance of a Labour Party as a screen for the Communists in the belief that the CP can only become a mass Party through the medium of a Labour Party (Alberta)." Since Moriarty had been leading the party work in Alberta in the recent past, this was a clear attack on him. Another passage condemned "the emphatic bourgeois pacifist ideas held by leading women comrades," echoing a charge made by Smith against Custance. In fact every charge made by the Buck-Smith faction against the MacDonald team found an echo in the Comintern letter: underestimation of the radicalization of the masses, failure to organize the unorganized, failure to develop an agrarian program, failure to recruit French Canadians, failure to recognize the role of the YCL in organizing foreign-born youth, and on, and on.

Virtually the only aspect of party work that did not come in for severe criticism was trade union work—Buck's special field. Although this area of activity had "shown serious signs of weakness," nevertheless the party had "done good work in the direction of organizing the unorganized automobile workers and in forming the industrial needle trades union" and had "participated actively in a number of recent strikes." And the resolution proposed by Tim Buck on Trade Union work "considerably helps to clarify and emphasize the important tasks of the Party in Trade Union Work."

The letter caused jubilation in the Buck-Smith faction and dismay among their opponents. Mike Buhay mildly criticized it as "confusing." MacDonald went further:

I stated when I read the letter first that I did not think the letter an impressive letter.... I could see in it, or thought I did, not the mature consideration of the leading elements in the Comintern, but I thought I saw the writings of Comrades Leslie Morris and Sam Carr.[20]

MacDonald was probably correct in suggesting that the letter was the work of Smith's successors in the Lenin School, but such remarks were not to be made in Stalin's Comintern. The leadership of the Young Communist League charged that MacDonald's comments showed "a complete misunderstanding of the collective work and leadership of the CI" and "can only result in undermining the prestige of the CI."[21]

The Comintern letter became *the* central issue in the faction fight. According to later CP mythology—a mythology which unfortunately has been accepted by even non-party historians— the debate was between Buck, who endorsed the CI line, and MacDonald, who did not. In view of the widespread acceptance of this view, it may be useful to consider how it was seen at the time. John Williamson, an American who attended the Canadian party convention in 1929 as a representative of the Young Communist International, described it this way:

The Convention and the Plenum were divided into *three tendencies*, 1. those who declared their acceptance of the C.I. Letter (*Buck-Smith*) and made efforts to correct their own mistakes.... 2. those who resisted the C.I. line *M. Buhay, Moriarty*, etc.—associates of *MacDonald*, and 3. *MacDonald*, who while declaring he accepted the C.I. Letter and admitting his own mistakes, in his report repeated his basic errors and categorically refused to attack and dissociate himself from Buhay, etc.[22] [emphasis in original]

Similarly, at the convention itself the Young Communist League, under the control of the Buck-Smith faction, made a clear distinction between "such comrades as...M. Buhay, Custance and Moriarty," whom it branded as "open Right elements," and MacDonald, who was criticized primarily for "his categoric refusal to separate himself from such open Right elements."[23] The fraternal delegate of the U.S. Communist Party, Clarence Hathaway, distinguished between the "open Right tendencies expressed by Comrade Buhay and Moriarty," and the "conciliatory tendencies of Comrade MacDonald."[24]

The idea that there were *three* tendencies and not two flies in the face of everything the CPC has since written about the Sixth

Convention. As early as the fall of 1929 the Buck-Smith faction was describing the conflict as one between the Right Wing, led by MacDonald, and the Left Wing, led by Buck and Smith.[25] But a schema based on a two-way split makes the convention itself and the events that followed it completely incomprehensible. There were three distinct groupings: Buck-Smith, Moriarty-Buhay, and MacDonald's "conciliator" group.* Buck and Smith, of course, saw themselves as the only real supporters of the Comintern Letter, but MacDonald also endorsed it, withdrew his Draft Theses, and defended it in party meetings and at the convention.

It was Mike Buhay and William Moriarty who led the real opposition to the CI Letter. Both were particularly disturbed by the tendency of the International to accept "dual unionism." As early as the October 1928 plenum of the Canadian party's CEC, Buhay had criticized "the tendency to get away from the fight against the bureaucracy in the Unions, and some Comrades tried to solve this the easy way by forming new Unions."[26] This was a direct challenge to the party's move to create the Industrial Union of Needle Trades Workers—a move the CI letter explicitly endorsed. (This project is discussed more fully in Chapter 15.) At the same meeting Buhay said that in general in Canada "Left errors" were more serious than the Right Danger.[27] During the discussion of the Comintern's letter, Buhay also opposed the turn away from involvement in the Canadian Labor Party.

Moriarty did not contribute to the written discussion, and no transcripts of his oral contributions have been found, but from remarks made by others about him, and from his subsequent emergence as the central leader of the Lovestoneite organization in Canada, it is quite certain that his views were similar to Buhay's— if anything, he was stronger in his opposition to the ultraleft turn demanded by the Comintern.

After the Political Committee's first discussion of the Comintern letter, Tim Buck presented a resolution endorsing its main points. He was instructed to edit his resolution and have it mimeographed for final discussion and presentation to the convention. But, according to MacDonald, Buck's editing produced unexpected results:

---

*Custance, who was bitterly hostile to Buck and in general supported the Buhay-Moriarty group, fell ill before the convention and played no role in it. She died on July 12.

...the following morning the resolution was in the office, a fundamentally different resolution than the first one. It singled out certain comrades, some of the remarks of comrades Buhay, Moriarty, Custance, characterized them as right elements, asked that at, and following the convention, organizational measures be taken against these comrades....[28]

Buck's resolution raised a bitter dispute to the level of a major crisis. He and Smith wanted the expulsion or suspension of three of the party's founders: MacDonald would not accept such measures against people he had worked with for a decade.* With Buck and Smith determined to force a major organizational confrontation, and MacDonald determined to resist, the possibility of a split loomed. At the very least, it seemed that the Political Committee would face the convention with majority and minority reports on all major questions.

That eventuality was prevented by the arrival, a week before the convention, of Clarence Hathaway, representing the U.S. Communist Party, and John Williamson, representing the Young Communist International. Hathaway in particular came armed with instructions from his party (which had far more regular contact with Moscow than the Canadians did) to "take a position firmly opposed to the maintenance of factions in the Canadian party," and to point out that the Right danger could only be defeated "with the abolition of faction activities and group formations."[29]

Hathaway and Williamson negotiated a compromise. Buck and Smith withdrew their demand for organizational measures against Moriarty, Buhay, and Custance, and a subcommittee composed of MacDonald, Buhay, Smith, Buck, and the two Americans was established to draft a single resolution for the convention.[30] The resolution produced declared "unequivocal acceptance of the line of the C.I. [as] the basis for unity in the Canadian Party." It endorsed "all the corrections of the mistakes made by our party" in the C.I. Letter. For the most part the resolution consisted of word-for-word repetitions of the charges and criticisms made in the Comintern's letter.[31]

For the convention itself, a compromise arrangement had the

---

*There was an obvious contradiction between his attitude here and in the case of Spector. Spector, however, was a Trotskyist: the very label was anathema. There was no similar ban, yet, on people who simply hesitated to accept a major shift in policy.

main report divided into two parts, with Stewart Smith reporting on the international situation, followed by MacDonald speaking on the "Present Situation and the Tasks of the Party." With these arrangements, a united convention seemed possible.*

But the compromise did not last through the first day.

The Convention

The convention opened smoothly with the reading of greetings from the Comintern and from Britain, and adoption of the credentials report. There were 41 delegates with voice and vote and another 23 (mostly members of the outgoing Central Executive Committee) with voice and consultative vote. It was one of the most representative conventions the party had ever held, with delegations present from every part of the country except the East Coast.

Smith's report on the international situation was as close to contemporary Comintern orthodoxy as might be expected. Everything was predicated on the view that the entire world had now entered "the 3rd period of Capitalist development" in which "conditions are intensifying and developing for a new frontal attack against the capitalist class of the world."[32]

According to later Communist Party mythology, the Buck-Smith faction correctly forecast the coming economic crisis, while MacDonald denied that it would take place. In fact everyone predicted an economic crisis in some form, but the main theme of Smith's economic analysis was not that a crisis was due, but that "we can see one fundamental tendency above all, that is the increase of production, this rise of the productivity of world economy, of world capitalist economy above the prewar level."[33] Until after the stock market crash in the fall of 1929, Stalinist theorists consistently described the Third Period as one of capitalist *growth*; only later did they announce that the Third Period meant capitalist decline. But they drew the same conclusions—immediate revolutionary prospects—from both analyses.

---

*Hathaway and Williamson were undoubtedly carrying out Comintern instructions in arranging this compromise. In contrast to other countries, where the Stalinists forced splits, in Canada there was no major group in the leadership actually allied with Bukharin: this may have been a critical factor in deciding the International's policies.

Smith's report endorsed the purges then going on in the major parties of the Comintern, called for the removal of the Right Wing from the CPSU (without mentioning Bukharin by name) and otherwise hewed to the Stalinist line. No one who valued membership in the Communist Party was likely to criticize it in any way—and no one did.

Jack MacDonald would long regret the report he presented to the 1929 convention. He had been a leader of the labor and socialist movements in Canada for almost two decades. He had more understanding of the problems of building a mass movement than any ten of the other delegates present—and certainly more than the little committee of Comintern bureaucrats and Lenin School students who were dictating strategy and tactics to him. MacDonald had fought to break the party from its early ultraleftism and sectarianism. He had led it into united actions with non-Communists, and had steered it clear of attempts to split the existing unions. He had learned his own lessons, and had taught them to others.

But MacDonald was also intensely loyal to the Communist International. He was one of a whole generation of labor leaders for whom the Russian revolution was a bright light in the darkness, and who were determined to build a single world-wide revolutionary party. For that cause to be successful, disclipline was needed, and MacDonald was nothing if not disciplined. Discipline, however, had come to mean something very different in Stalin's Comintern than it had meant while Lenin was alive. By 1929 it meant unhesitating and uncritical acceptance of Moscow's orders, not intelligent cooperation in developing a commonly-accepted program. The transition from one form of discipline to the other had taken place gradually during the 1920s, so gradually that few Communists noticed the change until it was too late. MacDonald, who had never been inclined to probe political issues very deeply, now found that Comintern discipline required him to advance policies which contradicted everything he had learned in the past. Gritting his teeth, he did so.

There can be no doubt that the line of the Comintern letter stuck in his throat. To defend it, he had to declare for "a perspective of the liquidation of the American Federation of Labor" and to endorse the creation of "revolutionary unions." He had to declare that "one of the main tasks" of the party was "the exposure of Social Democracy" and pronounce J.S. Woodsworth, Labor Member of Parliament, "one of the most dangerous elements in the working class of this country." (MacDonald had no illusions about Social Democracy, but for him the main enemy was the capitalist class, not the social democrats.) His report called for "eventual liquidation of the Canadian Labor Party"—and if the labor movement should ever try again to form such a party, the CPC would have to resist with all of its strength.[34]

As well, MacDonald was expected to "self-criticize." This practice, new to the Comintern after Lenin's death, became a substitute for discussion under Stalin's leadership. Instead of discussing the line, party members criticized themselves for failing to apply the line: the line itself was inviolable. MacDonald's report was filled with this sort of thing:

I plead guilty to leaning towards the viewpoint that the crisis of Canadian capitalism will develop from the outer contradictions in the framework of world capitalism and Imperialism rather than from the inner contradictions....

My approach to [the Labor Party question] was wrong, many other comrades also took this viewpoint. I was not able quickly enough to re-orient myself to this line....

I realize that I may have been super-sensitive to the criticism of certain comrades, I may have played the role of a conciliator.[35]

For a man of MacDonald's stature—indeed for any serious revolutionist—this was a tragic, even pathetic, performance.

Perhaps because they scented weakness, the Buck-Smith faction broke the compromise agreement immediately after MacDonald's report. Unable to conduct anything resembling a serious political debate, since there were no clear differences,* they resorted to vague generalizations ("failure to properly comprehend the radicalization of the masses," "underestimation of the war danger") coupled with personal abuse. Mike Buhay, who repeated his hesitations about the new line, came in for particularly rough treatment. MacDonald, who made only a slight effort to defend himself, protested the "unnecessary and unprincipled hounding" of Buhay by the Buck-Smith forces.[37]

The Buck-Smith faction demanded again and again that MacDonald denounce Buhay: MacDonald refused to do this.

---

*"...to the rank and file delegates to this convention it became difficult to see what was the serious difference if we could all accept one resolution."— Tim Buck[36]

I believe Comrade M. Buhay to be an honest proletarian revolutionary comrade, loyal to the Comintern and honestly endeavouring to orientate himself on the C.I. letter and making no attempt whatsoever to organize the least resistance to same.... If it came to a question of having Buhay on our C.E.C. or not, I would prefer him to certain followers of the self-appointed bearers of the true line of the C.I. ... [who] would have a demoralizing effect on our C.E.C.[38]

MacDonald and Buhay had already endorsed a resolution which stated that "unequivocal acceptance of the line of the CI is [the] basis for unity in the Canadian Party."[39] It followed that anyone who questioned the line would have to be excluded from the CEC. Buck and Smith demanded the exclusion of Buhay, Moriarty, and Custance, and MacDonald agreed that the latter two should not be re-elected.* But Mike Buhay was quite another matter. He had taken over as editor of the *Worker* after Spector's expulsion, and was part of MacDonald's team on the party staff. MacDonald was determined to keep him in the CEC—but Buhay's doubts about the Comintern Letter made that impossible. Finally, near the end of the convention, under heavy pressure from MacDonald, Buhay made a formal statement to the assembled delegates. It was a classic piece of self-criticism.

After a further study of the C.I. letter, I have come to the conclusion that I have made incorrect interpretations on the question of Canadian prosperity and the coming crisis, the growing radicalization of the workers and the attitude of the C.P. to the C.L.P.... I placed most emphasis on the outer contradictions of Canadian Capitalism...I underestimated the internal contradictions...I have underestimated the growing radicalization of the Canadian working class.... My previous attitude underestimated the role of the Social reformists....[41]

This appalling statement reeked of insincerity (Buck and Smith immediately denounced it as such), but it met the minimum requirements for inclusion of Buhay's name on the incoming CEC.

The atmosphere at the convention remained poisonous. J.B. Salsberg, the party's leader in the needle trades, felt compelled to make a formal protest. He had, he said, come to the convention determined to decide questions on their merits, and not to become involved in the factional infighting.

---

*MacDonald: "Comrade Moriarty was never considered a political leader. Comrade Moriarty was more or less a party speaker. ...he will have to go from our leadership."[40]

But it became alarmingly evident, during the course of the convention, that a group headed by Comrades Buck and Smith are most factional in their almost every utterance and stand at this convention.... It was obvious to every delegate that the Buck-Smith group repeatedly left the session en masse and disappeared without trace.

In his later accounts, Buck would present his supporters as having been the proletarian core of the party, resisting the petty-bourgeois policies of MacDonald's supporters, but according to Salsberg's protest they showed little respect for the working class delegates present.

The snobbish attitude, the uninterrupted jeering and ridiculing of the healthiest proletarian elements in the party by such unproletarian elements at the Buck-Smith table as [Charles] Marriott and Beckie Buhay was the most provoking and intolerable behaviour at this convention. Whether those Ukrainian delegates from the mines of this country speak English correctly or not, whether they always grasp the correctness of a certain policy swiftly or not, does not justify the attitude of B. Buhay and Marriott, who should bow in reverence to those miners, to whose height they will never rise.[42]

It was this atmosphere, rather than the incomprehensible political debates, that produced a major crisis at the convention. Towards the end of the week-long gathering, the Ukrainian delegates held a secret caucus meeting to discuss how best to respond to the "uninterrupted jeering and ridiculing" they had faced for several days. John Stokaluk of Edmonton, vice-president of the Mine Workers Union of Canada, was the spokesman for a group of delegates who favored a Ukrainian walkout—a split in the party.* His views did not carry, but the overwhelming sentiment among the Ukrainians was for exclusion of all members of the Buck-Smith faction from the new Central Executive Committee. They presented that demand to Jack MacDonald on the evening of June 4.

The following morning, before the convention began, Jack MacDonald gathered together about twenty opponents of the Buck-Smith faction, including Matthew Popowich from the Ukrainian delegation, Finnish leader John Ahlqvist, labor leaders Fred Peel and J.B. Salsberg, and others. They met on the stage in the hall in

---

*The meeting, and Stokaluk's role in it, was described by a Ukrainian party member in the *Worker*, January 10, 1931.

which the convention was being held, and discussed the situation in the party for more than two hours. By the end of the meeting, MacDonald had persuaded those participating to stay in the party, and to accept a CEC which included all viewpoints.

Like Spector's Alhambra Hall meeting, MacDonald's meeting with his supporters on June 5, 1929 has become a major element of Canadian Stalinist mythology. Buck and Smith, whose supporters regularly left the convention floor in a group to caucus, denounced the meeting as proof of MacDonald's factionalism. The meeting marked, they declared, "the consolidation of all the right opportunist elements of the party into an unprincipled faction for the purpose of resisting the line of the Co[mmunist] Inter[national]." Every subsequent official account of the 1929 convention has held up this meeting as a major crime committed by MacDonald. There is no more convincing proof of MacDonald's factionalism, it seems, than a meeting held to protect the party's unity.

The New CEC

At the 1927 convention, the election of the Central Executive Committee took the form of open nominations, followed by balloting. Such a method had worked satisfactorily when the party was united on all major questions, but it was obviously subject to manipulation during a faction fight: the majority could easily take all of the positions on the executive. To meet this problem, the outgoing Political Committee had proposed establishment of a "Nominations Committee," charged with the task of producing a unified slate for the new CEC. The elected committee included nine members: it was balanced not only to represent the two major political currents, but also the Ukrainian, Jewish, and Finnish wings of the party, all of whom would have to be included in the slate.*

The Nominations Committee included Jack MacDonald, Bruno Tenhunen, Jacob Margolies, John Nykyforuk, and John Navis for the majority, and Tim Buck, Stewart Smith, Charles Marriott, and Malcolm Bruce for the Buck-Smith minority. As might have been expected, the committee was hopelessly deadlocked, unable to produce a unanimous report. Buck and Smith insisted that Matthew Popowich and Mike Buhay be excluded from the new

---

*A constitutional change had eliminated the previous practice of election of the language-group representatives by the groups themselves. Now the whole CEC was to be elected by the convention.

executive: MacDonald, just as vehemently, insisted that they be
included. After days of debate, during which the members of the
committee were unable to play any part in the discussions on the
convention floor, the committee decided to present two slates to the
delegates.

Buck's later accounts of this election have accused MacDonald of
using his majority to severely limit the representation of the
minority on the CEC. On two different occasions Buck stated that
only three of his supporters were elected.*

The official *Convention Report* gives a different picture of the
election. The chart on pages 245-6 lists the delegates according to
the slate they voted for. The majority slate, presented by
MacDonald, received 27 delegate votes and 13 consultative votes, a
total of 40. The minority slate, presented by Buck, received 13
delegate votes and 8 consultative votes, a total of 21. Buck and
Smith had, therefore, 21 votes out of a possible 61, slightly more
than one third.

Each slate included 23 names. Seven of the 23 nominated by
MacDonald were Buck-Smith supporters—Tim Buck, Malcolm
Bruce, Beckie Buhay, Stewart Smith, S.G. Neil, Tom McEwen, and
Fred Rosenberg (Rose). With the addition of a YCL representative,
who would certainly side with Buck, the minority would have
exactly one third of the membership of the Central Executive
Committee. MacDonald's slate gave them proportional representation.

Buck's slate would have removed Mike Buhay, Harry Guralnick,
Albert Graves, and Matthew Popowich, and replaced them with
four of his own supporters. This would have given them 50 percent
of the Central Executive Committee, considerably more than their
strength in the party justified.

The voting for the CEC illustrates the divisions in the party very
clearly. MacDonald received all of the votes of the delegates from
Timmins, Sudbury, and Port Arthur districts. The party
membership in those areas was overwhelmingly Finnish, as were
their delegations. Similarly, MacDonald's slate received the
support of all of the Edmonton delegates who voted: Edmonton was
a center of Ukrainian strength. Buck and Smith, on the other hand,
received the votes of only four of the more than thirty Ukrainians

*In 1952 Buck named the three as himself, Stewart Smith, and Malcolm
Bruce. In 1965 he said that they were himself, Malcolm Bruce, and Tom
McEwen.[43] Between 1952 and 1965 Smith had left the Communist Party of
Canada: henceforth he was a nonperson in CP historiography.

and Finns present. Ukrainians and Finns made up more than 80 percent of the party membership: their hostility to Buck and Smith would be a major factor in the continuing party crisis after the convention.

Buck's slate received all four of the YCL votes, two regular and two consultative; Buck's support in the YCL has already been noted. More important, Buck received all of the votes of the delegations from Winnipeg and Vancouver. This reflects the activity of two of Buck's closest allies, Tom McEwen and Malcolm Bruce, in those cities. The Winnipeg delegation did not reflect the strength of the Ukrainian wing of the party there: the Ukrainians from Winnipeg who attended the convention, including Lobay, Navis, and Popowich, all had consultative votes and all voted for MacDonald's slate.

Roscoe Filmore, a long-time Socialist and a founder of the Workers Party who seems to have been given a consultative vote solely in recognition of his long service, voted for MacDonald's slate.

This, then, was the line-up of forces as the convention ended. MacDonald had the support of a two-thirds majority of the party, including the solid backing of the Finns and Ukrainians, and important figures in the "Old Guard" such as Peel and Buller. Buck's support was in the West and in the YCL. Although he had the voting strength to force Buck and Smith out completely, MacDonald compromised: he gave Buck-Smith proportional representation in the CEC, and agreed to refer the main convention resolution to a subcommittee composed of himself and Smith, for re-drafting. With that, the convention came to a close—but the battle had barely begun.

**THE 1929 ELECTION TO THE
CENTRAL EXECUTIVE COMMITTEE**

	MacDonald Supporters	Buck-Smith Supporters	Not Voting
Full Delegates			
District 2 (Montreal)	Gold Sthalberg	Rosenberg	
District 3 (Toronto)	Shur Peel Marshall Ahlqvist Stefansky	Aristoff	
District 4 (Timmins)	Smeek Thachuk Sivula Maamba Helin Wuori Parnega Oksonen		
District 5 (Sudbury)	Wirta Tenhunen Rinne Korpenin Halewach Wilen		
District 6 (Port Arthur)	Biniowsky Bryan Hautamaki		
District 7 (Winnipeg)		Davy Wiggins Prodanchuk Forkin	
District 8 (Edmonton)	Klebenousky Stokaluk Nykyforuk		Lakeman
District 9 (Vancouver)		Bennet Porter Balo Bruce M. Clarke	
YCL		Marriott Farbey	

**THE 1929 ELECTION TO THE
CENTRAL EXECUTIVE COMMITTEE (continued)**

	MacDonald Supporters	Buck-Smith Supporters	Not Voting
Consultative Delegates			
YCL NEC		Freed Andrews	
CEC	Hill Popowich Boychuck Latva M. Buhay MacDonald Buller	Buck Ryan Halperin Smith	Moriarty Custance Menzies
Enlarged CEC	Margolies		
Editor of *Furrow*	J.M. Clarke		
For C.I. Congress	Navis	Neil	
Ukrainian Labor News	Lobay		
U.S. fraternal Delegate			Hathaway
Industrial Organizers	Salsberg	Murphy	
Other	Filmore		

MacDonald's slate: T. Buck, M. Buhay, A. Graves, H. Guralnick, A. Gault, A.T. Hill, Kostaniuk, J. Lakeman, J. Margolies, J. MacDonald, S.G. Neil, M. Popowich, Pastuch, A. Skaara, S. Smith, Salo, B. Buhay, M. Bruce, T.E. Ewen [McEwen], Lehtinen, Rosenburg [Rose], Silinpaa, A. Vaara.

Buck's slate: Same as MacDonald's, except: remove Popowich, Guralnick, Graves, M. Buhay. Replace with S. Sarkin, C. Marriott, C. Sims, P. Halperin.

Source: *Report of the Sixth National Convention of the Communist Party of Canada.* pp. 1-2, 137-138.

13. Buck's Coup

For five months the Communist Party had been torn apart by charges and counter-charges, by debates and polemics marked by a ferocity unequalled in the party's history. As the delegates returned home, there must have been a sense of relief that it was all over. The political disputes had been settled by a compromise, and the party's traditional leadership (except for Spector) was back in office. The party could get back to work.

Just as things were settling down, however, the membership learned that everything was up in the air again. The new CEC, meeting in plenary session six weeks after the convention, elected a Political Committee on which the Buck-Smith forces had an absolute majority—six out of nine members. Only one of the new district organizers had supported the majority at the convention. And, most remarkable of all, the newly elected General Secretary was...Tim Buck!

Inevitably this development has played a major part in the official histories of the Communist Party. Not until the July 1929 plenum of the CEC did Tim Buck hold the highest office of the party. Any account of "Tim Buck's Party" would be incomplete without an explanation of that event.

But how to explain it?

The earliest accounts of the plenum, published about six months after the event, refer only to the "desertion" of party responsibility by the right wing. But that rather inadequate explanation required fleshing out. By the time he wrote his first major account of party history, Buck had developed a much more coherent story of his own rise to power.

The "Lovestonites," Buck says, had won a majority at the convention, "but the position of the minority had corresponded with the basic economic and political realities." Although MacDonald was supported by some party leaders,

the minority was winning ever wider support among the most active members of the party as a whole.... The membership of the party was recognizing that the minority was fighting for a correct Communist position. With that recognition support for the minority was growing rapidly.[1]

MacDonald, according to Buck, saw that he was losing his majority and so resigned. In a later account, perhaps realizing that six weeks was a very short time for the accomplishment of such a change in the views of the membership, Buck argued that the convention delegates had been elected before the membership learned what MacDonald's real views were. The convention, he implied, did not represent the actual views of the majority of party members. "The contradiction between the majority of the members and MacDonald's record became so sharp that, on July 12th...he resigned."[2]

MacDonald's resignation was not, however, a selfless gesture designed to bring the leadership into line with the thinking of the majority of the party membership. It was a maneuver carefully calculated to split the Communist Party.

The following day [July 13], a carefully prepared statement over the name of MacDonald and naming several members of the Central Committee as being aligned with him, appeared in papers edited by his supporters, calling upon the workers to abandon the Communist Party of Canada and establish a new organization.[3]

MacDonald's new organization was a flop—he was compelled to join forces with the Trotskyite Spector, "in an unprincipled but futile attempt to form an anti-Leninist organization. They failed, and passed quickly into political oblivion."*[4] Leninism had triumphed and the Communist Party, under Buck's leadership, could go forward with the correct line.

Buck presented variations of this story in *Thirty Years*, in his *Reminiscences*, and in *Lenin and Canada*. It is repeated by Tom

---

*In another version "MacDonald...joined Spector and the two of them, with Bill Moriarty, tried for some months to organize."[5]

McEwen in his autobiography *The Forge Glows Red*, and in Oscar Ryan's *Tim Buck: A Conscience For Canada*, not to mention many lesser works. It is, beyond doubt, the official version of the Buck takeover.

Frequent repetition, however, does not create truth: there is virtually no truth at all in this official version of the events of July 1929.

THE CONVENTION ENDED IN THE EARLY MORNING on June 7. The deep-seated hostilities it had exposed remained, poisoning relationships among the party leadership. The Ukrainians in particular felt that the convention should have crushed Buck and Smith, rather than compromising with them. Those whose opposition to Buck and Smith was more ideological felt very uneasy about the political direction implied in the few resolutions the convention had adopted.

The first casualty was Michael Buhay. He had taken over the editorship of the *Worker* following Spector's expulsion: now his position there was untenable. Even with his "self-criticism" on record, Buhay clearly could not count on the support even of MacDonald in political disputes. Whether Buhay resigned or was forced out is not known: after the convention the *Worker* missed an issue, and when it reappeared there was no editor named on the masthead.* Buhay left Toronto and returned to the needle trades in Montreal.

Buhay's resignation was followed by a convention of the Young Communist League, at which the Buck-Smith fraction demonstrated that it had no intention of abandoning hostilities. The YCL convention repeated all of the attacks on the "right wing," singling William Moriarty out for particular criticism.

Buck and Smith were encouraged in their intransigence by events south of the 49th parallel. The Communist Party of the United States had entered a period of extreme crisis, leading, on June 27, to the announcement that the Comintern leadership had ordered the expulsion of Jay Lovestone, and was turning the leadership of the CPUSA over to the Foster-Browder minority. In the face of a direct Comintern assault, Lovestone's former majority evaporated. The *Daily Worker*, issue after issue, carried statements from party units dissociating themselves from the "former

---

*Stewart Smith edited the paper until the end of July, when Malcolm Bruce took over.

majority." Earl Browder became the new party secretary, and the U.S. party began its long career as a totally loyal element of the international Stalinist movement.*

The purge of the U.S. party was, for the Canadians, the most dramatic illustration of Stalin's general policy of purging the "Right Danger" from the International, but it was not the only one. Attacks on the right wing leaders in some of the European parties had begun during the winter, leading to a general attack on Stalin's rivals in the Soviet Union itself. At the beginning of June 1929, Mikhail Tomsky, Bukharin's closest ally, was removed from his position as head of the Soviet trade union movement. This was followed by the attack on Lovestone and, on July 3, by the removal of Bukharin himself from the chairmanship of the Comintern.

These events could not but increase the Buck-Smith faction's confidence. They saw themselves as—and in fact they were—the Canadian spokesmen for Stalin's faction in the Comintern. They decided to press the attack.

Buck's various accounts of the CEC plenum that opened on Friday, July 12 all state that MacDonald's resignation was the first order of business. In fact, the minutes of the plenum show that two full days of business were transacted before MacDonald's announcement that he was not going to stand for re-election.[6]

The plenum began with a discussion of the Political Thesis written jointly by MacDonald and Smith. This wholly orthodox Third Period document was adopted unanimously, after a few amendments. The remainder of the first day was devoted to organizational reports, covering changes to the Constitution which the convention had not had time to deal with, and reports on the proposed activities of various party departments. All of the reports were adopted—there was little controversy.

The first report on Saturday morning, by Finnish leader Tom Hill, dealt with a proposal to create an "Anti-Imperialist League." Again there was little controversy. But as that discussion came to a close, the plenum was interrupted by a young party member from

---

*Lovestone and his closest associates formed an organization optimistically named Communist Party (Majority Group), launched a newspaper named *Revolutionary Age*, and established international connections with a number of groups which had been expelled from the Comintern, notably the Communist Party (Opposition) led by Heinrich Brandler in Germany. Lovestone's group moved steadily to the right during the 1930s, and dissolved at the beginning of the war. Lovestone himself later became prominent in the AFL-CIO as a political advisor to George Meany.

Toronto, Joseph Zrodowsky, who asked permission to make a statement to the CEC. Permission was granted.

This was, to say the least, a highly unorthodox procedure. The plenum's function was to deal with organizational matters, take care of unfinished business from the convention, and in general to plan activities for the coming months. It was, by definition, a gathering of the party leadership: aside from Zrodowsky no one who was not either a CEC member or a leader of a "mass organization" addressed the meeting.

We will probably never know what led Zrodowsky to approach the plenum, and what led the plenum to let him speak. In view of what he said, it is quite possible that the Ukrainian wing of the party leadership put him up to it. Be that as it may, his brief statement caused an uproar.

Zrodowsky identified himself as a party member, a member of the YCL, and a member of the party fraction in the Ukrainian Labor-Farmer Temple Association in Toronto. In that capacity, he said, he had for some time "opposed the policy and the false approach of the group led by Comrade Ryan and Buck." He charged that Buck and Ryan were the inspiration behind a factional grouping in the Ukrainian section of the YCL, led by "Kosinsky and Colly." He and others had opposed this group's activities but "all our warnings, complaints and demands were ignored."

Charging Buck and Ryan with organizing factions in the YCL was serious enough. But Zrodowsky went on to drop a major bombshell. Kosinsky and Colly, identified as allies of Buck and Ryan, had left the YCL, joined the right-wing Ukrainian nationalist movement, and were now "leading attacks against the Ukrainian Labor Temple and against the YCL and Party in particular."

The YCL did not expel these members. Naturally there exists a bitter feeling among the Ukrainian comrades, Party and YCL members and among the non-Party members of the mass organizations against those comrades who condoned this attitude and were assisting those elements against which we are now fighting.

I consider it necessary that immediate steps be taken to remedy this situation. Otherwise the influence and the prestige of the YCL and the Party among the Ukrainian workers in Toronto will be entirely undermined and for some time destroyed.

The minutes of the plenum do not record the immediate reaction of Buck and his allies to this statement, but in all probability they protested vehemently. Whether or not the Zrodowsky statement had been prompted by the Ukrainians on the CEC, Buck would charge that it had been: the statement gave him the perfect excuse to reopen his offensive against the majority.

When the next session opened, Tim Buck took the floor, and on behalf of himself and Oscar Ryan introduced a formal resolution demanding an investigation into Zrodowsky's charges, which he described as "the culmination of a consistent series of slanders" made against him by the Ukrainian wing of the party. He mentioned the Ukrainian wing's resolution to the Sixth Congress of the Comintern, which had demanded his removal from the party leadership, and a "lying story" which had circulated in the party accusing him of participation in the beating of a Ukrainian comrade earlier in the year. He charged that a "lying telegram... signed by Comrades Popowich and Boychuck" had been sent to the CEC on February 3, with the object of keeping Buck away from the ULFTA convention in Winnipeg.

Whatever the truth of the charges and counter-charges, the long-standing hostility between Buck and the Ukrainians was now a major issue in the plenum. MacDonald announced that a "special closed session" of the plenum would be held the following day, Sunday, July 14, to discuss the question. After a brief discussion of the perspectives for the Canadian Labor Defense League, the plenum broke up for the evening.

The minutes for the session that began at 3:00 p.m. on July 14 are extremely terse—so terse as to mislead the reader about the events that took place. *The discussion of the Zrodowsky statement, scheduled for that time, is not mentioned at all.* It is possible that the discussion did not take place—but it is more likely, in light of what happened next, that the discussion was considered too inflammatory to report, even in the CEC minutes.

What happened next was the election of party officers. The minutes record only that Popowich requested to be left off the Political Committee for reasons of ill-health, and that "Comrade MacDonald made verbal statement, stating his reasons as to why he believed it would be in the best interests of the party that he be released from duties of Executive-Secretary." They report that a "lengthy discussion" took place, followed by a motion to carry the discussion over to the following morning. The next day MacDonald's resignation was accepted, and a new Political Committee elected. The new committee gave Buck and Smith an absolute majority—Buck was elected executive secretary (also sometimes termed general secretary).

If the minutes were our only source of information about the plenum, we would be completely in the dark about this bloodless coup. Non-party historians who have used only the minutes have been forced to accept Buck's claim that MacDonald resigned because he had lost the support of the membership. No other explanation seems to make sense.

There are, however, three other accounts of the election of the Political Committee that have been overlooked. They point to a very different explanation of MacDonald's resignation.

The first account is by Tim Buck himself, in the form of an unpublished report to the Anglo-American Commission of the Comintern early in 1930:

When the Plenum came the majority submitted a slate for the Polcom. We fought against this slate, we fought against Comrades Popovich [Popowich] and Hill...we objected categorically against Popovich. We also protested categorically against Hill and nominated in his place Vaara, who always previously stood for an aggressive Party line, and just previously had come out of jail. In the enlarged executive there was quite a struggle over Vaara, Popovich and Hill. MacDonald then faced us with the fact that he would not stand for the secretary's position.[7]

The second account appears in a document entitled "The Right Danger in the Ukrainian Mass Organizations of Canada." It is undated and unsigned—but on internal evidence it was written in 1930, and the literary style is very similar to Stewart Smith's. It too seems to have been addressed to the Comintern.*

During the election of the Political Bureau of the new Central Committee, the Minority objected to the nomination of Comrade Popowich...on the grounds of his open Right Wing position, and that we hold him chiefly responsible for the unscrupulous factional activities of the Right Wing among the Ukrainian leadership. As a result of our categorical opposition, the Rights withdrew the name of Popowich. We were then faced with the impossibility of getting another Ukrainian comrade in his place.[8]

This third account, much briefer, appears in a "self-criticism" made by Matthew Popowich in 1931:

---

*In the fall of 1930 there was a Comintern investigation of CPC-ULFTA relations.

I admit, condemn and repudiate my own very serious mistake...[consisting of] stating, in my declaration, that I was in favor of the list of candidates in the Polburo as presented by comrades Smith and Buck, in order that we may convince ourselves in their abilities and honest desires to follow the Comintern line and build the Communist Party and Communist movement in Canada.[9]

These accounts, together with the minutes of the plenum, provide a coherent picture—one which for the first time makes the disappearance of MacDonald's majority understandable.

MacDonald came to the plenum with a proposal for a new Political Committee which reflected the balance of forces on the CEC. Buck and Smith made a counter-proposal, giving themselves a majority, and backed it up with vehement denunciations of Popowich, the leader of the Ukrainian wing of the party, and of Tom Hill, a Finnish leader whose main crime was voting with MacDonald at the convention. The Zrodowsky statement was in all probability introduced by the Ukrainians as a counter to Buck's attack on Popowich, demanding as it did the removal of Buck from the Political Committee.

MacDonald would have done as he did at the convention—insist on a slate with all groups properly represented—but this time his allies refused to go along. Since they could not get Buck and Smith off the Polcom, the Ukrainians decided to leave it themselves, and announced their intention of voting for the Buck-Smith slate in order to prove to the party that Buck and Smith were dangerous and incompetent. Popowich's claim of illness was a pretext only—his illness certainly did not prevent him from playing a central leadership role in the ULFTA in the months following the plenum.

The Ukrainians' action left MacDonald in a completely untenable position. He had said at the convention that the bitterness of the faction fight had frequently tempted him to resign from the Polcom to "do rank and file work."[10] Now he would be in a minority on a Political Committee dominated by Buck and Smith. Resignation was the only course open to him.

MacDonald's resignation caused panic in the Buck-Smith camp. They were quite prepared to take a majority on the Political Committee, but they had assumed that MacDonald would continue as executive secretary. Now they feared his resignation would lead to a split in which they would be left with a small minority of the party membership. The entire afternoon was devoted to attempts by the minority to convince MacDonald to stay on, but he was adamant. That evening, according to Buck, "the various comrades gathered together and we concluded to accept MacDonald's resignation."[11] The following morning, with considerable concern about the possible consequences, the Buck-Smith faction announced their decision.

MacDonald, however, had no intention of splitting the party, or even of joining the Ukrainians in their boycott of the party leadership. He agreed to a compromise in which he would be on the Political Committee and serve as acting executive secretary until Tim Buck was able to assume the position. MacDonald continued in that position for three months after the plenum.

Buck in 1929 feared that MacDonald would lead a split. In his later histories, Buck treated that fear as though it was fact, reporting several times that MacDonald led a split the day after the plenum. Other CPC historians have made the same claim. As even a cursory glance at the evidence shows, that story is pure fiction.

Buck did not fully replace MacDonald until October 1929, but that was only a formality. MacDonald was a prisoner of the Buck-Smith majority from the moment the plenum ended: he had only one sure ally on the Political Committee, Albert Graves, a shoeworker who had played no role in the party leadership before. The majority included Buck and Smith, plus Tom McEwen, Malcolm Bruce, and Beckie Buhay from the CEC, and YCL representative Fred Rosenberg (Fred Rose).* Bruce was to become editor of the *Worker*, Smith headed up the Agit-Prop department, and Tom McEwan took over Trade Union from Buck. These and other appointments gave Buck and Smith full control of party policy.

They had fought for the "Comintern line." Now the party could learn what they had meant.

---

*A ninth Polcom member, Aarvo Vaara, was an unknown quantity. He had played no role in the faction fight, having been in jail for sedition until just before the plenum.

14. The Third Period in Canada: United Front From Below

The takeover of the Communist Party of Canada by the Buck-Smith faction in July 1929 was no simple change of personnel, but a total change in the policies and program of the Canadian Communist movement. For the next twenty months the party was in constant turmoil, as the majority attempted to resist the policies imposed by the new leadership.

Between Buck's accession to the office of executive secretary in 1929 and the plenum of the CEC in February 1931, the party changed its course on every important question of Canadian and international politics. It abandoned completely the principles on which it had been built, replacing them with nothing more or less than complete subordination to the foreign policy goals of the Stalinist leadership of the CPSU. In 1929 that meant acceptance of the madness known as the Third Period.

The policies of 1929-1935 have long been an embarrassment to the CPC—the Third Period is usually mentioned only in passing in official accounts of the party's history. Tim Buck, who was in prison from February 1932 to November 1934, has tried to suggest that the ultraleft policies of the Third Period were the result of errors made while the real leaders were in jail.[1] His role in formulating those policies, and in implementing them from 1929 until early 1932, is passed by in silence. In fact, the policies and practices of the Third Period were decisive in shaping the Stalinist movement in Canada for years to come: although the specific set of policies that characterized the Third Period was abandoned with unseemly haste in 1935, the conception underlying them, one of unswerving support of Kremlin policy, did not change and has not changed to this day.

It is not possible here to present a full history of the Third Period in Canada. What follows in this and the next chapter focuses on major themes that remained relatively constant through the years 1929-1935. This account concentrates, for the most part, on the years 1929 through 1931, when Tim Buck was in direct personal control of the party.

"Mass Radicalization"

According to the Stalinists, the end of World War I had ushered in a first period of revolutionary uprisings. This gave way in the 1920s to the second period, in which a "partial stabilization" of capitalism occurred. The third period, in the words of the 1929 Political Thesis of the CPC, was "characterized by the development of the conditions of a new frontal attack of the proletarian world forces against capitalism." As a result of the "fantastic intensification of the contradictions within the capitalist world," on one hand, and, on the other, of the "growth and construction of Socialism in the Soviet Union," there was taking place "a growing wave of radicalization of the workers of the whole world, the decisive swing of the masses to the left."

The leftward swing of the masses and the sharpening of the class struggle find their expression in the growth of gigantic strikes thruout the capitalist world, which inevitably develop in this period into political struggles of the workers against the capitalist state.[2]

This perspective, however, was manifestly untrue. (Indeed it would be difficult to name any country for which this analysis held true in 1929.) There were no "gigantic strikes taking place in Canada." In fact, fewer workers took part in strikes in 1929 than in any year since 1915. Never was the ideology of class collaboration and labor peace as strong as it was at the end of the 1920s—it was the official policy of the major labor federations, and the accepted ideology of the working class, organized and unorganized.

It is often suggested that the strength of Buck's position was that he forecast the stock market crash of October 1929 and the radicalization it would bring. That suggestion is based on two invalid assumptions.

First, it assumes that the stock market crash led directly to a major radicalization of the Canadian working class. Nothing could be further from the truth. The year 1930 saw no change on the industrial front—the number of workdays lost in strikes remained at the 1915 level. In fact, if coal-mining strikes are eliminated from the statistics, 1930 is seen to be one of the worst years for labor militancy in this century. It was not until the latter half of the decade that Canadian labor resumed its forward march. Nor was a left turn evident in electoral politics. 1930 saw the election of the Conservative Party to office under the leadership of R.B. Bennett; Labor representation did not increase, and the independent Farmers' parties continued their decline.

The second invalid assumption is that Buck and his faction forecast the coming economic crisis. One will search in vain through the documents and articles of 1929 for such a forecast. There were, to be sure, general comments about the cyclical nature of capitalist production and the inevitability of a downturn, but these were common to all participants in the discussion, and were couched in extremely vague terms. Indeed, the Political Thesis spoke not of an impending economic crisis, but of the "tremendous growth" of Canadian capitalism and the "growth of new industries." In general the Stalinist Comintern was extremely conservative in its economic forecasts: it was not until late 1932 that the "end of partial stabilization of capitalism" was proclaimed by the ECCI and reported by the *Worker*.[3]

What the Buck-Smith faction predicted was not radicalization resulting from an economic crisis, but radicalization resulting from a war in which Canada would become a battlefield. Stewart Smith first enunciated this perspective late in December 1928, not in an internal party discussion, but in an interview with the *Toronto Star*:

The hope of The Communist Party in Canada lies in a war in which Canada shall take part. If the war is against our brother workmen in Russia then we will not offer passive resistance as we did in the last war. Our members will join the Canadian army, then take their rifles and turn them on the capitalist class of Canada....

There are people in this city, and newspapers too, confident that there will be a lasting peace, that war is impossible. Little do they realize that in a very short time the streets in Toronto will be running with blood.[4]

One might attribute this remarkable statement to misquotation by the press—but Smith did not claim he had been misquoted, and the *Worker* maintained an embarrassed silence. In any event, Smith provided a theoretical justification for such a perspective in the

1929 Political Thesis.* The Canadian bourgeoisie, the Thesis stated, was divided into two wings—one pro-British, the other pro-U.S. War between Britain and America was inevitable, and this would have catastrophic results for Canadian capitalism. The United States would invade Canada and the Canadian capitalist government, hopelessly divided, would collapse. This would open up a period of civil war in which the working class would oppose the Americans, the British, and the Canadian bourgeoisie.

This fantastic schema provided Smith and Buck with a justification for the policies they imposed on the CPC in 1929. Although it was completely out of touch with reality, it did allow the CPC to talk about mass radicalization. So what if no such radicalization was taking place? The international contradictions of capitalism were producing the radicalization: the party's task was to be prepared.

One part of the schema proved to be shortlived. Although the prospect of a British-American war that would split the Canadian ruling class had been clearly enunciated in the Comintern's letter to the 1929 convention, by October 1929 the CI was taking a different tack. The Polsecretariat of the ECCI wrote that the CPC's Political Thesis betrayed dangerous tendencies:

There is evident in the Party's agitation a tendency to regard the outer contradictions as the sole factors determining the development of the political situation, leading to an underestimation of the inner contradictions (the narrowing of the home market, etc. and the growing class struggle) and thereby causing the danger of a similar underestimation of the possibilities of work in the present period of growing ferment among the masses.[5]

"Overestimation of the outer contradictions and underestimation of the inner contradictions." Behind these abstract formulations—so common in intra-Stalinist polemics—was the implied criticism that the CPC was placing all of its hopes on war, while the CI wanted Third Period policies regardless of the immediate international prospects facing the Canadian state.

The Comintern's insistence on "growing ferment among the masses" forced the CPC, in effect, to deny reality. The *Worker*, after the Buck-Smith takeover, became a thoroughly unreliable source of news about the Canadian working class. Defeats were reported as

---

*Although the Thesis was presented to the July Plenum as the joint work of MacDonald and Smith, both style and content mark it as Smith's work.

victories, small meetings as mass rallies. As Max Shachtman wrote, "every strike became a revolt, every demonstration a near-insurrection."[6] Anyone who read only the *Worker* in the early 1930s might have expected the revolution at any moment.

Although the specific schema of a British-American war was dropped from CPC propaganda, the war danger remained a vital part of the party's agitation. Now, however, the emphasis shifted. Instead of an inter-imperialist war, it was the danger of an attack on the Soviet Union, raised again and again in the party press. The Political Thesis had declared that the party's "central task" was "the fight against imperialist war and Defense of the Soviet Union."[7] The 1931 plenum spelled this out: "In this period with the sharpening menace of imperialist attack upon the First Workers' Republic, the fight for 'Defense of the Soviet Union' must be in the forefront of all Party work...."[8]

By now, "Defense of the Soviet Union" meant faithful adherence to all the zig-zags of Kremlin foreign policy. It has remained a leit-motif of the Canadian CP's program up to the present day.

The Conquest of the Streets

Late in 1928 reactionary circles in Toronto, emboldened by the CP's growing isolation, began a campaign to outlaw the party. The *Globe,* in December, urged the authorities to "step heavily" on the Communists, who were "devoting their energies to polluting God-fearing Canadian homes."[9] A group calling itself the Canadian Christian Crusade enlisted considerable support among Toronto's ruling elite for a policy of repression of the left. Early in 1929, Toronto Police Chief Daniel Draper declared his support for the anti-Communist campaign, and warned that his force would break up any meeting which featured "disorderly or seditious reflections on our form of government or the King or any constituted authority."[10] The Police Commissioners announced a ban on any Communist meeting "carried on in a foreign language" — threatening cancellation of the license of any hall in which such meetings were held.[11] Hall owners in Toronto began to refuse to rent their premises to the CPC: the regulation was, in effect, a ban on Communist meetings in Toronto. The party was forced to move its meetings to the suburbs. The 1929 convention, for example, was held in East York.

Reading the *Worker* in 1929, it would be easy to conclude that the CPC stood alone in its opposition to these attacks on civil liberties. This is not true. The Trades and Labor Council was quick to condemn Draper's actions: the labor leaders recognized his anti-Communist moves as a threat to all labor meetings in the city. A few months later, students at the University of Toronto, no hotbed of radicalism in 1929, approved a resolution stating that "Toronto is deserving of her reputation for intolerance." Many academic figures protested the ban on Communist meetings. Even the city's ruling circles were not unanimous: the *Toronto Star* in particular denounced Draper's police state policies. Nor were the courts in full support of Draper: many of the Communist Party members arrested in Toronto were released by the magistrates, or given minimal fines.

In such a situation an effective campaign attempting to unite all supporters of civil liberties in the city might well have stopped Draper in his tracks. There were many members of the CPC and of the labor movement who could remember when such a campaign had won the release of Watson and Cheeseman from jail in 1919.

Such campaigns do not spring out of the ground. They have to be built—and the victims of police repression have to demonstrate their willingness to organize their own defense. To defeat Draper, the Communist Party would have to show that it was ready to cooperate with disparate forces in the left and labor movements.

Third Period Stalinism forbade such campaigns entirely. As Smith expressed it in the Political Thesis of 1929, the slogans "To the Masses" and "United Front" had been appropriate in the "second period," but now had to be abandoned:

The radicalization of the workers has created new conditions in the working class, has created the condition where the basis for a united front of the working class no longer rests upon the reformist trade unions, upon the reformist organizations, but a real united front can only develop in this period of time with the development of a new frontal attack of the workers against the capitalist class on the basis of the masses of the workers, under the direct leadership of the Communist Party.[12]

The "united front," as understood when Lenin was alive, was by definition an alliance in action of two or more organizations, each of which had the allegiance of a section of the working class. It was a tactic specifically designed to meet the needs of a working class divided into Social-Democratic and Communist wings. A "united front...under the direct leadership of the Communist Party," usually referred to as the "united front from below," was of course no united front at all. A "united front" composed only of people who were prepared to accept the leadership of the CPC would be nothing more than a party front, if indeed it was anything more than a figment of the party's imagination.

With the policy of the "united front from below" as its only weapon, and the myth of the radicalization of the masses firmly fixed in its mind, the leadership of the Communist Party embarked on a suicidal attempt to defeat the police singlehandedly. The occasion for the battle was August 1—named "International Red Day" by the International. This was the day, according to the International, when the masses would avenge the police murder of several German Communists on May Day. Their vengeance would take the form of "conquering the streets."* The Communist Party of Canada called for demonstrations across Canada, in an appeal headed "Transform the Imperialist War of the Exploiters into the Class War for the Workers and Farmers Government!"[13]

Since there was no imperialist war in progress in the summer of 1929, Canadian workers might well have wondered just what the party expected them to do. Stewart Smith enlightened them in an interview with the *Toronto Star*. The Communist Party, he said, was organizing a rally in Queen's Park despite a formal police ban. The party fully expected the police to attack.

They'll ride horses upon us. They'll crash us. They'll do anything. But we're going to stick. We're going to see it through.... We're going to offer the maximum resistance along scientific lines. We're organized. We're fitted to put up a stand against them.... Two thousand workers are not going to be sat upon; they're not going under without putting up a stand.[15]

The Communists, Smith said, would organize the crowd into mobile groups as the police attacked, groups which would form a barrier around the speakers to defend them.

This was pure fantasy. The Communist Party, as events showed, was completely unprepared for a confrontation. It had no defense

---

*Trotsky: "Ordinary mortals wondered, why August 1, whose failure was forecast by the failure of May 1? What do you mean, *Why?* the official strategists answered excitedly: 'for the conquest of the streets!' Just what is to be understood by this, the conquest of the sidewalk or the pavement? Up to now we thought that the task of the revolutionary party is the conquest of the masses, and that the policy which can mobilize the masses in the greatest numbers and activity inevitably opens up the street, regardless how the police guard and block it. The struggle for the street cannot be an independent task, separated from mass political struggle and subordinated to Molotov's office schedule."[14]

guards organized, not even a marshalling squad. With his imaginary "scientific" defense Smith was in effect challenging the police to attack an unprepared, unarmed crowd.

When the time for the meeting arrived, police and curious onlookers considerably outnumbered the Communists. True to Smith's prediction, the police rode horses into the crowd, attempting to clear the park. Jack MacDonald, who had been out of Toronto when the plans were made for the demonstration, quite sensibly refused to make a target of himself: he refused to get on the speakers' platform. The other scheduled speaker, A.E. Smith, also refused to speak. Tim Buck, who did attempt to speak, was hit in the face with a police billy club. The meeting did not take place, and many bystanders were injured in the mounted police assault.[16]

The August 10 *Worker* headlined its report of this fiasco "Toronto Cossacks Charge 10,000 Workers in Mad Riot to Crush Demonstration." The party promptly organized another Queens Park demonstration for August 13. The leaflet announcing it was filled with ultraleft rhetoric, condemning "the Labour fakirs and reformist trade union bureaucrats" equally with the capitalists and the police. The slogans it advanced were scarcely calculated to win mass support for civil liberties:

Demonstrate Against Police Terrorism! Fight the Ban on Free Speech and Assemblage! Fight Against Imperialist War! Defend the Soviet Union! the Socialist Fatherland! Join the Communist Party! the Party that Fights! Young Workers! Join the Young Communist League!

The unstated but obvious conclusion of the CPC's leaflet was that only by joining the Communist Party could the workers defend free speech. This was the path to defeat.

The August 1 demonstration had been routed, but police violence was limited. By comparison, August 13 was a bloodbath. Jack MacDonald, instructed by the Political Committee to be the principal speaker of the day, was the main victim of the police attack. As he approached the speakers' stand, he was tackled by the police and wrestled to the ground. Several cops punched and beat him repeatedly, although he offered no resistance. Mounted and motorcycle police rode repeatedly into the crowd, lashing out indiscriminately. Dozens of people, most of them bystanders, were injured in the police attack. Once again the CP meeting was prevented from taking place.

An immense public outcry followed. Publications as varied as the

New Outlook, published by the United Church, and *The Beaver*, published by the Canada First movement, condemned the Toronto police. The Toronto Trades and Labor Council denounced the police violence and called for a royal commission to investigate the situation. Letters to the editors of the Toronto papers ran heavily against the police.

Once again the CPC refused to organize a united defense of democratic rights. Another demonstration was called for Queen's Park, on August 27, under the exclusive sponsorship of the CPC and the YCL. In spite of the TLC's condemnation of police violence, the party declared that "The Boss Class and their lickspittles—the social-reformists and American Federation of Labor misleaders— lead the present bloody attack on the Communist Party."

"Jimmy Simpson and the vile crew of A.F. of L. misleaders," it seems, were worse enemies than the police. Once again the "united front from below" was urged: "Smash the Bosses' Offensive! Rally to the Communist Party!"

The number of real participants (as opposed to onlookers) had been smaller on August 13 than it was on August 1. On August 27 it was smaller still. This time the police simply surrounded the park in advance, keeping out spectators and demonstrators alike. There was no violence: the demonstration the CPC had predicted would be "the greatest demonstration in the history of the Toronto Labour Movement" simply fizzled out.

The Communist Party's tragic error in 1929 was not its determination to challenge Draper's police-state policies; that was the elementary duty of every revolutionist, indeed of every democrat. What the CPC did was to carry out that challenge in a way that guaranteed defeat in advance. The party's go-it-alone policy, its contempt for all possible allies, its constant overestimation of its own strength, its arrogant challenges to the cops—these things left it hopelessly isolated in a battle it could not win alone. The outcome was not just the breaking up of a few rallies: it was the virtual outlawing of labor protest meetings from the streets and parks of Toronto until 1933, when the labor movement, with little or no CPC support, was able to challenge and defeat the ban.

The campaign for "conquest of the streets" was typical of the Third Period. The Comintern was attempting to create a mass movement by command from above. The attempt was doomed to failure. As Trotsky wrote:

...you cannot fool history. The task is not to appear stronger, but to get stronger. A noisy masquerade will not help. When there *is no* "third period," it is possible to *invent* it. It is possible to pass dozens of resolutions. But to *make* the third period on the streets, according to the calendar, is impossible. On this road the Communist parties will find only defeats, in some cases tragic ones, in most simply stupid and humiliating ones.[17]

Social Fascism

The Communist International's aboutface on the tactic of the united front—its adoption of the mis-named "united front from below"—required a theoretical rationalization. The united front tactic had been established as one of the most important weapons in the CI's arsenal following long debates between the Leninists and the ultraleft. Although Lenin's writings themselves would soon undergo a complete purging at the hands of Stalin's tame intellectuals, the united front was too deeply imbedded in his works and in the collective consciousness of the International to be simply cast aside.

The rationalization for abandoning all attempts at joint activity with Social Democracy was found in an obscure 1924 article by Stalin, written during the brief ultraleft turn the Comintern made under Zinoviev's guidance in the aftermath of the 1923 defeat in Germany. "Social Democracy is objectively the moderate wing of fascism," Stalin had written. "They are not antipodes, they are twins."*[18]

In 1924 this type of statement, meaningless and stupid as it might be, served as little more than exaggerated abuse directed at the Social Democrats. At the Tenth Plenum of the Comintern in 1929, however, the idea that Social Democracy was nothing more than a form of fascism—that it was in reality "social-fascism"— emerged as a fundamental doctrine of the Stalinized Comintern. According to the new "theory," the war drive of the capitalist class, and the victories of the USSR, had forced Social Democracy to choose sides—and it chose fascism. From the Tenth Plenum until 1935, the claim that Social Democracy was fascist became standard fare in the Stalinist press. This paragraph, from *Pravda* in 1931, is typical:

---

*Similar statements were made by other members of the post-Lenin leadership in 1924. Zinoviev, for example: "International Social-Democracy has become a wing of fascism."[19]

Social democracy is carrying out the fascisation of the bourgeois state under the pretext of defending bourgeois democracy, as the alleged "lesser evil," compared with fascism. The role of social-democracy, which in words comes out against fascism and which is praised in the press of the right wing and the Trotskyists as an opponent of fascism, must be ruthlessly exposed. There can be no compromise or bloc with the social democratic workers against fascism and social fascism, to support the capitalist offensive against the working class, to support the preparations for war against the Soviet Union.[20]

Nor was Social Democracy simply a subsidiary part of fascism. According to the ideologists of the Comintern, social-fascism was the *main enemy*. In the words of the Twelfth Plenum of the ECCI in 1932:

The sections of the C.I. must therefore direct the *chief blow against social democracy*, because the isolation of social democracy from the proletariat is a prerequisite for the winning over of the majority of the working class, a prerequisite for the victory over fascism and the overthrow of the dictatorship of the bourgeoisie.[21]

Just four months after this resolution was adopted, Hitler came to power in Germany, his way paved by the Comintern's refusal to form an anti-fascist united front with the Social Democrats. The German catastrophe demonstrated conclusively the utter bankruptcy of the Stalinized Comintern, and prompted Leon Trotsky's call for the formation of a new International.

The theory of social-fascism, though not the term itself, appeared very clearly in the resolutions of the 1929 convention and plenum of the Communist Party of Canada. Not only was the policy of supporting the Canadian Labor Party abandoned (no one could object to that, since the CLP was virtually defunct) but the very idea of such a policy was denounced. "Our task is to combat the whole idea of a Federated Labor Party," the CEC declared. "Establishing a united front with the reformists would amount in essence to a betrayal of the true interests of the working class."[22]

From there it was only a small step to describing the Independent Labor Party, which included such individuals as J.S. Woodsworth and Agnes MacPhail, as "a social-fascist, third party of capitalism."[23]

The role of the social democrats of all countries today, including the Canadian brand, is a role of social-fascism; they are the open agents of Capitalism; and no word twisting, or glib radical phrases can make them anything else....[24]

When Woodsworth urged an end to such attacks and adoption of a policy of united labor action, the CPC replied:

No! Mr. Woodsworth, we will be unable to support your united front. In fact, we declare that it is the task of every honest man and woman in the Canadian labor movement to fight with might and main against your united front. Your united front would be a united front of betrayal, of unscrupulous, though cunning, attacks upon the working class.[25]

In 1930 and 1931, when the Canadian labor movement was in disarray and the organized forces of Canadian Social Democracy were at an all-time low, the Communist Party's sectarian policy had little practical effect—except insofar as it isolated the CPC itself and left it open to government attack. In 1932, however, the labor left began to revive. In August the founding meeting of the Cooperative Commonwealth Federation (CCF) was held in Calgary, and in a matter of months the new Social Democratic party spread across the country. The first public CCF meeting in Toronto, on November 30, 1932, drew more than 3,500 people, 1,000 of whom signed membership cards on the spot.[26]

It is sometimes suggested, even by people who consider themselves Marxists, that the birth of a mass Social Democratic party was inevitable. The assumption seems to be that Marxism is an alien force in Canadian life, while Social Democracy is somehow natural, the spontaneous product of Canadian labor's collective consciousness. In fact, however, revolutionary Marxist parties have a long history in this country, while Social Democracy of the CCF-NDP type is a relative newcomer. Prior to World War I and again during the labor upsurge of 1919, Marxist parties had the support of large sections of organized labor. During the latter half of the 1920s, Social Democracy in Canada all but collapsed, and the Communist Party was the largest organization on the left.

The formation of the CCF, and its success in creating a mass Social-Democratic organization, owes little to the wisdom of its leaders or the natural inclinations of Canadian workers. The CCF became dominant on the left in large measure because the Communist Party in 1929 abandoned any serious attempt to hold or win the leadership of the left. By 1932 the policies of the Third Period had made the CP a thoroughly unrealistic choice for the thousands of Canadians who had begun to question the existing social order. The appearance of the CCF gave them an alternative.

Much had already been lost by 1932, but even then a correct

approach could have won a hearing for Marxist ideas in the ranks of the CCF. The CCF was not a labor party (its main base was in the agrarian West), but a party which proclaimed itself to be socialist, and which could sign up 1,000 members in a single night, certainly deserved the attention of a party claiming to be Communist. The CP could have proposed united actions to the CCF, perhaps attempted to arrange a mutually acceptable division of constituencies for election campaigns. The CCF in its first year was very open to overtures from the left—and the Communist Party, more than any other Marxist current in Canada, had the forces to make such overtures count.* Sensitively-posed calls for united action were on the order of the day.

Whatever else might be said about the CPC's response to the CCF, it was certainly not a sensitively posed call for united action. The *Worker* called the new party "A New Unholy Alliance." The CCF, said an editorial, "is composed of proven traitors to the workers and small farmers and will provide a detriment and a menace to the interests of all toilers."[27] The party rushed out a book which purported to prove that "a fundamental community of ideas exists between the fascism of Hitler and the social-fascism of the CCF." It concluded:

We have summarized the role of the C.C.F. as the twin of Fascism, paving the way for the organic growth of Fascism out of capitalist 'democracy.' ...It is a reactionary force, an indispensable instrument of dying capitalism for perpetuating the enslavement of the people. It is the main bulwark of the rule of finance capital in its drive towards Fascism and war.†[28]

Certainly no working class organization would propose united action to "the main bulwark of finance capital!" The CPC combatted the CCF at every turn, refused united action with those who supported it, and ran candidates against it at every opportunity. The party cut itself off from the first stages of a new

---

*Both the Trotskyists and the Lovestoneites were active in the Ontario CCF in 1933-34. The former in particular won many of their recruits there.

†This book, *Socialism and the CCF*, by G. Pierce (Stewart Smith) was removed from circulation by the CPC in 1935, but as late as 1952 Buck claimed that "the role played by the C.C.F. leadership...was fully explained... [in] *Socialism and the C.C.F.*" In 1965, however, after Smith had left the CPC in disgrace, Buck disowned the book, attributing it to errors that crept into party policy while Buck was in prison.[29]

wave of radicalism—and cut the new radicals off from Marxism.

Defending Civil Liberties

As the battle for "freedom of the streets" progressed from disaster to disaster, the Communist Party faced a steadily increasing number of prosecutions. In response to these attacks, the party in 1929 decided to revitalize the moribund Canadian Labor Defense League. The CLDL had originally been founded in 1925

to unite all forces willing to cooperate into a broad National organization that will undertake to provide means for the defense and support of workers, regardless of their political or industrial affiliations, race, color or nationality, who are indicted and prosecuted on account of their activity in the Labour movement.[30]

While the League could not claim any great victories in its first years of activities, it did raise money to defend a variety of victims of antilabor prosecutions and to support their families while the trials and jail terms proceeded. It brought together defenders of civil liberties from different political currents, including Social Democrats (James Simpson was on the executive board) and leaders of the All-Canadian Congress of Labor.

That, however, was before the Third Period. Under the new order, the CLDL made little pretense of being more than a Communist Party front. The first issue of the *Canadian Labor Defender* featured an article by Stewart Smith which declared that the Depression would lead the workers to "sweep away the capitalist exploiters and their servants, the social-reformist traitors."[31] The next issue insisted that "every worker who understands the purpose for which the CLDL was founded...must line up with the election program of the Communist Party."[32] This was no way to build a united defense of civil rights.

The CLDL's primary activity was the organization of "united front" conferences in cities across the country. These one- or two-day gatherings would be hailed in the *Worker* as proof of the growing mass resistance to incipient fascism in Canada—but the published attendance lists showed that few participated other than members of CP-dominated organizations. Non-Stalinists would be barred at the door or subjected to constant abuse in the ritual speeches and resolutions of the conferences. When J.S. Woodsworth protested against an anti-ILP resolution adopted at one such conference, pointing out that he had often spoken out in defense of civil liberties, Beckie Buhay replied:

If Mr. Woodsworth has brought up the cases of the deported and arrested workers in the House of Commons, he was forced to do so, in order to deceive the workers and make them keep their illusions about him....

It is the duty of the Canadian Labor Defense League...to expose to the working class all who are actively or passively helping the fascist henchmen of the bourgeoisie.[33]

One could scarcely blame the "fascist henchmen of the bourgeoisie"—and their supporters—for refusing to have anything to do with the CLDL after this type of attack.

Reading statements such as Buhay's, it would be easy to conclude that the CP was not serious about defending civil liberties. Though it gave lip-service to the cause of democratic rights, the Communist International and its Canadian section leaned strongly towards the view that police terrorism and repression were inevitable—and that they would perform a positive role by radicalizing the working class. This conclusion was explicit in the ECCI's evaluation of the 1929 "struggle for the streets" in Canada:

These demonstrations denoted a growing sympathy of the working class for the USSR, their growing antagonism to the bourgeoisie, and their readiness to struggle. These events show that the inner class contradictions within Canada are sharpening, resulting in the police terror of the bourgeoisie. The political education of the masses received a great impetus as a result.[34]

Similarly, at the 1931 CEC plenum, Tim Buck declared that "with every demonstration that is smashed the prestige of our Party grows."[35]

The party seldom missed an opportunity to announce that fascism was imminent, or that it had already arrived: the obvious differences between a liberal-parliamentary system and a fascist system were glossed over with the generalization that both were forms of capitalism. Implicit or explicit in every such statement was the conclusion that the growth of fascism would assist the party, by "exposing" capitalist democracy.*

Such conceptions made it impossible for the CPC to mount any

---

*In the International, this conception reached its nadir with the ECCI's statement on Hitler's takeover in Germany: "The establishment of the open fascist dictatorship, which is destroying all democratic illusions among the masses and liberating them from social democratic influence, is accelerating the rate of Germany's advance towards the proletarian revolution."[36]

serious defense of democratic rights. The party won fewer and fewer court cases as it isolated itself from all possible allies in or out of the working class. By 1931 the process was complete: the Communist Party of Canada stood alone.

IT WAS THIS ISOLATION THAT MADE POSSIBLE a joint attack of federal, provincial and municipal governments on the Communist Party in 1931. On August 11 a joint force of officers from the RCMP, the Ontario Provincial Police, and the Toronto Police assembled in the Ontario provincial parliament buildings. They were addressed by OPP Commissioner Victor Williams. "Gentlemen," he said, "We are going to strike a death blow at the Communist Party."[37] The police raided the offices of the party and the homes of its leaders, confiscated all documents they could find, and arrested nine men: Tim Buck, Malcolm Bruce, Tom McEwen, Tom Hill, John Boychuck, Matthew Popowich, Sam Carr, Tom Cacic, and Michael Golinski. They were charged under Section 98 of the Criminal Code, a law originally passed as a response to the Winnipeg General Strike. Two months later the first seven named were sentenced to five years in prison. Cacic received a two-year sentence, to be followed by deportation. Golinski was not convicted. The judge concluded his sentencing by declaring the Communist Party of Canada to be an illegal organization.

This is not the place to discuss the trial itself. It was, beyond doubt, one of the greatest travesties of justice in Canadian history. The judge was openly biased against the defendants, and the law under which they were charged violated the most basic principles of justice. As Frank Scott pointed out in the *Canadian Forum,* Section 98 declared that anyone who even attended a meeting of an "unlawful association" was presumed to be a member of the association "in the absence of proof to the contrary."

None of your old-fashioned ideas that a man is presumed innocent until proven guilty.... You won't escape gaol unless you can prove that you are not a member of the party. And think what it will be like trying to make this proof! Obviously no member of the party will dare to testify that you are a non-member, because by coming forward he would at once give notice to the police that he is a criminal. [Section 98] really gets down to business and should rid our radicals forever of the obsolete idea that under the Canadian constitution the personal liberties of the subject give the subject any personal liberty.[38]

Section 98 was enormously unpopular. The House of Commons

had voted several times to repeal it, only to have repeal defeated by the Senate. Every section of the labor movement was opposed to it. Seldom has there been a civil liberties case with such potential for uniting broad sections of the population in support of democratic rights.

The Communist Party utterly failed to organize such a campaign. Its defense in the courtroom was lacklustre; its defense outside of the courts was self-defeating. In the face of a major government attack on its right to exist, the CPC did little more than organize routine CLDL "united front" conferences. These, to no one's surprise, had no impact on government policy or the court's verdict.

The court's ruling that the CPC was an "unlawful association" had little practical impact. The party continued to function, the *Worker* continued to publish. But now the party took on the trappings of illegality. Public meetings of the party were called "united front" campaigns—although there was never a genuine united front involved. The *Worker's* reports on party meetings would begin with the note, "The following has been received through the mails."

This was all charade. No one—certainly not the RCMP—was fooled by the play-acting. Instead of fighting for legality, instead of denying the government's right to drive it underground, the CPC was using its formal illegality to prove its right to the label revolutionary. The party had, in effect, reverted to the "undergroundism" of 1921. The absurdity of it all was clearly shown when the line changed. In 1935 the CPC started functioning as a legal party—with no adverse legal consequences. The defeat of 1931 and the following three years of "illegality" were as much a product of the party's own sectarianism as of the government's determination to crush communism.

15. The Third Period in Canada: Red Unions

The Communist Party's sectarian refusal to work with other groups on the left in defense of democratic rights was not the only factor that aided the anticommunist witch-hunters in securing the Section 98 convictions. Another factor, perhaps even more important, was the party's self-imposed isolation in the trade union movement, resulting from the creation of the misnamed "Workers Unity League."

The WUL is the one major exception to the Communist Party's general policy of suppressing all mention of the policies of the Third Period. In contrast to the "struggle for the streets" lunacy and the suicidal "social-fascism" line, the WUL retains an aura of romantic militancy, of hard-fought union battles when the going was tough in the depths of the Depression. CPC histories like to claim that the WUL pioneered industrial unionism in Canada, paving the way for the CIO. Tom McEwen, for example, claims that "the Communist Party and the WUL" led "the first major attempt to organize the steel workers on an industrial basis...the strike of the workers at the National Steel Car Company of Canada in Hamilton, Ontario, in the late summer of 1928."[*1] The WUL's role in organizing miners, garment workers, and lumberworkers is cited in most accounts.

These claims have had an impact on non-Party historians, who have tended to view the WUL as a model of militant unionism: the Canadian nationalist wing of the left has been particularly

---

*McEwen makes no attempt to harmonize this claim with the fact that the WUL was not formed until 1930.

enamored with the WUL in recent years. Irving Abella, for example, describes the dissolution of the WUL in 1936 as "a blow from which the national union movement was not to recover."[2] Robert Laxer writes that "the ability of the WUL to organize workers during the depths of the depression shows the strength of militant Canadian unionism." According to Laxer, "with a minimum of finances and no previous union base, the WUL organized at least 25,000 workers between 1930 and 1935."[3]

The idealization of the Workers Unity League by sections of the left is based, to a considerable extent, on lack of knowledge. Despite its fame (or notoriety) the WUL's history has never been told. Most accounts of the history of Canadian labor mention it only in passing, as Laxer does, perhaps with references to the Estevan miners' strike in 1931, the Stratford furniture workers' strike in 1933, or the unemployed workers' On-to-Ottawa Trek in 1935. These events have achieved semi-legendary status for labor historians— few of them seem aware that despite the exceptional heroism of the workers who participated, the Estevan and Stratford strikes went down to defeat, and the On-to-Ottawa Trekkers, with the exception of a few party leaders, never got within 2,000 miles of Ottawa. These struggles are testimony to the courage of the Canadian working class in exceptionally difficult circumstances—but they are by no means proof of the great abilities of the WUL leadership.

The Workers Unity League constantly combined a readiness to enter all-out combat, regardless of the balance of forces involved, with a total refusal to seek allies beyond its own ranks. This combination of adventurism and sectarianism led to defeat after defeat. The only lasting achievement of the WUL was the isolation of thousands of left-wing labor militants from the mainstream of Canadian labor.

Revolutionary Unionism

As we have seen, the Communist Party of Canada rejected "revolutionary unionism" very early in its history. The party's founding convention concluded that the attempt to split the existing unions had only isolated the left, leaving the workers in the old unions "more nakedly at the mercy of the A.F. of L. officialdom than before."[4] The major debate at the founding convention of the Workers Party in 1922 was on precisely this question—and the party voted overwhelmingly against red unions.

This position, it should be noted, had nothing in common with the opposition to "dual unionism" as interpreted by the North

American labor bureaucracy. Under Samuel Gompers's guidance, the unions of the American Federation of Labor (and the Trades and Labor Congress of Canada) spent more time in jurisdictional disputes than they did in defending workers' rights: the question the union leaders asked was not "How can we best organize these workers?" but rather "Who will get their dues?" In the AF of L, each union had absolute control over its "jurisdiction"—and the union brass decided whether or not to organize workers within their jurisdictions. It took a very powerful "dual union," the Congress of Industrial Organizations (CIO), which organized in a way that cut right across jurisdictional lines, to break out of the dead-end craft unionism of the AFL-TLC.

The revolutionary position took as its first concern the necessity for revolutionaries to work in the organizations of the working class. The problem with the One Big Union (OBU) was not that it split the labor movement—it was so small by 1921 that the split did not weaken any of the major unions—but that it took the radicals out of the labor movement, into isolation. The purpose of working in the existing unions, whatever they might be, was to build a class-struggle-oriented left wing that could fight for the leadership of the working class.

This objective was somewhat obscured in the late 1920s by the Communist Party's adaptation to a nationalist wing of the labor bureaucracy, organized in the All-Canadian Congress of Labor (ACCL). Nevertheless the Communists did cling to the Leninist policy of working where the masses were to be found, no matter how reactionary the organizations might be.

The Communist Party held all or part of the leadership of two ACCL unions by mid-1929: the Mine Workers Union of Canada and the Lumber Workers Industrial Union. The former was discussed in chapter 6: it was the product of the collapse of the United Mine Workers in Western Canada. The latter had existed since the end of World War I. Originally based in B.C., the LWIU had gone into decline early in the 1920s: by the end of the decade it was based primarily in Northern Ontario among Finnish workers, and had between one and two thousand members.

The party also led two unions which were not in the ACCL. The Auto Workers Industrial Union was formed in Windsor in 1928, during an unsuccessful attempt to organize Ford. The Industrial Union of Needle Trades Workers (IUNTW), which was also formed in 1928, was led by militants in Montreal, Toronto, and Winnipeg who had been expelled from the International Ladies Garment

Workers Union and the Amalgamated Clothing Workers. It was probably about the same size as the other garment unions in those cities in 1928.

WHILE MANY CRITICISMS could be made of the CPC's union policies in 1928, it cannot be doubted that the party was making important advances. The formation of the IUNTW was an indication that the party had the leadership of a considerable body of urban workers in a major industry. An effective organizing campaign, coupled with a fight for consolidation of the IUNTW, the ILGWU, and the ACW into a single garment workers' union, could have produced major gains for the party in 1929 and 1930. And it would have been consistent with the policies the Trade Union Educational League, under Tim Buck's leadership, had been defending since 1922.

The Communist International, however, was in the process of dumping the effort to influence the existing unions. Stalin had laid the basis for the new policy in December 1928:

> If the reformist leadership is identifying itself with capitalism... while the working class is waging a struggle against capitalism... a situation is quite conceivable in which it may be necessary to create parallel mass associations of the working class, against the will of the trade-union bosses who have sold themselves to the capitalists. *We already have such a situation in America.*[5] [Emphasis added]

The Trades and Labor Congress of Canada was indistinguishable from the American Federation of Labor. If the TLC had been the only union federation in existence in early 1929, the Buck-Smith faction might have become champions of "revolutionary unions" immediately on learning of Stalin's speech. Their counterparts in the United States certainly moved quickly to adopt such a policy in December 1928 and January 1929.[6]

But Canada had the All-Canadian Congress of Labor, which the CPC, and Buck in particular, had been defending for two years as a "progressive" union center. The Buck-Smith group, therefore, adopted a position which gave a great deal to the new policy, but kept hold of the ACCL. Thus Sam Carr wrote:

> My opionion is that while we will affiliate new unions to the ACCL and not form a new centre at present, we must understand that the reactionary leadership will sooner or later embark upon an expulsion policy against Communists and Left-wingers, and in general reach the condition of the AF of L (unless we succeed in completely changing the leadership and policies

of the new congress in the near future, which is highly improbable). In such a case, the question of forming a new revolutionary centre in Canada may arise...At present, however, the immediate organization of a new center is untimely and out of the question.[7]

Similarly, Tim Buck wrote, "To withdraw from the ACCL *now* and to set up a revolutionary centre would be contrary to all Leninist principles in trade union work."[8] [Emphasis added]*

The International also hesitated. In February the Red International of Labor Unions (RILU) urged the Canadian Communists to devote their efforts to building a revolutionary opposition *within* the ACCL and the TLC: "It is especially necessary to point out that the opposition does not aim at the creation of the Third trade union center.... The greatest care must be exercized that we do not isolate ourselves from the workers belonging to one or the other center."[10] The ECCI letter in April urged more criticism of the ACCL leadership, and confirmed that the comments made by the RILU in February "should serve as the basis for further developing and improving the line of trade union work."[11]

The Trade Union Resolution adopted by the CPC convention in June adopted the formation of a "revolutionary center" as a long-term goal. It did so, however, in terms which implied no major break with past policy. In reference to party and TUEL policy towards strikes, it said:

The line to be followed in each specific case [is] to be of course in line with the general program of winning the decisive majority of the rank and file of the whole trade union movement for the goal of a single united independent Canadian Center affiliated to the R.I.L.U.[12]

This was no different from the policy adopted by the party and TUEL at the beginning of the decade: fighting for the adoption of class struggle policies by the decisive majority of the trade union movement. Six months later this policy was jettisoned entirely.

The Turn

When the change came, it came with startling suddenness. An October 3, 1929 ECCI letter to the party still spoke of building a "broad Left wing movement" which, together with the new unions established under CP leadership, would "eventually...develop

---

*There is a valuable discussion of this turn in Norman Penner's *The Canadian Left*.[9]

into a revolutionary trade union center." The letter insisted that the "immediate task" of the party was to gather its forces to provide "the basis for opposition to the trade union bureaucrats in both centers" and the organization of unorganized workers into "revolutionary unions."[13] Despite the "revolutionary union" rhetoric, the letter clearly posed the creation of a revolutionary center as a long-range task.

One month later, in November, a letter from the RILU arrived. It announced that both the TLC and the ACCL were now "component parts of social-reformism in Canada and are the bulwark of the Canadian and Anglo-American bourgeoisie." The letter described this as a recent development, and drew immediate organizational conclusions:

The latest development in Canada, the final and complete transformation of the Canadian Congress into a tool of capitalism etc.—force us to take up the question of establishing a revolutionary trade union center. Your perspective must be one of the organization of a revolutionary trade union center that will unite all the workers for the struggle against capitalism and its agent, the social reformist trade union bureaucracy.[14]

Nothing whatever had happened that might have justified a change in the CPC's evaluation of the ACCL. The ACCL was no better than it had been in the past—but it was certainly no worse. In fact, during the summer of 1929 Aaren Mosher had attended the founding convention of the Industrial Union of Needle Trades Workers, and had written a friendly article for the convention's souvenir program: he was clearly signalling his willingness to have the CP-led union join the confederation. The change in policy had nothing to do with Canadian conditions. It was decided thousands of miles away, by people whose primary concern was not the advancing of the Canadian class struggle but the imposition of uniform Third Period tactics on every party in the International. The minutes of the CPC Political Committee for December 16, 1929 are brief and clear:

Discussion of RILU letter and the formation of opposition Center in Canada. Decided name of organization, "Workers Unity League of Canada."[15]

The party moved quickly. Early in 1930, a meeting in Toronto attended by no more than 75 people—according to Tom McEwen, "probably a half or more were members of the Communist Party"—

founded the Workers Unity League.[16] Tom McEwen became Acting National Secretary, rented an office, and had letterhead printed, and the Canadian working class learned through the pages of the *Worker* that a new trade union federation had been born.

What kind of an organization was the WUL to be? It was, the propaganda insisted again and again, a *revolutionary* trade union center. The League's Draft Constitution, published in June 1930, tried to give this a concrete political meaning. The WUL, it said, was

pledged to a program and policy of revolutionary struggle for the complete overthrow of capitalism and its institutions, and the setting up of the State Power of the Workers and Poor Farmers through a workers' and farmers' government.[17]

But calling an organization "revolutionary" does not make it so. As Norman Penner has pointed out, this terminology indicated that the party was abandoning the trade union policies of the early Comintern:

...why did the Communists insist on calling the WUL the "revolutionary trade union centre?" What was "revolutionary" about its activity? After all, Lenin had called the trade unions in capitalist society the "most rudimentary class organizations" and declared that any attempt to try to invent "brand new, clean little workers' unions...guiltless of bourgeois-democratic prejudices" was "foolish."

Despite all the revolutionary rhetoric, Penner notes, "the aims and objects of the WUL were the same as those of other trade-union centers and could be accomplished within the existing society."[18]

The only excuse for calling the WUL "revolutionary" was the fact that it was led by the Communist Party to the exclusion of all other political currents, and it devoted its efforts to splitting and smashing the "reformist," "social-fascist" unions. The object of the WUL was to do just what the party had resolved *not* to do in 1921: to create "brand new, clean little workers' unions...guiltless of bourgeois-democratic prejudices." As Leslie Morris wrote:

Our party cannot any longer lend support to the building and strengthening of the reformist trade unions, for to do so is to strengthen the reactionary bureaucracy of these unions, to lend support to the bourgeois prejudices of the "labor aristocracy," and to strengthen the influence of this aristocracy among the ranks of the working class.[19]

On another occasion Morris wrote, "all talk of capturing the apparatus of the reformists' unions is hopelessly wrong; . . . the reformist
bureaucracies are an integral part of the bourgeois machinery of
state." The *One Big Union Bulletin* quoted Morris's statement and
remarked sarcastically: "Gee whiz! it's too bad it took the [ECCI]
Plenum nine years to find this out. The O.B.U. told these
masquerading revolutionists the same thing nine years ago."[20]

One could scarcely ask for a clearer illustration of the distance
Tim Buck's Party had travelled from its Leninist beginnings.

The Trade Union Educational League, the instrument of CP
trade union policy in the 1920s, was established to make the
existing unions "ever more clear-sighted, *cohesive*, militant and
powerful."[21] (emphasis added) It repeatedly moved to dissuade
unionists from carrying out splits in their unions as a response to
the conservatism of the bureaucracy. Only after a split had been
imposed by the bureaucracy (as in the needle trades) or the existing
union had collapsed (mine-workers in Alberta) did the party
attempt to form "dual" unions. Even then it carried on a constant
campaign for unity of the workers' organizations. Compare that
stand to Tim Buck's in 1930, set out in a letter to Jim Barker, CPC
organizer in Nova Scotia, referring to unrest in the United Mine
Workers:

Our policy should be to convene a conference of all Left-Wingers . . . at the
same time as the district convention [of the UMW] . . . as a rallying point for
the Industrial Union to break with the U.M.W. by declaring itself the
representative conference of the miners of Nova Scotia . . .

The program must be SMASH THE UMW with all energies centered on
the building of the Industrial Union, using the slogan of REFUSING TO
PAY PER CAPITA as the main lever against the UMW.[22]

This policy led directly to the split in the mine workers' ranks in
Nova Scotia. The Communists walked out of the UMW, creating the
Amalgamated Mine Workers of Nova Scotia under J.B. McLachlan's leadership, a step which was directly contrary to the policy
the party had defended through most of its first decade. In 1935,
when the "Third Period" was abandoned, the Amalgamated was
ordered to dissolve and return to the United Mine Workers:
McLachlan, unwilling to make another 180-degree turn, resigned
from the Communist Party in protest.

Communist Party historians have done their best to play down
the splitting, "red-union" tactics of the WUL, and to emphasize the
successes it had in "organizing the unorganized." While no one can

deny the dedication, even heroism, of the CPC militants who fought to create new unions against nearly insurmountable odds, the fact remains that the WUL, even at its peak, encompassed only a small minority of the organized workers in Canada. Most of the League's growth came in the last two years of its six-year existence, when the working class had begun to move again and the AFL and ACCL leaders were still failing to respond—the WUL, in effect, won members by default.

And it must be pointed out that the organization's main membership base, for most of its existence, was not in the new unions, but in the Mine Workers', Lumber Workers', and Needle Trades Workers' unions—*all organized before the Workers Unity League was created.*

Organizing the WUL

The Workers Unity League was a completely artificial creation. It had no particular reason to exist, other than the directives of the Comintern, and it had virtually no life other than that which the party gave to it. The Political Secretariat of the ECCI said as much in its letter to the February 1931 plenum:

The organization of the Workers Unity League was not preceded by a mass campaign with the object of providing it with a mass base in the factories.... In its development the WUL was to a great extent, especially as it appeared before the masses, a duplicate of the Party.... Of special importance is the neglect by the revolutionary unions of the work of building the unions on a factory basis and also of developing district organizations.[23]

Norman Freed, then a party leader in Winnipeg, wrote:

The organization of the Workers Unity League has been very mechanical. We established committees at the top (District, National Committees, Local Committees, etc.) without having any real contact with the shops, mines and reactionary trade unions.[24]

The party's 1931 plenum pointed out the "entire lack of national and local cadres" in the WUL,[25] and Tom McEwen remarked that "the WUL, as far as the Center is concerned, it still a one-man job."[26]

Yet this organization, without a base, without national or local leaders, was supposed to create a mass revolutionary union center! Its only affiliates in its first year were the Industrial Union of

Needle Trades Workers and the Lumber Workers Industrial Union.
At the end of 1930 it succeeded in splitting the Mine Workers Union
of Canada, taking a majority into the WUL. Later it did the same
with the United Mine Workers in Nova Scotia. Later in the 1930s,
when the working class began to recover from the blows of the
Depression, the WUL did organize some unorganized workers into
new, if short-lived, unions. At the beginning, however, it could only
grow by splitting the existing labor movement. Smashing the other
unions became the prime consideration in setting WUL policy. In
1930, for example, Tim Buck wrote to Harvey Murphy that CPers in
the Mine Workers Union should press for strike action, regardless
of the consequences:

We are governed not merely by the consideration of whether or not the
probabilities are for a "successful" strike. Under the cicumstances
"success" might not be so important. The basic consideration now is that of
the fight against the U.M.W. of A. and the strengthening of the Left-wing
leadership.[27]

This approach, in which smashing the ALF-TLC unions was given
priority over the needs of the workers involved, had disastrous
effects for thousands of workers during the first years of the Third
Period. A particularly blatant example of the sectarian blindness of
Communist Party policy in the early 1930s occurred in Toronto,
during the garment workers' strikes of 1931.

Organizing the Needle Workers

Early in 1930, in part as a response to the activities of the
IUNTW, the International Ladies Garment Workers Union
launched a drive to extend its organization in Toronto. Had it been
following the policies of the TUEL in the 1920s, the Industrial
Union would have hailed this organizing drive, supported it, and
pressed for united action against the bosses. Such an approach
would have strengthened the left, regardless of the response of the
ILGWU leaders. Instead the CP-led union denounced the ILGWU's
organizing drive, and did its best to obstruct it at every turn. The
"National Needle Trades Commission" of the party, at a meeting
which Tim Buck attended, decided that

It is not the task of the I.U. of N.T.W. of Canada to draw workers into this
fake movement. To do so would be tantamount to supporting the
International fakers in their treachery. We are with the Cloakmakers in all

their struggles, and one of the most serious of their struggles today is that of exposing the International fakers and destroying their influence in the working class movement. We will fight them all through the present campaign with this end in sight.[28]

At the 1931 plenum McEwen stated the policy clearly:

On the question of what the Industrial Union should do in those shops where we had effected an Agreement and the International Union calls a strike, our policy where we have a majority, is that our comrades pay no attention to the call of the International....[29]

In other words, the fight against the leaders of the ILGWU took precedence over the fight against the employers. Throughout 1930 the workers of Toronto were treated to the spectacle of the two unions fighting with each other, scabbing on each other's strikes, and raiding each other's memberships. Perhaps little better could be expected from the ILGWU, which operated in the Sam Gompers tradition of jurisdictional disputes, but for a "revolutionary union" this was appalling behavior.

The ILGWU, with superior resources at its command, signed up a majority of the 2,000 garment workers in Toronto. It proceeded with plans for a general strike of the city's needle trades in February 1931—the main object of the strike would be to win union recognition and a first contract.

The IUNTW was not going to be outdone in the militancy department. Although it had signed up at most 500 members, it prepared a general strike for January 13, 1931, just one month before the ILGWU's planned strike. If the party had been primarily interested in organizing the unorganized, in winning union rights for garment workers, it would have planned its strike to coincide with the ILGWU. But the CPC was only interested in being one-up on its labor opponents, not in building genuine unions.

The IUNTW's "general strike" was doomed from the start, if only by the party's organizing procedures. The strike was planned and organized by a handful of party members, behind the backs of the workers! Buck later admitted:

We certainly had plenty of preparations for the Toronto strike, but nobody knew anything about it. It was too secret. We have, for instance, a YCL Trade Union Buro member. He is a needle trades worker. I asked him how the strike was getting along and he had not even known there was a strike on. Our leading comrades...were afraid the International [union] might learn of the strike. Consequently, they kept all preparations to themselves, and we did not have enough publicity, not even among the needle trades workers themselves, so we had no chance of carrying through a really successful strike.*[30]

On January 13 only ten of the dozens of garment factories in Toronto responded to the IUNTW's call. The strike collapsed in less than a week and the IUNTW members returned to work, having lost some pay and gained nothing. The *Worker* tried to claim that the defeat was a victory, that they had now "gained the confidence of the honest worker in the needle industry" and established "a healthy foundation for the Industrial Union," but few workers were fooled. In the course of the next five years the WUL would often claim victories that no one else could see—but calling a defeat a victory does not make it one. The party was only deluding itself and the workers who followed its lead.

On February 24, Local 72 of the International Ladies' Garment Workers Union went on strike, demanding union recognition, a 15 percent wage increase, and a forty-four-hour week. Some five hundred workers, most of them women, walked out on the first day: eventually more than one thousand took part.

Whatever disagreements they might have had with the International, it was the elementary duty of the Communist Party and the IUNTW to support the strike. Criticism of the ILGWU's policies should have been expressed *within* the union, and from a basic position of support for the strike and its demands. If the IUNTW had superior tactics to offer, it could have proved their superiority in practice by supporting the strike. Any other policy would weaken the strike and isolate the radicals from the strikers.

The Communist Party ignored such considerations. Not only did it condemn the ILGWU and the strike, it openly called on garment workers to cross picket lines, to scab on the strike. "ILGWU Conducts Dressmakers' Strike for Establishing Its Company Union Yoke on Necks of Workers," read the headline in the *Worker*. "Close your ranks against your enemies, the International Scab Agency and the bosses," said the IUNTW executive. "The striking

---

*Such bureaucratic, high-handed procedures were characteristic of the WUL. Referring to the Estevan strike, for example, a WUL resolution (*after the fact*, of course) noted that "the strike demands were not discussed by, or even known to the miners when the first rank and file committee negotiated with the coal operators."[31]

dressmakers should make their own settlements, should go over the heads of the officials," declared the party.[32]

An editorial in the *Worker* illustrates the tone and content of party propaganda:

The fascist trade union bureaucracy of the so-called "Internationals" that have fastened themselves like a leech on the necks of the needle workers have been the main protagonists of capitalist rationalization and sweatshop exploitation. Thru these fascists, the "Internationals" have been transformed into efficiency [*sic*] adjuncts of capitalist exploitation. By the extensive use of gangsterism and thuggery and job control these degenerates have sought at all times to terrorize the needle workers into submission to starvation standards and to drive the militant needle workers and the Industrial Union from the shops.[33]

Communist Party leader Annie Buller reported the impact of the party's antistrike campaign to the May 1931 convention of the Industrial Union:

The statement we issued during the International strike, exposing the betrayal and telling the Dressmakers to make their own settlements, was well received and several shops held meetings and actually wanted to carry this through in life. But there the International stepped in with gangsterism and the strikers were actually afraid to return to work. The strike, however, was demoralized, and the International lost out.[34]

The ones who really lost out were the garment workers. After two-and-a-half months the ILGWU called the strike off. The defeat was a result, at least in part, of the policies of the CPC and the IUNTW, which amounted to organized strike breaking. The only winners were the bosses.

This is only one example. Time and again the Workers Unity League, through a combination of adventurist tactics and sectarian refusal to cooperate with other labor organizations, led groups of workers into defeat. There could be nothing more absurd than to label this policy "revolutionary." Its main result was weakening of the labor movement—and a weakening of the influence of the left within the labor movement.

Isolation of the Left

The essence of Communist policy towards the trade unions, from the Second Congress of the Communist International on, had been to maintain and strengthen a revolutionary presence in the mass organizations of the workers, to carry on tireless propaganda for a class-struggle policy. An attempt was made in Germany in 1920 to establish "revolutionary unions" and the Comintern decisively repudiated it. The task of Communists, the Third Congress of the CI insisted, was "to work steadily, energetically, and stubbornly to win the majority of the workers in all unions, not to let themselves be discouraged by the present reactionary mood in the unions, but to seek, despite all resistance, to win the unions for communism by the most active participation in their day-to-day struggles."[35] As late as 1927 the Organization Department of the Comintern warned the Canadian CP about the dangers involved in creating revolutionary unions:

The experience of the revolutionary international trade union movement (concretely, France, Czecho-Slovakia and Holland) has shown that with the use of the revolutionary trade unions, existing side by side with the reformist unions and under the influence of the direct guidance of the Communist Parties, work in the reformist trade unions diminishes and the influence of the Party in these unions remains at a standstill or diminishes.[36]

The Workers Unity League never formally repudiated this policy. Its constitution declared that work in the "reformist" unions was to be an essential part of WUL activity, and provision was made for the affiliation of opposition groups within the ACCL and TLC. Despite this, the WUL and the CPC constantly noted that work in the non-WUL unions was almost nonexistent. The February 1931 plenum noted "the recently developed tendency to liquidate all our activities in the reformist unions."[37] A resolution of the WUL in 1932 criticized "underestimation of the tremendous importance of work in the AF of L and ACCL unions," and urged "a decisive improvement in the work within the AF of L and ACCL...."[38] In January 1933 the WUL Executive Board resolved that "the WUL must immediately intensify its work to build up organized opposition movements throughout the reformist unions, destroying all pessimism, underestimation and neglect on this important part of WUL work."[39] The WUL National Congress in September 1933 "raised the alarm about our weak and insignificant work within the AF of L, ACC of L unions, the Railroad Brotherhoods, etc...."[40]

Even in 1934, when the WUL's membership was reaching its highest point, a party member wrote that "we can count the Communist fractions that carry on daily work inside of the reformist unions *on the fingers of your hands.*" He added, "in no city can we speak about systematic work within the reformist unions."[41] And the party's Seventh Convention, during the summer of 1934, complained that

The turn to work in the factories, to mass revolutionary work has only been commenced, and is carried on as yet only by a small section of the party. A fundamental improvement in the work in the reformist unions has not been carried out, particularly in the railways. . . .

The Party must decisively overcome the underestimation of and serious lagging behind in the work in the main A.F. of L. and A.C.C.L. and Catholic unions. . . .[42]

As these statements illustrate, there was no lack of awareness of the problem. But the problem could not be overcome by resolving to "work" in the trade unions, so long as the character of that "work" was determined by the sectarian and adventurist policies of the Third Period.

The Third Congress of the Comintern spoke of active *participation* in the "day-to-day struggles" of the unions. The object of CI policy was to prove the superiority of Communist policies *in practice*, and thus to forge a left-wing current in the unions, centered around the party but including a broad range of trade unionists who saw the need for class-struggle policies.

From mid-1929 on, however, the Communist International and the Canadian CP approached the existing unions differently. The constitution of the WUL spoke not of winning the ranks of the labor movement to a class struggle program, but of making "every effort. . .to win the membership of the reformist unions for the revolutionary industrial unions."[43]

There is a substantial difference between winning the workers to a revolutionary *program* and winning them to a revolutionary *union*. The latter required that the WUL build its caucuses in the existing unions on a *split perspective*: their objective was to pull workers out of those unions, not to encourage them to fight for militant policies in their unions. Far from trying to prove to the workers that Communist leadership would better build the unions, the Comintern's policy opposed building the existing unions:

Today we no longer advocate indiscriminate entering of all workers into the reformist trade unions. We advocate only the entering of class conscious revolutionary workers to strengthen the revolutionary opposition.[44]

The "revolutionary opposition," by its very nature, was limited to the Communist Party and its immediate periphery. The oppositionists were quickly identified by the union bureaucracy and expelled—or else they left voluntarily to work in the revolutionary unions, since the attempt to build a mass labor organization with limited resources required a constant influx of organizers ready to work for little or nothing. The result was complete abandonment of work in the "reformist unions" from 1930 to 1935. The policy which was supposed to win the party a mass following isolated it from the masses more than ever.

16. The Making of "Tim Buck's Party"

Tim Buck led the struggle against this right wing development. This struggle manifested itself sharply at the Sixth Convention of the Party in 1929 and during some months following it. Under Tim's guidance this critical situation was overcome without the Party's ranks being thrown into disorder and without the secession of more than a handful of people from the Party.

—*The Worker,* June 24, 1933

As we have already noted, the crisis of 1929-1931 resulted in rather more than the secession of "a handful of people" from the Communist Party. During those years party membership plummeted: some members declared their objections to the inner-party situation to all and sundry; others simply stopped paying their dues. The circulation of the *Worker* fell, *Canadian Labor Monthly* ceased publication. The crisis had begun late in 1928, with the expulsion of Maurice Spector and the opening of the preconvention discussion, but the party organization remained reasonably stable until July 1929—until the plenum which selected Tim Buck as executive secretary and turned control of the party over to the Buck-Smith faction. That plenum saw the beginning of a boycott of the party leadership by the Ukrainian leadership, a boycott which spread rapidly through the party as the real import of the policies advocated by Buck and Smith became clear. The party membership may not have known just what was happening—but they knew that the Buck-Smith line meant disaster, and they voted with their feet.

A number of individuals who had voted with MacDonald at the

convention joined the boycott during the summer of 1929. In August J.M. Clarke, editor of the party's farmers' magazine, *The Furrow,* announced his resignation. When Tom McEwen tried to persuade him to reconsider, Clarke wrote:

No, Tom, it's no damn use. What in hell is the need of trying to persist and subjecting yourself to unlimited hardships in the face of Goddamn driveling shit like this? Words, words, words; oceans and oceans of empty verbosity; miles of trollop; reams of junk; hours of scatter-brained blah that in no way indicates the slightest understanding of conditions as they actually exist out in the country among the rank and file of the workers.[1]

Clarke's resignation was followed by a more serious one. J.B. Salsberg, the party's principal leader in the Industrial Union of Needle Trades Workers, announced that he was withdrawing from activity. Salsberg's sit-down strike (he was expelled in December) led to the almost-total collapse of the IUNTW in Toronto.*

The group led by William Moriarty also withdrew from party activity during the summer of 1929, pleading a variety of excuses to escape the responsibilities imposed on them by the Third Period. And, as the steadily-declining attendance at the party's battles in Queens Park showed, there were many members who quietly absented themselves from what they justly saw as suicidal confrontations with the cops.

These individual defections did serious political damage to the party, especially when they involved people with decades of trade union experience behind them. Organizationally, however, the greatest damage was done not by the secession of individual trade unionists, but by the all-out revolt of the language federations against the new Political Committee.

THE BOYCOTT OF BUCK AND SMITH by the Ukrainians ought not, in retrospect, to have surprised anyone. While Buhay and Moriarty were the most vocal and prominent of the opponents of the Third Period, they represented at most a handful of party members, most of them trade unionists who were comfortable in their unions: they were more like left-wing Social Democrats than Communists. For them "unity" went beyond tactics: it was a strategy, even a fetish. But that small group, although it was prominent, was not the real danger to the hegemony of the Buck-Smith faction. The real threat

---

*Salsberg rejoined the party in 1932 and remained one of its most prominent spokesmen until 1956.

came from the language federations. Ninety percent or more of the party's membership was Ukrainian, Finnish, or Jewish: those members were organized in federations which provided a major power base for their spokesmen. A report by Matthew Popowich to the Sixth Convention showed just how powerful that base was:

> ...the U.L.F.T.A. has 88 general branches with 2,651 members; 52 branches of the Women's section with 1,355 members; 40 branches of the Youth section with 1,262 members; 5 affiliated societies with 190 members, or a total membership of 5,438. It has...63 buildings valued at $696,717.00. The Workers Benevolent Association of Canada (Ukrainian Workers Organization)* has 116 Branches with over 8,000 members. The Finnish Organization of Canada has 65 Branches with 2,505 members; 53 buildings valued at over $300,000.00.... There are 28 Co-operative consumer societies affiliated to the Canadian Co-operative Union with a membership of about 9,000 and a further 2,500 members are unaffiliated.[2]

Vapaus, the newspaper of the Finnish Organization, was a daily, based in Sudbury. *Ukrainian Labor News* published ten thousand copies, three times a week—the ULFTA also published separate papers directed towards farmers, women, and youth. For thousands of workers and farmers who spoke no English, the FOC and the ULFTA and their associated cultural and economic organizations were life itself; they were not just political bodies, but entire cultural milieus.

The opposition of the language federation leaders to the Buck-Smith faction and the Third Period had a contradictory character. On one hand, they had a responsibility to protect their members from victimization—and the policies of Buck and Smith made such victimization inevitable. Anglo-Saxon party members arrested at demonstrations received fines or short jail terms: immigrant workers were faced with deportation. The language federation leaders had had long experience with the repressive policies of Canadian governments and knew what to expect if they carried out Comintern policy as interpreted by Stewart Smith.

On the other hand, there was a considerable element of outright conservatism, of concern for protection of their comfortable jobs and incomes, in the policies adopted by the language federation leaders in 1929. They had a vested interest in not rocking the Canadian boat too much. This had been manifested, for some years, in constant opposition to all attempts to bring their

---

*A mutual insurance organization.

organizations under centralized party control. Since 1925 there had been regular efforts made to eliminate "federalism" in the CPC. Originally the party's central executive had included direct representatives of the FOC and the ULFTA, and those organizations had paid dues for their members *en bloc*. That was eliminated in 1925. The ULFTA and FOC became independent organizations: Finns and Ukrainians who wished to join the party had to do so directly. Party activity in those communities was to be directed by party "Agit-Prop Committees." But in reality there was no change. The Agit-Props elected their own delegates to the CEC directly, and ran the independent organizations as their own private fiefdoms. One of the major conflicts between Buck and the Ukrainians occurred when the YCL (where Buck was party representative) tried to organize Ukrainian youth: the ULFTA would have none of that, and the Ukrainian Agit-Prop demanded Buck's recall. Each CPC convention voted to abolish federalism, and the Ukrainian and Finnish leaders dutifully agreed, and nothing was done.

In Winnipeg, the center of the ULFTA, the conflict between the Ukrainians and the Anglo-Saxons had almost reached the point of split in 1928. The legendary attack Tom McEwen made on Jack MacDonald early in December 1928, supposedly for "American Exceptionalism," seems to have been connected with this ethnic conflict: when MacDonald arrived in Winnipeg the Anglo-Saxon wing of the party, knowing him to be friendly to the Ukrainians, did not want to allow him to speak.[3]

Even MacDonald, who worked closely with the Ukrainian leaders and sympathized with their situation, had to agree that they looked on the ULFTA as "an institution and not as a means or medium of work for drawing the masses into the struggle and into our party."[4] Stewart Smith, who had no sympathy for them at all, was much more harsh, but no less accurate:

...we must see that the spontaneity of our Ukrainian comrades in following the expedience of their administrative posts is absolutely incompatible with work in a Communist Party. There is finance, there is money, there is certain consideration for the administrative interests, for the organization in which they are involved, and the tendency growing up is to sacrifice their role as Communists to their interests as administrators of property institutions....[5]

The Comintern's letter had reiterated the CI's longstanding demand that the party eliminate federalism in its organization; a separate letter from the Organization Department of the ECCI insisted that "the convention should pass a series of firm decisions on the question of reorganization of the party from the federation of national sections such as it is today into a centralized Party."[6] A special resolution on Organization, adopted by the convention, demanded "complete liquidation of all social-democratic, federalist elements in the structure of the Party." The resolution insisted that the activities of the language groups should be strictly subordinated to the control of the Central Executive Committee and Political Committee.[7]

Resolutions of this type had been passed before. Now, however, the party leadership was in the hands of a group of determined factionalists who had no political or personal ties to the leaders of the language groups, and who had shown their complete disregard for those leaders on many occasions. When the Buck-Smith faction showed signs of wanting to carry out the policy approved at the convention, all hell broke loose.

The Calm Before the Storm

During the three months following the July 1929 plenum, despite the growing "Right Wing" boycott, faction fighting died down in the CPC. In part this was because the "struggle for the streets" was taking place: Buck, Smith, and their associates were too occupied with that adventure to launch a new battle within the party. As well, they feared the consequences of such a conflict. As Buck later wrote, "we were in the position where we had to choose between a measure of conciliation with MacDonald, or wrecking the Party."[*8]

During this period MacDonald, as Acting Executive Secretary and a member of the Secretariat, continued to have some influence over party policy. Early in October, while Smith was on a speaking tour in Western Canada and Buck was out of action with a recurrent illness, MacDonald was able to demonstrate the potential of a united front response to police repression.

Following the judicial overturn of several attempted prosecutions of CP members, Toronto Mayor Sam McBride introduced a bylaw that would require all groups planning public meetings to apply to the police for approval. He assured City Council that the

---

*Buck made this statement in a "self-criticism" to the Comintern early in 1930. By then he had his priorities straight, for he continued, "And we chose wrongly. We chose conciliation with MacDonald." Wrecking the party was apparently preferable to compromise with opponents of Stalin's line.

bylaw would be used only to stop communist meetings. A public hearing on the new bylaw was set for October 1.

When the meeting convened, the authorities discovered that an impressive array of individuals and organizations had assembled to defend civil rights in Toronto. The Trades and Labor Council was represented, as were the Ontario Labor Party, several local Labor parties, the Salvation Army, the Rationalist Society, and the Methodist Church. All these groups stood to lose if the bylaw were passed.

After several officials, including Police Chief Draper, testified in favor of the new bylaw, the opposition took the floor and held it. Jack MacDonald's masterly defense of free speech was the sensation of the evening. He ridiculed the authorities' attempts to declare the Communists criminals by definition. If they had broken any laws, he said, the authorities should bring them to trial.

We workers are like the revolutionary leaders of old, like the grandfather of Mackenzie King.... Whether the law permits it or not we are going to hold meetings in the parks and streets. We have got to maintain our rights. If we are talking sedition, you have your courts.

MacDonald was followed by a variety of speakers, each attacking the bylaw from his own point of view. The Salvation Army declared that it would be humiliating to have to apply to the police for permission to speak. A preacher declared that he took his orders from God, not the police. The famous and enormously popular Methodist minister Salem Bland declared that introduction of the bylaw amounted to an admission that the police had acted illegally—and he suggested that Christianity might never have survived its meagre beginnings if the Apostles had required police permits to speak.

It was clear that the City Council would be in serious difficulty in the coming elections if the bylaw were passed. It was quietly shelved, and the defenders of civil liberties celebrated a major victory.[9]

The broad mobilization against the bylaw constituted a major challenge to the Third Period politics of Buck and Smith. Their attitude towards this victory for united action may be inferred from the fact that the *Worker* maintained a stony silence about the only significant victory the Free Speech campaign had won.

A few days after the bylaw hearings, two events, probably related, stirred Buck and Smith to new factional vigor. One was a visit to Toronto by William Z. Foster, whose faction now controlled the U.S. Communist Party. The other was the arrival, quite possibly in Foster's hands, of a letter from the Political Secretariat of the Executive Committee of the Communist International.* Foster gave a solid Third Period speech in public, and in private apprised the Canadian leaders of the current thinking of the International. The ECCI letter was sharply critical of Buck and Smith for their policy of compromise with MacDonald.

The refusal of the old leading group to carry on their work practically amounts to desertion of their Communist responsibilities, and has resulted in a weakening of the apparatus at the Centre during a very critical period of the Party's development.

The comrades who now have the leadership of the Political Bureau made a great mistake in not taking a firm stand against the resignations. Their attitude should and must be one of severe criticism. The Party must emphatically condemn such non-communist acts as an integral part of the fight against the Right danger, and for the further education of the Party membership. The party must demand from those comrades who have resigned that they unreservedly accept and work for the decisions of the Convention and the CI letter, failing which decisive measures must be taken against them.

The letter also instructed the new leadership to move immediately against the Ukrainian and Finnish organizations:

The chief task confronting the new executive will be that of converting the CPC from a federation of language groups into a genuine bolshevist centralized party. The chief activities of the CPC are still based on the language federations... unless the old federalist structure of the party is radically altered, the CPC will not be able to become a real Bolshevist party.[10]

Suitably encouraged, Buck and Smith moved into action. During the two weeks following Foster's meeting, Buck assumed the office of executive secretary and the Secretariat was dissolved. A previous decision to have MacDonald run as a candidate for the

---

*The ECCI letter was dated October 3. Foster's visit took place the weekend of October 7-8. Communications between Moscow and New York were always better than between Moscow and Toronto, and the Canadian CP often received directives from the Comintern via New York. Ruthenberg's 1926 visit (see page 190) was a previous example of this practice.

party in Toronto's Bellwoods riding was revoked; he was replaced by Tim Buck.*

Buck and Smith had good reason for moving quickly. All plans for an offensive against the language federations had to be scrapped, because the Finns had seized the initiative.

The Finnish Crisis

At the July Plenum, Aarvo Vaara, long the editor of the FOC newspaper *Vapaus*, had been named to the Political Bureau as Organizational Secretary. This removed Vaara, who proved to be a MacDonald supporter, from the Sudbury headquarters of the Finnish Organization. In his place the Political Committee appointed Sula Neil, one of the very few Finns who supported the Buck-Smith faction. Neil set about converting *Vapaus* from an FOC house-organ concerned primarily with Finnish community activities and events in the old country, into "an instrument for the bolshevization and activization of the Finnish members of the Communist International."[11] The FOC executive, upset that Vaara had been transferred without their agreement, was even more upset that the new editor was not prepared to submit to their political control.

On October 15 Vaara and John Ahlqvist, the chairman of the FOC, having seen the ECCI letter and convinced that a drive against the FOC was on the agenda, decided on open defiance. They walked into the offices of *Vapaus* in Sudbury and took over. Neil and two of his assistants were fired, and Vaara resumed the editorship. The battle was joined.

For three weeks the battle took place in silence. Circular letters from both groups attempted to win support within the Canadian party and in the Finnish organization in the United States. In one such letter, Ahlqvist stated that the Finns were fully prepared to accept the consequences of their actions:

---

*Although no public announcement was made, it is possible to date this final takeover by Buck and Smith with considerable accuracy. MacDonald represented the party on the platform at the Foster meeting October 8, and his name appeared on a list of candidates published in the *Toronto Star* October 18. Buck made his first major public appearance after his illness at a Queens Park demonstration on October 19, and was listed as CP candidate in Bellwoods in the *Toronto Star* October 21. Between October 18 and October 21, then, Buck and Smith took the final action necessary to oust MacDonald.

If they will not endorse our action we will at the very least be censured, and a demand will be made upon us to reverse our decision. If we will not do this, we will probably be finally expelled, and then an inner and open struggle will begin.[12]

On November 7 Stewart Smith went to Sudbury to speak to the FOC membership, only to find himself excluded on the grounds that the meeting was open only to FOC members. (The *Worker* charged that "three policemen were elected and Smith was shoved out of the meeting."[13]) The meeting, without Smith present, endorsed Vaara as editor of *Vapaus* and expelled Sula Neil from the Finnish Organization.[14]

Smith went directly from the FOC Hall to the *Vapaus* plant, where the *Worker* was printed. Without consulting anyone, he wrote a long statement in the name of the Political Committee, announcing the suspension of Finnish leaders Vaara, Ahlqvist, and John Wirta. The statement, under the headline "Defeat the Attempt of the Right Wing to Split the Revolutionary Movement of the Canadian Workers," took up almost a full page in the November 16 *Worker*, which came off the presses on November 9. It warned that "Vaara, Wirta and Ahlqvist are leading in the direction of the camp of the worst enemy of the working class movement, the snake of Social Democracy," and it traced their crimes back to the Sixth Convention:

The splitting tactics followed by the comrades in the leadership of the Finnish Organization of Canada were revealed to the Party openly at the National Convention of the Communist Party of Canada in June. The leading Finnish comrades participated in the secret caucus of the MacDonald forces at this convention. Along with MacDonald and all the other factionalists who organized this caucus, these comrades refused to repudiate this caucus and admit the open right wing character of the caucus. On the other hand they, like the other factionalists, had the effrontery to tell the Party that their caucus had been organized to save the Party. Obviously these comrades had embarked on the policy of right wing factionalism in order to "save" the party from the line of the Communist International.

This statement was the first public attack on MacDonald since the convention: it was the beginning of an attempt to drive him out of the party. The next issue of the *Worker* accused him of direct complicity with the Finnish leaders. Under the headlines "Right Opportunists Exposed as Foes of Communist Party" and "The

Pathway from Right Wing Factionalism to Betrayal of the Revolutionary Movement," Stewart Smith charged that

Comrade MacDonald, who was the central figure of the secret caucus of the right wing at the last national convention of the party, has become the connection of the Finnish splitters on the Polburo of the party, giving them all the decisions of the Polburo and information concerning the line of the party to combat their factional activities.[15]

Following his removal as executive secretary in mid-October, MacDonald had been out of Toronto. Buck later charged that he had met with the FOC leadership on November 3. This is quite possible: it would have been reasonable to expect MacDonald to confer with other members of the CEC, especially in view of the ECCI's call for Buck and Smith to launch war on the party majority.

MacDonald returned to Toronto on November 10 and demanded the right to reply to the charges which had been made against him. When this request was denied, he wrote a statement and mailed it to party branches and to Communist newspapers across the country. It was published in the November 26 *Vapaus*:

Concerning the Vaara, Wirta and Ahlqvist situation:

To my knowledge, no Political Committee meeting was held regarding this situation.... Although I am a member I had not been given an opportunity to express my opinion concerning this.... So, at the meeting of Nov. 16, 1929, I brought the matter up....

Secretary Buck informed me that Smith had prepared the report concerning this matter and had mailed it from Sudbury, as the topmost priority had been to publish it in the *Worker*. Only four persons had been aware of its contents—Buck, Bruce, Graves and Smith. This happened on Nov. 8th; Graves tells me that he received it on Nov. 9.

If I had been given the opportunity to consider the report, I would have asked for changes to be made in it. In my opinion it contains many things which are not true. I will go over the most important points....

My name has been drawn into the report for reasons I do not know. I assume that it has been done in an attempt to involve me with Vaara, Wirta and Ahlqvist. The report states that I and others were involved in right-wing activity, while pretending to be strongly in favor of the CPC. It accuses me of having taken part in group meetings, against the CPC. I have also been accused of influencing Salsberg's decision when he left the Needleworkers' Union Organizing Committee. This is not true.

I feel that it is necessary to write this letter, for the sake of truth and clarity.... The spreading of falsehoods does nothing for the unity of the CPC....[16]

Meanwhile, the war between the CPC Political Committee and the Finnish Organization was heating up. Three supporters of the Buck-Smith leadership were expelled from the Communist Party in Sudbury on November 13.[17] *Vapaus* declared:

This is not a fight against Communism, but a fight against the clique that has placed itself at the head of the Communist Party. There are *no* Sudbury members who actually side with this clique. And anyone who does *not* side with this clique is labelled a right-winger.[18]

The November 30 *Worker* added Bruno Tenhunen, political editor of *Vapaus*, to the list of those suspended. According to an unsigned article,

Tenhunen...who has consistently opposed the line of the Party in connection with Red Day and the struggle against Police Terrorism, and who is perhaps, the most out and out expression of social democratic ideology in a developed form among the right wing splitters, called for the expulsion of all members who supported the line of the Political Bureau of the Party from the Finnish Organization of Canada.[19]

Despite the length and virulence of the polemics, it is remarkably difficult to discern any real programmatic differences in the fight between the Finns and the Polcom. Charges of "cliquism" and "right-wing policies" abound, but a serious discussion of real differences is absent. The only concise summary of the Finnish position appeared in an article by Stewart Smith: it is therefore highly suspect, but it does seem to present the Finns' case, and to illustrate its strengths and weaknesses. Smith headed the summary "The Platform of the Splitters."

1. The Communist International does not understand the situation in Canada, underestimates the power of Canadian capitalism, overestimates the strength of the revolutionary movement, and hence the carrying out of the CI policy leads to "adventurism."

2. The Central Committee of the C.P. of C. does not understand the policy which must be pursued among the Finnish masses, and should leave this entirely to the Finnish leaders, who alone understand the correct approach to the Finnish masses, and what is "good" and what is "bad" for the Finnish masses.

3. The minority at the national convention, which fought against the majority, is a "clique," which desires to gain control of the party for personal ends, and has not the confidence of the party membership.

4. Federalism can never be eradicated from the Canadian party because of the immigrant composition of the Canadian working class. A united, centralized Communist Party in Canada is impossible.

5. In general the policy of the party is disruptive, while they (the Finnish leaders) are constructive.

6. Opposition to centralized leadership is growing in every country, and must be strengthened in Canada in order to establish "control from below."[20]

An editorial in the same issue of the *Worker* quoted Ahlqvist as objecting to "breaking up unions on Party instructions," and as replying to the suspensions with the statement that "those who have done most for the movement, like Trotsky and Bukharin in the Soviet Union, and others elsewhere, have met the same fate."[21]

Reading between the lines here, it seems evident that the Finns' objective was to protect their organization and membership from the imposition of the Third Period policies. Ahlqvist's reported reference to Trotsky and Bukharin suggests that at least some of the Finns were aware that broader issues were involved, but this reference is the only one of its kind: the Finns did not, generally speaking, question the wisdom of the International. On the contrary, their statements imply that either Moscow was being misinformed about Canadian conditions, or that Buck and Smith were misinterpreting Comintern policy. Whether this was political naïveté or opportunism, it weakened their position in the long run.

But in the short run they enjoyed great success. The Polcom claimed it had support among the rank and file of the FOC, and named several prominent Finnish Communists—including Tom Hill and Lumberworkers Union president Alf Hautamaki—as supporters of their position, but statements of support from Finns were few and far between in the *Worker*. The pages of *Vapaus*, by contrast, listed local after local of the FOC as endorsing its stand. The struggle seemed to be reaching a climax early in December, with a Polcom statement announcing that Wirta, Ahlqvist, and Tenhunen had been expelled from the party, and three "factional organizers and agents of the renegades" had been suspended. The same statement claimed that Vaara had capitulated to the Political Committee.[22]

Then, suddenly and without explanation, the polemics stopped. The Finnish dispute vanished from the pages of the *Worker*.

Both sides had asked for intervention by the International. In mid-December the ECCI acted—and rapped everyone's knuckles. Both sides were ordered to cease all polemics, and the expulsions were annulled. The U.S. Finnish Communist newspaper *Tyomies* was ordered to cease attacks on *Vapaus*, and the Canadian party leadership was ordered to stop circulating *Tyomies* in Canada.

Each side was instructed to send a representative to Moscow to discuss the issues with the ECCI Political Secretariat. The Finnish Organization sent John Latva; the Political Committee chose Tim Buck, who was already on his way to Russia, as its representative.*

The Crisis Spreads

For several months the Finnish situation remained in limbo, but the Buck-Smith faction was given no time to catch its breath. The rebellion against the Polcom was spreading to new fronts. By the spring of 1930 there were major crises in both the Ukrainian and Jewish wings of the party.

The Ukrainian boycott of the party leadership continued through the fall and early winter of 1929-30, but it remained passive in form. There was no mass defiance of the Polcom—simply a continuing refusal to cooperate, accompanied by a whispering campaign against the new leadership. The Ukrainians did not, despite the obvious similarity of their interests, support the Finnish leaders against the Polcom.

The first sign that the Ukrainian resistance might go beyond the boycott occurred early in December, when the Winnipeg Organization of the CPC was presented with a statement condemning the Finns. The statement, drafted by the Political Committee, was adopted, but one important change was made. The Polcom resolution read, in part:

With the sharpening of the class struggle in the present period, the fight against the right danger and social reformism must be sharpened. The old Federalist structure of the C.P. of C. in the mass organizations of the Finnish, Ukrainian and Italian workers must be shattered....[23]

The Winnipeg membership voted 44 to 25 to delete the word "Ukrainian" from the second sentence. The party's Ukrainian wing was quite willing to denounce the Finns as splitters and federalists—but it was determined to protect its own turf.

The simmering conflict with the Ukrainians came to a boil at the national convention of the Ukrainian Labor-Farmer Temple Association in February 1930. When the Communist delegates met prior to the convention, they were presented with a letter from the

---

*Buck was going to Russia for a congress of the RILU, and to recuperate from his recent illness. In his absence Tom McEwen served as National Secretary.

Political Committee. Leslie Morris later described the contents of the letter:

It stated openly and clearly that serious and fatal mistakes have been committed by the Party comrades who are the ideological leaders of the ULFTA, mistakes that express far more clearly than mere words the attitude of these comrades of the Party; mistakes in the cooperatives, indicating a Utopian approach to these types of organizations; mistakes in their work of educating the children (since rectified but nevertheless characteristic); mistakes in relations [sic] to the problem of the poor farmers, (advocating "unofficially" the formation of farming "communes" in Peace River); errors in their attitude to the property of the Ukrainian workers, the Labor Temples, expressed in the refusal to utilize them for the general interests of the working class in the fight against the police terror.*

This catalogue of errors and mistakes was followed by demands that the ULFTA begin "orientating towards the class struggles of the Canadian working class."

[The letter] stated that the chief activity of the majority of our Ukrainian members still consists of cultural and educational and dramatic work within the four walls of the ULFTA buildings, and that a sharp turn must be made to the masses at the point where struggles develop, in the factories, upon the streets, in the unions.[24]

Morris later admitted that there was "opinion to liquidate mass organizations" in the Buck-Smith faction.[25] With relations between the Polcom and the Ukrainians already strained, the letter sent to the ULFTA fraction can only be seen as a deliberate attempt to provoke a confrontation.

The Ukrainian fraction reacted predictably. By an overwhelming 81 to 6 vote it rejected the Polcom letter and adopted its own resolution, which, while endorsing in general terms the political line of the Polcom letter, denied all of the concrete charges it made. It turned fire on the Political Committee, and renewed the old demand "that Comrade Buck be withdrawn from the CEC for his unpardonable carelessness and tactlessness which endangers the interests of the Party."[26]

Having been burned once in an attempt to discipline a language organization, the Political Committee moved cautiously now. In

---

*The last point is a reference to the refusal of the ULFTA to rent halls to the party in Toronto for fear of losing their licences. The FOC took similar action.

place of the full-page blasts that responded to the FOC's defiance of discipline, the Ukrainian crisis was marked, publicly, only by two brief and surprisingly restrained articles in the *Worker,* suggesting that the Ukrainian leaders did not properly understand the line of the Comintern. The party leadership undoubtedly hoped to win points with the Comintern by this approach—but their restraint was interpreted by the Ukrainians as capitulation.

The scene of battle shifted to Alberta, where Buck-Smith supporter Harvey Murphy had been appointed District Organizer. Murphy had gained a reputation for arrogance and insensitivity towards Ukrainian workers during the Hamilton Steel Car strike of 1928, and he did nothing to correct that reputation in Alberta. Shortly before the ULFTA convention the Drumheller local of the party had written the Political Committee urging Murphy's withdrawal, charging that instead of building the party he was "idling around and at slot machines gambling," causing the workers to "lose their faith in the C.P. and working class movement as a whole." Drumheller's demand was endorsed by the Alberta District Executive Committee.[27]

After the ULFTA convention the atmosphere grew increasingly tense. On March 5 Murphy wrote to McEwan:

We are head over heels in the mining situation and have so far been unsuccessful in getting cooperation from the local Ukes, harder now since the delegates returned from the ULFTA, its a buggar. I learned that they made some first class attack on Smith as being irresponsible ect they are wipping up a real campaign against the CEC.[28] [Spelling and grammar as in original]

Chief organizer of the campaign against the CEC was John Stokaluk, who, in addition to being a leader of the right wing within the Ukrainian Communist fraction, was vice-president of the Mine Workers Union of Canada.

Stokaluk's main challenge to the party leadership was on union policy. The early 1930s saw another round of "rationalization" in the mines, marked by reduced wages and shorter hours. Party policy was to conduct strikes against these measures wherever possible, with little regard to the possibility of winning. Stokaluk and his supporters opposed this policy, seeing it as a direct road to destruction of the union. In union locals across the province—and in particular in the Crows Nest Pass region, Stokaluk agitated against party policy.

On March 17 the Alberta Dominion Executive Committee, now under Murphy's control, expelled Stokaluk from the party. The Political Committee, still concerned to tread softly, set aside the expulsion and cabled Stokaluk for a statement accepting party discipline. It demanded that he support party policy in the unions, and leave Crows Nest Pass. Stokaluk replied on March 25:

Will not support your policy on strike question because it means smashing of the union. Will not comply with your order to leave Crows Nest. I fought this policy in the Party and now I will fight outside the Party because I'm convinced that it is entirely wrong.[29]

Faced with direct refusal to obey instructions, the Political Committee had to act or lose all credibility. Stokaluk was promptly expelled, along with party locals that supported him. A statement in the *Worker* declared that Stokaluk had placed himself "in the ignominious role of a traitor to the Revolutionary cause he pretended to uphold, and on the side of the enemies of the miners of Alberta."[30]

The Ukrainian Party Fraction Bureau in Winnipeg immediately protested the "expulsion based on false charges," and Ukrainian CEC members John Pastuch and Matthew Popowich demanded Stokaluk's reinstatement, labelling the Polcom statement a "perversion of truth."[31] The ULFTA condemned the expulsion and refused to publish the Political Committee's statements in its newspapers. As a final gesture of defiance, Stokaluk was hired as a teacher at the ULFTA school in the spring of 1930.[32] For all practical purposes, a Ukrainian split had followed the Finnish split.

THE CRISIS IN THE ETHNIC ORGANIZATIONS was not limited to the Finnish and Ukrainian groups: the Jewish auxiliary was also a source of concern.

During 1929 the party's main concern was the influence of the Trotskyists in the Jewish Labor League. This was identified in the May 1929 ECCI letter as a matter to be dealt with, and the 1929 convention resolution on "The Press" placed "special importance" on strengthening the party's Yiddish newspaper *Der Kamf* "owing to Spector's connections with some Jewish workers."[33] The Workers Sports Association, a largely Jewish organization, was also identified as an area to be dealt with: "Party and YCL fractions within this organization must carry on a relentless struggle against Trotskyism and remove the present Trotskyist leadership."[34] This was a reference to the role played by Maurice Quarter and Joe Silver in the WSA: both were expelled from the CPC as Trotskyists, but the non-party members of the WSA executive refused to support a party proposal to expel them from the Sports Association. It was nearly a year before the CP regained control of this group.[35]

The problem in the Jewish organizations spread beyond the influence of the Trotskyists, who were organized only in Toronto. In February 1930 the party leadership in Winnipeg, headed by Jacob Penner and Leslie Morris, expelled four prominent party members for "a long series of Right-wing anti-Party acts that have marked the work in the Jewish mass organization for some time." One of those expelled was Max Dolgoy, the organizer of the Industrial Union of Needle Trades Workers in Manitoba. He immediately appealed to the Political Committee for reinstatement, charging that the real "Right Danger" in Winnipeg came from Jacob Penner and John Navis. Of recent Lenin School graduate Morris, Dolgoy could only say that he "specialized in writing resolutions with this in mind, that he *is* the Comintern."[36] The Political Committee, however, backed Morris, Penner and Navis, leaving Dolgoy, temporarily at least, in the wilderness.*

The expulsion of Dolgoy from the party meant, inevitably, his removal as organizer of the IUNTW—there was no pretence made that the WUL unions had the autonomy to determine their own leaders. After trying unsuccessfully to find a replacement for Dolgoy in Winnipeg, the Political Committee instructed Toronto Jewish Agit-Prop leader Sam Lapidus to leave the *Der Kamf* staff and go to Winnipeg as an organizer for the Needle Trades Union. When Lapidus refused to do so, he was removed from the staff of the paper, publicly censured, and removed from the list of candidates for the Lenin School in Moscow.[38] This is an early example of the use of trips to Moscow as a means of keeping recalcitrant members in line: the power to grant or deny such petty perquisites is the stuff of which bureaucracies are made.

Canada's Lovestoneites

The leaders of the Ukrainian, Finnish, and Jewish groups that defied party discipline in 1929-1930 did so as much to defend their

---

*I have been unable to discover when Dolgoy returned to the CPC. The February 1931 plenum minutes report that Winnipeg CPer Martin Forkin stated that "Dolgoy [is still] fighting party and has influence over ideologically weak comrades."[37]

respective power bases as out of political conviction. They were, in general, willing to pay lip service to the Comintern line if they were left alone to run their organizations as they saw fit.

There was, however, a small current in the party that objected to the Comintern line as such. The party's later habit of describing *all* opponents of the Political Committee as "Lovestoneites" tends to obscure the fact that there actually was a Lovestoneite group in the party in 1929-1930: it was the group led by Michael Buhay and William Moriarty.

An unsigned letter on "The Situation in the Canadian Party" appeared in the January 15, 1930 issue of Lovestone's newspaper *Revolutionary Age.* The letter discussed the deepening crisis in the Canadian CP in some detail, including some facts about the Finnish controversy which had not yet been made public. (It mentioned, for example, that a Finnish delegation had been sent to Moscow "to stop the operation of the destructive line in Canada.") The author must have been a party member: on the basis of internal evidence and subsequent experience, it is most probable that it was written by Moriarty. In view of later charges that MacDonald was a Lovestoneite, it is instructive to note that the letter was very critical of MacDonald for following a "conciliatory and passive policy" towards Buck and Smith.

The *Revolutionary Age* article concluded that "it is time that the foundations were laid for a clear and conscious Communist Opposition movement in Canada." Almost simultaneously with the appearance of the article, such foundations were laid in Toronto.

Late in December 1929 or early in January 1930, a "Workers Recreation Club" was established in Toronto. Ostensibly formed "to develop a social center for those who are interested in the working class movement," the club announced a regular program of Saturday night activities in a rented hall at the corner of Winchester and Parliament streets, featuring dancing, cards, badminton, and quoits. A drama group was also established. Membership was open to anyone, but the executive reserved the right to refuse admission. The executive included J. Valin, Mrs. A. Rimmer, T. Kilner, W. Moriarty, and R. Shoesmith.[39]

Despite its apparently harmless nature, the club was, quite certainly, a "front" for the Lovestoneites, and that is how the party saw it. In mid-February the Toronto Executive of the CPC ordered all party members to sever any connections they might have with the club. William Moriarty, Fred Peel, and Robert Shoesmith, all founding members of the party, refused, as did J. Valin. Peel told the Executive that "this club offers me and my associates the chance to meet many comrades who have been hounded and slandered by the party leadership."[40]

The March 1 *Worker* reported the expulsion of the WRC leaders, under the headline "Right Wingers Cleaned Out of Communist Ranks."

None of those expelled were members of the Central Executive Committee, so they could be removed with very little fuss. One case was more difficult: that of Jack MacDonald. He had not been one of the organizers of the club, nor had he played a leading role in it. He had attended some of its Saturday night social events, paying 25 cents admission: this was viewed as a membership fee. Unlike the others, MacDonald did not refuse to accept the instructions of the City Executive. He agreed to drop his nominal membership in the club, but he refused to promise not to attend any of the Saturday night socials in the future. Such participation, he said, could not possibly interfere with his party responsibilities, and the party had no right to forbid it.[41]

Charles Sims, secretary of the Toronto Executive, immediately wrote to Tom McEwen, Acting National Secretary in Buck's absence, demanding MacDonald's expulsion from the party. The March 15, 1930 *Worker* announced that MacDonald had been suspended from the Political Committee for "refusal to dissociate himself from the Workers Recreation Club, an organization created by right-wing sabotagers and disrupters for the purpose of crystalizing their anti-party line and policy." The statement reviewed all of MacDonald's crimes, including opposing the line of the Comintern, organizing a "secret fraction meeting" at the 1929 convention, leading the desertion of the party by the right wing, refusing to accept party instructions, vacillating on the question of Salsberg, and "holding secret conferences" with the Finnish splitters. It concluded with the announcement that "a final statement on the case of Comrade MacDonald" would be issued by the coming plenum of the Central Executive Committee.

In Montreal, Mike Buhay and Jake Margolies protested the expulsions and suspension and found themselves suspended in turn. The list of charges against them was quite remarkable. They were accused of every conceivable crime from "open disagreement with line of CI" to "refusing to address meetings of unemployed" to "undermining and slandering the leadership of the party" to "stating that greatest danger confronting party is labelling as right wingers those who are not."[42]

With the exception of MacDonald, the Communists expelled and suspended in early 1930 formed the basis of the Canadian Lovestoneite organization. Operating under various names, including Marxian Educational League, Workers League, and Communist Party (Opposition), the small organization had branches in Toronto, Montreal, and Hamilton throughout the 1930s. In Ontario its principal activity was in the Cooperative Commonwealth Federation (Moriarty was a delegate to the CCF's founding Regina convention); in Montreal it was deeply involved in the International Ladies' Garment Workers Union. Moriarty died in 1936. Mike Buhay, who was the organization's principal spokesman in Montreal, returned to the Communist Party late in the decade, after the party's line had swung far back to the right. Like its counterpart in the United States, the Canadian Lovestoneite organization collapsed at the beginning of the war.

The Comintern Intervenes

During the winter of 1929-30 many Communists were wondering if their party could survive the Buck-Smith leadership. The Finnish split, the *de facto* Ukrainian split, the expulsion of Dolgoy, the expulsion of Moriarty's group, and the suspension of MacDonald, Buhay, and Margolies—all of these, and dozens of lesser disciplinary crises, occurred in just over four months. The party anxiously awaited the outcome of the Comintern's discussions with Buck and Latva: the decisions of the International would decide the party's future.

In Moscow, Buck was in trouble. He went prepared to argue the case for the expulsion of the Finnish leaders, but he found his own political judgment being called into question. The major issue, to his surprise, was the nature of Canadian capitalism.

In 1929 the Canadian CP had abandoned the "Canadian Independence" slogan, replacing it with a perspective of an Anglo-American war that would split the Canadian ruling class and lead to civil war and proletarian revolution. The October 3 ECCI letter had been sharply critical of that perspective, but Buck and Smith had failed to see the danger signs. Not only did they not change their line but they adopted a new resolution, "Strengthen the Struggle Against the Right Danger," which attempted to defend the Political Committee's line in more detail. This resolution, known in party history as the "24-page Document," became a major point of contention in Buck's discussions with Otto Kuusinen, who had replaced Bukharin as secretary of the Comintern.

Having failed to accept the Comintern's guidance on this issue once, Buck proceeded to deepen his error. While in Moscow, he wrote a "Statement on Political Perspectives in Canada" which again defended the perspective of an Anglo-American war and a split in the Canadian capitalist class as the only correct one for Canadian Communists. Worse still, Buck devoted much of the statement to a demonstration that the Canadian CP's shifting line—including the line on the Anglo-American conflict—originated entirely in the International's various letters to the Canadian leadership.[43]

It was bad enough to persist in error when the Comintern had illumined the path of righteousness. It was even worse to suggest that the infallible Comintern was responsible for the error. Buck had yet to learn that the price of leadership in Stalin's Comintern was unquestioning submission to Stalin, without concern for consistency.

Kuusinen refused to endorse the actions of the Buck-Smith leadership—but he could not endorse the indiscipline of the Finns in Canada. Instead he upbraided both sides, overturned all disciplinary actions, and appointed a commission to investigate the situation in Canada. The single commissioner appointed was Kullervo Manner, former leader of the Communist Party of Finland, who had headed the short-lived Soviet government in Finland in 1918. Manner's chief qualification for the task seems to have been that he spoke Finnish: he spoke no English. (Otto Kuusinen's estranged wife, Aino, accompanied Manner to Canada: she was on a Comintern mission to New York. She later wrote that the Comintern secretary, himself a Finn, had selected Manner in order to get him out of Russia during a faction fight in the exiled Finnish CP.[44])

Manner arrived in Toronto in mid-March and held a series of hearings into the party crisis. He investigated not only the Finnish dispute but the Stokaluk case and the party's intransigence on the Anglo-American conflict question. As Tom KcEwen later commented [the wording is from a stenographic memo], "The [24 page] Document appeared at an untimely moment of struggle with Finns and Ukrainians, giving Right elements chance to cover up own errors."[45]

Manner's decision on the Finnish dispute was announced in the

April 12 *Worker*: it amounted to a compromise. The FOC fraction agreed to cease all polemics against the party, admitted its error in the matter of Vaara, and promised to promote the party line in *Vapaus*. The party agreed to respect the FOC's independence, and to refrain from intervening in its internal affairs except through the medium of the fraction.

The CEC's choice of Vaara as Organizational Secretary was declared to have been an error, because "1) he wasn't equal to the task and 2) it provoked a split in the FOC." The FOC was censured for attacking the party, and Bruno Tenhunen was removed from the FOC staff.

Everyone involved made statements of self-criticism, accepting the Comintern commission's decision. Reading these, there is no doubt that the Finns thought that they had won a victory. One wrote: "I suppose that party leadership has received a lesson, how to consider mass organizations, if it continuously endeavours to carry out matters by mechanical instructions, then it may result to new differences."[46] The Buck-Smith faction, on the other hand, although they formally agreed to accept the decision of the commission, were furious: they wrote a detailed letter of protest to the ECCI, describing Manner's decisions as "purely mechanical and formal" and accusing him of having a conciliatory attitude towards the Finnish organization.[47]

There remained the conflict with the Ukrainians. Although the Ukrainian fraction urged Manner to reinstate Stokaluk he did not do so. As a result the Ukrainian dispute continued to simmer for several months. Twice in the fall of 1930 the Comintern sent representatives to Canada to mediate the differences between the ULFTA and the Polcom: one of the mediators was French CP leader André Marty. On another occasion that fall Tom McEwen and John Navis went to Moscow to argue their cases. Eventually an agreement much like that arranged with the FOC was reached. The Ukrainians agreed to accept the party's line and leadership; the party agreed to keep out of the internal affairs of the ULFTA.[48] An informal compromise was reached on the Stokaluk case: he would remain outside of the party for an interval before reapplying for membership. He was readmitted in August 1931.[49]

Despite the decisions of the commission, many Finnish party members still found the Third Period line impossible to swallow. Their resentment came to a head in October 1930, when the miners at Inco's Frood Mine were confronted with wage cuts. As in Alberta, the party line was for an immediate strike by the Mine

Workers Union of Canada (Metal Miners Section). Since the MWUC represented only a minority of the Frood miners, this would have been a suicidal venture. The Finnish party members in Sudbury, on the initiative of Nestori Luoto and Bruno Tenhunen (respectively president and district secretary of the MWUC Metal Miners), campaigned against a strike. According to a statement by the party's District Bureau:

Luoto spoke and fought against such strike action, using all of the old arguments in [the FOC Right-Wing's] declaration that they had pledged themselves to discard—lack of preparation, the Winter upon us and the Miners faced with starvation, Unemployment, over-production of nickel, no response to such a call for strike action, splitting the revolutionary movement, provocation by International Nickel Co. in order to blacklist the militant section, Bureau agents of Inco, etc, and a campaign of slander in general designed to discredit the party leadership in this district.[50]

The Frood union voted overwhelmingly against strike action. Their vote was condemned as "strike-breaking" by the party leadership, and Tenhunen and Luoto were expelled from the party.[51]

This began a prolonged hemorrhaging of the Finnish wing of the party, leading in 1932 to a full-scale split in the Finnish Organization. The minority, based in Sudbury, launched a new newspaper, *Vapaa Sana*, and affiliated to the CCF.

The Expulsion of Jack MacDonald

In addition to negotiating the compromise with the FOC, Manner made one other, unpublicized decision: he rescinded the suspensions of Jack MacDonald, Jacob Margolies, and Mike Buhay, and instructed the Political Committee to attempt to reintegrate MacDonald into the leadership.

MacDonald, however, had had all he could take. From the beginning of the crisis, MacDonald had played an independent role, quite distinct from that played by the other opponents of Buck and Smith. Unlike the Finns and Ukrainians, MacDonald was not trying to protect his administrative position or his property; unlike Moriarty, Buhay, and Margolies, he did not agree with the Right Opposition of Lovestone, Brandler, and Bukharin. MacDonald had welcomed the Third Period turn as a correction to the Comintern's rightward course in 1925-1928, a course which had the Canadian CP campaigning for national independence, subordinating itself to the Canadian Labor Party, and abandoning all efforts to build a left wing in the unions. Not until he saw what the Third Period meant in practice did MacDonald realize that this was not a return to Leninism but an even more drastic break with Lenin's policies than the previous period had seen.

At the Sixth Convention MacDonald emerged as the spokesman of all those who were appalled by the crude factionalism of the Buck-Smith group. Temporarily, this gave him majority support. But after the convention, and particularly after the catastrophic situation in the Finnish Organization in the fall of 1929, MacDonald's majority vanished. The Right Opposition went its own way; the ethnic groups won the independence they wanted, and so accepted the leadership of the men who had Moscow's blessing. MacDonald, who had only wanted to maintain party unity, was left isolated. He was still strongly opposed to the organizational policies of Buck and Smith and he was increasingly critical of their political line—which was Moscow's line.

Discouraged and demoralized, MacDonald refused to resume political activity. Invited by Stewart Smith on May 23 to attend a Political Committee meeting to discuss his suspension, MacDonald wrote that he could "see no useful purpose to be served by me attending this meeting."

So far as I am personally concerned, I have no statement nor appeal to make to the Pol-Bureau. They are quite well aware of the facts concerning my case.

The Pol-Bureau has indulged in a campaign of lies and slander concerning me, distributed through the columns of the Party Press, while at the same time refusing me the privilege of making a statement or repudiating same, either publicly or through the Party Press.

I have absolutely no confidence in the outcome of any "discussions" with the present Pol-Bureau or in adding to the numerous statements or declarations that have already been made—statements that are superficial in their character and solve nothing.[52]

This letter was Jack MacDonald's last formal statement as a leader of the Communist Party of Canada.

Still he was not expelled. Unnerved by their experiences with Comintern commissions and investigators, the Political Committee hesitated to act without express instructions from Moscow. These finally came in November, in the form of a telegram from Fritz Heckert, secretary of the Comintern's Anglo-American Secretariat:

PLACE BEFORE MACDONALD DEMAND THAT HE AS MEMBER OF

PARTY AND CC MUST OPENLY ADMIT AND IMMEDIATELY
ABANDON RIGHT OPPORTUNIST POSITION COMMA UNCONDI-
TIONALLY AGREE TO CARRY ON RESOLUTE STRUGGLE IN DEED
AGAINST ALL RIGHT ELEMENTS IN PARTY COMMA AGAINST THE
LOVESTONEITES AS WELL AS TROTSKYITES UNCONDITIONALLY
ACCEPT CI LINE AND PARTY LINE AND DISCIPLINE INFORMING
HIM FAILING TO ACCEPT THESE CONDITIONS OF THE TENTH ECCI
PLENUM MEANS EXPULSION FROM THE PARTY STOP. IN CASE HE
DOES NOT COMPLY WITH THIS DEMAND CC SHOULD TAKE ACTION
PUBLISHING STATEMENT ON HIS POSITION.[53]

On November 22 the Political Bureau gave MacDonald ten days
to reply to the Comintern's ultimatum. The December 17
Secretariat minutes record his request for an extension, which was
granted.[54] The exact date of his expulsion is not recorded, but the
January 3, 1931 *Worker* announced the Comintern's decision to
"put before MacDonald an ultimatum of conditions for his
continued membership in the Party." The "Enlarged Plenum" of
the Central Executive Committee which assembled in Toronto on
February 6 confirmed his expulsion from the party, as well as that
of Buhay and Margolies.

There was no opposition.

The 1931 Plenum

The February 1931 Plenum marked the final consolidation of
Stalinism in the Canadian Communist Party. Buck had obtained
special permission from the International to conduct the plenum
with "appointed delegates...regardless of formal status."[55] As a
result, more than one third of the CEC members elected by the 1929
convention were excluded: in addition to MacDonald, Buhay and
Margolies, those not present included Graves, Gauld, Lehtinen,
Salo, Silinpaa, and Skaara. In their places sat loyal Buck
supporters, most of them from the Young Communist League.

More surprising was the conspicuous absence of Stewart Smith.
Whether he was recalled by the ECCI or sent to Moscow to advance
the Polcom's cause is unclear, but by the summer of 1930 he was in
Moscow, and he was not allowed to return. On September 29 he
wrote to Buck:

As to myself, there is to date no final decision, but it is proposed that I
remain here and the reasons are: (1) The mistakes in Canada made by
myself. (2) To strengthen the apparatus of the A[nglo] A[merican]
Secretariat. (3) To gain some international experience.[56]

Smith eventually returned to Canada late in 1931, properly re-educated, to become Buck's second-in-command and the party's principal theoretician.

The plenum was a veritable orgy of "self-criticism." Every aspect of party work was examined and found wanting—every aspect, that is, except the political line handed down by the Comintern. Beckie Buhay's comments during the discussion of the YCL illustrate the tenor of the discussion:

When we call meetings and the workers do not respond, it is not because the workers do not want to come, but because our approach is not correct. We do not bring forth the demands and the slogans which would interest the workers, and that is why they keep away.[57]

Despite two years of steady decline in membership and support, no one questioned the Comintern's view that a "mass radicalization" was in progress. "We may have lost a few thousand members," said Buck, "but this is not decisive."[58] Any failures were due not to the line itself, but to failures to implement the line properly.

The Ukrainian and Finnish leaders contributed volubly to the self-critical chorus. They pleaded guilty to federalism and sectarianism, to secret opposition to the Comintern line, and they voted with both hands for a resolution codifying the compromises reached during 1930. The Finnish fraction agreed to "unconditionally accept the line of the Comintern resolution on the Ukrainian question, which clarifies our understanding of many mistaken conceptions and shortcomings in the Finnish situation, particularly as to the major mistakes of holding to the federalist attitude in the Party."[59] Matthew Popowich confessed to "the unbolshevik approach" and "lack of bolshevik understanding," among Ukrainian party members.[60]

But most important of all was the vigorous and repeated self-criticism of Buck and his associates on the question of Canadian independence, the Anglo-American conflict, and Canadian imperialism. "Without the condemnation and repudiation of the 24-page Document there can be no correction of the error and no understanding of the new line," Buck insisted.[61] Wherever possible, Buck shifted responsibility for the errors of the past onto Maurice Spector's back—Spector took full blame for the Canadian independence line. But on the question of the Anglo-American conflict there could be no equivocating. The Political Bureau's Draft Resolution pleaded guilty in a most convincing manner:

It is of vital importance that every Party member understands the significance of the correction of the false conception held previously by the Political Bureau of the Party, concerning the path of the proletarian revolution in Canada.

This position . . . was maintained by our Pol-Bureau for a period of several months even after the Comintern had denounced it as incorrect. . . .

Under pressure of frank criticism of this position by the Comintern backed by the close co-operation in analysis and discussion of all questions involved, the Political Bureau has been able to throw off these false conceptions, and to estimate Canada and the Canadian bourgeoisie in a Leninist manner.[62]

This theme—the error of the Polcom and the wisdom of the CI in correcting it—appeared again and again in the plenum discussions. No one could take the podium, it seemed, without raising it.

Speaker after speaker [wrote Tim Buck in the *Worker*] emphasized the correctness of the Comintern characterization of Canada as an imperialist country and condemned the criminal error of the Pol-Bureau in its resistance to this characterization of the Comintern. Our (now notorious) twenty four page document, which marked the culmination of the resistance and placed the political bureau in objective opposition to the Comintern, was analysed and condemned.[63]

Notably absent from these discussions was the point Buck had made a year before in Moscow: that the "error" had originated with the Comintern. No one pointed out that the ECCI's letter to the 1929 convention had insisted that "Canada is today a battleground between British and American imperialism," and that "The approach of war and the sharpening world struggle between the two imperialist giants will bring this antagonism inside the Canadian ruling class to its highest pitch."[64] The Comintern was acknowledged as an infallible guide.

The specific issue in dispute was really not important: the party would repeatedly change its evaluation of the Canadian capitalist class over the following decades. What was important was total submission to the Comintern line. Never again would the Canadian party leadership challenge in the slightest way the decisions of Stalin's Kremlin.

In exchange for total submission, Buck was given full backing as the unquestioned leader of the Canadian CPC. He held that position longer than any CP leader outside of the "socialist" countries. Until 1957 his leadership never faced a serious challenge within the party—and even then the challengers went down to ignominious defeat.

The Canadian Communist Party had been destroyed. Tim Buck's Party—which meant Stalin's party—had taken its place.

17. Conclusion

Class against class is the order of the day, and we who are the
subjected class must learn to fight our battles just as viciously
as do our oppressors.
> —*Workers Party of Canada, December 1921*[1]

Some comrades...want a class versus class position, a point of
view the international communist movement moved away from
many years ago.
> —*William Kashtan, National Leader, Communist Party of
> Canada, May 1974*[2]

I

The Third Period, with its suicidal ultraleftism, proved to be a
shortlived episode in the evolution of the Comintern. Reacting in
panic to Hitler's 1933 triumph in Germany, Stalin veered sharply to
the right. The pseudorevolutionary policies of the early 1930s gave
way, in 1935, to a strategy that was explicitly opposed to
proletarian revolution. In the name of "antifascist unity" and the
"defense of democracy," the Communist parties now actively
sought alliances not just with Social Democrats, but with bourgeois
parties and governments that in Moscow's view might be induced
to adopt a more favorable attitude toward the Soviet Union as a
counterweight to Germany. In place of the Leninist tactic of the
united front—in which the Communists sought to ally with other
currents in the workers movement in pursuit of common goals,
while maintaining full freedom to criticize and oppose the overall
programs of those currents—the Stalinists substituted the strategy
of the Popular Front. According to this conception, elaborated by

the Seventh (and final) Congress of the Communist International in 1935, the Communists were to subordinate their own program to the programs of their hoped-for bourgeois and petty-bourgeois allies, and fight for a "minimum program" that did not challenge capitalist property relations or pose the need for socialist revolution. It did not take long for this new policy to bear fruit.

In September 1934 the Soviet Union joined the League of Nations. Under Lenin's leadership, opposition to the League had been a condition of membership in the Comintern; it was seen as fundamentally an alliance of the major imperialist victors at Versailles. But now the Soviet Union was an advocate of "collective security"—against Germany. Early in 1935 Stalin signed pacts with France and Czechoslovakia. In May he issued a joint communiqué with French Premier Pierre Laval: "M. Stalin understands and fully approves the policy of national defense undertaken by France by maintaining her armed forces at the level necessary for security." The French CP followed the lead, abandoning its antimilitarist policies in favor of support for French rearmament. In France, and soon in every country, the Comintern's policies had but one aim: to support those sections of the capitalist class that favored alliances with the USSR, or that could be "neutralized" on the diplomatic plane. Under various names (Popular Front, peaceful coexistence, détente) that has remained the goal and the program of the Communist parties to this day.

An early test of the new turn came in Spain, where Stalin showed his good faith by using the Comintern to strangle the revolutionary upsurge that erupted when Franco's fascists launched the civil war. The Spanish CP, supporting the Popular Front government and participating directly in it, moved to suppress and disarm the unions, mass workers parties, and all independent initiatives by the workers and peasants behind the Republican lines. Its policies ensured the victory of the fascist counterrevolution. As with Stalin's previous maneuvers, the Popular Front strategy in Spain served not to aid the defense of the Soviet Union, but to further endanger it.

The essential content of the Comintern's line was not its support of the "democratic bourgeoisie" against fascism, but more fundamentally a firmly established opposition to independent class political action by the workers and a desperate search for even the most "conjunctural" diplomatic and military allies for the Soviet Union. That is why Stalin's 1939 pact with Hitler, which might appear to be in contradiction to the Popular Front, was only its complement.

With war very clearly on the horizon, and Stalin's hoped-for allies failing to promise to defend the Soviet workers state if it were attacked by Germany, Stalin abruptly moved to negotiate a deal with Hitler. In the summer of 1939, he fired his Jewish Commissar of Foreign Affairs, Maxim Litvinov, appointing in his stead the thoroughly Aryan Vyacheslav Molotov. On August 23, 1939 the Stalin-Hitler pact was signed. Germany and the USSR agreed not to wage war against each other. Germany was given a free hand in Western Poland, Russia in Eastern Poland and the Baltic countries. Hitler was now free of Soviet pressure on his eastern flank, and World War II began a few days later.

Molotov announced the new Comintern policy in unmistakably clear terms:

Today, as far as the European great powers are concerned, Germany's position is that of a state which is striving for the earliest termination of war and for peace, while Britain and France, which but yesterday were declaiming against aggression, are in favor of continuing the war and are opposed to the conclusion of peace.[3]

The Communist parties, after some initial confusion, fell into line. They denounced the war and fought to keep their countries out of it. The "antifascists" of yesterday were the imperialists of today. In occupied France, the CP issued statements against the collaborationist Vichy government, *but not against the Nazi occupiers.*

Whether or not Stalin himself believed this line, the evidence is now overwhelming that between 1939 and 1941, he did little to strengthen the military position of the Soviet Union. And he was taken totally by surprise by the German invasion. As late as June 1941, one week before the German invasion of the Ukraine, Stalin issued a special statement denouncing rumors of war and insisting that Russo-German relations were proceeding well. Clearly, the Stalin-Hitler pact, like all the other maneuvers, was expected to protect the USSR from intervention.

The German invasion rudely ended this interlude, and Moscow reverted to its earlier stance of allying with Germany's imperialist enemies. The Communist parties were now for conscription and the war. No one could equal their patriotism. Anything that hindered the prosecution of the war had to be stopped. In the name of defending the Soviet workers state against Hitler's counterrevolutionary assault—a necessary task—the Comintern and its member parties sought to suppress the class struggle in the imperialist countries and their colonies. Strikes by inflation-squeezed workers, resistance to British rule in India, the Québécois' opposition to conscription were denounced by Comintern parties in the name of the war effort. The Comintern policy was the polar opposite to Lenin's call in 1914 to turn the imperialist war into a class war.

When the parties of the Comintern were forced to make sudden 180-degree turns in 1925 and 1928, many Communists objected. The reversals were carried out only with great upheavals, in many cases entailing the wholesale expulsion of party leaderships. Until 1930, the Soviet leadership could not rely on the Comintern to follow its lead without question: the Communist parties were led by dedicated revolutionists who took their right to think for granted.

The sharp turns of 1935, 1939, and 1941, however, took place with virtually no disruption. The new lines—the exact opposite of what the CI had been saying to everyone—were accepted without question. The Comintern had been tamed. Its parties were led by men who were broken to the bureaucracy's saddle. They would go where they were told, even without the threat of discipline.

By 1935 it was clear that the Comintern was of little value to the Soviet bureaucracy: it was only in the way when big power negotiations took place, an unwanted reminder of the USSR's revolutionary past.

As the war pressed on, Stalin's allies constantly urged him to rid himself of this encumbrance. Unless the Soviet leadership explicitly renounced the goal of world revolution, the capitalist powers said, they would be reluctant to open a second front against Germany. A *New York Times* editorial warned of the "subversive and, in the result, suicidal activities of a Communist International guided by the Trotskyist ideology of the proletarian world revolution." U.S. Vice-president Henry Wallace also called on the USSR to give up "the Trotskyist idea of fomenting world-wide revolution."[4]

Let it never be said that Stalin was insensitive to the desires of his capitalist allies. On June 8, 1943, without a Congress, without even a meeting of the Executive Committee, the Communist International was dissolved.

"The announcement of the formal dissolution of the Comintern," said U.S. Trotskyist James Cannon, "is simply the news account of a burial that is ten years overdue. It serves a certain purpose in that it puts an end to a fiction and clears the air of illusions and misunderstandings, to say nothing of very bad odors."[5]

The Comintern was created, in 1919, to take advantage of the epoch of wars and revolutions to extend the soviet system. It was dissolved twenty-four years later in order to preserve Stalin's alliance with the capitalist West. In reality, the international revolutionary organization founded by the Bolsheviks had died many years earlier.

The postwar creation of new workers states—in Yugoslavia and China, in particular—was to lead to conflicts within the Stalinist camp, provoke the formation of new power centers in the international Stalinist movement and lead to deep schisms and open splits. More recently, new non-Stalinist revolutionary leaderships with Cuba's Fidelista current in the lead, have come to the fore in several countries of the so-called Third World, further aggravating the crisis of the world Stalinist movement. But through it all the Canadian Communist Party has remained loyal to Moscow.

WHAT THE NEW COMINTERN LINE after 1934 meant for the Canadian CP is most clearly exemplified by the party's approach to the issue of working-class political action. The revolutionary CP of the early 1920s had been known above all for its uncompromising commitment to the principle of the class political independence of the workers. It had fought long and hard to build the Canadian Labor Party, the first faltering attempt by the workers through their trade unions to establish a mass political party of the labor movement. It had campaigned in the unions and the working class as a whole for the principle of labor unity, against the class-collaborationism of the reformists and the sectarian divisiveness of the syndicalists. Many of its militants had won their credentials as leaders in the labor movement through their firm opposition to the imperialist world war of 1914-1918 and their refusal to subordinate workers' needs to the prosecution of the war.

The Popular Front policy represented a complete break with all this. It was not long before the CP, in the interests of the antifascist alliance, was pressing for "progressive unity" not just with the CCF but with the Liberals, Conservatives, even Social Credit.* By 1939, on the eve of the war, the CP was proclaiming that in the

---

*In December 1938 Leslie Morris spoke at a victory party for a Social Credit candidate who had won a federal by-election in Edmonton. The *Edmonton Journal* reported: "Leslie Morris...declared that people all over Canada will view the Social Credit victory with pride and enthusiasm. 'It's a national victory for all who stand for a free-progressive, democratic Canada,' the Communist Secretary said."[6]

coming federal election "our guiding policy will be...to re-elect Premier [Prime Minister Mackenzie] King." After a brief interruption during the twenty-two months of the Hitler-Stalin Pact, in which the Liberal prime minister was denounced as "Iron-Heel King," the CP returned to its now-established multiclass reformist perspective. In 1944, it called for

election of a government based upon a coalition of democratic forces— uniting the mass support of the CCF, the Labor-Progressive Party (the CP), the progressive farm organizations, with the trade union movement and the progressive reform Liberals who supported Mackenzie King.[7]

Within the labor movement, the CP was among the foremost opponents of moves during the 1940s to affiliate the unions to the CCF and to support that party as a means of rupture with the Liberals.[8] At one point, in 1945, Alex Parent, a member of the Labor-Progressive (Communist) Party, won election in a previously-CCF riding in Ontario on a Liberal-Labor ticket and sat *as a member of the Liberal caucus* in the Ontario legislature for nearly a year.[9]

Nor was this policy confined to the war years. In the early 1960s, when the unions took the initiative in forming a new labor-based party, the New Democratic Party, the CP strongly opposed efforts to root the party in the unions, calling instead for the new party to be only a "parliamentary united front of Canadians...from different economic and social groups who unite around the need for a mass parliamentary party to defeat monopoly and its parties."[10]

The CP's opposition to working-class political action, and its virulent support of the war—to the point of fighting for a no-strike pledge and campaigning for conscription—discredited the party among many class-conscious workers. This facilitated its victimization in the postwar witch-hunt, when the CP's erstwhile allies in the union bureaucracy turned on it and sought to drive it out of the unions. The party suffered further blows with the collapse of the Stalin cult in the Soviet Union and the Kremlin's brutal suppression of the Hungarian workers' uprising in 1956. In the 1960s and '70s, the new generation of radical youth who turned toward Marxism as a result of their experiences in the anti-Vietnam war movement or the women's movement were largely unattracted by the Communist Party with its heritage of Stalinism and cynical support of totalitarianism.

II

The founders of the Communist Party of Canada were committed to class-struggle socialism. They were neither angels nor devils: they were working class leaders who sought to unite their class with the poor farmers in an all-out battle against the ruling capitalist class. They were prepared to form alliances with non-Communist groups and individuals, indeed they went out of their way to forge such alliances, but they would not cross the class line that separated them from the capitalist class. They would have been appalled to learn that the party they founded would one day set as its goal the forging of an alliance of "wage- and salary-earners, farmers, professionals, intellectuals, small businessmen and non-monopoly capitalists" to form "a large progressive bloc in Parliament."[11]

The Communist Party of 1921 was composed of men and women who had past records of political and union activity which they were proud of. Many of them had more than a decade's experience as labor leaders. They saw the Russian Revolution as a confirmation and extension of their own political views; they looked to the leaders of that Revolution for guidance, but they accepted dictation from no one. If they were wrong, they wanted to be convinced, not ordered to change. When they disagreed with the leaders of the Communist International—as on the question of "Trotskyism"—they were not afraid to say so.

By contrast, the Communist Party of Canada today is one of the most servile of the world's communist parties. It never deviates from total support to the policies of the rulers of the Kremlin, even when that support means making a sudden unexplained about-face in policy, even when it means seriously damaging the party's credibility among its supporters. Any party member who objects—witness the members who opposed the 1968 invasion of Czechoslovakia—is soon found outside of the party's ranks.

What happened to destroy the Communist Party of Canada? What caused the degeneration of a party with such promise?

The usual explanation is "domination from Moscow." According to this explanation, the Canadian Communists were doomed from the moment they hitched their wagon to Russia's red star. If only they had kept themselves free of foreign ties and influences, none of this would have happened.

Those who blame the party's international ties for its degeneration forget that it was the Bolshevik leaders who put the Canadian Communists on the right track in the first place, pointing them away from dead-end sectarianism and into the unions and the labor parties. The Canadian left had a long and admirable tradition, but the Russian Revolution gave it a program and a strategy for the first time.

The Communist Party of Canada was formed as a result of the intersection of national and international influences: it represented, from the beginning, a fusion of the Russian Revolution with the native tradition of Canadian radicalism. The party's decline was also caused by a combination of international and national social forces.

The long isolation of the Russian Revolution and its consequent degeneration was certainly a primary factor. The corruption of the Russian Communist Party was transmitted, through the Comintern, to the Communist parties that had accepted the Russians as first among equals. But just as the Russian Revolution needed receptive individuals and groups in Canada to learn its lessons before a party could be built, so the corruption of Stalinism could not have spread had not the ground been prepared for it by conditions in Canada.

The degeneration of the Communist Party of Canada began not in 1929 when Tim Buck took over, and certainly not (as some Maoist writers claim) in 1935 when the Third Period ended, but in the mid-twenties, when the party was only a few years old. The conservatism of the twenties, brought on by the post-war boom and the collapse of the labor movement, weakened and demoralized the party, and sent it in search of new paths to revolution. The adoption of the "Canadian Independence" slogan was one such path: when the party leadership, on the initiative of Buck and Spector, approved that line, they were setting aside the class-struggle principles they had fought for, in quest of an easier road. They drew back from actually supporting the Liberals as "anti-imperialists," but their analysis implied such support.

A strong, revolutionary International could have corrected that error just as it had corrected the ultraleftism of 1920-1921. But the International itself was in trouble.

The causes of the degeneration of the Russian Revolution and the Comintern are similar to those that weakened the Canadian CP. The Canadian Communists were isolated in a conservative society: the Russian Revolution was isolated in a conservative world. The failures and defeats of 1918-1920 weakened the USSR. That in turn weakened the International. The action became reciprocal: a weakened International proved unable to meet the challenge of the German revolution of 1923. That defeat pushed the International further off track. The policies the International followed from 1923 on reinforced the conservative bureaucracy in the USSR by weakening the international working-class movement. At first it was a matter of narrow-mindedness, of bureaucratic incompetence: later the anti-revolutionary activities of the Comintern became a matter of deliberate policy.

Added to this was the fact that the bureaucratic degeneration of the Soviet workers state—a new phenomenon unforeseen in the classic writings of Marxism up to then—was not easy to analyze and understand. It took years for the remnants of the Russian Bolsheviks, led by Trotsky, to develop a comprehensive theoretical appreciation of this development. Small wonder that so few leaders of the Canadian CP grasped its implications and reacted in time.

The Canadian Communists were caught between a rock and a hard place. The conservatism of Canadian society on one side and the bureaucratization of the Soviet Union on the other caught the party, paralysed it, and squeezed the life out of it. By the time the working class began to move again in Canada, the Communist Party was no longer a communist party.

III

A transformation as complete as that which took place in the Canadian Communist Party does not occur as a smooth, unbroken evolution. As in society at large, great changes in political organizations occur as a combination of gradual evolution and sudden crises. Prior to November, 1928, the Communist Party's drift away from Leninism had been gradual, so much so that few party members or leaders saw it, let alone questioned it. Beginning with the expulsion of Maurice Spector, and continuing until the final consolidation of the Tim Buck regime in February 1931, the party passed through a crisis that brought about a qualitative change in every sphere.

1. The first and most obvious change was a change in leadership. In two years the party's founding cadre was decimated. Maurice Spector, Jack MacDonald, Mike Buhay, Bill Moriarty, Fred Peel, Bob Shoesmith... these and many others were driven out. The leaders of the Finnish Organization were expelled and readmitted only when they repudiated the policies they had been fighting for. A similar process occurred with the Ukrainian leadership. *Tim Buck was the only member of the leading group from the 1920s to come through the crisis unscathed.*

In place of the party's traditional leadership there now appeared a new group, composed entirely of people who had entered the party in the mid-twenties—who, in other words, had no pre-Stalin political experience. Stewart Smith was the first of these to come into prominence, but he was quickly followed by Leslie Morris, Sam Carr, John Weir, Oscar Ryan, Charles Sims, and others. Many of them, following a pattern repeated in many countries, were groomed in Moscow's Lenin School to take over their parties.* They were expressly trained in Stalinist ideas and Stalinist methods, and they never questioned them. With the major exception of Stewart Smith, almost the entire group that took over with Buck in 1929-1931 remained in the party for the rest of their lives. Some of them are still a force to be reckoned with in the Canadian Stalinist movement.

2. The new leaders introduced what seemed to be a new style of leadership in the party. Again and again in the years 1929-1931 party members complained about the rudeness and arrogance of the supporters of the Buck-Smith faction. At the Sixth Convention they bullied and ridiculed delegates who had difficulty with English. In the trade union movement they plowed ahead, consulting no one. The Ukrainians wanted Buck removed on the grounds of his insensitivity. Harvey Murphy, another long-term Buck supporter, won no friends in Alberta in 1930; according to Tom McEwen, "Com. Bruce...stated that Murphy would be lynched if he ever went back there, because of his bureaucratic, black-jacking methods."[13]

What was involved was not just a new style, or inexperience. The leadership tactics of the Buck-Smith group were modeled on those of the Soviet bureaucracy. They replaced education and persuasion with commands. Democratic centralism was supplanted by bureaucratic centralism; unquestioning submission to the apparatus replaced collective decision-making. The first four congresses of the Comintern had featured discussion and debate, often heated, between independent revolutionists who sought to hammer out a program for the world revolution. Thereafter the congresses were little more than rituals at which the line was handed down from above. What was true for the International became true for the

---

*Italian Communist Party leader Togliatti is reported to have said, during an early discussion of the implications of the Third Period, "If we don't give in, Moscow won't hesitate to fix up a left leadership with some kid out of the Lenin School."[12] This type of thinking bred infinite cynicism in Communist parties around the world.

national parties, and for the Districts and Branches of those parties. For the Canadian party, 1929 saw the beginning of commandism as a way of life.

3. Official Soviet theory, since 1956, has ascribed all of the evils of the Stalin period to the "cult of personality," which Stalin fostered. While this is a deliberate attempt to conceal the social roots of Stalinism, there can be no doubt that the virtual deification of Stalin was an important aspect of Stalinism. A similar process took place in each of the Communist parties: small-scale leader cults were established around each party leader. Beginning in the early 1930s, the Communist Party began to develop a Tim Buck cult. The *Worker* began a regular feature called "Tim Buck Says," which used a photo of Buck and a more-or-less banal quotation from his writings and speeches. Major articles hailed him as the founder of Canadian Communism. He was acclaimed as the "most beloved leader of the Canadian workers." A pamphlet on party history was named "The Story of Tim Buck's Party." "Comrade Buck," wrote one apostle, "if he had pursued the arts, had the qualities which would have made him a great surgeon; he could have become a very clever lawyer; in science, he would have been one of those who have travelled the stoney road to the atomic bomb."[14]

A regime that rules by command must justify its rule by the claim that the supreme ruler is uniquely qualified to give commands. Stalin was the greatest Marxist-Leninist of the epoch: Buck was his image in Canada.

4. Closely related to the establishment of a regime that ruled by command was the outlawing of all dissent within the party. During the 1920s there were seldom any major political disagreements in the party—but it was never suggested that the disagreements that did exist were grounds for excluding anyone from the party. Spector's "Trotskyism" provides the clearest example of this: although he was the only member of the Central Executive who expressed sympathy for the Left Opposition, he was re-elected party chairman and editor of the *Worker*.

This was characteristic of the Comintern in Lenin's time. The Bolsheviks never pretended to be running a pacifist discussion circle: they were building an International of revolutionists, and they fought hard for their ideas in that International. But within that framework they recognized that differences would occur. Those who comment adversely on the harshness of Lenin's criticisms of the ultraleft in *"Left-Wing" Communism* seldom note that after the pamphlet was published the Communist Workers Party of Germany (against whom much of the pamphlet was directed) was welcomed into the International to defend its ideas. Similarly, even when the Bolsheviks found it necessary to temporarily ban factions in their party during a period of crisis, Lenin nominated the chief spokesman of one of the banned factions for the Central Committee.

Under Stalin's rule, the "monolithic" International and Party became the order of the day. All dissent was hunted out of the party: eventually all dissenters and even potential dissenters faced the firing squad. The same process took place in every party. Tim Buck's attempt to defend the party's 1929 thesis on the Anglo-American conflict illustrates very graphically what happened. Buck first made the mistake of defending a line the Comintern was against, and compounded his error by pointing out that the Comintern had imposed the line on the Canadian party in the first place. As a result, the party leadership found itself in disfavor in Moscow: its moves against the Finns were undermined, and it was investigated by commissions. By the time of the 1931 Plenum Buck had learned his lesson. There was no mention of the CI's responsibility for the line in any of the Plenum documents or speeches. The International was infallible: all error flowed from failure to understand the line.

5. The change in party leadership was paralleled by a rapid turnover in membership. As we have seen, about three quarters of the party membership dropped out or were expelled in 1929-1931. Those who remained adapted to the new regime: those who returned humbled themselves before it. The routine for a returning prodigal was a public "self-criticism" in the pages of the *Worker*, admitting real and imaginary errors, accepting the infallibility of the party line, and promising to obey in future. Only those whose revolutionary spirit was broken—or who never had any to begin with—could submit to such terms, The mass exodus of party members in 1929-1931 provided the basis for remaking the party on the Stalinist model.

6. Finally, the Third Period entailed a process of political re-education that may justly be described as the destruction of thought and of the ability to think. In place of carefully worked out propaganda and agitation, party militants were armed with the weapons of physical and verbal violence. Name-calling replaced political analysis. Humble acceptance of the dictates of Moscow replaced Marxist analysis of the realities and needs of the class

struggle in Canada. This sort of thing, from the main resolution adopted at the 1934 CPC Convention, passed for Marxism:

The bourgeoisie is fascizing its state...Canadian social reformism is the main support of the bourgeoisie....The social-fascist officials of the A.F. of L. and A.C.C.L. and C.C.F. aid every line of the capitalist offensive....The social fascists play the role of a cover behind which the bourgeoisie organize their fascist forces....[15]

And on and on and on. Rote repetition of the current slogans replaced any form of thought, let alone Marxism. People who were educated to accept this drivel could easily be persuaded to accept the exact opposite a few months later.

The Communist Party began drifting away from its original program in 1925. In 1929 the drift became headlong flight. The United Front policy developed by the Comintern was built around two central axes: the need to unite the largest possible number of working class forces in action against the capitalist class, and the need for the Communist Party to maintain its independent political position within the united front. That policy served the party well in the unions, in electoral activity, and in other forms of radical activity such as aid to political prisoners. In 1929 the first half of the policy was jettisoned. Any form of unity with non-Communists was forbidden. Political cooperation between working class parties was banned; Communists abandoned the "social-fascist" unions. In 1935 both halves were thrown aside. In place of working class unity in action against the capitalists, the party promoted "progressive" unity against "reaction." The few vestiges of revolutionary politics which remained in the party program were jettisoned: Stewart Smith pledged to "cement together all the fragments broken apart by the great betrayal of 1914" if the CPC were allowed to join the CCF.[16] The Workers Unity League was dismantled with as little ceremony as it was created, and its members were sent scurrying back into the unions they had denounced for half a decade as unreformable agents of imperialism. Soon the "Communists" were distinguishable from other trade union "progressives" only by their steadfast loyalty to the Kremlin.

With the single exception of James McLachlan, who refused to return to the United Mine Workers, no party leader questioned the 1935 about-face. The rank and file accepted the turn unhesitatingly. There was no political integrity left in the Communist Party of Canada.

IV

What is to be done when a major attempt to build a revolutionary party fails? When the Second International collapsed in 1914, Lenin immediately called for the building of a Third. There was no time to mourn: new tasks were at hand.

Such was the approach of the founders of the Canadian Communist Party to the destruction of their party. Jack MacDonald and Maurice Spector devoted themselves in the 1930s to the cause of a new revolutionary party and a new revolutionary International. In 1934 they established a new party, the Workers Party of Canada. In 1935 they were among the signers of an appeal, initiated by Leon Trotsky, for the creation of a Fourth International, and their organization assisted in the establishment of that International in 1938.

Two other pioneer Canadian Communists, Max Armstrong and Malcolm Bruce, joined the Trotskyist movement after World War II, contributing their talents and experiences to the effort to rebuild the party that was destroyed at the end of the 1920s.

Fighting against the stream, against the overwhelming influence of Stalinism and Social Democracy in the workers movement, these pioneers and new generations of revolutionists kept the revolutionary program alive. The experiences of the 1920s are not part of a dead past. Learning from the successes and failures of the first generation of Canadian Communists is a major part of the effort to translate that program into reality.

DOCUMENTS

The documents reproduced here have been chosen to illustrate the three principal phases of Communist politics in the years covered in this book: the underground ultraleft period, the Leninist period, and the birth of Canadian Stalinism. The full texts appear as originally published or written, with only minimal changes in spelling and punctuation to ensure clarity.

I. The Underground

Peace and the Workers

Soldiers and Workers:

After more than four years of slaughter, starvation and misery for the workers of the world, the rival factions of capitalists have come to terms. Fifteen millions of workers have been killed in order to settle which gang of

---

"Peace and the Workers" was distributed in Southern Ontario in November 1918, shortly after the armistice. It seems to have been the first public statement of the organized underground. Two subsequent statements, similar in form and content, were distributed early in 1919 and signed "Provisional Council of Soldiers and Workers Deputies of Canada."

The formula "means of wealth production" used in this statement provides a strong clue to the origin of part of the group that wrote it. Most of the left referred to the "means of production"—only the Socialist Party of North America, for reasons that remain obscure, insisted on the insertion of the word "wealth."

Originals in Chief Censor's Files, Public Archives of Canada, Ottawa.

exploiters shall exploit the workers of the world. Fifteen million more have been disabled, blinded or stricken with disease in order that a crew of parasites could get control of new markets, sources of raw material, and trade routes. Many millions of women and children have died of starvation while fat capitalists have rolled in luxury and have accused you of squandering your miserable wages, their fat and silk-clad women have urged your overworked wife to "conserve food"—you must know that you have been forced to "conserve" all your life and yet you kept silent under the sneers of these people who rob you of nearly all you produce! You have gone through all this for what? Read the speeches of the spokesmen of the rival gangs and see. Do they intend to make your life easier? No, even returned soldiers who were supposed to have "fought for their country" are being forced into factories because of the small pensions they receive after their "glorious sacrifice." Are they out to establish Democracy? No, ask the hundred of workers who have been thrown into prison for daring to speak the truth about this war of conquest; ask the crippled soldier who is imprisoned for daring to wear his uniform after he is discharged; ask the soldiers who are discharged with a pension insufficient to keep them alive. Could these, soldiers and workers, honestly say that this war is to "make the world safe for democracy"? No! Then do not let yourself be fooled by the lying press and the prostitute public speakers. All that concerns the capitalists is the destruction of a dangerous trade rival; the capture of colonies and new markets and cheap labor.

Slimy-tongued speakers have told you during the war that you were "saving the Empire." The "Empire" has been saved, but it does not appear to have helped the workers. Those who fought for the "Empire" are being got rid of as cheaply as possible; those who slaved in munition factories are being turned adrift by the thousands. The Empire has been saved! The capitalists do not need you any more, they need not care what becomes of you now—the sooner you die the sooner you will receive your share of the "Empire." You know these things are true; then why don't you start out and work for your freedom?

You are celebrating the victory of your masters over another set of masters; you are cheering over the death of fifteen millions of your comrades. You are doing exactly what your masters want you to do, that is, keep yourself in a state of excitement over your masters' victory, while your masters are preparing to suppress you when, in a few months' time, you are howling for bread. This victory means nothing to you except the same daily grind of hopeless toil, poor food, poor clothing, poor shelter, and an early death. Wake up! Show yourself to be worthy of more than a slave's position. Sweep away the capitalist class; conquer supremacy for the working class; and then get down to the serious business of building up institutions necessary for carrying on the business of the country where the workers will own and control all means of wealth production and distribution. You must now choose between revolution for the establishment of Socialism or degradation and misery.

Your Example

The workers in Russia have been in power for one year—the soldiers and workers joined together and overthrew the Czarism; then the capitalists tried to gather the fruits of the workers' action, and again the soldiers and workers co-operated and overthrew the capitalist government. They established their councils and set about building up Socialism. They were faced with great difficulties, the productive machinery was almost at a standstill; the transportation system was ruined by the war, and the workers practically starving. Besides these difficulties every capitalist government in the world was opposed to these workers, every capitalist newspaper in the world sought to discredit them, and some governments, the British amongst others, financed counter-revolutionary plots. Despite all these obstacles the Russian workers have triumphed. They have brought order out of chaos; they have increased the food supply, but great care is taken that only those who work get any of it; and they have reorganized the railways. The factories have been handed over to the workers, who elect committees to direct production; and the land has been taken away from the landlords and handed to the peasants. Remember that these things are actual facts which can be proven, while the accusations of the yellow press have never been proven.

The Russia of the Czar was pointed to as Black Russia, the workers of Russia have built up Red Russia, and it is from the workers of Russia that you must take your example. You have spilled your blood like water for the benefit of your masters, surely you are prepared to take decisive action for your own benefit? Workers and soldiers unite for the overthrow of the parasites who fatten upon your labor. Take action and build up your councils to conduct the business of the country; take over and run all industries for the benefit of the working class; establish revolutionary discipline and crush the capitalists as they have crushed you since you were born. These actions MUST be taken if you want to be more than food for cannon in times of war and work beasts in times of peace.

The flames of revolution are spreading over Europe; the workers of Germany have risen and overthrown their master class and the allied capitalists are going to try [to] crush them and help the capitalists of Germany despite the fact that they were deadly enemies a short time ago. The capitalists of the world are helping each other—the workers must unite and overthrow them. Workers and soldiers, the issue is clear—either revolution for Socialism or degradation and misery under capitalism.

What to Do

It is a usual saying with those who are anti-Socialist that "Socialists are impossibilists." This has been refuted by the events in Russia during the last year or so. There the workers have taken the line of action advocated by the Socialists and have succeeded in defeating the capitalists and building up a system of society where only the interests of the workers are consulted.

Qualities of statesmanship have been displayed by the Socialists which have effectively smashed the frantic efforts of the capitalist governments of the world [in] their efforts to reduce the Russian workers to slavery again.

We desire to impress upon you the practicability of the action we urge. No abstract theories are necessary. All that is necessary is that you, soldiers and workers, should recognize that while a few men own the means whereby you live, you must be slaves to these men; once you see this then you must be prepared to take action to accomplish your freedom. You know that the government uses the police force and soldiers to crush you every time you try to do anything for yourselves. These men are members of the working class like you are, efforts must be made to win them over to the side of the workers. This is your first step, and it is not so hard as it may appear; the workers in the army suffer under a system which is worse than factory life, also, [and] they are coming to understand that when they are discharged from the army they can only expect a miserable pension. You can show them the difference which would take place if they support the workers' revolution, how the soldiers would elect their own officers; how the soldiers' committees would participate in conducting the affairs of the country; in fact, everything about which they only dream now could become a practical certainty through the co-operation of the soldiers and workers for the defeat of the capitalist class. You must show the soldiers that the only ones who have interests in common with them are their fellow-workers; all the capitalists think about is how cheaply the soldier can be kept. The soldiers have everything to gain by the overthrow of the capitalists and nothing to lose.

The uprising of the soldiers and workers against their oppressors will make it necessary for a new kind of administration, to conduct the business of the workers' republic, to come into being. We have seen [how] the workers in Russia and Germany managed this by the formation of Soldiers' and Workers' Councils. Only members of the working class can stand for election, and the electorate has the right of recall at any time; besides that, a general election is held every three months. This is a truly democratic form of representation, nothing can be done unknown to the workers. These councils will take over all power from the existing governing bodies whose great function is the suppression of the working class. Capitalist officials will be given a chance to co-operate with the workers and if they refuse will be imprisoned until everything is settled. The men who so gladly imprison the workers will taste their own medicine.

The business of the Soldiers' and Workers' Councils is, firstly, to suppress the capitalists and their followers; secondly, to transfer all private property in the means of wealth production into the property of the working class to be used for the benefit of the worker class alone. This cannot be done all at once and the first steps in this direction will be to hand over the factories to the workers, who will elect committees to direct production; in this work the technical experts will be made to help. The farms will be taken over by the agricultural laborers and poor farmers (who will be glad to get rid of this slavery to financial capital through mortgages). Committees will be appointed by the Councils to co-ordinate the efforts of these local committees, and in that way the industrial life of the community will be placed upon a firm foundation, with the result that in a short time the capitalist will be completely shorn of his power to rob and exploit the workers.

This is how the workers of Europe are moving, and succeeding in their task of ridding the world of the system of society which means only misery for the workers. But the first essential is revolutionary action by the working class, nothing short of the complete overthrow of the capitalists and their institutions can prepare the ground for the building of the Workers' Republic where the workers shall control their own destiny.

Workers and Soldiers! Upon your shoulders rests this mighty work, your whole future depends upon its success.

"May Day!"

To the Workers of Canada:

The First of May is regarded by the workers of the world as a day upon which they must attempt to express the solidarity of the international working class fight against capitalism. Demonstrations are held all over the world, and defiance is hurled at the capitalist class in all languages. Even the contemptible "moderate Socialists" are forced upon that day to use phrases which, if carried into effect, would destroy capitalism and enthrone the workers as rulers of society. But they are only phrase-makers, and the lesson for you workers to understand is that May Day is not only a day for bold speeches, but also a day for bold action. We have enough succeeded in seizing power and establishing their own rule.[sic] In Germany an exceedingly bitter struggle is going on—the workers have been defeated many times, but always rise again stronger than ever. Those scoundrels, Ebert and Scheidemann [leaders of the Social Democrats] and their gang of cutthroats are trying to save the capitalist of Germany from defeat—they are traitors to the workers just like their brothers in other countries: Henderson in England, Albert Thomas in France, Gompers in United States, and Thomas Moore in Canada.

In France, Italy and England the decisive moment is fast approaching: Reforms are thrown to the workers in order to deceive them, but conditions are getting worse every day, and the workers are being forced to rise in revolt against their capitalist oppressors.

"May Day" and "Programme of the Communist Party of Canada" were two sides of a single sheet distributed in Montreal and in Southern Ontario on April 30, 1919. The Programme was printed at least one month earlier: copies of it were confiscated during the arrest of Samsonovitch, Ewart and Zoborowski on March 23. See chapter 2.

Originals in Vertical Files, Department of Labor, Hull, Quebec.

Either starvation and death, or revolution—these are the only alternatives. The workers must choose the path of revolution. The sham of parliamentary action has been destroyed, tinkering with reforms does not help the working class, only the complete overthrow of capitalism can emancipate the workers—the workers of France, Italy and England will soon choose the true road to Freedom—Revolution!

But on this continent, fellow-workers and soldiers, what a dismal picture presents itself to us! Here there is no workers' triumph to celebrate—only a blood-thirsty ruling class has anything to celebrate. Unemployment, hunger, disease and death stalk amongst the workers here. Soldiers who have fought for the exploiters under the delusion that they were fighting for themselves are being turned into the streets penniless, diseased and wounded. On the other hand, the capitalists are bloated with luxury, their wives dressed in silks and jewels—you are starving and your wives are in rags. Fellow-workers, are you content with this? Are you willing to be a slave all your life, driven and starved? Are you willing to see your children half-starved, whipped into factories, where they become physical wrecks? Are you content to let your daughters be driven into prostitution in order to live? You, soldiers, who fought so bravely for your masters; you, workers, who have slaved all your lives so that other men could enjoy themselves while you starved; can you not see that you must rise up and put an end to this system of exploitation? You cannot celebrate any victory on May Day, but you can resolve not to stay slaves any longer, but to struggle uneasingly [sic] against the capitalist class until you conquer power and establish the rule of the workers.

Your only hope lies in revolution—the sweeping away of this rotten system of exploitation. You must achieve a victory over the capitalist class so that you can celebrate May Day along with your fellow workers in Russia.

Long live the revolution of the workers against the capitalists. Workers, Unite!

Published by the Central Executive Committee of the Communist Party of Canada.

Programme of the Communist Party of Canada

The object of the Communist Party of Canada is to organize and prepare the working class in Canada for the Social Revolution and the establishment of the Dictatorship of the Proletariat. The revolutionary section of the working class must take the lead in the class struggle against the bourgeoisie, and by agitation prepare the mass of the workers for the decisive struggle for the establishment of communism.

The tactics of the Socialist parties hitherto have been to use the political institutions of capitalism. Two reasons are usually given to support these tactics: (1) That all the workers have to do is to elect a majority to the House of Commons and "legislate the capitalists out of business," and in the meantime advocate social reforms which will make the process of growing into Socialism easier. (2) That the House of Commons can be used for agitation purposes. Both of these reasons were shown to be useless by the events of the war of 1914-18. These Parliamentary Socialist parties either collapsed into one or the other of the Imperialist camps or degenerated into mere pacifist organizations howling about the horror of bloodshed and the abolition of "elementary right" such as free speech and press. Both groups demanded peace, but did not demand, or work for, a workers' peace based upon the triumph of the workers over the capitalist class. Their whole conduct proves that they could not conceive of any action not based upon the use of the institutions of capitalism. The destruction of the capitalist State machinery and the building up of workers' institutions never occurred to them—the majority Socialist forgets nothing and learns nothing.

The seizure of power by the workers of Russia under the leadership of the Bolshevik Communist Party in November, 1917 marks the turning point in the conception of Socialist tactics. The old parliamentary programs were subjected to criticism and slowly in each country arose groups of workers advocating the tactics of the Bolsheviki. Of course, many of these groups consisted of "revolutionary phrase makers" who accepted these tactics in word but not in deed. These phrase makers are typified by wanting to use parliament for "agitation".

The tactics of the Bolsheviki are based upon the fact that we do not need the institutions of capitalism for our emancipation, but we must destroy them and substitute our institutions in their place, and the success of the social revolution can only be assured by the arming of the workers and the disarming of the capitalist class and its followers.

The Communist Party of Canada builds its facts upon this basis. We oppose the use of parliamentary action as a snare and delusion. We know that parliament, even when filled with capitalist representatives, is only a debating chamber, and has no executive power whatever. The parliamentarians are the best safeguard of capitalism against the attacks of the workers. Instead of relying upon capitalist institutions, our business is to urge the workers to seize power and destroy the rule of the bourgeois.

The Communist Party does not worry about reorganizing the Trade Union movement; we do not propose to fritter away our forces in guerrilla warfare with the capitalist class about better conditions under capitalism. It is inevitable that the workers, in their instinctive revolt against the conditions imposed upon them under capitalism, should seek some means of defence against this oppression. Thus rises trades unionism and later industrial unionism. It is our duty to point out the limitations of these means of defence and urge them to take offensive measures against capitalism.

The role of the general strike in the social revolution is that it prepares the way for the civil war between the workers and capitalists. To say that by the general strike alone the workers can emancipate themselves is ridiculous—it is only part of the action necessary for the overthrow of capitalism. It is a common saying that the workers control in industry, their "economic power" and so on, but we must recognize that the workers, by refusing to work do not demonstrate their control of industry. They demonstrate the fact that they can destroy industry by refusing to work. To destroy a thing is one thing, to control it is another. A strike by the workers could make it impossible for the capitalist to extract profits—but that does not give the workers control of industry. The workers must not only make it impossible for the capitalist to rule—they must take over society and rule themselves.

The Communist Party of Canada entirely support the Communists of Europe in their actions, not only in words, but we are determined to take the same actions in Canada. The elemental revolt of the mass of the workers against the Imperialist Autocracy is coming soon on this continent, the autocracy will fall and some "popular" leader from the "labor movement" will be called in to save capitalism, supported by the moderate Socialists. Then the Communists must step into action and destroy capitalism and establish communism.

Then will come the time for the putting into practice of our program as follows:

(1) The first act in the revolution of the proletariat is the forcible seizure of the governmental power and the establishment of the dictatorship of the proletariat.

(2) The complete destruction of all capitalist political institutions, and the substitution of Workers', Peasants' and Soldiers' Councils as the governing authority.

(3) The abolition of the standing army, disarming of the capitalists and their followers (especially police officers and army officers), and the arming of the fighting proletariat leading to the establishment of the Red Guard.

(4) The abolition of all law courts, and the substitution for them of revolutionary tribunals.

(5) The confiscation of all private property without compensation, secret or open, including factories, mines, mills, railroads and real estate owned by individuals or corporations and used for profit-making. This confiscated property to be socialized, that is, to be made the property of the working class under workers' control.

(6) The confiscation of all banking accounts (excluding the small accounts of the workers), and the nationalization of the banking system.

(7) The handing over of the land to the agricultural laborers and poor farmers.

These are the first steps we must take in order to establish the rule of the proletariat. Society must be run in the interest of the worker alone (this constitutes a dictatorship of the proletariat) until such time as the bourgeoisie disappears and every member of society is a worker; then, the dictatorship of the proletariat will become unnecessary.

Published by the Central Executive Committee, Communist Party of Canada.

II. The Leninist Period

The Constituent Convention of the Workers' Party of Canada February 1922
By Maurice Spector

I.

The Workers' Party Convention which took place in the third week of February laid the foundations of the first actual political organization of the militant workers of Canada. It is true that there have been other socialist parties in the past, but in the light of developments it is clear that these were merely the elementary stepping-stones for a more serious political evolution of the workers of this country. The Social Democratic Party, which attracted greatest attention during the war period for its pacifist attitude, dimly attempted to be a mass party by its program of maximum and minimum demands. It attempted to go down to the level of the workers just emerging to political consciousness without seeking to raise that level. It attempted to get its "immediate demands" realized through electioneering and legislation, rather than through the pressure of proletarian struggle. The Social Democratic Party vanished from the political scene for two reasons. First, the right wing perceiving that the war had sufficiently quickened the sense of independent political action among the moderate trade union elements, threw themselves into the work of getting control of that development by the organization of an Independent Labor Party; secondly, the left wing developed by the repercussion of the Russian Revolution succeeded in putting a successful referendum on affiliation to the Communist International (1919). But this achievement was in effect little more than a revolutionary gesture, a demonstration of ideal revolutionary solidarity, since the party was rapidly disintegrating, and was finally liquidated by its revolutionary Central Committee to prevent the treasury funds and party name being exploited by the former Social Democratic element in the I.L.P. for its own political ends.

The other Socialist Party, the Socialist Party of Canada, was a sectarian body and not a revolutionary political party in the European sense. For instance, its official organ, the "Western Clarion", declared editorially that

---

"The Constituent Convention of the Workers Party of Canada," by Maurice Spector, has never been published before. By its contents, it must have been written in March or April 1922: it appears to be a report by Spector to the Fourth Congress of the Communist International, which he attended.

Original in Kenny Papers, University of Toronto Rare Book Room.

the function of the party was purely educational, consisting that is, in the holding of study classes, lectures, etc. In general its party attitude was purely critical of labor developments, and its criticism was characterized by abstruse pedantry. The effect of the party teachings on some of its members was to instill in them a contempt for the everyday "wage struggle" of the workers. The real class struggle was, so to speak, considered postponed until a majority of the workers were ready to accept the S.P. of C. program, or if the class struggle was at all being waged currently it was done so at the S.P. of C. headquarters. Another section if its membership, however, was active in the trade union movement, the position of the S.P. of C. members of this section as workers proving stronger than the doctrinarism of their party. Working steadily, they became influential in the Western trade union movement (it should be pointed out here that the S.P. of C. never extended materially into Eastern Canada). But because these S.P. of C. workers were not carrying on under centralized control, because the conception of the role of the party of the proletariat was as yet very vague, their activity in the everyday struggle tended to give them consciously or unconsciously a syndicalist outlook. For real action and leadership in the class struggle they looked to the trade union movement rather than to the organized political vanguard of the proletariat. The S.P. of C. has finally split on the rock of affiliation to the Communist International.

II.

The Communist Party of Canada was formed in the summer of 1921 on an illegal basis, for several reasons. The comrades were still living in the memory of the ruthless government Orders-in-Council suppressing revolutionary movements during the war and demobilization period, the brutal measures that the State took to break the Winnipeg strike and gaol the strike leaders were still fresh in mind, and the Canadian Communist groups were still in the shadow of the terroristic means adopted by the American bourgeoisie to outlaw the American Communist Party. The underground character of the Party, however, combined with the inexperience of the leading elements, led to its isolation from the Canadian Labor movement. No matter how active certain Party members may have been, the Communist Party as such played a negligible role. It began to dawn more and more clearly on the Party comrades that unless the Party adopted a new orientation in the question of public activity, the Communist Party would be condemned to stagnation. The formation of mere legal workers' societies, as planned in a resolution at the Constituent Convention, was proving utterly insufficient. This feeling was clarified and organized when the decisions of the Third Congress on the American situation became known. Any lingering fears there may have been among some comrades of the Party that broad public activity was necessarily associated with the compromise of principles and would lead to Centrism, were rapidly dissipated. It became manifest to all that the essence of the policies of the Communist International was Communist activity rather than the pure and punctilious phrase. Consequently, the decisions of the Comintern were welcomed unanimously in Canada as being absolutely in accord with the demands and realities of the situation.

That situation, moreover, made it imperative that the Communist Party act quickly and assume the initiative or be wholly left behind in the organization of the left elements of the Canadian Labor movement which were beginning to stir. The left wing of the S.P. of C., growing tired of the interminable discussion on affiliation to the Third International carried on by their party organ, along with consistent sabotage of every effort to arrive at the decision, were leaving the S.P. of C. Various organizations, such as the Finnish Socialist Federation, were unattached but yet ripe for affiliation to an open Communist organization. The retrogression of the O.B.U. in the West was leaving great numbers of workers outside of any political or economic organization. The "labor parties" had met with disappointing results at the polls in the Federal election. Wage reductions and unemployment were the order of the day. And finally the labor bureaucracy were laying plans to canalize the mass movement, which is beginning to pick up again, by the organization of the "safe and sane" Labor Party.

A call was sent out for a preliminary conference to consider the question of establishing a Workers' Party of Canada on militant lines. At this preliminary conference a rough program and constitution were adopted and the Provisional Organization Committee was appointed to prepare plans for the Constitutent Convention of the Workers' Party. The upshot was the recently held convention of February 17th-20th.

III.

This convention was characterized chiefly by the spirit of fundamental unity and earnest desire for activity. The Communists did not direct this convention by virtue of any "mechanical control" but simply because they were best prepared, were aware of the issues most distinctly, did the most thinking, worked most energetically, and had in general the best organization. The independent elements like the Finnish organization accepted this Communist leadership without question. But the Western, former S.P. of C. elements, came with an original program calling for an open Communist Party with frank acceptance of the twenty-one points [Theses on the conditions of admission to the Communist International]. They suspected that the Eastern delegates were working for a moderate, milk-and-watery program, and since these S.P. of C. Left-wingers had split from their party on just this very issue of the twenty-one points, they felt that they would be placed in an impossible position if they went back West with any program short of their original conception. A frank explanation, however, that a Canadian Section of the Comintern already existed and that an open Communist Party would not at the present moment be oppor-tune, along with the explanation of the Communist delegates that an open Communist Party was their objective also, after the experience, activity and mass contact of the Workers' Party for a year or so, enabled both sides to reach an accord. It was agreed, however, that the time was ripe for the Workers' Party to recognize more or less openly the spiritual leadership of the Communist International and the principle of proletarian dictatorship.

The only discordant moment at the convention, if it can be called discordant, in view of the fact that the delegates were almost unanimous in their rejection of his attitude, was the debate on Labor Union policy precipitated by R.B. Russell of Winnipeg strike fame and fraternal delegate of the O.B.U. As is perhaps generally known, the overwhelming majority of the Canadian workers belong to the "International" unions affiliated with the American Federation of Labor, and finding a national expression in the Canadian Trades and Labor Congress. Then there are various independent unions like the Canadian Federation of Labor, which bases itself upon the principles of national organization, refusing to send union moneys out of the country. There are French-Canadian Catholic unions of Quebec dominated by the clergy. There is the Lumber Workers Industrial Union, strong and radical, originally syndicalistic but now affiliated with the R.I.L.U. And then there is the "One Big Union" balloted upon by the Western workers at the time when the revolutionary wave in Europe was at its crest, and when syndicalism and Bolshevism were often confused, and actually formed after the Winnipeg general strike. Since its formation the O.B.U. movement in some way becomes isolated from the main body of the trade union movement, it becomes easier for the capitalist class to harry and destroy it. The O.B.U. movement did not arouse the enthusiasm of the workers of the industrial East, who remained attached to the A.F. of L.; the government's clubbing of the Winnipeg strike intimidated numbers of even the Western workers. Finally, the ideas of the Communist International and the Red Trade Union International, which make the consolidation and unity of the Trade Union movement the great revolutionary desideratum, have awakened a desire in the militant workers for a unification of all forces of the Canadian Trade Union movement, a healing of the splits of the past. Russell spent his time trying to demonstrate the superiority of the O.B.U. "structure" over the A.F. of L. structure, shirking the main issue which is the consolidation of the Trade Union movement and its re-organization from within the existing unions by amalgamating related crafts on an industrial union basis. The Western delegates, some of whom had been as prominent as Russell himself in the formation of the O.B.U., stood solidly with the Eastern delegates in repudiating his point of view.

IV.

What are the prospects of the Party? The Workers' Party should be regarded as the potential Communist Party of today, and the open Communist Party of the near future. It is the only militant political organization of the workers in the field. With the exception of the Maritime Provinces it has established nation-wide connection. The membership of the Party is thoroughly imbued with the necessity of striving to mould the

Party into a party of action, a party of the masses. The Party recognizes the urgent necessity of wresting the control of the organized labor movement from out [of] the hands of the labor bureaucrats. It recognizes that the organized labor movement gives the political tone to the working-class of the country. It is therefore embarking on becoming an integral part of the labor movement without losing its own party integrity and identity. It will strive to swing the Canadian Labor movement into line with the revolutionary labor movement of the world. The Party has been organized but a very short time, yet it is already admitted even by the leaders of the Canadian Labor Party to be a potential force to be reckoned with. At the same time it is being watched by the workers of the whole country, those, that is, not yet of the militant vanguard, to see what the calibre of its activities and influence will be, and there is little doubt that if the Party continues to work in the spirit of the program and policies adopted by the Convention it will indeed not disappoint expectations and will become the leading political force of the workers generally.

Manifesto of the Workers' Party of Canada

To the Workers of Canada:

FELLOW WORKERS—At a conference held at the Labour Temple, Toronto, on Sunday, December 11, 1921, 51 accredited delegates from points between Winnipeg, Montreal, Guelph, and Timmins, decided unanimously to endorse the call for the formation of the Workers' Party of Canada. The general feeling of the conference was that the need for a party of strength, of action, of feeling, was never more urgent than now.

The Development of American Imperialism—The frantic efforts of Imperialist diplomats at Washington to form alliances strong enough to hold up under the shock of the recent world war, the sparring for position in the world's markets without actually causing open conflict must prove to the workers of the world that another "last" war to end war is inevitable.

The capitalist class of the United States are having it brought home to them forcibly that they cannot maintain the industries created by their peculiar position during the war, while the economic structure of Europe crumbles under their noses. With the menace of bankruptcy facing many of their class, with the added menace of nearly 6,000,000 unemployed, the American capitalists are beginning to question their false sense of economic security, and seek to strengthen their position by imperialist alliances.

Britain's Insecurity—The future position of Britain's vast emporium, which she fondly calls her empire, is more uncertain. However Washington

---

The "Manifesto of the Workers Party of Canada" was adopted by the preliminary conference held in Toronto, December 11, 1921.

Initially printed in *Workers Guard* and reprinted in *Labor Organization in Canada 1922.*

may help to solve the immediate problems, there will remain several serious obstacles to permanent peace. Australia can never regard Japan as an ally, while Canada's possible development as an industrialist capitalist power makes her more and more dependent upon the United States.

The growing influence of Wall Street is making itself felt, at the expense of the "Mother Country", and young Miss Canada is becoming positively ungrateful in this respect by flirting with her powerful neighbour, and already shows signs which indicate that the wooing of Uncle Sam is affecting the economic position of John Bull in this country.

The Weakness of the Workers—Japan, France and Germany all present their problems, and the capitalist form of production prevents a peaceful solution of these problems. In the face of this, whither are we of the working class drifting? Drifting is an expression which covers our position clearly. Betrayed during the war by the false promises of capitalist statesmen, we sacrificed ourselves by the million. Those who stayed at home were accused of riotous living, of bleeding the country in her hour of need by demanding wages which would break the Empire, but which we know never once overtook the mad increase in the cost of living.

Our organizations and parties of working class tendencies succumbed to the atmosphere of looseness, of inactivity, during the period following the armistice. We neglected to avail ourselves of the opportunities for consolidating our forces, and when the after effects of the war began to be felt we were powerless to act. Winnipeg is the one bright spot in our development since the war, and we have failed to follow up this example of what is possible by organized effort, in a most unsatisfactory manner.

The Unemployment Situation—And now we are suffering for our sins by seeing hundreds of thousands of unemployed in Canada and scarcely a whimper coming from them. The unemployed are not alone to be condemned for this, but we also, the advanced, class-conscious section of the working class, must share the blame to no small extent. The time has come for a movement which will link up all forces willing to work for the emancipation of the workers. It is not enough to tell the unemployed the cause of their miserable plight, and then to sit back with our arms folded and feel that our revolutionary fervour has been expressed in the best possible manner.

The Workers' Party of Canada proposes to line up the forces of the unemployed, who will eventually learn the folly of sitting back, waiting for paternal assistance from our governing bodies. We can never obtain assistance without a fight, and the fight must be waged upon the battle cry of "Work or Compensation at Trade Union Rates of Wages." Undoubtedly the capitalist state will raise its ugly head during such agitational struggles, and then, and only then, will the masses realize the full power of the state together with its qualities of oppression and suppression which are the reasons for its existence.

Our Appeal to Trade Unionists—The W.P. of C. appeals to all progressive trade unionists to come into its ranks. The trade union movement must be strengthened preparatory to the coming struggles. The universal campaign by the bosses for the open shop has not been abandoned. The fight has only now commenced and we are but experiencing a lull in the storm of attack, which will only break out with increased fury next spring.

The capitalist class refuse to accept the responsibility for the present crisis, and are vainly hoping for the revival of trade which will bring the sunshine into their lives and profits to their pockets. The international complications touched upon above will not permit a revival of any consequence, and they will turn upon organized labour. They know that organized labour is the last stumbling block in their path, which, once removed, will allow them to ride rough-shod over our fellows and will permit them to grind us down into the depths of poverty, misery, and starvation.

The W.P. of C. seeks to prevent this by strengthening the unions, by striving toward making them fighting organizations, by perfecting the available machinery, and by endeavouring to develop the feeling of militancy which will cause them to fight back when attacked by the wolves of capitalism.

To those industrialists who are as yet but members of industrial organizations, and who, through a desire to ignore political parties, or who are dissatisfied with existing political parties, remain aloof, we direct our appeal for support.

The bitter class struggle now being waged must prove that we shall use every avenue of approach, every possible opportunity, to weaken the capitalist state. The issue was never more clear than now. Class against class is the order of the day, and we who are of the subjected class must learn to fight our battles just as viciously as do our oppressors. The industrial weapon is not enough, we must organize our forces so as to take advantage of every weak point in the armour of our oppressors if we are to progress.

To Members of the Socialist Party of Canada—To members of the S.P. of C. we make special appeal. For over a year now your party has talked on the question of affiliation with the Third International and the referendum is only now being submitted. This method of action, while pleasing, no doubt, to our sense of comfortable discussion, is too comfortable to make for progress. If progress is to be made the workers must be taught to reason from the basis of action, rather than that of academic discussion.

We appeal to you to reconsider your position and to decide whether it is in conformity with the needs of the day. These have been briefly outlined and the Workers' Party of Canada claim that they call for a geater degree of virility than has been shown by your party up to the present.

To Members of Labour Parties—To all members of labour parties throughout the Dominion we point out the weaknesses of your position. The recent elections, fresh in your minds, with the added sting of ignominious defeat, emphasize how poorly equipped you are with the necessary machinery for progress.

Recent events should have the effect of making you reconsider your attitude. The W.P. of C. are satisfied that you are not merely playing with the question of the struggle between capital and labour. We also feel assured that you are open to adopt new methods of action shown to be necessary by reason of changed conditions.

The rank and file of the labour parties have trusted to leaders who are unable to carry on a vigorous fight against the exploiters of labour. For example, the miserable compromise made with the farmers in Ontario only resulted in some "leaders" gaining cabinet rank—as far as the working masses are concerned, nothing tangible has resulted from the fusion. A party with such a record cannot possibly hope to gain the confidence of the workers.

As for the platforms of labour parties, there exists a marked resemblance between that of the I.L.P., for instance, and the Conservative party. They both agree that the principle of "public ownership" is correct, for the Conservatives are now swearing that nothing short of government ownership will satisfy their thirst for progress. Thus, by reason of this agreement of principles, labour parties become mere tails of the capitalist parties, and, as such, have no reason for existence.

Workers of labour parties! leave those leaders who are eagerly trying to squeeze into capitalist politics and come over to the W.P. of C., which is determined to stand up and fight the battle of the workers, shunning the efforts of other parties to patronize us by adopting a few of our leaders.

Is there not evidence enough at hand to prove that "democracy" is at best a miserable sham, and Parliament one of its most miserable expressions? Your present political beliefs only tend to destroy the militancy of the workers, who, under the influence of such beliefs, betray inclinations to trust to leaders to emancipate them from their miserable conditions rather than develop a feeling that the general rank and file themselves must act in order to produce results.

To Unattached Workers—Finally, we appeal to all workers who are unattached. We put the question of a Workers' Party squarely before you. Are you sufficiently blind to your class interests as to be able to ignore our call to action? With the increased determination of the ruling class to grind the workers down, we must offer more keen resistance upon the part of the workers. It is no longer possible to remain outside of the fight. All are concerned and all must prepare to participate.

So we address our manifesto to all workers. We cannot sit down and wait patiently for capitalism to collapse. Conditions call for fight, for action, and with the prospects of further unemployment, a more intensified open shop campaign, and, in the near future, Imperialist war, the Workers' Party of Canada issues this call. If we are to survive we must be free from capitalist domination. If the capitalist class is to dominate we must suffer more bitterly.

The issue is clear, therefore, between Unemployment and Prosperity; Organized Tyranny and Political Freedom; Capitalist State and Workers' Republic.

There is no half-way line, and the W.P. of C., recognizing that unity of action is essential if the workers are to triumph, call upon all to rally to the banner of progressive action.

PROVISIONAL PLATFORM OF THE WORKERS' PARTY OF CANADA

1. *Workers' Republic*—Clearly the problems which call for working class action centre about the capitalist system; the alternative to the capitalist system is a working class government. The Workers' Party shall lead the workers in the struggle toward the establishment of the Workers' Republic of Canada.

2. *Political Action*—The role of the Workers' Party in electoral campaigns shall be to expose the sham democracy, with which we are afflicted. The Workers' Party shall take part, whenever possible, in all such campaigns with this end in view, so that ultimately the real issue will be laid clear, and we, the working class, shall eventually triumph at the expense of the enemies of the working class, their capitalist oppressors.

3. *Trade Unionism*—To help educate the Trade Unionists to appreciate the possibilities of their organizations as definite factors in carrying on the class battles caused by capitalist oppression, to initiate a movement to expose the tyranny and treachery of the reactionary labour bureaucrats and to definitely create real fighting working class units.

4. *Party of Action*—The party shall be composed of militant class-conscious workers who shall be subject to the discipline and direction of the national executive committee, which shall be the highest expression of the party between conventions. Democratic centralization shall be the guiding principle of the Workers' Party, and all members will be required to submit to the direction of the party in all struggles affecting the workers, such as unemployment, wage reductions, open shop campaigns, etc., etc.

5. *Party Press*—The party shall eventually acquire a party press in order to give expression to our needs. This press shall be owned by the party, and under the control and direction of the national executive committee.

Working Men and Working Women! We call upon you to play your parts in the establishment of a real live working class party which shall ultimately produce a fighting machine able to organize and direct the opressed masses in their struggles for political and economic freedom. Rally to the call for complete emancipation! In answer to the oppression of the capitalist class let our battle cry be:

"Workers of the World, Unite! You have nothing to lose but your chains; you have a world to gain."

Programme and Platform of the Workers' Party

The outbreak of the world war marked the close of a great historic period.

"Programme and Platform of the Workers' Party" was adopted by the

Capitalism, the social system based on the class ownership of the means of production and maintained by the coercive power of the bourgeois state, was then in its period of expansion. That was a period of mass production, accumulation of capital, extension of the world market by the acquisition of colonies and spheres of influence to absorb the surplus of commodities and capital. It is true that, as a result of its anarchic production, capitalism suffered from current crises even then, but assisted by the safety valve of immigration it was able regularly to recover its equilibrium. It is also true that there were always great masses of workers on the poverty line; but it was not these masses that determined the policies of the working class.

For that was also the great period of the development of the organized labour movement with its trade unions, cooperatives and political parties.

And since the enormous profits that the capitalist class derives from the exploitation of the workers both at home and abroad disposed it to share a little of the spoil rather than invite a fundamental challenge to the capitalist system, the policy of organized labour tended to be conservative, reformist, and opportunist.

Imperialism and the Labour Movement Today—For this policy of adaptation to the social and economic conditions of capitalism the workers were to pay a terrible price. In spite of peace tribunals and their hypocritical professions, [owing to] the economic rivalries engendered by the monopolist tendencies of the great Imperialist powers [the] subsequent explosion came, the bewildered working class was caught completely off its guard, and the organized labour movement transformed by the treachery of the reactionary labour leaders into an adjunct of the Imperialist war machine.

As a result of the prolonged slaughter that followed, international exchanges collapsed, factories closed down, millions of workers were thrown into the ranks of the unemployed and the very foundations of capitalism undermined. Faced by this situation the capitalist class is making frantic efforts to re-establish the equilibrium of capitalism by a general attack on the living standards of the workers.

Wages have been cut, agreements broken and concessions withdrawn. Finally in order to make its systematic campaign for the reduction of the workers' living standards effective, they have launched an equally ruthless offensive for the destruction of the mass organizations of the workers.

Under these changed conditions the international labour movement is of necessity being transformed into an organ of revolutionary struggle against capitalism.

The Russian Revolution and the First Workers' Republic—The general revolutionary movement at the close of the imperialist war, and during the succeeding period, was marked by unprecedented intensity and

---

founding convention in February 1922.

Initially printed in *The Worker* and reprinted in *Labor Organization in Canada 1922*.

particularly by the Russian revolution which established the first workers' republic. Although this first revolutionary wave was checked in other countries, the Russian Soviet Republic has, nevertheless, been able to withstand the united efforts of the imperialist powers to overthrow the rule of the workers, and remains the incarnation of the struggle of the world proletariat for its emancipation.

The Workers' Party recognize in the Russian revolution the first section of "the world revolution". Basing its policies on the international character of the revolutionary struggle, it will strive to make the Canadian labour movement an integral part of the revolutionary movement of the world. Disillusioned by the treacherous conduct of their own leaders and inspired by the proletarian revolution of Russia, the workers of the world have organized the Communist International. Despite the bitter opposition of the capitalists and their labour lieutenants, the Communist International has grown rapidly, and become a world power, the citadel and hope of the workers of every country. The Workers' Party will expose the Second International, which is continually splitting the ranks of labour and betraying the working masses to the enemy. It will also warn and guard the workers against the attempts of the so-called two-and-a-half international [a centrist grouping] to mislead the workers. Further recognizing that the Communist International is the only real centre of world revolutionary activities, the Workers' Party will strive to rally the workers under the banner of the Third International.

PLATFORM

The Workers' Party has arisen in consequence of the failure of the hitherto existing parties to co-ordinate and lead the working class in its struggles against capitalism. The Socialist parties have practically disappeared from the political scene owing to their sectarianism. The reformist labour parties have failed to recognize the class struggle and function chiefly as electioneering machines. In opposition to the principles and tactics of the above parties the Workers' Party will strive to be at one and the same time a party of action which is also the party of the masses.

The general programme of the Workers' Party shall be:

1. To consolidate the existing labour organizations and develop them into organizations of militant struggle against capitalism, to permeate the labour unions and strive to replace the present reactionary leadership by revolutionary leadership.

2. To participate in the elections and the general political life of the country. Its representatives in the various legislative and administrative institutions will expose the sham democracy of capitalism and help to mobilize the workers for the final struggle against the capitalist state. They will give conscious and public expression to the every day grievances of the working class in concrete demands upon the capitalist governments and their institutions.

3. To lead in the fight for the immediate needs of the workers, broaden and

deepen their demands, organize and develop out of their every day struggles a force for the abolition of capitalism.

4. To work for the overthrow of capitalism and capitalist dictatorship by the conquest of political power, the establishment of the workng class dictatorship and of the workers' republic.

Workers' Party Resolutions on Labour Unions

1. The trade union movement of Canada in common with the trade union movement of the world is experiencing the gravest crisis in its history. Already before the world war the policies and structure of the trade unions were being proved inadequate to cope with the growing concentration and solidarity of capital. But the changes wrought in the very basis of capitalism as a result of the world war have made it impossible to postpone any longer a re-examination and solution of the problems that confront the trade union movement, particularly the problems of policy and organization.

In order to re-establish the equilibrium of capitalism, the capitalist class has launched a general offensive for the reduction of the workers' living standards, making at the same time a determined onslaught for the destruction of the trade union movement itself. Utterly unprepared for this attack, the trade unions are almost everywhere in disorderly retreat. All along the line wage reductions are being enforced with only the slightest resistance on the part of the unions. With equal helplessness the trade unions face the problem of unemployment. Unless the unions begin to understand that the era of conciliation and arbitration in the class struggle is passed, and recognize the changed conditions of the struggle between capital and labour, there is danger that the efforts of the capitalist class will succeed.

Under these circumstances the most vital task which confronts the working class is the establishment of a united front to resist the aggressions of the capitalist class. It follows that the role of the labour unions in the building up of this united front is to bring about the co-ordination and consolidation of the entire labour union movement of the country on the basis of militant struggles. Not only, however, is this consolidation necessary, but equally essential is the international organization of all the militant unions of the world. The only force that has proven itself capable of recognizing the needs of the trade union movement imposed by the changed conditions, and capable of rallying all the militant forces of the world labour movement, is the Red International of Labour Unions.

2. To accomplish the tasks indicated above, not only must the policy pursued by some groups in the past of seeking to revolutionize the labour movement by splitting away to form new ideal unions be completely

---

Resolutions adopted by the WPC founding convention, February 18, 1922.

Originally printed in *The Worker* and reprinted in *Labor Organization in Canada 1922.*

abandoned, not only must dual unionism be vigorously combated, but all tendencies to consolidate the trade union movement by amalgamating the related crafts on the basis of one union for each industry must be positively fostered within the existing trade unions. Towards this end the membership of the Workers' Party will work in co-operation with all militant elements in the unions for the formation and development of a left wing. Along with this effort, towards the formation of industrial unions, goes the policy of strengthening the local and district councils for the purpose of co-ordinating the activities of the various labour unions in matters confined to the local situation. In all localities and industries, where the old trade unions are definitely the predominant bodies, the Workers' Party will oppose all dual unions or secessionist efforts. In localities or industries where the independent unions have achieved some measure of constructive organization, and where the old trade unions are weak, the membership of the Workers' Party will work within their respective organizations for the purpose of bringing about united action in all struggles, while seeking at the same time to bring about their unification with the general labour union movement. In these instances, where for various reasons the dominant union is outside the general labour union movement, the Workers' Party will support such unions in all regular organization matters while endeavouring at the same time to align them with the general organized movement.

The Workers' Party calls attention to the difference in function between the Workers' Party and the labour unions. The unions necessarily include even the most backward and politically unconscious elements of the working class. The Workers' Party, on the other hand, confines its membership to the more politically conscious. Nevertheless the attitude of seeming political neutrality adopted by the trade unions really plays into the hands of the capitalist class, and must be abandoned and the trade unions brought into alignment with the militant international labour movement finding its expression in the Red International of Labour Unions. The membership of the Workers' Party will assist in the consolidation of the labour unions on militant lines by permeating these organizations with a revolutionary spirit, exposing the reactionary and treacherous policies of the labour unions' bureaucracy, stimulating the sense of aggressive rank and file control, and resisting to the utmost the expulsion of militants and the splitting up of the unions in general.

Report on Industrial Activity

In presenting his report the industrial organizer drew attention to the fact that our industrial policy, being as it was, a new departure in the field of

---

The "Report on Industrial Activity" was presented to the Second Workers Party Convention in February 1923 by Tim Buck, the party's "Industrial Organizer." It was printed, in slightly modified form, in *The Worker* and then reprinted in *Labor Organization in Canada 1923*.

revolutionary politics, presented the party with new tasks and problems, a fact which it was necessary to bear in mind when reviewing our work and measuring our accomplishments.

Adopting a broad viewpoint and advocating unity of action on the part of all workers regardless of the name of the organization to which they belong, the progress we have made in industrial activity during the past year is very gratifying. In face of the apathy and in many places actual hostility to co-operation in any form whatsoever, it is almost sufficient to challenge belief.

With organized groups of party members in sixteen central labour councils, over sixty local railroad bodies, throughout both districts of the coal miners, in two big metal mining camps, and a great many of the largest lumbering centers, it can be safely said that our membership constitutes a continuous thread of militant activity stretching from coast to coast. While the work is still of necessity in its initial stages, positive results so far are such as to justify us in the belief that we are on the high road to becoming the dominant influence in the left wing union movement all over the country. The miners of Nova Scotia, the Edmonton strike and the Alberta Federation convention are three of the outstanding activities upon which the party membership made their influence felt. Even more important, however, in its implications is the fact that we have no less than fifty-six organized groups of railroad workers stretching from coast to coast and including representatives of thirteen out of the sixteen standard crafts with three of the so-called Big Four.

Co-operating with the rebel element in the railroad, building trades, needle trades and other unions, our members are finding a common ground of struggle in the programme of the Trade Union Educational League, and wherever possible our members are urged to take the initiative in organizing lead groups and arousing interest in the rank and file movement for amalgamation. The left wing movement is developing into a broad mass movement and our party, having been by its clear and correct policy and aggressive activity one of the principal factors in developing the left wing movement to this point, it is vitally necessary that the work be intensified in every possible way.

While our policy was correct and we have been, on the whole, extremely successful, experience of the past year has demonstrated two tendencies present in almost every locality against which we must be on our guard, namely: The tendency to drop into the old position of negative opposition to officialdom and everybody else who is not a revolutionist or a good left winger. In many cases our membership are being forced into this position by the skillful manoeuvring of reactionaries and conservatives in the skirmishes which are to-day taking place in every local preliminary to the real struggle for rank and file control. It is essential that we study this problem carefully, and rather than being forced into opposition let us take the initiative on a positive programme of concrete demands, fight for something the rank and file want such as amalgamation (in the case of miners, loggers, etc., international affiliation). These today are real needs and slogans expressing the desires of the rank and file. Organize a group around these slogans and far from dogmatically opposing officialdom, officialdom will quickly declare itself and give you a clear-cut issue. The other danger is the tendency of lining up with centrists, twisters, fakirs and all who pay lip service to revolutionary ideals and progressive trade unionism. This is the greatest danger of all and can only be guarded against by making it impossible for any man to align himself with you without declaring definitely for a programme at least as advanced as that of the T.U.E.L.

Our immediate tasks are to make industrial work one of the principal activities of every branch; smash down the dogmatism and fatalism with which many of our members are still imbued, and co-operate with all rebel elements on an immediate programme of militant unions, leading the workers ever leftward, ever into greater unity and clarity, inspiring the rank and file with the desire for self-expression, thereby insuring success in the great struggles of the future for Communism.

RESOLUTION

The second annual convention of the Workers' Party of Canada reaffirmed its labour union policy adopted at the first convention. Experience of the past year has definitely proved the soundness of this policy, particularly in combating the disruptive influence of dual unionism and secession, setting up in their place a policy of unity through amalgamation of the craft unions into industrial unions powerful enough to protect the workers, and broad enough to include every worker in the industry. The policy of fighting for militant leadership, as against the passive and reformist bureaucracy, has yielded great results and has proved that the workers of Canada are ready for a forward step in labour unionism. They are preparing to take this step in conjunction with the militant unionists of the United States, under the leadership of the Workers' Party of Canada, which has been the outstanding exponent of unity in the labour movement. The slogans of amalgamation, the Labour Party, and the Red International, have taken firm root in the Canadian Unions.

United action of Workers' Party members with all other sincere and progressive workers for our trade union programme has been brought about through the medium of the Trade Union Educational League. We call upon all our members to participate in the activity of the league, and whole-heartedly support its work; to identify themselves with the international industrial committees being established, such as the International Committee for the Amalgamation of the Sixteen Standard Railway Unions, and to keep the Canadian movement firmly united in one uniform movement covering the North American continent; with one common programme of amalgamation, militant leadership and the rest of the league programme. The fate of the Canadian left wing is entirely bound up with that of the United States. National autonomy is an illusion; international unity the need.

Experience of the past year has proved that we must definitely oppose certain tendencies in the labour movement. Particularly is this true of such disruptive efforts as those of officials of the One Big Union, which, through the so-called Western Shopmen's Committee, attempted to set up claims to represent railroaders, not by bringing them into the organization, but merely on the strength of an indiscriminate collection of signatures. This is on a par with the rankest peonage system of the most reactionary unions, and cannot be tolerated in a healthy labour movement. We will fight such destructive tactics with all the strength at our command.

The party pledges itself to support all real organization campaigns to organize the unorganized. In those fields and industries where there are no unions, party members will form themselves into propaganda nuclei, to prepare the ground and give active assistance to the unions. Particularly do we call upon our foreign-born members to take hold of this work with vigor. The solidarity of the native-born with the foreign-born workers is a crying need in the union movement.

Unity of the Canadian with the American left wing, as well as unity of the native with the foreign-born worker, necessitates a systematic campaign of education. One of the principal means to this end is the labour press. Our party press should give special attention to these problems, and *The Worker* should be given a prime place in trade union work. In addition, the organs of more general circulation and importance must be circulated as much as possible. This is particularly true of the "Labour Herald" among all trade unionists, of the "Amalgamation Advocate" among the railroaders, "The Industrialist" of New York among the printing trade workers, etc. Party branches, as well as T.U.E.L. groups, should regularly sell and distribute these papers, especially the "Labour Herald". Members should maintain the closest possible relations with *The Worker* and left wing press in general, furnishing them with all news and information concerning developments in Canada, such as the adoption of amalgamation resolutions and decisions, etc.

We recognize the labour unions as the basic organizations of the working class, and are convinced that no party can become the guiding influence in the revolutionary movement except it is rooted deeply in these organizations. The Workers' Party calls upon its members everywhere to continue and intensify their trade union work, which is rapidly giving our party this necessary foundation. This is the basic and fundamental preparation which alone can build up the necessary power leading to the establishment of the workers' republic.

Resolution on the United Front

1. Labour throughout the world finds itself confronted with a vicious

---

The "Resolution on the United Front," probably written by Maurice Spector, was adopted by the February 1923 WPC Convention.
Original in *The Worker,* reprinted in *Labor Organization in Canada 1923.*

offensive of capital to crush its spirit, destroy its organizations, and reduce its living standards. This capitalist offensive takes different forms at different times; now it is an attack on the eight-hour day, now a reduction in wages, or an attempt to establish the open shop, and finally the utter throwing overboard of the mask of democracy and the ruthless terrorism and destruction of the labour movement by the Fascisti dictatorship, those elements of the bourgeoisie which tear up their own constitution and keep labour down by open force of arms, burning of trade union halls, etc. This latest Fascist form of capitalist offensive is not unlikely even in America in the developing conditions. Labour in Canada has the experience of the Citizens' Committee of the Winnipeg strike.

2. Owing to various historical reasons, the labour movement is, unfortunately, in a split up and demoralized condition today, under the active political and industrial oppression of capital. If labour is to put up an effective resistance to save itself (this attack is sometimes allegedly directed only against the so-called "extremist" organizations, but it is really an attack against labour as a whole), the workers, no matter how much they differ as to final aims and principles, must establish a common front of struggle and resistance on both political and industrial fields.

3. In Europe, where the working class has a longer development behind it, where there are already great political mass parties of labour to form a coalition and where there is a developing shop council movement to provide such a coalition with its driving force, the united front can already find expression in the desire for the labour government as the means of resistance. Here, where the labour movement has been so backward that craft unionism still prevails on the industrial field and the majority of our workers have not as yet developed even the notion of independent political action, our united front task consists (a) on the industrial field, of working for the amalgamation of the existing craft unions into a series of massive industrial unions (in this connection we endorse the work of the Trade Union Educational League); (b) to be in the forefront of the development of the Labour Party. As the Labour Party is organized on a federated basis, inclusive of industrial as well as political organizations, it becomes the instrument for establishing a common front on all the vital issues of the labour movement. The Workers' Party not only re-affirms its resolution to work inside the Labour Party, but clearly recognizes the necessity for making it a really effective instrument of aggressive political action. The Workers' Party will join and strengthen the sections of the Labour Party, wherever there are such, take the initiative in their creation where these are absent, will attempt to bring about their greater co-ordination throughout the country; in short will strive for a strong, united, Dominion-wide party, filled with a truly proletarian spirit, and broadened conception of political action, in place of the present narrowly parliamentarian conception. The basis and guarantee for a real proletarian development of the Labour Party must be the redoubled effort to renovate the trade union movement.

All this does not, of course, mean that the Workers' Party will sink its distinctive aims, principles and organization as a Communist Party. On the contrary, it regards the maintenance of its aims and principles, its freedom of criticism and agitation and its identity as an organization, to be the guarantee of further progress in the labour movement. But a common programme of action on which to unite the workers can be worked out on the basis of the immediate struggles of the working class, such as: (a) the fight against unemployment; (b) against the open shop; (c) for the eight-hour day; (d) against espionage, whether by government or employers; (e) for free speech; (f) for the freedom to picket; (g) against injunctions as a means of intervening in labour struggles; (h) against the intervention of the police and military forces of the State in labour struggles; (i) for the establishment of complete political and economic relations with Soviet Russia.

III. The Birth of Canadian Stalinism

Maurice Spector: Letter to the Political Committee

Toronto, November 6, 1928
To the Political Committee,
Communist Party of Canada

Following upon the motion at yesterday's session of the Polcom to endorse the expulsion of the three comrades, J.P. Cannon, Max Shachtman, and Martin Abern, from the Workers Party of America for their stand on behalf of the opening of a serious discussion of the fundamental problems of the Communist International, a motion which I was unable to support, certain questions have been directed to me by the Polcom as to my own position. These may be boiled down to the following:

First, whether I believe that the ideological line of "Trotskyism" is correct and whether I am prepared to carry on an aggressive campaign against "Trotskyism" and the comrades who had been expelled from the W.P. for their solidarity with the platform of the Russian Opposition.

In reply, I wish to state that the bureaucratic expulsion of these comrades and the attempt to ratify their expulsion by our own Polcom in mechanical fashion has precipitated [and] crystalized my own stand. Since 1923 I have had reservations about the line of the Communist International, but I have

---

Maurice Spector's "Letter to the Political Committee" was written immediately after his suspension from the Communist Party for refusing to support the expulsion of James Cannon, Max Shachtman, and Martin Abern from the U.S. party. He was expelled a few days later.

A shortened version of the letter appeared in *The Militant* in 1928. The full text was found and made available to me by Professor William Rodney.

always relegated my own doubts into the background in the interests of Comintern and Party discipline and unity. I was not fully convinced that the discussions of the Lessons of October "catastrophe" in Germany had been carried on in the way it would have been while Lenin was an active participant in the life of our International. I was not satisfied that the estimation of the International situation made by the Fifth Congress was correct. In my view the fight against the Russian opposition dating back from 1923 was confused by the unreal issue of "Trotskyism." The conception of Bolshevization was mechanical. The "discussions" that were carried on on this issue were mostly farcical; a one-sided presentation of the documents of the majority and the systematic suppression of the documents of the Opposition. As an instance of the bureaucratic method of "discussing," there was the demand made for a stand by our Political Committee condemning "Trotskyism" during the period of the discussion of L.D. Trotsky's "Lessons of October," before even any of us here had read the very preface about which the whole controversy raged in the Soviet Union. I believe that our Polcom took a correct stand in the cablegram it sent in reply on this question.

I had always hoped that the "pressure of events," the logic of history in the present period of relative stabilization of Capitalism, would straighten out the official line of the Comintern. It is now clear to me that it is insufficient for a revolutionist to "wait and see." His active ideological intervention is necessary if a correct line, failing which all discipline is hollow, is to be arrived at.

An additional reason for my hesitation was that I, along with hundreds of thousands of other members of the sections of the C.I., had no first hand information as to the position of the Russian Opposition, but only the garbled extracts contained in the official thesis. On my way back from the Sixth Congress, however, I fortunately came into possession of the suppressed documents of the Opposition, which I have carefully studied since and which have resolved all my doubts and brought me to my present unequivocal position.

In reply to the question whether I am prepared "to wage an aggressive campaign against 'Trotskyism,'" I can assure the Polcom that I am prepared to wage an aggressive campaign for Leninism. Historical Trotskyism was liquidated with the entrance of L.D. Trotsky into the Communist Party and his collaboration with Lenin following his return to Russia in 1917. Trotsky has declared before the Russian Party that in all questions bearing any character of principle at all in which he had differences with Lenin prior to 1917, Lenin was correct. The revival of the issue of so-called "Trotskyism" by the majority in 1924 and 1925 was an attempt to obscure the real issues by an artificial issue. Zinoviev, who was one of the leading comrades in the fight against Trotsky, has not only admitted since that the latter was correct in his fight for internal Party democracy in 1923-4, but also that the issue of "Trotskyism" was then invented by himself and a few other comrades for strategical purposes, to link up the current differences with differences that had long passed into history.

The comrades in the vanguard of the fight against "Trotskyism" were most of them further removed from the position of Lenin on his return to Russia and his presentation of the April Theses of 1917, than L.D. Trotsky. Zinoviev and Kamenev, Rykov, Losovsky, etc., were opposed to the insurrection by which the Bolsheviks conquered power and were for a coalition of all the Socialist parties. Comrade Stalin, prior to Lenin's return, had written articles for co-operation with Tseretelli. When so much is made of the differences between Trotsky and Lenin in the course of the revolution itself, it should be borne in mind that all these differences are being exaggerated for factional ends, and that silence is maintained on the differences that other comrades, Bukharin for instance, had with Lenin, but who is nevertheless regarded as a one hundred percent Leninist. Comrade Bukharin not only fought Lenin on the Brest Litovsk issue but also on the Trade Union question and on the question of State Capitalism. On the Peasant question he was the author of one of the most dangerous slogans ever put out by a leading comrade: the slogan of "enrich yourselves," the objective significance of which meant a call on the Kulaks to intensify their exploitation of the poor peasantry. The present leader of the C.I., Bukharin, had to be overruled on the question of the validity of partial demands in the Communist Program by the intervention of Lenin, Trotsky and others at the Fourth Congress.

Not only did Lenin during his lifetime deny all slanderous rumors of any differences between himself and Trotsky on the Peasant Question, but up to his last days he considered L.D. Trotsky his closest collaborator as may be seen by the correspondence which passed between these two leaders of the revolution in the "Letter to the Institute of Party History" by L.D. Trotsky. Lenin called upon the latter to defend his views for him on the following questions: the National Question, the Question of Workers and Peasants Control, the Monopoly of Foreign Trade, the Struggle against Bureaucracy, etc. It is high time that a stop be put to the falsification of Party history that has accompanied the unscrupulous and demagogic campaign against the revolutionist who, next to Lenin, was the most authentic leader and organizer of the October revolution, and was so recognized by Lenin himself. Trotsky today stands foursquare for the maintenance of the principles of Leninism, uncontaminated by the opportunist deviations that have been smuggled into the Comintern and USSR policy by the present Rykov-Stalin-Bukharin regime and to which the lessons of the Chinese revolution, the economic situation in the USSR, the situation within the CPSU, and the experiences of the Anglo-Russian Committee bear eloquent witness.

For these are the real issues. In retrospect it is clear that the Sixth Congress, meeting after a delay of four years, nevertheless failed to measure up to its great tasks. Eclecticism and a zig-zag line replaced a real analysis of the rich treasures of political experience of the past four years. The discussion of the Chinese revolution, the greatest upheaval since the November Revolution, was utterly inadequate. As in the case of the discussion of the failure of October 1923 in Germany, the attempt to throw major responsibility for what happened on the leadership of the Chinese Communist Party will not down. The responsibility for the opportunism of our party in China lies in the first place with the ECCI and with the formulation of policy of Stalin, Bukharin, Martynov. Lenin at the II Congress proposed a clear line on the Colonial question, for the independence of the Communist Parties and the working class movement even in embryonic form; against the National bourgeoisie, struggle for proletarian hegemony in the National emancipation movement even when the National Revolution has only bourgeois democratic tasks to solve; constant propaganda of the Soviet idea and creation of Soviets at the earliest moment possible; finally, possibility of the non-capitalist development of backward colonial and semi-colonial countries on condition that they receive support from the USSR and the proletariat of the advanced capitalist countries.

Otherwise, Lenin pointed out, the alliance with the national bourgeoisie would be dangerous to the revolution. This alliance could only be effected on the basis that the bourgeoisie carried on an effective struggle against Imperialism and did not prevent the Communist Party from organizing the revolutionary action of the workers and peasants. Failure to exact these guarantees would lead to a repetition of the Kemalism of the Turkish national struggle which has made its peace with Imperialism. Nearly every one of these cardinal points of Lenin's revolutionary colonial policy was violated in China. By throwing up the smokescreen that the creation of Soviets would be tantamount to the dictatorship of the proletariat, despite the fact that Lenin proposed the Soviets already as a form of the democratic dictatorship of workers and peasants in the 1905 revolution, the leadership of the Comintern misrepresented the criticism and theses of the Opposition and covered up their own opportunist mistakes.

Our Chinese party was subordinated to the National bourgeoisie in the Kuomintang under the cover of the old Menshevik Martynov's policy of the "Bloc of Four Classes" (renunciation of the right to criticize Sun Yatsenism, renunciation of an illegal fighting apparatus and of the creation of cells in the National Army). The working class movement was subordinated to the Government of the National bourgeoisie (prohibition in certain cases of picketing and strikes, disarmament of the workers, etc.). The CP maintained silence at the beginning of the repression period (coup d'état of Chiang Kai-shek etc.). The Enlarged Executive of the CI did not subsequently straighten out the line. The slogan of Soviets was issued not when the revolutionary movement was at its height but when the bourgeoisie had already betrayed the movement against Imperialism and the workers and peasants were being decimated. Stalin was making a speech still hailing Chiang Kai-shek as a revolutionary warrior only a few days prior to Chiang Kai-shek's coup, in a speech which was criticized at the time by Comrade Radek, and which was of course suppressed to avoid compromising himself.

The opportunist line followed in the Chinese revolution is of course by no means isolated. I have dwelt at some length on the revision of Lenin's principles contained in the Stalin-Bukharin policy in China, and one could dwell with equal length on the opportunist line followed in the refusal to break with the traitorous British General Council in the Anglo-Russian Committee. The Anglo-Russian Committee was a political bloc between two trade union centers. The proposal of the Opposition demonstratively to break with the General Council was falsely represented as being parallel to leaving the old unions. Any Communist who reads the resolutions adopted by the Anglo-Russian conferences of Paris, July 1926 and Berlin, August 1926, and finally of the Berlin Conference at the beginning of April 1927 should convince himself that an absolutely impermissible capitulation line was followed. At the latter meeting the Soviet representatives went on record recognizing the General Council "as the sole representative and spokesman" of the British Trade Union movement at a time when the traitors of the General Council were suppressing the Minority Movement. But at the Enlarged Executive of May 1927, Comrade Bukharin sought to justify the Berlin capitulation by the theory of "exceptional circumstances," that is, that it was in the diplomatic interests of the Soviet Union which was under threat of war danger from the provocation of the British Government.

Such an attitude has little in common with the instructions of Lenin to the Soviet delegation that went to the Hague Conference, to ruthlessly unmask the Pacifists and Reformists. By the policy pursued in the Anglo-Russian Committee the British Communist Party developed such a degree of opportunism that it was at first even opposed to the Soviet Trade Union manifesto denouncing the treachery of the Left as well as the Right Labor fakers of the General Council, and wanted to continue a fight for the re-establishment of the moribund Anglo-Russian Committee. The whole line followed in the Anglo-Russian Committee was, like that in the Chinese Revolution, based on maneuvers with the Reformists at the top instead of regard for the unleashing of the mass movement below.

What is the social basis of these opportunist deviations? Unquestionably, the retardation of the World Revolution, the relative stabilization of Capitalism, the defeats in China, Germany, Great Britain, Bulgaria, etc., and the difficulties of socialist construction in the USSR have exercized their telling influence, and have provoked a desire upon the part of certain elements in the RCP to follow the line of lesser resistance, to solve the difficulties, National and International, not by the harder road of hewing to Leninism, but by the apparently easier theory of "socialism in one country."

Up to 1924, Stalin understood "that for the definitive victory of socialism, for the organization of socialist production, the efforts of one country and above all, of an agricultural country such as ours, are not sufficient. For this the efforts of several advanced countries are necessary." But after 1924 a theory was developed based obviously on a conviction that the stabilization of capitalism would last for decades, that the construction of Socialism could be completed within the USSR alone, granted only freedom from military intervention. This theory has nothing in common with Lenin's conception of the revolutionary character of the present epoch, and is akin more closely to the theory of Narodnikism (populism). It is a theory which, if its implications are followed is bound to lead to a form of National Socialism. From the economic point of view it is a Utopian mirage for which neither Marx nor Engels nor Lenin are responsible, and the program of the Comintern will never be a completely correct guide to the revolutionary movement unless it breaks with this theory.

The economic analysis of the Opposition on the situation within the USSR, on the danger of the growth of the kulak, the Nep man, and the bureaucrat has been completely vindicated. Undoubtedly there are Thermidorean elements in the country which are striving to bring their class pressure to bear on the Party. The highest duty of a revolutionist is to warn of these dangers and to propose the necessary measures to combat them. That was always the case while Lenin was alive.

The crisis last February in connection with the grain collection proved strikingly the danger of the Kulak. The events in Smolensk, the Don Basin, the Ukraine, etc., proved the absolute necessity not only for such a campaign of self criticism as Comrade Stalin felt the need to initiate, but for effective internal Party democracy. One of the first guarantees of such real Party democracy would be the return of the exiled revolutionary Oppositionists, and their reinstatement with full rights to their former positions in the Party.

In 1921, Lenin wrote the golden words, "It is necessary that every member of the Party should study calmly and with the greatest objectivity, first the substance of the differences of opinion, and then the development of the struggles within the Party. Neither the one nor the other can be done unless the documents of both sides are published. He who takes anybody's word for it is a hopeless idiot, who can be disposed of with a simple gesture of the hand..." I therefore consider it my duty to call upon the CEC of the Communist Party of Canada to set an example by carrying on a real discussion of the decisions and resolutions of the Sixth Congress and by publishing in the Party Press all the documents, Theses on China, on the Anglo-Russian Committee, etc., of the Opposition which have hitherto been suppressed. I further call upon our Party to take a stand for the unity of the Comintern and all its sections on the basis of Leninism and for the return of L.D. Trotsky and his comrades to their rightful positions in the Party.

I have been a foundation member of the Communist Party of Canada since its organization, in which I took a joint part. I have also been a member of the CEC practically all the time since. Regardless of the immediate organizational consequences, I find myself compelled to make the above statement and to further register the fact that nothing on earth can separate me from the Revolutionary Communist movement. Everything that I have stated flows from my conviction that the deviations from Leninism in the CI can and must be corrected by a struggle within the International and its sections.

Long Live the Communist International!
Long Live the Proletarian Revolution!

(signed)

Maurice Spector
Member CEC, C.P. of C.

Tim Buck: Report to the Comintern

Comrades, on account of the fact that the most important problems confronting our Party in Canada today are inner Party problems and on account of the fact that the fight against the Right Wing has resulted in an attempt on the part of the bureaucracy of the Finnish mass organisations to split the Party, this report will deal mainly with inner Party questions.

* * * *

I do not think it is correct to say we based all our possibilities for work upon the approach of an immediate economic crisis. Some of the fiercest arguments that took place in the CEC on this question were the debates whether the workers were becoming radicalised or not. During the [sixth] convention some of the sharpest struggles took place actually over this question, we fighting against the right wing attempts to minimise radicalisation and the possibilities in revolutionary work. The leading right wingers accepted the Comintern letter unconditionally. MacDonald accepted the Comintern letter even before any discussion on it. It is true that on one question he declared the criticism of the Comintern letter was not fundamental, but he immediately corrected himself; he said he should not have said it. Buhay resisted it until the last day of the convention, but the last day of the convention he accepted it. His first position was that the Comintern letter was wrong because of false information.

Following the convention we came to the question of the CEC. It was finally settled on the proposal of Comrade Hathaway and Williamson that we should elect a nominating commission of nine to draw up a slate for the new Central Executive Committee. Unfortunately the minority had a minority representation on this commission. We had adopted a resolution. The Central Executive Committee fought over this resolution all of one week before going into the convention. The resolution as originally drafted

---

Tim Buck's "Report to the Comintern" is previously unpublished. Dated January 23, 1930, it was written as a defense of the Buck faction during the Finnish dispute. This account of the 1928-30 crisis contradicts all of Buck's later versions.

The original document, from which this excerpt is taken, was found and made available to me by Ron Adams.

categorically branded the right wingers and demanded organisational measures against them. Comrade Williamson, representative of the YCI, and Comrade Hathaway, representative of the American Party, endeavoured to smooth over all possible difficulties existing between us, while completely accepting the CI letter, and finally succeeded in securing an arrangement whereby MacDonald and Buhay for the majority and Smith and myself for the minority, would sit in a small commission to go over the resolution. In this small commission certain changes were made in the resolution. The demand for organisational measures against individuals was dropped and the names of individuals (excepting in the case of MacDonald) were stricken out, which rendered this an expression of one group of the Central Executive Committee against the other. And to the rank and file delegates to this convention it became difficult to see what was the serious difference if we could all accept one resolution. In this respect while we have no complaint and no defence to make, I feel we were not the only people to blame. The pressure of Comrades Williamson and Hathaway was all to the effect of securing a political document upon which we could agree, rather than a political document which would differentiate between us. Their point was that we should adopt a political document which would lay the line and the real struggle would be the fight for the line. We therefore adopted the tactic of insisting in all our speeches that this marked only the beginning of the struggle against the Right wing. In each of our speeches we emphasised this point. Unfortunately we came out of the convention with very little of the forces of the party, faced with the necessity of immediate preparations for Red Day and carrying our policy into effect.

We settled down to routine work of the party waiting for the Party plenum. When the Plenum came the majority submitted a slate for the Polcom. We fought against this slate, we fought against Comrades Popovitch and Hill. Our position was that we had to make a sharp break with the past, we must bring to the centre the best and most aggressive Party elements of the various language groupings. To this end we objected categorically against Popovitch. We also protested categorically against Hill and nominated in his place Vaara, who always previously stood for an aggressive Party line, and just previously had come out of jail. In the enlarged executive there was quite a struggle over Vaara, Popovitch and Hill. MacDonald then faced us with the fact that he would not stand for the secretary's position. We then made a very serious error. We resisted his resignation, and after an afternoon's discussion, when it was impossible to arrive at any conclusion, it was unanimously agreed by the whole plenum to have an adjournment and to meet again the following day. In the meantime in the evening the various comrades gathered together and we concluded to accept MacDonald's resignation. The following day we agreed to accept MacDonald's resignation. Comrades, I realise now what a bitter mistake this was. During the Party convention we fought against the nomination of Buhay and nominated another comrade in his place. In the small commission for the nomination of the executive it was impossible for us to come to an agreement. Why did we agree to MacDonald and Popovitch? Because of the atmosphere that permeated our whole convention. The atmosphere of disintegration caused us to allow MacDonald and Popovitch to be elected onto the CEC with nothing but a statement from us. MacDonald also emphasised this "atmosphere" in a declaration defending the open caucusing of the Right Wing.

We were convinced at that time, that we must secure collective leadership, otherwise the language sections would withdraw from the Party. We made these mistakes and the mistake at the Plenum was made in the same sense and under the same pressure. The whole Party was in a state of suspended animation. It was a question of whether there was a Party or not. In a few months we paid a bitter price for the previous years of procrastination. During this time we were in the position where we had to choose between a measure of conciliation with MacDonald, or wrecking the Party. And we chose wrongly. We chose conciliation with MacDonald. The political committee we elected however, was undoubtedly the best political committee we had in our Party yet.

****

The composition of the political committee is good and the work of the political committee is superior to any polcom we ever had in our Party before. Comrade Ewen was working in the railroad shops and if we wanted him to retain his status in the union it was necessary that he should continue until September 2nd and we considered that it was very important that he should retain his status, particularly owing to the fact that he was to be head of the TUUL. The result was that for sometime we had difficulty in securing a meeting of the Political Committee. This creates an impression that the Political Committee was unable to function. We decided also that MacDonald should continue in his office as temporary acting secretary. We made this decision under the same pressure and under the same circumstance that we agreed that he be on the Central Committee and on the Political Committee, and we accepted his resignation as secretary because of this atmosphere of disintegration. Because of the fact that we conceived of his withdrawal as an attempt to violate the new political committee from the membership. We knew that he was desirous to utilise his withdrawal for the consolidation of the language organisation against us. These mistakes were all serious. Now when we look back upon it, it seems hard to imagine how comrades who have had 16-18 years experience could make such mistakes. But on the other hand while we suffered from these weaknesses and I myself was away from the office on account of sickness, at least our organisational policies and plans that we made during the Plenum have all been carried into effect.

****

Now to the question of the general fight against the Right Wing. The line of our struggle was to be for complete re-orientation of the Party toward concrete struggles, organisation of the unorganised, independent political action, abolition of all the federalistic remnants within the Party, and a sharper struggle against the Right tendencies of our language work. Also liquidation of the Labour Party and independent campaigns, etc. The policy of the leading comrades in the foreign language organisations has been to cling to the practise of Federalism, although formally the Federations were abolished in 1925. Utilising the language difficulties and the strength of the mass organisations, they focus the attention of the rank and file upon language work. So, while the members of the language organisations who are members of the Party now pay their dues to the local Party secretaries, they generally continue to look to the language leadership for directives.

There is a very strong basis for the Right danger in Canada, and a very strong basis for Right tendencies in our Party. Particularly in the foreign language-speaking organisations. The Finnish and the Ukrainian language speaking organisations in Canada are not mere radical working class organisations, they are considerably more than this. They are centres for all kinds of assistance. Political, and also economic assistance. They are real centres to which they draw the workers, on the basis of language needs, and definite advantages to immigrants. In addition there has developed a "superiority complex" among the members of the Finnish and Ukrainian language organisations, in relation to other immigrant workers. This is partly a petty bourgeois attitude of superiority to those members who are not members of revolutionary organisations, and partly a certain cultural superiority. All this is in the hands of a very narrow leadership and a bureaucratic leadership, and this is more important in Canada than it is in some countries. I think this is more important to our Party in the sense that foreign language workers in America are much more Americanised than foreign workers in Canada are Canadianised. The foreign born workers in Canada are still living to a great extent (mentally) in their home countries. They still want to speak their own language, they cannot effectively participate in trade union meetings or Party meetings on the basis of their language, but in contradistinction to this, they are a decisive element in Canadian industry.

Previous to the war the foreign born worker was employed on railroad construction, on rough unskilled work of the steel industry, in agricultural work—during the war, they were taken out of the concentration camps and put in munition factories. During the war they were thrown into various productive processes and from that time onward, the percentage of foreign born workers in industry has increased rapidly. They are in every industry. Instead of having foreign born only in the Needle trades industry, and doing heavy unskilled work, you have them in every single industry, even in the printing trades, in the automobile industry, in the electric, in the mining, textile, etc. etc. And on the most highly skilled jobs. This also accentuates the class differentiation already advanced in their ranks. We have very little contact with these workers, except with the Ukrainians, Finnish and to some extent Hungarians. But the Ukrainians, due to the fact that they come from the oppressed provinces of Poland, Roumania and the Carpathian district of Czecho-Slovakia have contact with the best elements from all nationalities of Central Europe. They (the Ukrainians) are highly organised and most active. They have an effective press, and have strong general influence among foreign born workers.

Three years ago the bourgeoisie started with more than usual force an attack upon our Party. And naturally, in attacking our Party the bourgeoisie concentrated the attack upon the language organisations, which were close to our Party, and the main part of this attack was concentrated upon the Ukrainian Labour Temple. This attack took the form of speeches, articles in the capitalist press, interviews of capitalist politicians, Ukrainian priests, etc. The obviously correct policy for the leadership of the Ukrainian mass organisations of course, was to launch a counter-offensive, and to rally the masses of foreign born workers for defence. But instead of this, our comrades adopted a policy of systematic retreats.

The first sign of retreat was an article written by Comrade Popovitch in which he denied the relationship between the Ukrainian Labour Temple Association and the Communist Party and in which he over-emphasised the cultural aspect of the Ukrainian Labour Temple Association and excludes its political role. We criticised this article, but this was immediately followed by a whole series of very sharp deviations, such details as singing the national anthem at concerts, and even decorating the National headquarters with the National Colours of Canada. We did not know of all these things. In Canada owing to the long distances news is not always rapid in coming to the centre. This matter of the Union Jack I heard accidentally in a discussion at the City Central Committee of the Party. The same Comrade Popovitch opened an attack on the Party Polcom for Leftism, and in the discussion it came out about the digression of the Labour temple. No report had ever been sent by any comrades in Winnipeg to the Polcom. We started a fight on this. This started a fight all along the line on the question of Right Wing deviations in the Ukrainian organisations. Those comrades who have been for a long time in the Anglo-American Secretariat will remember the document sent demanding my removal from the Political Committee for alleged factional activity against the Ukrainian leadership. This document was circulated among the Ukrainian membership. The whole struggle was represented as a struggle to smash the language organisations. However, this to some extent was settled by a letter from the Anglo-American Secretariat to the Canadian Party in which was laid down a line for the work in our language sections. This letter established the line but this letter was not sufficiently specific. While it gave us a clear mandate for fighting against the Right wing tendencies it was so general that everybody accepted it. One thing to be done here is that we should have a clear and specific settlement on the whole question of work among the foreign born workers. At the present time it is almost impossible for us to break down the conception that these mass organisations are permanent organisations.

When Vaara first came to the centre, as I explained before, there were only two members of the Polcom in the Centre, Smith and myself. Vaara agreed with us absolutely, and it appeared to us that Vaara stood with us 100%. Nine days after Vaara appeared in Toronto the Executive of the Finnish organisation of Canada sent a letter to the Polcom demanding that this decision be reversed. At a meeting of this executive—where Smith and myself were present—they finally agreed that we were correct. At least without admitting its correctness, they agreed that the decision should stand. I was then away on sick leave for almost two months. Two days previous to my return, the Finnish Organisation Committee had again demanded reconsideration of this decision and the sending of Vaara back to Sudbury. Of course it was quite clear that insofar as the Finnish Organisation Executive were concerned, they were interested in the political implications of Vaara being a member of the Polcom. This meant the transference of the centre of gravity for the Finnish movement from Sudbury to the Political Committee of the Party. The Polcom again decided against them. MacDonald supported their position. However the Political Committee decided against them. A few days after this we received word from the comrades in Sudbury that Vaara and Ahlqvist had appeared in Sudbury, walked into the editorial office, announced that Vaara was to be editor, and that any person who refused to accept the decision was summarily fired. They immediately fired three comrades who stood with the Polcom. We had a hurry up meeting and made a series of 16 decisions, which are on record in the files of the Anglo-American Secretariat.

To start this struggle we sent Smith to Sudbury to speak to the membership. The reply of the splitters was to throw him out of the hall. Following this—immediately, the next day—"Vapaus," the organ of the Finnish organisation, came out with a long statement from the executive of the Finnish organisation, that they had done this for the protection of the organisation. They stated that the Communist International did not demand that their organisation should be a 100% class struggle organisation, and that they remained loyal to the CI but they would insist upon the right to decide who should be editor of the Vapaus. They opposed Vaara's appointment as fraction bureau secretary, on the ground that he was not qualified for this work, he had a very poor command of English, etc. But they were very careful not to oppose the principle involved. They immediately sent out factional agents to various centres where we sent organisers. After one week, Vaara disappeared. We do not know where he is and what he is doing. He wrote a letter to the Political Committee explaining to us that if he has done wrong he must be subjected to the most severe discipline etc. From this letter, it appears that he does not know what it was all about. He refers to a meeting with the Secretariat in which he agreed with us, and he says that he changed his mind when we decided to send Smith away from the centre, as he considered this showed insincerity in the matter of strengthening the centre.

Certain mistakes were made by us also, for instance, on the purely concrete tactical side of the conflict, and we failed also to utilise it sufficient for political enlightenment. This also has to be understood from the viewpoint of the composition of the Finnish membership, their very low political level and the necessity of reaching them immediately with very concrete factual material. The statement that we issued on the Finnish question was issued under stress. They sent out some factional agents after throwing Comrade Smith from the meeting. We were having our paper published illegally in their plant. Type for this issue was almost all set and we decided we must get a statement into this issue. Comrade Smith sent a copy of this statement and asked if we would approve of it and we advised Smith to go ahead and publish it in the paper. MacDonald came into town and at the following meeting of the Polcom moved a motion condemning our action of putting this into the paper and endeavouring in the most naive way to separate the caucus in the convention, from the present split and the Right wing, and demanded the right to publish a statement in the paper. He sent this statement and the Polcom decided it should not be published. He then informed us that he had already sent copies to all language papers. We decided that we would wire the language papers not to publish it and he also should wire the editor of the Vapaus not to publish it. It did not appear in any of the other language papers, but it did appear in the Vapaus. Ahlqvist made a statement to the membership in the party that they did not have to worry about our Polcom and they did not have to worry about the statement, and that Buck and Smith were acting on behalf of the Polcom, because there should be an article in the Vapaus written by a leading member of the Polcom that these decisions were decisions of "the clique". The article appeared over the signature of MacDonald. We had a closed meeting on this account with the Finnish membership. During the discussion at this meeting it transpired that MacDonald had been in close association with them. We were discussing the whole question of the development of the split. One comrade very naively stated that on the evening of November 3, Comrade MacDonald came up there and had a conference with Wirta and the rest of the comrades of the Finnish Executive. This exposed his role. I immediately went back and challenged him with this and he did not deny it.

Fineberg raised the question personally about suspensions. In Canada suspension is definitely provided for in case of disciplinary action. It is a definitely different status than expulsion in the Party. To the present time we have not received any intimation that this should not be so. The idea of suspending some and expelling others was to differentiate between their political status. Our action on account of Vaara's status among the Finns and his proletarian origin, the fact that before we had a party he was still one of our most active left wingers in the trade union movement, etc., our policy was to differentiate between him and the yellow journalists and the professional functionaries who were leading the split. We therefore expelled some and suspended others. When Ahlqvist refused to accept the statement we changed his suspension to expulsion. The idea was to help create a differentiation among the rank and file. That concludes the actual report of work and activity.

Statement of Jack MacDonald

After a careful and extensive study not only in retrospect of the pre-October polemics and activities of Bolshevism and the literature and general ideological activity of the Communist International, particularly up to the death of its founder and leader—Lenin—and the opening of the struggle against "Trotskyism", but also of the more immediate and pressing situations and struggles of today, viz., Germany, China, Spain, etc., and the official C.I. programs, strategy and tactics therein, I have become convinced that the position, program and general criticism of the "Left Opposition" under the brilliant, untiring and courageous leadership of comrade Trotsky are fundamentally correct; and that the Left Opposition is the historical bearer and custodian of true Marxist-Leninism.

In this necessarily brief statement I have no intention of reviewing at length the attitude of the Canadian Party during my association with its leadership or my personal attitude during the "discussion" and subsequent fight against "Trotskyism".

Suffice it to say, that the ideological campaign against Trotskyism— charged with the attempt to revise Leninism—consisted of the scant distribution among the membership of occasional official bulletins from the C.I. containing alleged excerpts from the writings and speeches of Trotsky, counterposed with the official "true Leninist" rebuttal from the leading scribes of the International.

Honest comrades, with their faith in the revolutionary integrity of the central leadership unimpaired and who therefore resent and reject any suggestion of bureaucratic intrigue, falsification or degeneration, accept these official communications at their face value and act accordingly; search with the official microscope, flaying and uprooting in the name of Communist discipline and democratic centralism any tendencies, deviations, or suspects that would weaken or dilute the revolutionary movement in the face of its class enemies. In this so-called ideological campaign (if self-criticism is still in vogue) I accept my full share of responsibility and error and admit its travesty. What organizational and ideological crimes have been committed in the name of discipline!

For some time I have had occasion to compare these "excerpts" as published in official bulletins, with the actual writings of Trotsky. Many are completely false; others torn from their context are deliberately

---

Jack MacDonald's "Statement" announcing his adherence to the Trotskyist Left Opposition originally appeared in *The Militant*, May 28, 1932.

misinterpreted; while others correct in text are presumably demolished with the dud bombs of anti-Leninist theory.

I recall the first appeal which came to the C.E.C. of the Canadian Party to record itself against the Russian Party Opposition. This was during a session of the Enlarged Executive of the C.I.—a Canadian delegate being in attendance. The delegate had recorded himself against. Why not? There are few exceptions. A cable was dispatched to Canada requesting the C.E.C. to solidarize itself with the majority. Little if anything was known by the Canadian Party of the theoretical substance of the questions at issue. No liaison was in existence in those days where one could imbibe the latest on tap through "Lenin" students, etc. This honest unschooled proletarian center dispatched a return cable withholding decision until adequate information pro and con was received by them. The Canadian center fell into very bad grace over this incident. They might at least have adopted the course of one C.E.C. member, who, being unable to be present wired the C.E.C. to record his vote against Trotsky, but protested lack of information.

In brief the so-called question of Trotskyism was approached in a purely superficial and burocratic manner. This was in the days prior to deportations, exiles, etc. How far the regime has developed burocratically since those days must be obvious to all sincere comrades.

It is positively criminal in the best revolutionary sense to close one's mind against the Left Opposition's trenchant criticism and charges of the growth of a burocratic regime in the C.I. The autocratic and mechanical removal and superimposition of leadership on sections of the Comintern; the hounding of old and tested bolsheviks on the pretext of some discovered heresy in writing or speech, but in reality to make way for a substantial prop for the present regime; the stifling of initiative and discussion; the parody of workers' universities where "leaders" are molded and manufactured to standard current pattern, etc., are evidences, if only in an organizational and limited sense, of the truth of this criticism.

One had only to attend the Sixth Congress of the C.I. and that was several years ago, to have proof of the opposition's contention in its broad international sense, not to mention the alarming burocratic growth since in virtually every section nor the tragedy of the internal party situation in the Soviet Union. I have a vivid recollection of this "corridor" congress. I recall the session of the Standing Committee where the Pol-Bureau of the C.P.S.U. made its declaration, drawn from it, in its own words because the delegations were "speculating" on the rumored differences within the Bureau. No such principle differences existed, ran the declaration signed by all members of the bureau and implemented by remarks from Stalin and Bucharin. Hardly had the delegations reached home before news broke out that not only were there principle differences, but that actual factions existed. And this after the lie had been given to delegates who had probed beneath the surface of official declarations and reported the existence of groupings and factions.

The creation of the "third period" at the Sixth Congress, as justification for the left about-face, unquestionably under the blows of the opposition—a period that has apparently passed into history or been conveniently forgotten to avoid the creation of a "fourth" period; the rejection of the united front tactic with the non-party workers organizations in the slogan of the "united front from below", as an apology for the unprincipled maneuvering with the leaders of the Social Democratic and reformist trade union organizations; the tragic and catastrophic caricature of a bolshevist-Leninist policy in China, with its complete subordination of the Communist Party to Chiang Kai-shek and its corollary of subsequent adventurist and putschist insurrection; the eclectic and mechanical creation of the "war danger", which led the parties to orientate their activities solely on the imminence of war from which the proletarian revolution would be born; the swing back to the "right" with its glaring legalistic and parliamentary activity, just as the world economic crisis broke, only to find the parties isolated from the consequences to a great extent of the third period tactics; the acrobatics on trade union policy, etc., etc.—all this is at least ample proof of the zig-zag centrist policy of the present regime.

The appalling debacle of the Communist forces in the recent German presidential election with the enormous growth of the Fascist forces; the almost complete isolation of the party from the trade unions; its insignificant influence over the social-democratic workers, despite the deep internal crisis in Germany; the theory of "social Fascism"; the flirting, to put it mildly, with certain Fascist leaders; the apparent developing theory that a Fascist victory with its demagogic program and slogans means rapid disillusionment of the workers, which will be followed by a flocking to the Communist standard, Italy, Poland, etc., notwithstanding; all this in the German situation if nothing else must impel a general stocktaking and inner searching in the ranks of Communism.

One looks in vain for any keen analysis of these phenomena in the official Communist Press. In the Canadian "Worker" after the first presidential vote in Germany, there appeared a leading editorial that for trifling, irresponsible, poltroonish approach is, I believe, without parallel. Two main points were made. Firstly, the Opposition was "disarmed" with the assertion many times repeated that the "renegades" would possibly find cause to rejoice. Just why, wasn't stated. Secondly, finally and primarily, the most outstanding and significant result of the election was the gain of half a million Communist votes over last election. What humbug! The second vote with its loss of over a million Communist votes, still remains to be "explained", so far as I am aware.

The wealth of literature issued by the Left Opposition from the pen of Trotsky is something that no worker or student of Marxism or Leninism can afford to ignore or neglect. One listens in vain for the voice of Stalin on the outstanding events of today. Here in the opposition press and literature every question is approached and analyzed, clearly, fearlessly and dialectically. I recollect how in certain so-called discussions we used to blast and damn the theory of Trotsky's Permanent Revolution with an arsenal of quotations given to us by Bucharin. How the polemical differences between Lenin and Trotsky were magnified. How Trotsky underestimated or denied the role of the peasantry. How he would leap across historical stages. "Down with the Czar!" "Up with the Labor Government!" How during Lenin's leadership he was held in check and did great service for the revolution. But since Lenin died his old false theories had cropped up again, his old Permanent Revolution which was the source of all evil.

Every worker today can read Trotsky's Permanent Revolution for himself. Let us understand what the "differences" between Lenin and Trotsky were on the role of the peasantry, the "democratic dictatorship", etc. Acquire a knowledge of the rearming of the Party on the return of Lenin to Russia before October—in short have done with fabrication and misrepresentation and read history.

The theory of the Permanent Revolution is not an attempt at a leap of the proletariat over definite historical stages, but the transformation of the nation under the leadership of the proletariat. Here I may quote section two of the fundamental thesis of the Permanent Revolution: "With regard to the countries with a belated bourgeois development, especially the colonial and semi-colonial countries, the theory of the permanent revolution signifies that the complete and genuine solution of their tasks, democratic and national emancipation, is conceivable only through the dictatorship of the proletariat as the leader of the subjugated nation, above all of the peasant masses." The tasks of the "democratic dictatorship of the proletariat" were realized not before October, not in the "dual power", but by October—through the dictatorship of the proletariat supported by the poor peasants.

It will be instructive at some other time to retrace the directives to the Canadian Party, given by the opponents of the permanent revolution in their desire to find historical stages that might not be "skipped over". These run the whole gamut, from the fight against the British monarchy, demand for constituent assembly, farmer-labor government, farmers political parties, national independence, etc., etc.

I reject the theory of national socialism—of socialism in one country— evolved in the struggle against Trotsky in 1925, as contrary to all the teachings of Marx and Lenin. The inevitable social patriotic errors that the Left Opposition warned against are strikingly evident today. The appeal to the international proletariat against Japanese Imperialism, in its general formulation is a recent indication of this. A still more recent example is the advancement by the *Daily Worker* of the justification (based on an article in *Izvestia*) of an alliance between the Soviet Union and American Imperialism against Japanese Imperialism. The propaganda and agitation surrounding the slogan of "Defend the Soviet Union" is saturated with pacifism. All this is the logical outcome of the false theory of "socialism in one country".

This statement is made in support of the Left Opposition after thoroughly probing all doubts and reservations, slowly, calmly and deliberately. I make it with the sincere hope that any influence I may have with the workers, through my association with and work in the working class movement in this country, may lead the advanced workers to a critical examination of the Communist movement today, in all its ramifications, theoretical, organizational, strategical and otherwise; and to an examination of the literature and theoretical position of the Left Opposition and particularly to the works of Trotsky.

From this I am convinced there will inevitably come again another "re-arming" of the movement—a re-establishment of the advance guard of the international working class movement, on the solid bed-rock of the theories of Marx and Lenin.

—J. MacDONALD

Notes

Chapter One

1. *Industrial Banner,* December 18, 1914.
2. Ibid., February 7, 1913.
3. Babcock, *Gompers in Canada,* passim.
4. *Western Cla.ion,* August 15, 1914.
5. *Industrial Banner,* August 28, 1914.
6. *The Messenger,* July 1917.
7. *Western Clarion,* October 1917.
8. quoted in Troop, *Socialism in Canada,* p. 74.
9. quoted in *ibid.* p. 75.
10. *The Worker,* April 3, 1926.
11. *Western Clarion,* November 7, 1914.
12. Ibid., May 1915
13. Ibid., August 1916.
14. Ibid., October 1917.
15. See Chapter 7, p. 135.
16. *B.C. Federationist,* September 4, 1914.
17. *Toronto Daily Star,* December 26, 1914.
18. *Cottons Weekly,* August 20, 1914.
19. Max Armstrong Reminiscences.
20. *B.C. Federationist,* April 26, 1918.
21. *Labour Organization in Canada 1914,* pp. 19-20.
22. *TLC Proceedings,* 1915, pp. 13-15.
23. Ibid., 1917, pp. 42-43.
24. *Toronto Daily Star,* May 2, 1918; *Canadian Forward,* May 24, 1918.
25. *Western Clarion,* September 1915; *Toronto Daily Star,* December 10, 1915, September 28, 1918; *Canadian Forward,* April 24, 1917, September 24, 1917, June 10, 1918; *Toronto Daily News,* September 25 & 26, 1918.
26. See reports in *The Globe, Toronto Daily Star, Evening Telegram,* and *Toronto World,* June 4, 1917.
27. PAC Record Group 6, Box 609 File 279-23.
28. *Evening Telegram,* April 2, 1917.

29. *Toronto World,* May 2, 1917.

30. *Canadian Forward,* May 24, 1917.

31. Reed, *Ten Days that Shook the World,* pp. 171-2.

32. Cannon, *Speeches for Socialism,* p. 65.

33. *OBU Bulletin,* April 27, 1922.

34. Malcolm Bruce Reminiscences.

35. *B.C. Federationist,* February 23, 1918.

36. *Canadian Forward,* February 10, 1918.

37. *The Voice,* March 15, 1918.

38. *Toronto Daily Star,* November 8, 1917; Knightley, *The First Casualty,* p. 138.

39. *The Voice,* March 15, 1918.

40. *Canadian Forward,* February 24, 1918.

41. quoted in Penner, *The Canadian Left,* p. 59.

42. *TLC Proceedings,* 1918, pp. 44-46.

43. *B.C. Federationist,* February 8, 1918.

44. *The Worker,* April 3, 1926.

45. No copy of the September 1918 *Marxian Socialist* has survived. The first seven paragraphs were quoted in a Censors' Office memorandum (PAC RG 6, Volume 604). The seventh and eighth were quoted in *Western Labor News,* October 4, 1918.

46. *Western Labor News,* October 4, 1918.

Chapter Two

1. Borden Papers, Volume 104, Cawdron to Doherty, March 19, 1918.

2. quoted in Rodney, *Soldiers of the International,* p. 17.

3. Ibid., p. 17.

4. PAC-Justice RG 13, Volume 222.

5. Ibid.

6. PAC Justice, RG 13, Volume 229; D. Avery, *The Radical Alien,* p. 217.

7. *Western Labor News,* November 8, 1918, *B.C. Federationist,* November 29, 1918.

8. See reports in *Mail and Empire, Toronto Daily Star, Evening Telegram,* and *The Globe,* October 21, 1918.

9. PAC Justice RG 13, Volume 235.

10. PAC Justice RG 13, Volume 229; Avery, *The Radical Alien,* p. 217.

11. *Western Labor News,* January 17, 1918; *Evening Telegram,* January 13, 1918.

12. Rodney, *Soldiers,* p. 18.

13. This account of the Watson-Cheeseman case is based on reports which appeared in the Toronto daily papers in January 1919. The most important articles appeared in the *Toronto Daily Star* and *The Globe,* January 9, 10, 13, 17, and 25.

14. *Toronto Daily News, Evening Telegram, Toronto World, Mail and Empire, The Globe, Toronto Daily Star,* November 18, 1918.

15. Ibid., January 25, 1918.

16. Distribution of the leaflet was reported in the Toronto newspapers. The full text appears in the Documents section of this book.

17. PAC-RG 6, Volume 605. The full text of this leaflet appears in the Documents section of this book.
18. *Toronto Daily News,* December 22, 1918; December 9, 1918; *Toronto Daily Star,* December 18, 1918.
19. PAC-Justice, RG 13, Volume 209.
20. *Toronto Daily Star,* January 4, 1919; January 8, 1919.
21. *Toronto World,* January 13, 1919.
22. *Evening Telegram,* January 20, 1919.
23. *The Globe, Toronto Times,* April 7, 1919.
24. See reports in all Toronto dailies, April 29, 1919.
25. See reports in all Toronto dailies, June 2, 10, 19, 20 and July 11, 18, 1919.
26. *TLC Proceedings 1918,* p. 45.
27. *Toronto Daily News,* January 11, 1919.
28. *Toronto Times,* April 30, 1919.
29. *The Globe,* March 19, 1917.
30. Lenin, *Collected Works,* Volume 29, p. 562.
31. *Revolutionary Radicalism,* pp. 861-5.
32. *Mail and Empire,* October 21, 1918. Swigach had been chairman of the March 1917 meeting in support of the Russian Revolution at which Rotchyld spoke (see above, note 29). This is further evidence of his prominence in the S-R organization.
33. Draper, *Roots of American Communism,* pp. 65-6.
34. *Mail and Empire,* June 2, 1919.

Chapter Three

1. *Western Labor News,* August 2, 1918.
2. Ibid., December 27, 1918.
3. quoted in Friesen, "Yours in Revolt," p. 144.
4. Ibid.
5. *B.C. Federationist,* May 30, 1919.
6. *Winnipeg Citizen,* May 19, 1919.
7. MacEwan, *Miners and Steelworkers,* pp. 53-79.
8. *Mail and Empire,* May 19, 1919.
9. *The Globe,* June 23, 1919; *Toronto Times,* June 23, 1919; *The Globe,* July 18, 1919.
10. Robin, *Radical Politics and Canadian Labor,* p. 119.
11. *The Globe,* September 12, 1919.
12. A useful summary of the farmer-labor victories and fiascos of 1919-1921 is in Robin, *Radical Politics and Canadian Labour,* chapters 13-15.

Chapter Four

1. *Toronto Daily Star,* January 20, 1919.
2. *Labor News,* January 24, 1919.
3. Spector, "The Constituent Convention...," Kenny Papers, Box 1. See Documents at end of this book.
4. Rodney, *Soldiers,* pp. 31-32. Rodney gives the date of the formation of the Labor College as October 1920, but the founding of the College and its first class were reported in *The Globe,* January 26, 1920.

5. Rodney, *Soldiers*, p. 29.
6. Ibid., P. 32.
7. *The Globe*, February 2, 1920.
8. Robin, *Radical Politics*, pp. 234-5.
9. Reports of the two meetings appeared in both the daily press and the labor press. The most useful were those in *The Globe*, *The World*, and the *Mail and Empire*, January 24, 1921; *Labor Leader*, January 28, 1921; and *The Globe*, February 7, 1921.
10. For a full history of the complex splits and unifications which the U.S. Communists experienced in 1919-1921, see Draper, *Roots of American Communism*, chapters 10-13.
11. *The Communist Bulletin* is reported and reviewed in the *Western Clarion*, March 16 and April 1, 1921. No copies have survived.
12. Rodney, *Soldiers*, pp. 37-39.
13. *Western Clarion*, May 1, 1920.
14. Ibid., January 14, 1922.
15. Ibid., February 1, 1922.
16. Ibid., April 16, 1922.
17. Ibid., April 1, 1921.
18. POC Minutes. Kenny Collection, Box 1.
19. *Western Clarion*, January 14, 1922.
20. *B.C. Federationist*, January 6, 1922.
21. Buck, *Forty Years*, p. 27. See Rodney, *Soldiers*, pp. 29-30, and Avakumovic, *The Communist Party in Canada*, p. 12.
22. Buck, *Thirty Years*, p. 27.
23. Buck, *Reminiscences*, p. 85.
24. Ibid.,pp. 84-5.
25. Ibid., p. 54. *Lenin and Canada*, p. 14.
26. *Western Clarion*, May 20, 1911.
27. Buck, *Reminiscences*, pp. 43-44.
28. *Industrial Banner*, November 1, 1912.
29. Buck, *Reminiscences*, p. 67.
30. *The Worker*, June 24, 1932.
31. *The Worker*, December 21, 1935.
32. Spector to Birney, August 6, 1933, Birney Papers.
33. *The Vanguard*, May 1936.

Chapter Five

1. See Documents, p. 337.
2. *Revolutionary Radicalism*, pp. 759-61.
3. quoted in Draper, *Roots of American Communism*, pp. 216-7.
4. Lenin, *Selected Works*, Vol. 3, p. 404.
5. Ibid., p. 446.
6. Ibid., p. 678.
7. Trotsky, "The New Course," in *Challenge of the Left Opposition*, p. 94.
8. Cannon, *History of American Trotskyism*, p. 12.
9. quoted in *Industrial Banner*, May 6, 1921.
10. quoted in Rodney, *Soldiers*, p. 39.
11. *Industrial Banner*, May 6, 1921.

12. *Western Clarion,* July 16, 1921.
13. *B.C. Federationist,* January 27, 1922.
14. *Western Clarion,* Aug. 1, 1921.
15. Spector, "The Constituent Convention...," Kenny Papers, Box 1.
16. Kenny Collection, Box 1.
17. For a full discussion of the "legal party" debate in the U.S., see Draper, *Roots of American Communism,* chapters 16, 19.
18. *Manifestes, Thèses, et Résolutions des Quatres Premiers Congrès Mondiaux de L'Internationale Communiste 1919-1923,* p. 96. My translation.
19. Draper, *Roots,* p. 280.
20. Rodney, *Soldiers,* p. 45.
21. *Workers Guard,* November 5, 1921.
22. *Workers Guard,* November 19, 1921.
23. *Western Clarion,* December 1, 1921.
24. NcNaught, *A Prophet in Politics,* p. 149.
25. Kenny Papers, Box 1.
26. *The Worker,* March 15, 1922.
27. Draper, *Roots,* p. 342.
28. *Labor Organization in Canada 1922,* p. 178.
29. Avakumovic, *The Communist Party in Canada,* p. 31.
30. *Rex v. Buck,* p. 142.
31. Degras, ed., *The Communist International,* Vol. 1, p. 167.
32. *Rex v. Buck,* p. 142.
33. Spector, "The Constituent Convention...," Kenny Papers, Box 1.
34. *Western Clarion,* January 14, 1922.
35. *OBU Bulletin,* May 11, 1922.
36. Cannon, *The First Ten Years of American Communism,* pp. 69-70.
37. Ibid., p. 71.
38. *The Worker,* March 15, 1923.
39. *Rex v. Buck,* p. 139.

Chapter Six

1. Lenin, *Selected Works,* Vol. 3, p. 430.
2. *Workers Guard,* December 17, 1921.
3. *The Worker,* March 15, 1922.
4. quoted in Robin, *Radical Politics,* p. 213.
5. *Industrial Banner,* July 8, 1921.
6. *Revolutionary Radicalism,* p. 188.
7. *Labor Organization in Canada 1922,* p. 176.
8. Kenny Papers, Box 1.
9. *Industrial Banner,* February 24, 1922.
10. *Labor Organization in Canada 1922,* p. 223.
11. *The Worker,* August 1, 1922.
12. PAO-CP 1A-0009.
13. *B.C. Federationist,* June 9, 1922.
14. PAO-CP 1A-0008.
15. *B.C. Federationist,* December 15, 1922.

16. *The Worker,* June 27, 1923; *Labor Organization in Canada 1923,* p. 204.

17. Lenin, *Selected Works,* Vol. 3, pp. 400, 404.

18. Ibid., pp. 402, 403.

19. *One Big Union Bulletin,* May 21, 1921.

20. *One Big Union Bulletin,* May 7, 1921.

21. *The Communist,* June 1921.

22. *Labor Organization in Canada 1922,* p. 180; Bercuson, *Fools and Wise Men,* pp. 224-5.

23. *One Big Union Bulletin,* May 18, 1922.

24. *Labor Organization in Canada 1922,* pp. 179-180.

25. Ibid., p. 186.

26. *Labor Organization in Canada 1923,* p. 159.

27. quoted in Bercuson, *Fools and Wise Men,* p. 39.

28. *Labor Organization in Canada 1923,* p. 159.

29. Ibid., p. 159.

30. *Western Clarion,* May 16, 1923. See also November 16, 1922.

31. The most readily accessible accounts of the Cape Breton miners' struggles are David Frank, "Class Conflict in the Coal Industry: Cape Breton 1922"; and Paul MacEwan, *Miners and Steelworkers,* Chapters 7-11. Except where otherwise noted, the narrative and quotations given here are drawn from those works: the interpretation, throughout, is my own.

32. *The Worker,* August 1, 1922.

33. *The Worker,* September 15, 1922.

34. Bernstein, *The Lean Years,* pp. 117-136, provides a useful outline of Lewis's career in the 1920s.

35. Buck, *Reminiscences,* pp. 117-8; *The Worker,* August 1, 1922.

36. *The Worker,* March 1, 1923.

37. *Maritime Labour Herald,* April 21, 1923.

38. *Labor Organization in Canada 1923,* p. 186.

39. Ibid., p. 186.

40. Ibid., p. 187.

41. Ibid., p. 187.

42. Ibid., p. 188.

43. Lenin, *Selected Works,* Vol. 3, p. 403.

44. *The Worker,* October 3, 1923.

45. *Labor Organization in Canada 1924,* p. 182.

Chapter Seven

1. *The Worker,* July 19, 1923; *B.C. Federationist,* August 3, 1923.

2. Bernstein, *The Lean Years,* p. 90.

3. These statistics were published annually in the *Labor Gazette,* February issue, 1921-1933.

4. Bernstein, *The Lean Years,* pp. 53-4.

5. Niosi, *The Economy of Canada,* p. 60.

6. Abella, *The Canadian Labor Movement,* p. 15.

7. quoted in Frank, "Class Conflict in the Coal Industry," p. 182.

8. Cannon, *The First Ten Years of American Communism,* pp. 24-34.

Chapter Eight

1. Lenin, *Collected Works,* Vol. 28, p. 151.
2. Ibid., Vol. 27, p. 98.
3. Marx-Engels, *Collected Works,* Vol. 6, p. 352.
4. Marx, "Critique of Hegel's Philosophy of Right," *Early Texts,* p. 69.
5. Carr, *Socialism in One Country,* p. 198.
6. Trotsky, *In Defense of Marxism,* p. 25.
7. This account of the German crisis is based largely on material in James, *World Revolution;* Deutscher, *The Prophet Unarmed;* and Black, *Fascism in Germany.*
8. *Pravda,* February 2, 1924, as quoted in Trotsky, *Third International After Lenin,* p. 110.
9. Stalin, *Leninism,* pp. 52-3. This passage disappeared in later editions of Stalin's *"Collected Works."*
10. Block, ed., *Lenin's Fight Against Stalinism,* p. 136
11. Stalin, *Leninism,* p. 53.
12. Trotsky, *Third International After Lenin,* pp. 71-2.
13. Ibid., p. 61.
14. Stalin, *Works,* Vol. 8, p. 193.
15. Calhoun, *The United Front,* p. 171.
16. Stalin, *Works,* Vol. 8, pp. 194-95.
17. Trotsky, *Third International After Lenin,* pp. 133-34.
18. The best overall account of the Chinese revolution of 1925-1927 and its aftermath is Isaacs, *The Tragedy of the Chinese Revolution.*
19. Deutscher, *The Prophet Unarmed,* p. 326.
20. Stalin, *Works,* Vol. 7, p. 101.
21. quoted in Draper, "The Strange Case," p. 111.
22. *International Press Correspondence,* June 16, 1927.
23. Stalin, *Works,* Vol. 11, p. 210.
24. Shachtman, "Introduction" to Trotsky, *Third International After Lenin,* p. 377.
25. quoted in Deutscher, *The Prophet Outcast,* p. 143.

Chapter Nine

1. *Worker,* July 16, 1927.
2. Trotsky, *The Third International After Lenin,* pp. 119-21.
3. *Worker,* July 26, 1924.
4. Penner, *The Canadian Left,* p. 88.
5. quoted in Rodney, *Soldiers,* p. 118.
6. *Worker,* August 8, 1925.
7. *Worker,* July 17, 1926.
8. *Worker,* September 25, 1926.
9. *Militant,* May 28, 1932.
10. *Worker,* June 11, 1927.
11. Stalin, *Works,* Vol. 10, p. 163.
12. *Labor Organization in Canada 1923,* p. 159.
13. *Labor Organization in Canada 1924,* p. 144.
14. *1927 Convention Report,* p. 47.

15. *Worker*, January 9, 1926.
16. *Labor Organization in Canada 1927*, p. 50.
17. *Worker*, April 16, 1927.
18. *Worker*, September 10, 1927.
19. Ibid.
20. *Worker*, October 15, 1927.
21. *Labor Organization in Canada 1923*, p. 159.
22. PAO-CP 8C-0156.
23. *Labor Organization in Canada 1923*, p. 160.
24. *Worker*, April 24, 1926.
25. Martin Robin, *Radical Politics*, p. 262.

Chapter Ten
1. See Russell Block, *Lenin's Fight Against Stalinism,* and Moshe Lewin, *Lenin's Last Struggle*, for full accounts of this conflict.
2. Spector to CEC, January 14, 1924. Copy in author's possession.
3. Ibid.
4. quoted in Trotsky, *Third International After Lenin*, pp. 100-101, emphasis added.
5. Rodney, *Soldiers of the International*, p. 72.
6. Trotsky, *Challenge of the Left Opposition*, pp. 399-400.
7. Carr, *The Interregnum*, pp. 340-341.
8. Calhoun, *The United Front*, p. 63.
9. Bruce Reminiscences.
10. Spector to Political Committee, November 11, 1928. See Documents.
11. *Worker*, August 1, 1925.
12. *1925 Convention Report*, p. 6.
13. *Militant*, May 28, 1932. See Documents section of this volume.
14. quoted in Rodney, *Soldiers of the International*, p. 119.
15. Buck, *Lenin and Canada*, p. 51.
16. Rodney, *Soldiers of the International*, p. 125.
17. Draper, *American Communism and Soviet Russia*, p. 239.
18. Buck, *Lenin and Canada*, p. 54.
19. Ibid., pp. 55-56.
20. *International Press Correspondence*, January 20, 1927.
21. Rodney, *Soldiers of the International*, p. 129.
22. Buck, *Lenin and Canada*, p. 59.
23. Ibid., p. 60.
24. Draper, Interview with Spector, November 25, 1957.
25. *1927 Convention Report*, p. 109.

Part 3 Prologue
1. PAO-CP 8C-0462.
2. *Worker*, January 31, 1931; PAO-CP, 8C-0048.
3. PAO-CP 11C-2672; PAO-CP 4A-2730.
4. PAO-CP 8C-0284.

Chapter Eleven

1. *Worker,* July 9, 1927.
2. *1927 Convention Report,* pp. 58, 99, 10.
3. Ibid., p. 108.
4. *Militant,* June 1, 1929.
5. *1929 Convention Report,* p. 132.
6. Rodney, *Soldiers of the International,* p. 138.
7. Cannon, *History of American Trotskyism,* p. 41.
8. Ibid., pp. 41, 44.
9. Ibid., p. 44.
10. Ibid., p. 46.
11. Draper, *American Communism and Soviet Russia,* p. 363.
12. Cannon, *First Ten Years of American Communism,* p. 220.
13. Cohen, *Bukharin and the Bolshevik Revolution,* p. 293.
14. "Comrade X," as quoted in Black, *Fascism in Germany,* Vol. 1, p. 528n.
15. *Militant,* May 28, 1932. See Documents.
16. Draper, op. cit., chapters 17, 18.
17. Cannon, *History,* pp. 49-50.
18. Draper, Interview with Spector, November 25, 1957.
19. Cannon, *First Ten Years,* p. 225.
20. *Militant,* June 1, 1929.
21. *Worker,* January 19, 1929.
22. *Worker,* April 13, 1929.
23. *Worker,* December 2, 1928.
24. *Globe,* November 13, 1928.
25. *Globe,* November 14, 1928.
26. *OBU Bulletin,* November 29, 1928; *Labor Leader,* November 16, 1928; *Canadian Labor World,* November 28, 1928; *The Labor News,* November 29, 1928; *TLC Journal,* December 28, 1928.
27. *Worker,* November 24, 1928. The *Worker* was always postdated by one week, a common practice among weeklies. This issue was published on November 17.
28. *OBU Bulletin,* November 29, 1928.
29. *Worker,* December 1, 1928.
30. Buck, *Lenin and Canada,* pp. 47-48.
31. *The Clarion,* February 13, 1937.
32. The first issue of the *Worker* edited by Bruce was dated December 15, 1922. Spector's convention report appeared in the March 15 and April 2, 1923 issues. The April 2 issue announced his national tour, and the series on the united front began April 8.
33. Rodney, op. cit., pp. 71-2.
34. Smith, *All My Life,* pp. 94-95.
35. Buck, *Thirty Years,* p. 64.
36. Buck, *Reminiscences,* p. 130.
37. Buck, *Lenin and Canada,* p. 63.
38. Ryan, *Tim Buck,* p. 116.
39. Buck, *Thirty Years,* p. 64.

40. Buck, *Reminiscences,* p. 131.
41. Buck, *Lenin and Canada,* p. 63.
42. Buck, *Thirty Years,* p. 64.
43. Ibid., p. 65.
44. Buck, *Reminiscences,* p. 131.
45. Buck, *Lenin and Canada,* p. 64.
46. A full account of the break-in appears in Draper, *American Communism and Soviet Russia,* p. 144.

Chapter Twelve

1. Buck, *Thirty Years,* p. 65.
2. Ibid., p. 65.
3. Buck, *Lenin and Canada,* p. 69.
4. The charge against Lovestone was first made in the *Daily Worker,* May 20, 1929.
5. *Worker,* December 1, 1929.
6. PAO-CP 8C-0166.
7. Ibid.
8. *1929 Convention Report,* p. 133.
9. PAO-CP 8C-0126.
10. PAO-CP 8C-0166.
11. PAO-CP 12D-0118.
12. PAO-CP 12D-0077, 12D-0079.
13. Buck, *Reminiscences,* pp. 136-137.
14. *Worker,* March 24, 1929.
15. Ibid.
16. *Worker,* April 13, 1929.
17. *Rex. v. Buck,* p. 261.
18. *Militant,* June 1, 1929.
19. *1929 Convention Report,* pp. 6-14, contains the full text of the CI Letter.
20. Ibid., p. 129.
21. Ibid., p. 80.
22. *International Press Correspondence,* August 9, 1929.
23. *1929 Convention Report,* p. 80.
24. Ibid., p. 86.
25. e.g. John Porter [Leslie Morris], "The Struggle Against the Right Danger in the CP of Canada," *Communist International,* October 30, 1929.
26. PAO-CP 8C-0142.
27. Ibid.
28. *1929 Convention Report,* p. 130.
29. Ibid., p. 86.
30. See *Buck Report to Comintern,* in Documents, p. 362.
31. *1929 Convention Report,* pp. 15-18.
32. Ibid., p. 98.
33. Ibid., p. 99.
34. Ibid., pp. 112, 114.
35. Ibid., pp. 109, 114, 118.

36. See Documents, p. 363.
37. *1929 Convention Report*, p. 84.
38. Ibid., p. 83.
39. Ibid., p. 15.
40. Ibid., p. 131.
41. Ibid., p. 75.
42. Ibid., p. 79.
43. Buck, *Thirty Years*, p. 66; *Reminiscences*, p. 138.

Chapter Thirteen

1. Buck, *Thirty Years,* p. 67.
2. Buck, *Lenin and Canada,* p. 70.
3. Buck, *Thirty Years,* p. 67.
4. Buck, *Lenin and Canada,* p. 65.
5. Buck, *Reminiscences,* pp. 131-132.
6. The minutes of the Plenum, in both rough and mimeographed form, are in PAO-CP 8C-0171 et seq. Except where otherwise noted, the account in this chapter is based on those minutes.
7. See Documents, p. 363.
8. PAO-CP 9C-1295
9. *The Worker,* February 7, 1931.
10. *1929 Convention Report*, p. 134.
11. See Documents, p. 363.

Chapter Fourteen

1. Buck, *Reminiscences,* pp. 250-1.
2. *1929 Convention Report*, pp. 19-20.
3. *Worker,* January 28, 1933.
4. *Toronto Star,* December 27, 1928, first edition.
5. CI Letter to CPC, October 3, 1929.
6. Shachtman, "Introduction" to Trotsky, *Third International After Lenin,* 1936 edition, p. 377.
7. *1929 Convention Report*, p. 22.
8. *Worker,* January 3, 1931.
9. *Globe,* December 17, 1928.
10. *Mail and Empire,* January 31, 1929.
11. *Globe,* January 31, 1929.
12. *1929 Convention Report*, p. 106.
13. *Worker,* August 3, 1929.
14. *Writings of Leon Trotsky, 1930,* p. 58.
15. *Toronto Star,* August 1, 1929.
16. The factual details of the Queen's Park demonstrations given here are based on the account in R. Adams, *The CPC,* pp. 145-208. The interpretation is my own. is my own.
17. *Writings of Leon Trotsky, 1930,* p. 58.
18. Stalin, *Works,* Vol. 6, p. 294.
19. quoted in T. Draper, "The Strange Case," p. 122.
20. quoted in R. Black, *Fascism in Germany,* Vol. 2, p. 785.
21. quoted in Shachtman, op. cit., p. 378.

22. *1929 Convention Report,* pp. 15, 24.
23. *Worker,* August 9, 1930.
24. *Worker,* July 5, 1930.
25. *Worker,* November 22, 1930.
26. Caplan, *The Dilemma of Canadian Socialism,* pp. 12-14.
27. *Worker,* August 10, 1932.
28. G. Pierce [Stewart Smith], *Socialism and the CCF,* pp. 157, 195.
29. Buck, *Thirty Years,* p. 111.
30. CLDL Constitution, Article 2.
31. *Canadian Labor Defender,* May 1930.
32. *Canadian Labor Defender,* June 1930.
33. *Worker,* July 5, 1930.
34. CI Letter to CPC, October 3, 1929.
35. PAO-CP 8C-0470.
36. Quoted in Black, op. cit., p. 1032.
37. *Toronto Star,* August 12, 1931.
38. *Canadian Forum,* December 1931.

Chapter Fifteen

1. McEwen, The *Forge Glows Red,* pp. 143-4.
2. Abella, *Nationalism, Communism and Canadian Labour,* p. 4.
3. Laxer, *Canada's Unions,* p. 290.
4. *The Communist,* June 1921.
5. Stalin, *Works,* Vol. 11, pp. 314-5.
6. Draper, *American Communism and Soviet Russia,* pp. 394-5.
7. *Worker,* May 4, 1929.
8. *Worker,* May 18, 1929.
9. Penner, The *Canadian Left,* p. 132 et seq.
10. PAO-CP 10C-1846.
11. *1929 Convention Report,* p. 4.
12. Ibid., pp. 46-7.
13. ECCI to Polcom, October 3, 1929.
14. PAO-CP 9C-1462.
15. PAO-CP 8C-0210.
16. McEwen, *Forge,* pp. 137-8.
17. *Worker,* June 28, 1930.
18. Penner, *Canadian Left,* p. 137.
19. *Worker,* May 3, 1930.
20. *One Big Union Bulletin,* August 29, 1929.
21. *Labor Organization in Canada 1922,* p. 186.
22. PAO-CP 1A-0235-6.
23. *Enlarged Plenum Report,* p. 13.
24. *Worker,* January 31, 1931.
25. *Enlarged Plenum Report,* p. 26.
26. PAO-CP 8C-0626.
27. PAO-CP 1A-0627.
28. PAO-CP 10C-1847.
29. PAO-CP 8C-0495.
30. PAO-CO 8C-0492-3.

31. *Worker*, July 16, 1932.
32. *Worker*, March 7, 1931.
33. *Worker*, May 30, 1931.
34. IUNTW *Report of Second Convention.*
35. Degras, ed., *The Communist International, Documents,* Vol. 1, p. 277.
36. *1927 Convention Report*, p. 12.
37. *Expanded Plenum Report*, p. 24.
38. *Worker*, July 16, 1932.
39. *Worker*, January 7, 1933.
40. *Worker*, September 28, 1930.
41. *Communist Bulletin*, May-June, 1934.
42. *Worker*, September 15, 1934.
43. *Worker*, June 28, 1930.
44. Ernst Thaelmann, *Inprecorr*, October 4, 1929.

Chapter Sixteen

1. PAO-CP 1A-0918.
2. *1929 Convention Report*, p. 62.
3. There is an obscure reference to this event in Ibid., p. 133.
4. Ibid., p. 133.
5. Ibid., p. 124.
6. Ibid., p. 3.
7. Ibid., pp. 90-97.
8. See Documents, p. 364.
9. This acount of the fight against the bylaw is based on Adams, *The CPC*, pp. 211-217.
10. ECCI to CPC Polcom, October 3, 1929.
11. *Worker*, November 9, 1929.
12. quoted in the *Worker*, December 7, 1929.
13. *Worker*, November 30, 1929.
14. *Vapaus*, November 8, 1929.
15. *Worker*, November 30, 1929.
16. *Vapaus*, November 26, 1929.
17. *Vapaus*, November 14, 1929.
18. *Vapaus*, November 14, 1929.
19. *Worker*, November 30, 1929.
20. *Worker*, November 30, 1929.
21. *Worker*, November 30, 1929.
22. *Worker*, December 14, 1929.
23. *Worker*, December 14, 1929.
24. *Worker*, March 15, 1930.
25. PAO-CP 8C-0416.
26. PAO-CP 9C-1336.
27. PAO-CP 1A-0746, 1A-0751.
28. PAO-CP 1A-0760.
29. PAO-CP 1A-0780.
30. *Worker*, May 3, 1930.
31. PAO-CP 1A-0811, 1A-0812.
32. *Worker*, January 10, 1931.
33. *1929 Convention Report*, p. 59.

34. Ibid., p. 64.
35. Quarter interview.
36. PAO-CP 1A-0731, 0780.
37. PAO-CP 8C-0351.
38. *Worker*, October 28, 1930.
39. PAO-CP 1A-0715.
40. PAO-CP 1A-0710; *Worker*, March 1, 1930.
41. PAO-CP 1A-0717.
42. PAO-CP 1A-0711.
43. PAO-CP 9C-0731 *et seq.*
44. Aino Kuusinen, *Before and After Stalin*, p. 86.
45. PAO-CP 8C-0350.
46. *Worker*, April 2, 1930.
47. PAO-CP 9C-1259.
48. Adams, *The CPC*, p. 256.
49. *Worker*, September 5, 1931.
50. PAO-CP 8C-0078.
51. *Worker*, May 2, 1931.
52. PAO-CP 1A-0722.
53. *Rex. v. Buck*, p. 299.
54. PAO-CP 8C-0208.
55. PAO-CP 8C-0238.
56. quoted in Adams, p. 255n.
57. PAO-CP 8C-0661.
58. PAO-CP 8C-0605.
59. *Worker*, February 7, 1931.
60. Ibid.
61. PAO-CP 8C-0588.
62. *Worker*, January 3, 1931.
63. *Worker*, February 21, 1921.
64. *1929 Convention Report*, p. 6.

Chapter Seventeen

1. WPC *Manifesto*. See Documents, p. 345.
2. Kashtan, *The Decisive Question*, p. 3.
3. Degras, *Soviet Documents on Foreign Policy*, Vol. III, p. 389.
4. *New York Times*, December 20, 1942; March 9, 1943.
5. Cannon. *The Socialist Workers Party in World War II*, pp. 336-7.
6. *Edmonton Journal*, December 30, 1938.
7. *National Affairs Monthly*, October 1944.
8. Horowitz, *Canadian Labour in Politics*, pp. 92-102.
9. Ibid., pp. 111-3.
10. Morris, *Communists and the New Party*, p. 20.
11. CPC, *The Road to Socialism in Canada*, pp. 33, 45.
12. quoted in Hobsbawm, *Revolutionaries*, p. 50.
13. PAO-CP 8C-0489.
14. *Canadian Tribune*, September 15, 1945.
15. *Worker*, September 13, 1934.
16. *Worker*, November 5, 1935.

Bibliography

This bibliography identifies the primary and secondary source material used in writing *Canadian Bolsheviks*. Two sources were of particular importance.

The first was the Ontario Attorney-General's collection of Communist Party documents, deposited in the Public Archives of Ontario (abbreviated in the reference notes as PAO-CP). This collection includes all or most of the documents seized in the police raids on CP offices in Toronto in August 1931. It ranges from personal letters to official documents and periodicals, almost all of them from the 1928-1931 period. My chapters 12 through 16 make extensive use of this material.

The other source was the collection of microfilmed labor newspapers maintained by the federal Department of Labor in Hull. The vigorous labor press of the early decades of this century is a vital reference for any labor historian, and the DOL's collection comes very close to being complete.

I want also to identify two important collections of material that I was not able to use.

First, the archives of the Communist Party itself. I approached the CPC, requesting access to its files on the 1920s, and was informed that "the historical documents you wish to examine are unavailable to the public at this time." The explanation offered was that the CP is in the process of writing its own history and "we feel we have the right to use our own materials first." The party's research director assured me that they intend to deposit the party's records in a public archive, once the history is published.

The CPC of course has the right to do as it pleases with its own records, although I doubt that many historians would approve of a policy that withholds fifty- and sixty-year-old documents from study until an "official history" has been produced. It is to be hoped that if and when the records are placed in a public archive they will not be made subject to onerous access regulations.

My attempts to gain access to the historical records of the Royal Canadian Mounted Police were likewise fruitless. Although the Privy Council long ago ruled that thirty-year-old government documents were to be made available for research, the RCMP has refused to open files as much as seventy years old!

My efforts to examine the RCMP's records began with a visit to the Public Archives of Canada. Reviewing the list of RCMP files that are available, I found reference to a file No. 2447: "Summary of Crime Reports—Bolshevism." The reference had been deleted from the Archives' list, but it was still legible. Many other files on similar subjects were similarly deleted. When I asked the RCMP for an explanation, I was informed that the force had used the Privy Council's "Public Access Order" as an excuse for removing files previously deposited in the Archives!

Since that time the RCMP has allowed a few selected historians access to the massive files it maintains on the radical left, while denying access to other historians—presumably those whose political views the federal police force distrusts. Recently the RCMP Commissioner has stated that historians will not be allowed any access in the future: he cites "a growing concern by the Canadian public over the right for individual privacy" as his pretext. The RCMP's concern for privacy has nothing to do with citizens' democratic rights, of course. Canada's political police are simply determined to keep private all records pertaining to their longstanding practice of spying on and harassing the labor and socialist movements in this country—including the record of such activities half a century ago.

The RCMP's censorship of its own historical records is a barrier to the work of all historians. For many subjects, as the experience of other countries has shown, police records are a valuable (if extremely biased) source of information. I hope that Canadian historians will make a concerted effort to reverse the commissioner's ruling.

Manuscript Collections

Department of Labor (Hull, Quebec): Vertical Files
Library of Social History (New York): James P. Cannon Archives

McMaster University (Hamilton, Ontario): Canadian Radical
   Archives
Hoover Institution (Stanford, California): Draper Papers
Metro Toronto Public Library: James Simpson Collection
Public Archives of Canada   (PAC)
   Borden Papers
   Justice Records (RG 13)
   Labour Records (RG 27)
   Secretary of State—
      Chief Press Censor (RG 6)
   RCMP Records (RG 18)
   Toronto District Labor Council Minutes
   Woodsworth Collection
Public Archives of Ontario (PAO)
   Communist Party Collection
      (includes transcript of *Rex v. Buck,* 1931)
   MacDonald-Spector Collection
University of Toronto
   Robert S. Kenny Collection
   J.S. Woodsworth Collection
   Earle Birney Papers.

Contemporary Accounts, Reminiscences, Documents

Armstrong, Max. Reminiscences. Transcript in author's possession.
Bruce, Malcolm. Reminiscences. Transcript in author's possession.
Buck, Tim. *Lenin and Canada.* Toronto; Progress Books, 1970.
———. *Thirty Years: The Story of the Communist Movement in Canada, 1922-1952.* Toronto: Progress Books, 1952.
———. *Yours in the Struggle: Reminiscences of Tim Buck.* edited by William Beeching and Dr. Phyllis Clarke. Toronto: NC Press, 1977. (Transcripts of Buck's 1965 CBC interviews.)
———. *1917-1957: Forty Years of Great Change.* Toronto: Progress Books, 1957.
———. *The Road Ahead.* Toronto: 1936.
Cannon, James P. *The First Ten Years of American Communism.* New York: Lyle Stuart, 1962.
———. *The History of American Trotskyism.* New York: Pioneer Publishers, 1944.
———. *Notebook of an Agitator.* New York: Pioneer Publishers, 1958.
———. *The Socialist Workers Party in World War II,* New York:

Pathfinder Press, 1975.

Communist International. Letter to CPC Polcom, Oct. 3, 1929. Copy in author's possession.

—————. *Manifestes, Thèses et Résolutions des Quatre Premiers Congrès Mondiaux de l'Internationale Communiste*. Paris: Maspero, 1970.

Communist Party of Canada. *Enlarged Plenum Report 1931*. PAO-CP

—————. *1925 Convention Report*. Kenny Papers

—————. *1927 Convention Report*. Kenny Papers

—————. *1929 Convention Report*. Kenny Papers

—————. *Towards a Canadian Peoples Front*, Toronto, 1935.

—————. *The Road to Socialism in Canada*, Toronto, 1972.

Degras, Jane, ed. *The Communist International, Documents 1919-1943*. 3 vols. Oxford University Press, 1956, 1960, 1965.

—————. *Soviet Documents on Foreign Policy*. Oxford University Press, 1956.

Industrial Union of Needle Trades Workers. *Report of Second Convention*. Toronto: 1931.

Kashtan, William. *The Decisive Question*. Toronto: Communist Party, 1974.

Lenin, V.I. *Collected Works*. 4th ed. 45 vols. Moscow: Foreign Languages Publishing House, 1960-1970.

—————. *Selected Works*. 3 vols. Moscow: Foreign Languages Publishing House, n.d.

Luxemburg, Rosa. *Selected Political Writings*. Edited and introduced by R. Looker. New York: Grove Press, 1974.

Marx, Karl and Engels, Frederick. *Collected Works*. Vols 1-12. New York: International Publishers, 1975-1979.

—————. *Selected Works*. 2 vols. Moscow: Foreign Languages Publishing House, 1962.

—————. *Early Texts*. translated and edited by David McLellan. Oxford: Blackwell, 1972.

McEwen, Tom. *The Forge Glows Red: From Blacksmith to Revolutionary*. Toronto: Progress Books, 1974.

New York State Legislature. *Revolutionary Radicalism, Its History, Purpose and Tactics*. 4 vols. Albany: 1920.

Penner, Norman, ed. *Winnipeg 1919: the Strikers' Own History of the Winnipeg General Strike*. Toronto: James Lewis & Samuel, 1973.

Pierce, G. [Stewart Smith], *Socialism and the CCF*. Montreal: Contemporary Publishing Association, 1934.

Quarter, Maurice. Interview. March 13, 1975.

Ryan, Oscar. *Tim Buck: A Conscience for Canada.* Toronto: Progress Books, 1975.

Serge, Victor. *Memoirs of a Revolutionary.* Oxford University Press, 1963.

Smith, A.E. *All My Life.* Toronto: Progress Books, 1949.

Spector, Maurice. Interview with Theodore Draper, November 25, 1957. Hoover Institution, Draper papers.

Stalin, Joseph. *Leninism.* London: George Allen & Unwin, 1930.

————. *Works.* 13 vols, Moscow: Foreign Languages Publishing House, n.d.

Trades and Labor Congress of Canada. *Proceedings.* 1914-1931.

Trotsky, Leon. *The Challenge of the Left Opposition 1923-1925.* New York: Pathfinder Press, 1975.

————. *In Defense of Marxism.* New York: Pathfinder Press, 1970.

————. *On Britain.* New York: Pathfinder Press, 1973.

————. *On China.* New York: Pathfinder Press, 1976.

————. *The First Five Years of the Communist International.* 2 vols. New York: Monad Press, 1972.

————. *The Third International After Lenin.* New York: Pioneer Publishers, 1957.

————. *Writings, 1929-1940.* 14 vols. New York: Pathfinder Press, 1969-1979.

Periodicals

A. Daily
Daily Worker (New York)
Evening Telegram (Toronto)
The Globe (Toronto)
Mail and Empire (Toronto)
New York Times
The Spectator (Hamilton)
Toronto Daily News
Toronto Daily Star
Toronto Times
Toronto World

B. Weekly, Monthly
British Columbia Federationist
Canadian Forum
Canadian Forward

*Canadian Labor Defender**
*Canadian Labour Monthly**
Canadian Labour World
*Canadian Tribune**
*The Clarion**
*The Communist**
*Communist Bulletin** (1934)
The Communist International
Cotton's Weekly
Industrial Banner
International Press Correspondence (Inprecorr)
Labor Leader
The Labor News
*Maritime Labour Herald**
Left Wing
Marxian Socialist
The Messenger
The Militant
*Monthly Review** (1940)
*National Affairs Monthly**
One Big Union Bulletin
Peoples Advocate
Revolutionary Age (1930—superseded by *Workers Age*)
Trades and Labor Congress Journal
The Vanguard
*Vapaus**
The Voice
Western Clarion (During 1919 and 1920, *The Red Flag* and *The Indicator*)
Western Labor News
Winnipeg Citizen
*Woman Worker**
*The Worker**
*Workers Guard**

C. Annual
Canadian Annual Review
Labor Gazette
Labor Organization in Canada
Strikes and Lockouts in Canada

*Indicates periodical controlled by or published by the Communist Party of Canada.

Articles, Theses, Books

A: Canada

Abella, Irving. *The Canadian Labor Movement, 1902-1960*. Ottawa: Canadian Historical Association, 1975.

———. *Nationalism, Communism and Canadian Labour*. Toronto: University of Toronto Press, 1973.

Adams, Ron. "The Communist Party of Canada Confronts Canadian Authorities 1928-1932." Unpublished PhD. Thesis. University of British Columbia, 1977.

———. "The 1931 Arrest and Trial of the Leaders of the Communist Party of Canada." Paper presented to the 1977 Convention of the Canadian Historical Association.

Avakumovic, Ivan. *The Communist Party in Canada: A History*. Toronto: McClelland and Stewart, 1975.

Avery, Donald. *"Dangerous Foreigners": European Immigrant Workers and Labour Radicalism in Canada 1896-1932*. Toronto: McClelland and Stewart, 1979.

———. "The Radical Alien and the Winnipeg General Strike," in Carl Berger and Ramsay Cook, eds. *The West and the Nation*. Toronto: McClelland and Stewart, 1975.

Babcock, R.H. *Gompers In Canada*. Toronto: University of Toronto Press, 1974.

Bercuson, David Jay. *Confrontation at Winnipeg: Labour, Industrial Relations, and the General Strike*. Montreal: McGill-Queens University Press, 1974.

———. *Fools and Wise Men: The Rise and Fall of the One Big Union*. Toronto: McGraw-Hill, 1978.

Brown, Lorne and Caroline. *An Unauthorized History of the RCMP*. Toronto: James Lewis & Samuel, 1973.

Caplan, Gerald L. *The Dilemma of Canadian Socialism*. Toronto: McClelland and Stewart, 1973.

Copp, Terry. *The Anatomy of Poverty: The Condition of the Working Class in Montreal 1897-1929*. Toronto: McClelland and Stewart, 1974.

Frank, David. "Class Conflict in the Coal Industry: Cape Breton 1922" in G.S. Kealey and P. Warrian, eds., *Essays in Canadian Working Class History*, Toronto: McClelland and Stewart, 1976.

Friesen, Gerald. "Yours in Revolt: The Socialist Party of Canada and the Western Canadian Labour Movement." *Labour/Le Travailleur*, 1976.

Hansen, S.D. "Estevan 1931." in Irving Abella, ed. *On Strike*. Toronto: James Lewis & Samuel, 1974.

Horn, Michiel. "Keeping Canada 'Canadian': Anti-Communism and Canadianism in Toronto, 1928-1929." *Canada,* September, 1975.

Horowitz, Gad. *Canadian Labour in Politics.* Toronto: University of Toronto Press, 1968.

Laxer, Robert. *Canada's Unions.* Toronto: James Lorimer and Co., 1976.

Leach, James D. "The Workers Unity League and the Stratford Furniture Workers Strike." *Ontario History,* June 1967.

MacEwan, Paul. *Miners and Steelworkers.* Toronto: A.M. Hakkert, 1976.

McLeod, Catherine. "Women in Production: The Toronto Dressmakers Strike of 1931." J. Acton *et al.,* ed., *Women at Work, Ontario 1850-1930.* Toronto: Women's Press, 1974.

McCormack, A. Ross. *Reformers, Rebels and Revolutionaries: The Western Canadian Radical Movement, 1899-1919.* Toronto: University of Toronto Press, 1977.

McKean, Fergus. *Communism vs. Opportunism.* Montreal: In Struggle, 1977 (1946).

McNaught, Kenneth. *A Prophet in Politics: A Biography of J.S. Woodsworth.* Toronto: University of Toronto Press, 1959.

Morton, Desmond. "Aid to the Civil Power: The Stratford Strike of 1933." In I. Abella, ed., *On Strike.* Toronto: James Lewis & Samuel, 1974.

Niosi, Jorge. *The Economy of Canada: Who Controls It?* trans. by Penelope Williams. Montreal: Black Rose, 1978.

O'Brien, Gary. "Maurice Spector and the Origin of Canadian Trotskyism." Unpublished M.A. Thesis, Carleton University, 1974.

―――. "Maurice Spector, pioneer Canadian Socialist, on the national question." *Forward,* November 1974.

Penner, Norman. *The Canadian Left: A Critical Analysis.* Scarborough: Prentice-Hall, 1977.

Petryshyn, Jaroslav. "Communists, Courts and Campaigns: The Origins and Activities of the Canadian Labour Defense League, 1925-1940." Paper presented to the Canadian Historical Association, 1977.

―――. "From Clergyman to Communist: The Radicalization of Albert Edward Smith." *Journal of Canadian Studies,* Winter 1978-1979.

Phillips, Paul. *No Power Greater: A Century of Labour in B.C.* Vancouver: B.C. Federation Labor, 1967.

Robin, Martin. *Radical Politics and Canadian Labour.* Kingston:

Industrial Relations Center, 1968.

Rodney, William. *Soldiers of the International: A History of the Communist Party of Canada, 1919-1929.* Toronto: University of Toronto Press, 1968.

Troop, G.R.F. "Socialism in Canada." Unpublished M.A. Thesis, McGill University, 1924.

Upton, Jim. "The Origin and Evolution of the Young Communist League of Canada." Unpublished manuscript.

Wilson, J.D. "The Finnish Organization of Canada: The 'Language Barrier', and the Assimilation Process." *Canadian Ethnic Studies,* Vol. IX, No. 2, 1977.

B: General

Barltrop, Robert, *The Monument: The Story of the Socialist Party of Great Britain.* London: Pluto Press, 1975.

Berstein, Irving. *The Lean Years.* Boston: Houghton Mifflin, 1972.

Black, Robert. *Fascism in Germany.* London: Steyne, 1975.

Block, Russell, ed., *Lenin's Fight Against Stalinism.* New York: Pathfinder Press, 1975.

Calhoun, Daniel. *The United Front.* Cambridge University Press, 1976.

Carr, E.H. *The Interregnum.* Oxford University Press, 1954.

———. *Socialism in One Country.* 3 vols. Oxford University Press, 1958, 1959, 1964.

Cohen, Stephen. *Bukharin and the Bolshevik Revolution.* New York: Vintage, 1975.

Draper, Theodore. *American Communism and Soviet Russia.* New York: Viking, 1960.

———. *The Roots of American Communism.* New York: Viking, 1957.

———. "The Strange Case of the Comintern." *Survey,* Summer 1972.

Deutscher, Isaac. *The Prophet Armed.* New York: Vintage, 1965.

———. *The Prophet Unarmed.* New York: Vintage, 1965.

———. *The Prophet Outcast.* New York: Vintage, 1965.

Feldman, Fred. "Stalinism and Internationalism," in G. Novack et al., *The First Three Internationals.* New York: Pathfinder Press, 1974.

Frankel, Dave. "The History of the Left Opposition," in G. Novack, et al., *The First Three Internationals.* New York: Pathfinder Press, 1974.

Hobsbawm, E. *Revolutionaries.* London: Quartet, 1975.

Holton, Bob. *British Syndicalism, 1900-1914.* London: Pluto Press,

1976.

Isaacs, Harold. *The Tragedy of the Chinese Revolution.* 2nd revised edition, Stanford University Press, 1961.

James, C.L.R. *World Revolution.* London: Martin Secker and Warburg, 1937.

Kuusinen, Aino. *Before and After Stalin.* trans. by Paul Stevenson. London: Michael Joseph, 1974.

Lewin, Moishe. *Lenin's Last Struggle.* New York: Vintage, 1970.

Mandel, Ernest. *From Stalinism to Eurocommunism.* London: New Left Books, 1978.

Reed, John. Ten Days that Shook the World. New York: Vintage, 1960.

Index

—on counter-revolution, 129
—on internationalism, 154
—MacDonald on Trotsky, 369-73
—and Russian Revolution, 19, 181f
—on Soviet Union, 148, 325
—Spector on Trotskyism, 357-58
—on Stalinism, 145
—on ultraleftism, 90, 90f, 93, 100-101, 262f, 264
Truman, Robert, 35-36

Ukrainian Labor-Farmer Temple Association (ULFTA), 203, 253f, 254, 291; Buck's account of crisis, 366-67; crisis inside CPC, 292, 295, 301-4, 309-10, 214;
Ukrainian Revolutionary Group, 28
Ukrainian Social Democratic Party, 42, 44
United Brotherhood of Carpenters and Joiners, 31, 34, 79
United Communist Party of America. See Communist Party of United States
United Farmers, 59, 60, 68, 105f
United Mine Workers of America (UMWA), 110, 118, 121-23, 125-27, 140-41, 275, 280, 282
—District 14, 122
—District 18, 4, 51, 122, 131, 141
—District 26, 57, 118-27, 132, 141
United Veterans League, 59, 68

Vaara, Aarvo, 253, 255f, 296-97, 298, 300, 310, 363, 367, 368
Valin, J., 306-7
Vallerio, Andrio, 42
Vancouver General Strike, 54, 56
Vancouver Trades and Labor Council, 50, 54, 116-17, 132
Varley, William, 35
Vaskleck, George, 42

Wallace, Henry, 320
War Measures Act (WWI), 14, 27-29, 81
Watkinson, Frank, 31, 35
Watson, Charles, 30-32, 34, 42, 43, 44

Watters, James, 6
Wayman, Matthew, 13
Weir, John, 326
Wells, A.S., 50, 75-76, 97, 97f, 109, 116, 117
Western Federation of Miners, 78-79, 114
Western Labor Conference (1919), 51-53, 74
Westwood, Rev. Dr. Horace, 21
Williams, Victor, 271
Williamson, John, 234, 236, 237f, 362, 363
Wiltshaw, George, 70, 71
Winch, Ernest, 50
Winnipeg General Strike, 54-56, 57, 61, 86
Winnipeg Labor Church, 51
Winnipeg Trades and Labor Council, 6, 13, 30, 50-51, 53, 55
Wirta, John, 297, 298, 300
Wolfe, Bertram D., 205
Women's Labor League, 79, 108
Woodsworth, J.S., 60, 65, 105f, 238, 266-67, 269-70
Workers Alliance, 96
Workers Educational Association, 70
Workers League, 96
Workers Party of America. See Communist Party of the United States
Workers Political Defense League, 31, 39, 44
Workers Unity League (WUL), 273-74, 278-88, 305, 329
World War I, 7-16, 49-50, 146

Young Communist League (YCL), 170, 199, 203, 210, 215, 216, 229, 233, 234, 244, 249, 251, 264, 292, 313
Young Socialist League, 77

Zaborowski, Lita ("Annie Bancourt"), 39-41, 42, 46, 81-82, 335
Zinoviev, Gregory, 89, 93, 101, 144, 151, 155, 181, 182, 184, 190-92, 204, 265f, 357-58
Zrodowsky, Joseph, 251, 252, 254